THE **OBSERVER** BOOK OF PROFILES

EDITED BY
ROBERT LOW

First published in Great Britain in 1991 by
Virgin Books
338 Ladbroke Grove
London W10 5AH

Reprinted 1991

British Library Cataloguing in Publication Data
The Observer book of profiles.
1. Biographies
I. Low, Robert II. The Observer
920.02

ISBN 1-85227-357-7

Designed by Geoff Green
Set in Ehrhardt by
Phoenix Photosetting, Chatham, Kent
Printed and bound in Great Britain by
Mackays of Chatham PLC, Chatham, Kent

CONTENTS

Acknowledgements X
Foreword by Donald Trelford XI
Introduction XIII

THE PROFILES

THE SECOND WORLD WAR

Adolf Hitler, 31 January 1943 3
Joseph Goebbels, 28 March 1943 5
Aircraftman Smith, 4 July 1943 7
Albert Speer, 9 April 1944 9

ROYALS

HRH The Duke of Edinburgh, 4 January 1953 15
HRH Princess Michael of Kent, 21 April 1985 20
HRH The Duchess of York, 6 March 1988 24
HM Queen Elizabeth the Queen Mother, 5 August 1990 28

DIVINES

The Reverend Michael Scott, 4 December 1949 33
Dr Martin Luther King, 29 October 1961 35
Cardinal Basil Hume, 30 May 1982 38
Dr Robert Runcie, 12 September 1982 43
Bishop Desmond Tutu, 8 May 1983 46
Terry Waite, 13 January 1985 49
Pope John Paul II, 28 December 1986 52

ACADEMICS AND INTELLECTUALS

Professor A. J. Ayer, 15 September 1957 59
Bertrand Russell, 19 February 1961 63
Milton Friedman, 12 December 1976 66
Malcolm Muggeridge, 28 November 1982 69
Sir Isaiah Berlin, 11 June 1989 73

INTERNATIONAL

Fidel Castro, 11 January 1959 81
John Kennedy, 1 January 1961 84
Nelson Mandela, 19 August 1962 89
Mao Tse-tung, 6 January 1963 94
Jimmy Carter, 7 November 1976 98
Lech Walesa, 21 November 1982 102
George Bush, 6 February 1983 105
François Mitterrand, 21 October 1984 108
Mikhail Gorbachov, 11 November 1984 111
Yasser Arafat, 18 December 1988 114
Helmut Kohl, 11 March 1990 118

WRITERS, ARTISTS AND MUSICIANS

T. S. Eliot, 7 March 1948 125
Graham Greene, 27 November 1949 127
Sir Malcolm Sargent, 30 July 1950 130
Henry Moore, 24 June 1961 133
Evelyn Waugh, 31 July 1955 137
Maria Callas, 15 June 1958 141
John Betjeman, 8 February 1959 145
Kingsley Amis, 14 January 1962 148
Francis Bacon, 27 May 1962 152
Harold Pinter, 27 April 1975 155
Tom Stoppard, 14 November 1982 159
Jonathan Miller, 9 January 1983 163
Sir Richard Attenborough, 17 April 1983 167
Michael Frayn, 1 April 1984 170
Alan Bennett, 12 August 1984 174
Ted Hughes, 23 December 1984 177
Iris Murdoch, 11 May 1986 180
Margaret Drabble, 19 April 1987 183
Mark Boxer, 24 June 1988 186

BRITISH POLITICIANS

Sir James Grigg, 1 March 1942 193
Aneurin Bevan, 29 April 1951 194
Winston Churchill, 30 December 1951 199
Harold Macmillan, 8 June 1958 203
Enoch Powell, 5 February 1961 209

Jeremy Thorpe, 27 September 1970 213
David Owen, 14 February 1982 215
Roy Jenkins, 28 March 1982 219
David Steel, 19 September 1982 222
Neil Kinnock, 26 September 1982 225
Michael Heseltine, 3 October 1982 228
Shirley Williams, 10 October 1982 232
Norman Tebbit, 7 October 1984 235
John Smith, 2 November 1986 238
Denis Healey, 5 April 1987 241
Edwina Currie, 11 December 1988 244

SPORTS STARS

Don Bradman, 1 December 1946 251
Denis Compton, 6 June 1948 253
Stanley Matthews, 6 January 1957 256
Lester Piggott, 18 August 1957 258
George Best, 10 December 1972 263
Virginia Wade, 3 July 1977 269
Ian Botham, 18 July 1982 274
Diego Maradona, 29 June 1986 278

MISCELLANEOUS

Evan Edwards, 25 December 1960 285
Sir Timothy Cargill, 1 April 1962 288
Robin Day, 30 January 1972 291
Sir William Rees-Mogg, 19 December 1982 293
Elizabeth David, 5 January 1986 297
Denis Thatcher, 30 April 1989 300

SHOWBUSINESS

Mae West, 26 October 1947 307
Coco the Clown, 2 January 1949 309
Charlie Chaplin, 28 September 1952 312
Marlon Brando, 3 October 1954 317
Marilyn Monroe, 15 July 1956 319
The Goons, 23 December 1956 322
Tommy Steele, 21 December 1958 325
Brigitte Bardot, 27 September 1959 329
Tony Hancock, 30 March 1960 333

Peter Sellers, 6 November 1960 336
Albert Finney, 6 August 1961 339
Sir John Gielgud, 14 April 1974 342
Max Wall, 9 March 1975 346
Andrew Lloyd Webber, 18 March 1984 349
Ian McKellen, 16 December 1984 353
Bob Geldof, 7 July 1985 357
Dame Peggy Ashcroft, 20 December 1987 361
Barry Humphries, 27 December 1987 365
Lenny Henry, 26 February 1989 369
Madonna, 1 July 1990 372

ILLUSTRATIONS

HRH Princess Michael of Kent (*Mark Boxer*) 21
HRH The Duchess of York (*Nicholas Garland*) 24
Cardinal Hume (*Mark Boxer*) 39
Professor A. J. Ayer (*Jane Bown*) 60
Malcolm Muggeridge (*Mark Boxer*) 70
Sir Isaiah Berlin (*Wally Fawkes*) 74
Nelson Mandela (*Michael Peto*) 90
Yasser Arafat (*Nicholas Garland*) 115
Helmut Kohl (*Wally Fawkes*) 119
Graham Greene (*Camera Press*) 128
Henry Moore (*Jane Bown*) 134
Evelyn Waugh (*Jane Bown*) 138
Kingsley Amis (*Donald McCullin*) 149
Harold Pinter (*Tony McGrath*) 155
Jonathan Miller (*Mark Boxer*) 164
Michael Frayn (*Mark Boxer*) 171
Harold Macmillan (*Jane Bown*) 204
Neil Kinnock (*Neil Libbert*) 226
Michael Heseltine (*Mark Boxer*) 229
Edwina Curry (*Nicholas Garland*) 245
Lester Piggott (*Jane Bown*) 259
George Best (*Bryn Campbell*) 264
Virginia Wade (*Eamonn McCabe*) 270
Evan Edwards (*John Hedgecoe*) 286
Sir William Rees-Mogg (*Mark Boxer*) 294
Denis Thatcher (*Wally Fawkes*) 301
Tommy Steele (*Michael Peto*) 326
Albert Finney (*Camera Press*) 339
John Gielgud (*Jane Bown*) 343
Max Wall (*Tony McGrath*) 347
Ian McKellen (*Jane Bown*) 353
Bob Geldof (*Mark Boxer*) 358
Dame Peggy Ashcroft (*Jane Bown*) 362
Barry Humphries (*Nicholas Garland*) 366
Madonna (*Wally Fawkes*) 372

ACKNOWLEDGEMENTS

I am grateful to the following for their help and memories: David Astor, Donald Trelford, Michael Davie, Ken Obank, Anthony Howard, John Silverlight, Paul Ferris, Ivy Dunn and Peter Dunn. I was greatly helped in tracking down profiles from the archives by Jeffrey Care, the *Observer*'s chief librarian, and his staff; by Rhona Drummond, head of Observer Publications; and by the personnel of the paper's post room. I thank, too, Gill Gibbins, editorial director of W.H. Allen, for her support and advice; Anna Ford and Mark Amory, on behalf of Mark Boxer's estate; Nicholas Garland, and Wally Fawkes for permitting reproduction of profile drawings; Jane Bown for her photographs; Jill Thomas, Bridget Hornsby and Angela Burton for all their secretarial assistance; and Tony Mancini for his painstaking picture research.

R.L.

FOREWORD

To my predecessor, David Astor, the profile was the heart of each week's *Observer*. Except at times of national or international crisis, it seemed to be more important than the leading article. He certainly took more time over it, sitting hunched in his overcoat, sipping endless cups of coffee, late into Friday night.

He wasn't just seeking the precise adjective, though he fiddled with almost every word. To David, making judgements on another human being was a heavy responsibility. The questions he asked himself and those around him were: Is it right? Is it fair? Is it honest?

I admired him for this punctiliousness, though sometimes it seemed a shade over-fussy with deadlines fast approaching. On one occasion I remember, an editorial executive became exasperated with David's agonised search for *le mot juste*. 'What's the difference?' he finally asked impatiently. 'The difference is between amateurism and professionalism,' David replied coolly.

When I succeeded to the editorial chair on his retirement in 1976, one of the first things I did was to circulate a memorandum David had written on the preparation of profiles. These days no editor can spend so much time on any single feature in a newspaper that sometimes contains 200,000 words on more than 150 pages.

Even though other newspapers have imitated the format in recent years, we like to think that the *Observer* Profile retains a literacy, a vigour and a freshness that make it something special in British journalism. I hope readers of this overdue collection will form the same opinion.

DONALD TRELFORD

INTRODUCTION

The first *Observer* Profile appeared on Sunday, 1 March 1942. It was of Sir James Grigg. The profile was to become one of the most distinctive and distinguished of the *Observer*'s contributions to modern British journalism. Today, the *Observer* Profile is around 1,500 words long, sits on the first leader page, is unsigned, as the vast majority have been since its inception, and is illustrated by a drawing of the subject by the paper's cartoonist, Trog (Wally Fawkes). If imitation is the sincerest form of flattery, the paper can feel proud of itself: all the *Observer*'s Sunday quality rivals have since copied the format to an almost slavish degree. So have some of the dailies: the *Independent* on Saturdays, the *Guardian* on Mondays. All use caricatures rather than photographs as illustration; most are unsigned.

There is of course no copyright in newspaper ideas. The *Observer* Profile was itself inspired by another publication: the *New Yorker*, which ran (and still runs) lengthy occasional profiles of several thousand words which are clearly the result of months of research. It was David Astor, a great admirer of the *New Yorker*, who thought the formula could be adapted for the *Observer*. 'The *New Yorker* Profiles were lengthy and wonderfully intimate, wandering all through the subject's life, almost like a little book,' Astor told me when I asked how it all started. In 1942, he was an officer in the Royal Marines, and did not even have a formal link with the newspaper, which his family owned. The relationship was, in his words, 'strictly black market'. But he was already the most influential voice on the paper, and the first profile duly appeared, written by him. It was not until 1948 that Astor became Editor, a post he was to hold with the utmost distinction for 27 years. For much of that time, the paper flourished as never before and the profile was to become an integral part of its appeal.

The first profiles were short, compared with today's: around 800 words, understandable when the paper itself was only six pages because of wartime newspaper rationing. Those early profiles read today more like appreciations than the mini-biographies they were to become. They were written by a variety of people, although most were unsigned. The occasional one would carry the writer's initials at the end. Early writers included Arthur Koestler, Ivor Brown (Editor from 1942 to 1948) and Sebastian Haffner, who had fled Nazi Germany and been taken under the *Observer*'s wing, like so many brilliant Central European exiles of the time. Haffner's wartime profiles of the Nazi leaders still burn with informed hatred. He did not write entirely about Nazis: Astor described Haffner's 1951 profile of Churchill as 'an incredible document. It tells you nothing except Haffner's assessment of Winston. It was quite cheeky, lecturing him, threatening to remove his reputation if he didn't reform his ways. I think people read that fairly aghast.'

That sort of profile was to become an exception to the Astor rule, which was that it had above all to be fair. Astor did not really approve of Haffner's style of profile writing, calling it 'patronising and impressionistic'. In Astor's opinion, it gave the journalist too much power. Astor was a painfully fair Editor, one reason being that he came from a family and circle that was always being written about in the press. He therefore knew from the inside how hurtful or just plain annoying it could be when newspapers got it wrong. 'I preferred the researched profile – one that had a lot of originality about it and changed people's opinions, one that could make you feel what it must be like to be that person. I was always for treating people as objects of sympathy,' he said.

Outside contributors would often be asked to supply written notes. 'All sorts of people did so: ambassadors, enemies (very important), brothers,' recalls Michael Davie, Astor's deputy for a long period. Nowadays, the writer just rings them up in the normal journalistic way.

For better or worse, the profile's verdict on its subject was understood within the paper to be the *Observer*'s view of him too. This, and the fact that so many were a team effort, is why they came to be anonymous. They remain so today, although the lack of a by-line still puzzles many readers. Some of the profiles in this collection were by-lined. In those cases I mention the author in the section introduction. I also name the author of a few other, originally anonymous, profiles but, even allowing for teamwork, the authorship of the majority is unknown to me. There used to exist a series of albums in which the authors were carefully noted but they are no longer in the paper's archives. The profiles are still often a product of teamwork. To give one example: when we decided to do Diego Maradona, the brilliant Argentine footballer, on the day of the World Cup Final in 1986, in which he was leading his country, I was deputed to write it (having suggested it in the first place) but relied heavily on long telexed memos from our correspondent in Buenos Aires, Jimmy Burns, our chief sports writer, Hugh McIlvanney and sports news reporter, Peter Deeley, who were in Mexico covering the tournament, and the sage advice of sports editor Peter Corrigan. Whatever the merits of the eventual piece, it looked a good enough idea that Sunday afternoon when Maradona laid on the winning goal for Argentina.

One distinguished profile writer, Alan Moorehead, had his own way of defusing criticism from the people he was writing about: he would show hostile profiles to them. They would respond angrily and point out errors. Then, they had no grounds to criticise when the article was published. Hugh Massingham, the political correspondent, had an even more foolproof method: he refused to write profiles at all, though he would sometimes contribute thoughts. Thus he was able to look angry politicians right in the eye and say 'It wasn't me'. He was a rarity:

just about everybody on the staff was supposed to have a profile 'on their plate', says Michael Davie.

David Astor's thoughts about profile writing were contained in a long memorandum to the staff in the last year of his editorship, 1975. A profile should, he wrote, contain 'basics': age, parentage, education, religion and political affiliations. It should have a physical description of the subject, including 'special characteristics, i.e style of walking, kind of laughter, tone of voice'. On marital status, 'it should always be stated whether the subject is married, how often and to whom; what children there are'. The home should be mentioned and fully described 'if distinctive'. Under the sub-heading 'Evolution', Astor wrote: 'Every personality evolves. Usually there is some element of drama or of the unexpected in anyone's life story . . . The best profiles read like a journey with desired destinations seldom attained and with accidents, both fortunate and not . . . The worst profiles assume that the subject has an unchanging personality or that his life has followed a predetermined or predictable course.'

In the next section 'Over-simplification' we come to the heart of Astor's philosophy of profile-writing – and indeed of journalism: 'Clearly, no one is entirely good or bad. All pure heroes and all utter crooks should be taboo. The aim should be, rather, to describe how we are all good bad-bastards or bad good-guys. Over-simplifications usually come either from ignorance or prejudice and should be avoided.'

He advised the writer not to assume he was cleverer or better than his subject. 'The best profile-writing stance is that of a modest, fearless, self-effacing recorder of how things really are . . . The subject should not become the writer's victim. Nobody,' he added, 'should be written off as just a fool or a monster. That should normally be left to cartoonists.'

'Criticism should not be arbitrary . . . hostile judgments should always be expressed with restraint. It's a serious thing to condemn a person in print and should be done seldom and sparingly.' People, Astor thought, were worth writing about for what they did, not for what they were. Perhaps he paused here to re-read what he had decreed so far because he finished off by commenting: 'Obviously profiles can and should be written in many different ways. But they all need to have some theme (the little guy who made good, the big guy who came unstuck).' He warned, however, against imposing a theme on material selected to justify it.

Astor has since expressed amazement that he could have laid down the law in such a specific manner. Few profiles could possibly match up to the exacting standards he set in the memorandum but they are not a bad target to aim at.

Astor wrote that memorandum at a time when the *Observer* Profile had fallen on hard times. The early to mid-1970s were a period of financial crisis at the paper. The profile ceased to be a regular weekly feature and now appeared only intermittently. Astor gives the general sense of 'things falling apart' as one of the reasons for this. But it remained an important feature, sometimes signed, sometimes anonymous, for the first years of the editorship of Donald Trelford.

The arrival of Anthony Howard as Deputy Editor in 1981 heralded the revival of the profile as a permanent feature. Howard had always been keen on the profile genre. As Editor of the *New Statesman* he had run a number of long, anonymous profiles, illustrated with a caricature by Mark Boxer (Marc), and he revived the idea on the first *Observer* leader page (complete with Marc illustration), where the profile now joined the columns of Alan Watkins and Conor Cruise O'Brien (who was succeeded by Neal Ascherson and Michael Ignatieff successively). The profile had occasionally graced this page. Its arrival on a permanent basis cemented the page's authority and confirmed it as one of the paper's most popular and widely discussed ones. Although he was well aware of its importance, Howard did not take quite such a reverential attitude to the profile as Astor. While he naturally hoped it would be as authoritative as possible, he took the view that a 1,500-word newspaper profile could not be the last word on its subject.

Another change of emphasis from the heyday of the Astor profile is that the subject is frequently the Person of the Week and is not decided upon until the Wednesday editorial conference. This is probably a reflection of changing attitudes. In a news-dominated era, immediacy is a principal concern. It is not, however, the only one and at any one time, as in the old days, a number of *Observer* writers will be working on profiles to be run at an appropriate time – or possibly never.

It is rare nowadays to commission profiles from outside authors, a common practice 30 years ago. Today, they are usually written by the staff specialist with most knowledge of the subject or by a staff feature writer, of whom the most prolific profile author is Laurence Marks, one of the great unsung heroes of British journalism. Marks came to the *Observer* via the *Evening Standard*, where he edited the Londoner's Diary, and the *Sunday Times*, from which, typically, he resigned over a matter of principle. Of *Observer* Profiles in the 1980s, Marks wrote a good proportion. It is a body of work of an extraordinary breadth and quality and yet the public is unaware of its author. But Marks is one of those rare journalists for whom the by-line is the least important part of their work. He is a studious, intense and essentially private person with a tremendous appetite for work. Although he is not an anonymous man, the anonymity of the profile suits him. So do other requirements of the genre: he has a fine historical sense, which greatly helps to place his subjects in their proper context; a wide range of interests, which means almost anybody is within his scope; a fluent and pleasant writing style; a well-organised mind; and a highly efficient way of working, which renders him suitable for both the long-term profile, researched and written over several weeks, and the short-order version, which has to be turned around in a matter of days. The profiles of Sir Isaiah Berlin, Barry Humphries and the Queen Mother in this collection are good examples of Marks's work.

He is a worthy successor to a man who, for many of his contemporaries, symbolised the *Observer* Profile: Cyril Dunn. In the 1950s and '60s, Dunn thought up and wrote many memorable profiles. His forte was the offbeat. A key question to be asked when writing a profile in the Astor era was: 'How did they get where they are?' Michael Davie remembers Dunn having his own key question: 'What's the snag?' In his obituary of Dunn in the *Observer* in January 1988, Davie remembered: 'He once wrote a profile of Sir Malcolm Sargent, the fashionable conductor, identifying Sargent's weakness as snobbery. Carefully, he slid the knife into Sargent's back. He was appalled a day or two later to receive a fulsome scrawl from Sargent thanking him for the piece. To be thanked by anyone for a piece about them was, for Dunn, a clear proof of failure.' Dunn's widow, Ivy, remembers that he took about two weeks to research and write profiles. He always wrote at home and would shut himself away to write, fortified only by constant tea and tobacco. When it was finished, he would read it out to her, pausing at what he clearly regarded as the choicest passages to comment disapprovingly, 'You're not laughing'.

The choice of the person to be profiled was always one of the leading subjects thrashed out at the principal editorial conference of the week and it remains so today. Indeed, it could be argued that a disproportionate amount of time is spent discussing it, relative to the space it occupies. This is probably because it concerns people rather than issues and journalists like talking about people. It is probably the most enjoyable part of the conference and rarely fails to arouse strong feelings, for or against the proposed subjects.

In David Astor's heyday, as many as half a dozen journalists might contribute to a profile but Astor himself always edited and rewrote them. The verdict at the end was always his. Many *Observer* journalists of that time have similar memories of Astor fretting away over a galley proof of the profile, endlessly reworking it until he was satisfied with the final product. Ken Obank, Managing Editor for many years, noted:

'Particularly in his early editorship years, David and I . . . were often the only people still working in the office after eight or nine o'clock on a Friday night. David, with his jacket off but slung around his shoulders, would be sitting quietly at the big desk, polishing away at the week's profile. Halfway through the night, he would move across to the smaller W.T. Stead table, with its brass plaque stating that this was where the *Westminster Gazette* and *Pall Mall Gazette* had once been edited, to nibble his supper, a flask of hot soup and a sandwich tin of the thinnest toast imaginable. Then he would creep across the corridor to my room with the (ample) remnants and go back to his profile.'

The profile is still polished up on a Friday night, or sometimes on Saturday morning if it has been filed late, but on a computer screen nowadays. The Editor, Donald Trelford, takes as keen an interest in it as his predecessor and usually does a considerable amount of correcting and polishing – indeed, he occasionally rewrites it entirely – before releasing it to the page editor.

Perhaps Astor was loosening up by the 1960s. Paul Ferris was Profiles Editor for two years in that decade. The fact that such a job existed at all may be evidence that the profile was not as high on the Editor's list of priorities as before. Certainly, Ferris remembers that he was left alone to get on with it. He himself might 'top and tail' an essay written by someone else. Ferris's own preference, like Cyril Dunn's, was for the 'offbeat' profile, such as that of Evan Edwards, a Welsh shepherd, which he wrote for the Christmas issue of 1960. (He found him through R.S. Thomas, the Welsh poet, who was a clergyman in rural Wales.)

The profile remains a useful journalistic device, in a quiet week when the subject does not automatically suggest him- or herself. As Michael Davie notes, they can be 'an alternative and digestible way of telling readers about a subject or country or political situation . . . or a more palatable way of explaining difficult ideas on subjects remote from the ordinary reader'. Thus new developments in theology might be made more accessible by a profile of, say, Karl Barth.

Choosing 100 profiles from a total of, I calculate, nearly 2,000 by now, was a difficult task. I could just as easily have come up with 100 different names whose profiles are just as readable as those republished in this book. It was not hard to cut the list down to around 200; some names do not echo thrillingly down the corridors of history. Who now remembers Sir Thomas Barlow (Banker – 22 September 1946, as the card-index faithfully records)? Or Sir Norman Kipping (12 June 1960)? Or Mr Nobusuke Kishi, the Japanese Premier in 1959? In the 1950s there was a fad for profiling institutions (Kew Gardens, Henley Regatta, the Bank of England), which look rather dated now. I therefore excluded them. Some people were profiled more than once, inevitably over a long career. The record (four) appears to be held by Mao Tse-tung and Harold Macmillan. It is interesting to compare widely separated profiles of the same person, but I have reluctantly excluded such 'doubles' to give the widest possible spread of names.

To me, the most fascinating feature of just about every profile I have ploughed through in making this selection has been to see how their judgments have stood the test of time. I think the general answer is: pretty well, though I have included one or two which would probably make their authors blush on re-reading them. (The one of the young Fidel Castro, newly in power in Cuba, is, I believe, a classic case of the well-meaning liberal writer getting it all wrong.) It is easy to criticise journalists for getting things wrong when they are under pressure to produce a definitive verdict on someone in the space of 1,500 words or less. Profiles of that length cannot be much more than snapshots of a person who may be only halfway through a life. But it is intriguing nevertheless to see if the writer got it right.

Some great names will not be found in this book simply because the *Observer* has never profiled them. The biggest missing name in contemporary politics is that of Margaret Thatcher. I suspect this is because she rose to head the Conservative Party and then the Government at a period, the mid- to late 1970s, when the profile was not appearing regularly. So much has been written about her since then that a profile was presumably deemed to be redundant. During the two general election campaigns of the 1980s, the *Observer* Profile focused, not on the party leaders as might have been expected, but on more peripheral figures: on spouses in 1983, and image-makers in 1987. The theory was that the main players were having more than enough written and said about them, so readers might welcome something a little off centre in the profile slot.

In choosing these 100 profiles I have tried to provide a good spread from 1942 to 1990. I also aimed to make most of them names which will be instantly recognisable to today's reader, with a smattering of less well-known figures, whose presence I explain in the introduction to each section. I have also tried to present some of the best-written profiles, which I have either found in the archives or been personally involved with as an editor. I could easily have come up with a hundred others, equally interesting and well-written. I beg the forgiveness of readers who will search in vain for profiles they might remember and hope to find again here, and of my *Observer* colleagues, past and present, whose favourites I have passed over. I hope they all still enjoy this selection.

R.L.

THE SECOND WORLD WAR

It might seem odd that of four profiles selected from the Second World War, three should be of leading Nazis. But they are written with such power and informed detestation of their subjects that no collection of *Observer* Profiles would be complete without them. All are the work of Sebastian Haffner, a refugee from Hitler's Germany who was taken up by David Astor (and who, at the time of writing, is still active, in his eighties, back in his native country). These were of course early *Observer* Profiles: that of Speer is more in the style that was to characterise profiles from the 1950s onwards – informative and surprisingly dispassionate, given the author's natural feelings towards his subject. The profiles of Hitler and Goebbels, on the other hand, are more essay than profile, but none the less interesting for their insights into two demonic personalities.

The profile of Speer, as well as being an excellent introduction to the man, displays a prophetic awareness of the rising importance of the technocrat in modern society, of whom Speer was taken to be a perfect example. It was this aspect of the profile, indeed, that was to have an impact far beyond what its author could have imagined, for it gave Speer himself a few nasty moments, as he related in his book *Inside The Third Reich*. Of mid-May, 1944, he wrote:

'What was really bothering me that day was that Bormann might show Hitler an article from the British newspaper The Observer in which I was described as a foreign body in the party-doctrinaire works. I could easily imagine him doing so, and even the caustic remarks he would make. In order to anticipate Bormann, I myself handed Hitler the translation of this article, commenting jokingly on it as I did so. With considerable fuss Hitler put on his glasses and began to read.' (Here Speer inserted the concluding sentences of the *Observer* Profile, from 'For Speer is, in a sense, more important for Germany today than Hitler, Himmler, Goering, Goebbels or the generals . . .' to the end. In the paranoid atmosphere of the crumbling Reich, one can imagine how that sentence alone might have sealed Speer's fate.)

Speer continued: 'Hitler read the long commentary straight through, folded the sheet, and handed it back to me without a word but with great respect.'

The contrast between the Nazi profiles and that of 'Aircraftman Smith' could hardly be greater: this is an example of a series of profiles of Second World War types, composite characters rather than actual people. They are a mixture of propaganda and journalism: Aircraftman Smith is a shrewd portrait of all those aspirant servicemen who wanted something more than a return to the status quo when victory was finally won: they were looking for 'the square deal', the desire for which was to sweep Attlee to power in 1945. The profile got it half right: although it predicted 'Aircraftman Smith' would vote Conservative, it described him as 'a Conservative with a Socialist outlook'.

ADOLF HITLER

31 January 1943

It is a sign of the times that, after his Decade of Power, the person of Adolf Hitler has lost almost all interest. Those days when he was the most talked-of man in the world, when 'the riddle of Hitler' inspired whole libraries of books and articles, when even many of his opponents reluctantly agreed on his greatness, when every speech of his was keenly awaited and anxiously interpreted in every capital, when his day-to-day temper was carefully recorded in ambassadorial reports – where have they gone? They seem to belong to a remote past.

The man is no longer an actor of world history. He is a prisoner of fate. Every speech, every act of his, has become easily predictable. He can no longer surprise the world. Like Schiller's Wallenstein, he has immured himself with his own deeds. He can no longer make choices, he has left himself no way back and no way out. He is hardly any longer a free agent; the only function left to him is to make sure, by his continued presence in power, that Germany will travel with him down the steep road to utter doom to the very end.

There is hardly any political interest left in analysing his character and retracing the latest stages of its astonishing metamorphosis. But from an artist's viewpoint this change is a fascinating spectacle to watch. Shakespeare, in Macbeth or Richard III, has written no greater studies in damnation than this man Adolf Hitler is today enacting on the world's stage.

During his latest speech in the Munich beer-cellar, on 8 November 1942, when he announced, at the top of his voice, that Stalingrad had already been taken and that nobody would ever get him out of there, that he would exterminate the Jews 'wherever they may be,' and that he would never capitulate, his face is no longer the almost imperatorial face he had acquired during his years of triumph. It is the face of a maniac, puffed, unhealthy, pale, unkempt, with a glint of madness in the eye.

Nor is it a new face. Those who have followed Hitler's 23 years of public life will recognise in this haunted creature's mask the face of the earliest Hitler: the half-forgotten visage of the uncouth beer-cellar orator of 1920, that 'Beggar's Opera' mask, with its vague associations of doss-houses and outlaw's abodes, of that social underworld whence he emerged. Forsaken by his demon, Hitler returns to his origins.

Der Führer has vanished. That carefully stylised, well-groomed figure we remember from the newsreels of the thirties: standing erect in his black car, slowly walking along the front of paraded troops in his imperially draped tunic, smilingly shaking hands with foreign statesmen – this figure is no more. The grand mask has worn out; it has not stood the strain of disappointment, of adversity, and anguish.

Gone is even the Hitler of 1930–34 – the people's tribune risen to sudden respectability, the petty bourgeois awkwardly balancing a top hat on his knees; that queer Hitler suddenly falling back on the humble respectability of his childhood's background, the boy from Branau who had made good; the man whom Rauschning depicted, talking apocalypsis while sipping coffee and munching home-made cake – he is no longer recognisable in the Hitler of 1943. What now stares us in the face is again the Hitler of the early 'twenties, that poor creature with an appalling social record and a grievance against the whole world, who, from a two-hours orgy of denunciation and rage in some obscure beer-cellar, returned to his attic to let mice jump for crumbs of stale bread – and dream of his coming revenge on mankind.

Nor is it the face only which has reverted to its original stark ugliness. Listen to his speeches. There was a time when Hitler, however pervertedly, talked the language of a statesman; there was a time, before that, when he talked like an exceedingly shrewd and cunning demagogue. He knew how to take on his audiences at that time. He knew what to say and where to stop. If he flung himself into a rage, it was a well-considered rage. He would never let himself be caught in easily-refuted short-term prophecies; and when he lied, he lied with such brazen conviction that it took one's breath away.

Today he lies with cold sweat on his brow; he stammers and gropes for words like a man in the dock under cross-examination. His imprudent prophecies give hostages to fortune. Rage overcomes him at the wrong places. He has even lost his grip on his audiences; there is something pathetic about the jocularity with which he remarks on his speeches getting worse for lack of practice.

These are no longer the speeches of a statesman, or even of a first-class demagogue. Again they recall his earliest outpourings, those confused and half-crazy ravings against the Jewish world-conspiracy, the devilish alliance of Plutocracy and Bolshevism, those visions from apocalypsis and the eternal cry for blood . . .

The statesman Hitler is bankrupt. So is the general. So is even the demagogue. What re-emerges is the vulgar, sanguinary crank of 1920–23. His politics have become as irrational and as self-centred as at the time of his crazy beer-cellar putsch. 'I shall never capitulate' is their essence now. 'Tomorrow sees Germany free or me dead,' it was then.

But the morrow of his failure did not see him dead. In the face of physical danger the Hitler of 1923 ran away. Maybe this is the last surprise the Hitler of 1943 holds in store for the world.

JOSEPH GOEBBELS

28 March 1943

Paul Joseph Goebbels was born in 1897 in the small provincial town of Rheydt in the Rhineland, the child of poor, respectable, devoutly Catholic parents. He was from birth handicapped by a club foot, but displayed from his boyhood an unusually bright intelligence. He passed through school with distinction and had his higher studies financed out of a religious trust for the furtherance of poor, deserving Catholic youths of more than average gifts and promise.

As a student at Heidelberg University he enjoyed the tutorship of the eminent, Jewish scholar, Professor Gundolf, author of the German standard works on Goethe and Shakespeare, which are today banned in Germany. Politically the undergraduate Goebbels belonged to student clubs of a Radical Left complexion, mixed freely with Jewish and Catholic students of similar opinions, and showed the greatest enmity against both reaction and the incipient Nazi movement.

After his graduation Goebbels went through a hard time. He wrote several plays and novels, only one of which found a publisher, and that proved a failure. He applied in vain for a post as correspondent of the democratic, Jewish-owned *Berliner Tageblatt*. He lived the drab life of a provincial bohemian, earning a pittance by giving literary lectures, refusing to take up a bourgeois profession, and storing up the resentment of a misunderstood and rejected genius.

Then the local Nazi leader, possibly in one of his lectures, discovered his oratorical gifts and offered him a paid post, as a political platform speaker. Goebbels accepted and for a year toured the villages and small towns of the northern Rhineland to speak for the Nazi Party. This was in 1924.

One year later he caught the attention of the brothers Gregor and Otto Strasser, who at that time managed the Nazi Party in Northern Germany (Hitler was in prison after his beer-cellar *putsch*), and tried to make it a workers' party, competing with the more radical Socialists and Communists. Goebbels became editor of their weekly paper, *Nationalsozialistische Briefe*, and wrote leading articles, praising the genius of Lenin and looking forward to the Socialist Dictatorship of the future.

Up to this point there is hardly a break in his career – the career of a disgruntled, somewhat unstable, Left-wing intellectual, slowly and imperceptibly moving from idealism to cynicism. But now, in 1926, something happened to him. He met Hitler and came at once completely under his spell. The letters he wrote to him after their first meetings have since been printed; they are almost love-letters, filled with a glowing and delirious adoration. Under Hitler's influence, something was unleashed in him, that wild and demoniac power of demagogy which has since made him one of the most sinister forces in contemporary history.

He broke with his former friends. He deserted, betrayed, and fought the Strassers. He shed his former opinions. He even – most astonishing of all – changed his style. It is almost impossible to recognise the involved, serious, somewhat heavy style of his early leader writing in the incredibly vicious, vulgar, venomous pen which directed, after 1927, the newly founded paper *Der Angriff.*

The methods with which Goebbels, in that paper, made Nazi propaganda for six years are without parallel. He developed libel and vituperation to an unprecedented pitch. He swept his public out of its senses through the sheer breath-taking vehemence of the hatred he preached; the pure audacity of his lies. He developed the fine art of myth-creation, choosing as his first object the Jewish Deputy Police President of Berlin. In a sustained campaign of several years he made, without any factual basis at all, this highly respectable official, a former officer and holder of high decorations for valour, seem the very embodiment of every vice and corruption.

He gladly paid fine after fine for libel, heaping more enormous libels on those for which he had been convicted. He changed the Christian name of the unhappy man all of his own volition from Bernhard to Isidor, and made Isidor a battlecry to be howled by Nazi thugs wherever he made an appearance.

It was the first dress rehearsal for his later vilification of Churchill and Roosevelt.

Under Hitler's influence, Goebbels had discovered the black magic of propaganda. He had found out that it is possible to engineer whatever mass emotions are desired by a kind of precise and mechanical psychological pressure, and he has since wielded this new weapon with a boundless contempt for both truth and the human mind. It is almost pointless to reproach him with his inconsistencies and lies, because inconsistencies and lies are the very tools of his art; like an experimenting scientist he is constantly trying how to enlarge their scope of action and how to complete the paralysis and subjection of the human mind, which is his aim.

There is no doubt that Goebbels looks with a certain contempt on men like Goering, Himmler, Ribbentrop, or the German generals all of whom are his personal enemies. They all, he may say to himself, are only trying to do what has often been done: subject and coerce human bodies; he alone, as Hitler's greatest and truest pupil, is working at a task in which none has ever succeeded before. This is to subject and manipulate the spirit of man.

Meanwhile, this intellectual turned traitor to the intellect is no happy man. His life is full of curious, pathological contradictions. Though nobody wields a greater and more sinister power over the German public mind, nobody is personally more unpopular in Germany. He is universally hated, even throughout the Nazi party. His excess of anti-Semitic propaganda is turning against him. To the ordinary Nazi this uncanny figure is the very embodiment of diabolic Jewry as he himself depicts it, and there are unending – probably quite baseless – rumours in Germany which attribute a Jewish ancestry to him.

There are other even darker traits. This man, who owing to his physical deformity has never seen war and is reputed to have on several occasions shown a pathological physical cowardice, is positively seeking opportunities of surrounding himself with wounded soldiers, addressing them and posing with them for photographs. Similarly, the man who leads a notoriously dissolute life, the man whose affairs with alternating dancers and film stars are one unending public scandal, is publicising the regularly recurrent pregnancies and confinements of his wife in an altogether shameless manner.

In a pathetic bid for personal popularity he has posed for a great number of pictures which show him as a family man. These pictures are the height of surrealistic art: Victorian group-photographs, with the paterfamilias, surrounded by his faithful family, dangling a baby on his knees – but this paterfamilias is a swarthy, Mephisto-like figure, with a smile that cuts through his face like a knife. It sends a shudder down one's spine.

Nevertheless, this unhappy, perverted man is a great power in Germany, and a greater power than ever today. In his latest speeches he has almost reverted to his Radical Socialist beginnings. Is it a genuine reversal? Or is it his curse that he must consume and parody what was once his genuine belief in the service of that black magic of lies and deception of which he has become the high priest?

AIRCRAFTMAN SMITH

4 July 1943

Leading Aircraftman Smith – we take leave to call him so – is one of the million of his kind who are geographically behind the present battles, and very much in them in reality. The best of pilots owes as much to his machine as to his nerve and skill. The factories supply the tools, but planes don't look after themselves. That is Smith's job.

Smith is a rigger; he patches the bullet-holes and maintains the metal airframes, hydraulic systems, and the trimming and controls of aircraft. So he serves.

Let us take a closer look at him.

His age is 24. He came to the RAF as a member of a Lancashire auxiliary squadron five years ago. He joined, he says, because it was patriotic, and anyway he knew that war was inevitable. He preferred to do a job he liked rather than be conscripted for one he would dislike.

Smith was born in Liverpool. His parents were middle-aged and his youngest sister was twelve years his senior. Mr Smith could have sent him to a secondary school, but died while his son was still at an elementary school, so Smith never had that chance. His favourite subject was drawing, and his father taught him about colour and form while he was still in the primary class. Later he taught him to use tools.

Sometimes young teachers talked about the Great War, but only the story of the Battle of Jutland made an impression. They taught scripture like history and he liked it. Mrs Smith sent him to a Nonconformist Sunday school. He went willingly because there was a Friday night guild where he could learn leather and basket work. His father invented small things, from a folding perambulator to a patent lock; so young Smith thought it natural to buy saws and hammers with his spending money.

He liked science and history; preferred mathematics to Shakespeare, but read him because it was the right thing.

LAC Smith was fourteen and a half when he started work as a clerk in a building material firm. He disliked the job and became a contract clerk in the Liverpool corn trade. Until nineteen he went to night school to learn bookkeeping and English. He discovered that River Plate wheat is red and round and Danubian yellowish and rather flat. He learned about flour, rye, middlings, thirds, pollards, and maize from everybody who would help. When finished with night school he became a junior Corn Exchange salesman on the soft-goods side. Sometimes he dealt with orders for 5,000 tons of flour a week. He still spent his pocket-money on tools for his workshop.

Leonardo da Vinci was the historical figure who most impressed him because he was an artist and engineer, both of which Smith wanted to be. Among the painters he liked Rembrandt best. He admired Teutonic thoroughness and mechanical efficiency, but wished the Germans were not Nazis because the translations of German books given to him by a Polish friend convinced him war was coming.

LAC Smith was surprised, when war came, that there was not more bombing, though a year later, when he saw the damage on Merseyside, he knew what he had been fearing. He was happy when his own squadron destroyed German bombers as they flew along the North Wales coast to bomb Liverpool at dusk. Smith found he and the other mechanics worked best when they were pressed the hardest.

The food, Smith found, varied from aerodrome to aerodrome and was usually badly cooked. He sometimes longed, and still does, for his favourite meal of

Welsh lamb, green peas and new potatoes, with a few sliced peaches as a sweet. He earns 6*s* 6*d* a day as an LAC and allots part of it to his wife.

The married men, he finds, are most interested in what happens after the war. Most of his friends have heard of Beveridge; the proposals to raise the school-leaving age and build a lot of houses; but they do not worry about Parliament. They feel, says Smith, they are Communists, but like Smith most have had no political education. If he did vote it would probably be for a Conservative, for he regards himself as 'a Conservative with a Socialist outlook'.

He wants to go back to corn, middlings and flour after the war. He likes 'deals' and judges his efficiency by his commission cheque. He becomes civilian minded again in civilian clothes on leave, and once or twice has found himself getting off the tram at the Corn Exchange. Smith's friends, he thinks, look forward to having their old jobs back, and they all expect a square deal which they hope 'Big Business' will not stop.

LAC Smith dislikes compulsory religion, but likes the padre, who, he thinks, should advise and help but not preach. He occasionally goes with his wife to church, especially if it is an old one with some architecture about it, but wants Church Parades abolished. His philosophy, he explains, is: 'Do unto others as you would be done by.' Generally he avoids arguments on religion and politics because no one is convinced, and people sometimes lose their temper.

Smith has had little time to think about the causes of war. He thinks a United Nations with an international police force will prevent another war for the next generation. He often wishes he could invent something so devilish it would stop wars at once. In the RAF he is content and happy except for bouts of homesickness. After the war there will be the Corn Exchange and, he hopes, the square deal.

ALBERT SPEER

9 April 1944

As soon as the Nazis took over in Germany they began feverishly to build. There was in the early years a hierarchy of official master builders. First came technical construction work, motor roads, aerodromes, armament factories, fortifications. All this was under that able engineer, Dr Todt. Then there was the task of 'giving permanent evidence in concrete and marble of the greatness of our time': this meant gigantic fancy building. This fell to Herr Ludwig Troost, an old Party member. Finally on the lowest tier, there was the post of master decorator – the building of non-permanent decorative structures for rallies and public festivals, the plywood, canvas, and sawdust architecture, made to provide recurrent fleeting illusions of cheap splendour for the multitude. This went to Albert Speer, an unknown young architect, still in his twenties.

Speer was the typical representative of those tens of thousands of German middle-class youths who having finished their studies in the late 1920s settled down to an outlook of indefinite unemployment and, after some dreary years, joined the Nazis simply for bread and butter. He was born in 1905, one of a Mannheim middle-class family; he was educated at a technical secondary school, and studied architecture at the technical colleges of Karlsruhe, Munich, and Berlin; he passed his finals in 1927 and then, seeing little chance of a decent job ahead, marked time as research assistant to one of his tutors who found him 'gifted, pliable, but rather cocksure'. Finally, about 1931, he settled down in Berlin as a consultant architect. The outlook was still poor.

But in 1932 his chance came. The Nazi Party looked for an architect to redecorate the house which it had leased for its Berlin Party Headquarters. Of course, he had to be a Party member. Young Speer did not hesitate. His decorations were a success. Next year he got the chance to decorate the Tempelhof Feld for May Day. The Nazis had become the masters of Germany in the meantime. There would be a lot of similar jobs to do in the future.... Speer's decorations won the applause of his employers. Soon he was Germany's public decorator No. 1.

Luck remains with him. In 1935, Troost, the Führer's architect, died, suddenly. Speer, that modest, pliable, but enterprising young man, was chosen to be his successor. His now the chance to give evidence in concrete and marble of his time's greatness! Only one thing he had to do: to mould his style according to Hitler's personal taste. In this he succeeded to perfection. He now had an 'Unter den Linden' office to which Hitler had a passage built from the Reich's Chancellery. Here the Führer often came in a leisured hour, armed with pencil and rubber, to give the final polish of his artistic intuition to Speer's sketches of millennial buildings. The Hitler–Speer partnership soon produced an abundance of public buildings, all strangely similar: gigantic in scale, rectangular in shape, with columns in front and eagles on top. Among them were the Party buildings in Nuremberg and Munich, the German House at the Paris Exhibition, the new Reich's Chancellery (erected in world record time) and many others.

When, in 1938, Hitler tired of the mere building of houses and took in hand the re-building of whole cities, Speer became his plenipotentiary for this task. Late that year, he began with the large-scale pulling down of old Berlin. Innumerable photographs in the German newspapers showed the Führer and his architect side by side, admiring new models of rectangular buildings with columns and eagles about them.

Then came the war. For a time, little was heard of Speer. His smooth, smiling young face disappeared from the illustrated papers. The German public only vaguely remembered him as the Führer's peace-time pet. Suddenly, out of the blue at the crisis of the war, came his fantastic rise. On 1 February 1942 Todt, Germany's war production chief, died suddenly and mysteriously. To the general surprise, neither Goering nor any of the Army experts became his successor. Instead, this half-forgotten decorator became at one stroke Minister of Armaments and Munitions; Commissioner General for Building and Construction; Commissioner General for Water, Power and Electrical Energy; and Chief of the Todt Organisation, Germany's big labour army.

This was only a beginning. In eighteen months Speer gradually acquired the most complete industrial and managerial power that has ever been concentrated in one hand. First he was made Plenipotentiary for Armament under Goering's Four Year Plan. Then the Armaments Office of the High Command was transferred to Speer's Ministry. In June 1942 he was charged with the industrial reconstruction of Occupied Russia. Next, during 1943, supreme power over all German transport by land and water came his way. In August of that year he created the 'Ruhr Staff Speer' to restore and maintain the industrial production of the Ruhr area under air attack. Soon after he became Hitler's plenipotentiary general for the supervision of the planning of the reconstruction of bombed cities. Finally last October, the whole of Germany's industrial production – no longer only war production in the strict sense – was taken from the Ministry of Economics and put under Speer.

The list of his offices fills a long column. He is now, in fact, the dictator and supreme controller of all industrial, building, and transport activities, in the widest sense, in all German-dominated areas.

With what success he fills that gigantic office it is difficult, at present, to say. What is, at any rate, remarkable is the rapid process of power concentration as such – and perhaps even more that it is just a person of the type of Speer who comes forward in Germany's most critical hour to direct her decisive effort. For Speer is, in a sense, more important for Germany today then Hitler, Himmler, Goering, Goebbels, or the generals; they all have, in a way, become the mere auxiliaries of the man who actually directs the giant power machine – charged with drawing from it the maximum effort under maximum strain. And this man is that impersonal little smooth-faced technician, still under 40, that typical product of the new middle-class, who began as a versatile, 'pliable but rather cocksure' decorator and fancy architect. In him is the very epitome of the 'managerial revolution'.

Speer is not one of the flamboyant and picturesque Nazis. Whether he has any other than conventional political opinions at all is unknown. He might have joined any other political party which gave him a job and a career. He is very much the successful average man, well dressed, civil, non-corrupt, very middle-class in his style of life with a wife and six children. Much less than any of the other German leaders does he stand for anything particularly German or particularly Nazi. He rather symbolises a type which is becoming increasingly important in all belligerent countries, the pure technician, the classless bright young man without background, with no other original aim than to make his way in the world and no other means than his technical and managerial ability. It is the lack of psychological and spiritual ballast and the ease with which he handles the terrifying technical and organisational machinery of our age which makes this slight type go extremely far nowadays. The fate of nearly all these young men is circumscribed by the fact that they first find it very difficult to earn a living and then find it very easy to run the world. This is their age; the Hitlers and Himmlers we may get rid of, but the Speers, whatever happens to this particular specimen, will long be with us.

Royals

Since the war, the *Observer* has probably had a more respectful editorial attitude towards the Royal Family than one would guess from talking to many of its journalists. That said, the royals are always a good story, whatever one's political view. The profile of the Duke of Edinburgh catches him at the beginning of his long reign as the Queen's consort, between her accession and coronation, and is of interest in several respects: it accurately outlines the Royal Family's search for a new role in a new Britain; it rather depressingly shows how the Duke's urging of an 'industrial renaissance' failed to get the country to deliver the goods; and in describing the Duke casting around to define a proper role for himself independent of his wife, it was anticipating the problems their eldest son, Prince Charles, would come up against some 30 years later.

The ongoing drama of Royals in Search of a Role is highlighted in the profiles of two who joined the cast in the 1980s, Princess Michael of Kent and the Duchess of York (the tone of the latter being notably irreverent and an interesting contrast to that of the Duke of Edinburgh's 35 years previously). The profile of Queen Elizabeth the Queen Mother was published on the occasion of her ninetieth birthday in August 1990.

HRH The Duke of Edinburgh

4 January 1953

'It is a very grave matter that there are not enough qualified radio or electronic engineers and physicists coming from the universities and technical colleges to meet the industry's requirements.'

'An establishment which teaches science to soldiers and, at the same time, soldiering to scientists, is not an interesting novelty, it is an absolute necessity.'

'When some new discovery is made it is vitally important to see that it is passed into practice as soon as possible.'

'Only those companies who make full use of modern science and technology now will be able to withstand the cold winds of competition when they start to blow hard.'

'Let it never be said that Great Britain became the poor relation of the British Commonwealth in our time. No amount of talk will prevent this happening. Hard work with imagination is our only chance.'

'The solution of our industrial problem lies in the universities and technical colleges.'

Nobody reading these random quotations would easily guess that it is royalty speaking. But they are all taken from speeches made by the Duke of Edinburgh in the last two months, and they are typical of the speeches which he has been making up and down the country during the last half year or so. The occasions – openings, jubilees, exhibitions – have been conventional enough; the speeches have been anything but conventional. Drafted invariably by the Duke himself, delivered in the breezy but serious manner of an officer addressing his men before action, they are worlds apart from the dignified and tactful generalities traditionally put into the mouth of royalty. They are practical, urgent, and pointed – meant not just to grace an occasion, but to make a mark.

Moreover, it is nearly always the same mark they are hitting. What they are driving at is, in short, that this country stands in need of an industrial renaissance. Many of our industries are over-aged, inert, and stagnant. In many cases, the channels between science and industry, or between education and science, have got clogged. The vanguard of our industries is doing fine, but the gap between this vanguard and the average factory has become too large; and it is a gap we cannot afford.

The discovery is not new. What is new is to see the monarchy engaged, through one of its foremost representatives, in a crusade for an industrial and technological revival. Perhaps one could go farther and say: What is new is to see the monarchy engaged at all. In the last 50 years it has acquired an unprecedented prestige, serenity, and popularity through a policy of deliberate disengagement – of being, not doing. To depart from that policy, to put the imponderable, but clearly enormous, accumulated moral power of the monarchy into the service of a cause, is obviously not undangerous. It is also bold and magnificent.

The phrase 'a new Elizabethan age' is being much toyed with by speechmakers and leader-writers today; some of them may be undecided whether in modern conditions it can be more than an elegant literary metaphor. Whatever their doubts, one of those few exalted persons whom it concerns most nearly has clearly decided 'to do something practical about it'.

'It is all very well' – this comes from one of the most remarkable of the Duke's recent speeches, at the opening of Hatfield Technical College some three weeks ago – 'it is all very well to understand the problems which face this country and to have glib theories for their solution. It is quite another matter to have the foresight and courage to embark upon a scheme to do something practical about it.' In the same speech he gave a hint very clearly connecting what he had in mind with the first Elizabethan age: 'The characteristic of all the great periods of English history has been a nation-wide sense of confidence and adventure which went with a feeling of personal service to the sovereign.'

This link clearly existed, spontaneously, under the first Elizabeth. The idea of recreating it consciously, of fusing the sober and vital cause of technologicl progress, industrial rejuvenation, and scientific adventure, with the *mystique* of the Crown and the warmly personal feelings which surround the Royal Family: this idea is a new factor in our affairs; and it is a conception of which few would have thought before it made its appearance.

The man who thought of it and made himself its champion is obviously remarkable for personal qualities beyond the much publicised ones of glamour, looks, sportsmanship, and manners; and he might well make his presence felt on the contemporary scene even if he were not the Queen's consort and the First Gentleman of the land. The conjunction of personality and position makes him one of the most fascinating figures in the Britain of 1953.

Dr Kurt Hahn, the German educational reformer of the inter-war period who, after his emigration under Hitler, presided over most of the future Duke's education at Gordonstoun school, summed up his eighteen-year-old pupil in his school-leaving report as follows: 'Prince Philip is a born leader, but he will need the exacting demands of a great service to do justice to himself. His best is outstanding, his second best is not good enough.'

It is, of course, impossible to guess exactly what particular episodes lay behind this somewhat oracular pronouncement. But one can understand it when one realises two things: The Duke is a member of the between-wars generation – the rising generation of young men who grew up amidst the aimless fatuity of the

1930s and then gave the Second World War its air of sober and stoic fortitude. And he is, on his mother's side, a Mountbatten, and very much a member of that remarkable family, which has been the talk of three European generations, giving headaches to statesmen from the days of Bismarck to those of Roosevelt, alternately charming, annoying, and splendidly serving their contemporaries, and hiding tremendous thrust and energy under a deceptive surface of playboy charm. On both these counts it seems likely enough that his is the type of personal power which works best in response to strong impersonal demands of service. Nor have these demands been withheld.

On his father's side, Prince Philip is a direct descendant of King Christian IX of Denmark, whose children included two kings, one empress, and one queen. This royal background notwithstanding, his childhood and adolescence were spent in the unsettled and unhappy circumstances of exile.

Prince Philip had his first schooling in an American kindergarten and an American primary school in Paris; then his British and German relatives took a hand in his further education, and he went to school in Britain, in Germany, and then, when Hitler came to power in Germany, in Britain again. When not at school, he stayed with his grandmother or his uncle. When he left school and joined the Royal Naval College at Dartmouth as a cadet, in 1939, he is said to have confided in one of his fellow cadets that his one ambition in life was to have a home of his own one day. Whether or not he said it, these may very well have been his feelings at the time.

For the next six years, the navy became his home. He was still a cadet when war broke out. He served at sea throughout its six years, was mentioned in despatches after the battle of Matapan, rose to be second-in-command of two destroyers, and was present at the formal Japanese surrender in Tokyo Bay.

He was a junior naval officer on shore duty at home, living a life in no way different from that of hundreds of other modest-salaried young professional officers, in the years 1946–7 which were to change his life so decisively. These were, of course, the years of his courtship, engagement, and marriage. Nineteen forty-seven was also the year when he finally changed his status from that of an exiled Greek prince to that of a British citizen, and his name from Prince Philip to Lieutenant Philip Mountbatten.

This step was unconnected with his eventual engagement and marriage; there was no obvious need for a foreign prince to become a British commoner in order to marry the British heircss to the throne. Prince Philip had already applied for naturalisation in 1942, because he had to be a British subject to remain in the navy. His application indicated that he had, at last, found a home, a vocation, and an absorbing ambition; all of these were comprised in the Royal Navy. It is significant that even after his marriage he went back to sea for nearly two years, rose – 'entirely on merit,' the Admiralty insists – to the rank of Commander and for about a year commanded a frigate, the *Magpie.*

Some high naval officers who are in a position to judge think that but for his marriage, 'Lieutenant Mountbatten' might in time have equalled the naval achievements of his grandfather, the First Sea Lord of 1914, and his uncle, the present Allied Commander-in-Chief, Mediterranean. As for himself, there is no doubt that the navy completed his education. It brought out, in his mind, that scientific and technical bent which is his strongest intellectual trait, and it provided those opportunities for leadership and those 'exacting demands of a great service' which he needed if his character and temperament were to do full justice to themselves.

It is doubtful whether he felt the same about his position at court during the three-and-a-half years between his marriage and the accession of the new Queen. Perhaps the fact that for half the time he went back to active service at sea suggests a negative answer. He was successful at representative functions, and he made a splendid escort to his wife, especially on tours and visits abroad: the self-confidence and self-control of the naval officer, the natural cosmopolitanism of his upbringing, the Mountbatten dash and chivalry, all combined to make the right foil for the quieter Englishry of Princess Elizabeth's charm and shyness.

He conscientiously set about learning British life and administration at the local level. His chief means for doing so was his Presidency of the National Playing Fields Association, which he assumed at the late King's suggestion, precisely because it brought him into contact with local affairs in every part of the country, and into which he put a driving energy eloquent of underemployed powers. But perhaps the most striking indication of things to come was his presidential address to the British Association in Edinburgh in 1951 – a highly original review of British science in the last century, the fruit of furious research, written and re-written several times, and delivered with verve and force. The discoveries which the Duke made while working on this address largely engendered his interest in the development of science for industry.

The death of King George VI and the accession of Queen Elizabeth II brought perhaps the sharpest crisis in the Duke's official life and career. It meant a sharp separation of the status and working routine of husband and wife, governed by the fact that the Queen represents the highest – though normally inactive – constitutional and political authority in the realm, while the Duke has no part whatever in such constitutional authority. The Queen must know every State secret; the Duke must know none.

Present constitutional practice would make unlikely any arrangement like that by which Victoria and Albert came to share their study, the Prince Consort holding a position which oscillated between those of the Queen's confidential clerk, of her *alter ego*, and of a virtual king. Moreover, nothing in the Duke's life suggests a profound interest in politics or diplomacy, or a wish to play, let alone to extend, such part in them as falls to royalty at the present stage of British constitutional development.

But the Duke is a highly active and highly dynamic man, accustomed to responsibility and leadership, wholly unsuited to a life of mere formality and representation. Luckily for him, the same modern constitutional developments which have circumscribed the political functions of the sovereign more and more sharply have not only elevated the standing of the monarchy and vastly increased its undefined powers to set the tone of national life and to encourage, influence, and inspire activities in every non-political field; they have also spread these powers more and more widely from the person of the monarch over the Royal Family as a whole.

The precedents for this are not to be found so much in the virtually shared rule of Victoria and Albert as in the independent moral and cultural influence exerted by Queen Mary and Queen Elizabeth the Queen Mother; in the representative and almost ambassadorial role which Edward VIII played as Prince of Wales; and in the Imperial and Commonwealth tasks undertaken by the late King George VI as Duke of York and, more recently, by the Duchess and Duke of Kent; one might also, delving deeper into the past, think of the creative artistic or architectural patronage dispensed by past princes and royal dukes.

It did not take the Duke of Edinburgh long to strike out on his own line in this immense open field for the energies of active royalty; to find the point where his energies and his special gifts could be brought to bear, with the whole prestige and moral power of royal status, on a decisive department of national life, and to change the innocuous representative functions of the Royal Family in the patronage of science and industry into something like a royal crusade for national efficiency.

This activation of the monarchy, while taking place strictly within constitutional bounds, and initiated so tactfully as to have hardly been noticed till well under way, is doubtless a major innovation. It may arouse misgivings with those who saw, with admiration, the reigns of King George V and King George VI achieve their resplendent success by very different means. But the new style shows the vitality and adaptability of the ancient monarchic institution; it suits the uncommon gifts and energies of the dynamic man who is now at the Queen's side; and, most important of all, it happily meets an urgent need and a profound desire of the nation to be shaken up, to experience a renewal of its creative energies, its self-confidence, and its native optimism. By translating this desire into the sober terms of modern science and technology, the Duke of Edinburgh is today doing more than just symbolise it. He is in the front rank of those subjects of the Queen who 'have the foresight and the courage to do something practical about it.'

HRH Princess Michael of Kent

21 April 1985

There is a terrible irony in the fact that Princess Michael of Kent, who has cultivated the media with great charm and intelligence, should now be a victim of one of their periodic bouts of excess.

On Monday, she learned that her late father was to be exposed as an SS officer. On Tuesday, the circumstances of her marriage to the Queen's cousin were denounced in the *Daily Mirror* (and less directly in other papers), while the BBC TV News chivalrously illustrated her predicament with wartime film of the Nazis.

Then on Wednesday, unexpectedly, 10,000 swords leapt from their scabbards to avenge even a look that threatened her with insult – several of them brandished, without a pang of shame, by the previous day's denouncers.

By Thursday, her dignified self-defence on TV-am was itself being criticised on the grounds that Prince Michael, as a director of Aitken Hume, owners of the station, had a financial interest in scooping the rival BBC 'Breakfast Time'.

She adores the society of wits. Sir Roy Strong (she is a trustee of the V&A), Bernard Levin, Tom Stoppard and Ali Forbes grace her dinner table at Kensington Palace. She lunches with both George Weidenfeld and Nigel Dempster. She has sparkled at Alan Coren's *Punch* round table and on Maria Aitken's television chat show, and expressed her nostalgia for the vanished glory of the Habsburgs on BBC 'Woman's Hour'.

She has spoken guardedly in several long newspaper interviews, the latest on her fortieth birthday last January, about her difficulties in adapting to the unspoken rules and conventions of the Royal Family.

'There's not a tremendous amount of love lost between her and some of the cousins,' says a friend. 'It's slightly like showbiz: who looks good in photographs, who gets a magazine cover, and so on. Not with the Queen or Prince Charles, but with some of the others, there is a certain competitive tension. As in most families, they occasionally make sardonic remarks about one another.'

One of the keys to Princess Michael's personality is her high spirits. She enjoys such comforts and consequences as rank still affords in a democratic age, and sees no reason to dissemble her enjoyment.

'She's a natural,' says another friend. 'She adores playing the part of a princess on state occasions. She has great energy, great *joie-de-vivre*, great style. She laughs a lot. She looks the part and dresses the part. She's a marvellous actress.'

But another key lies buried in her Australian childhood and early youth, in nursery stories of lost grandeur and dispossession. Her friends say that she

seldom speaks of that part of her life, even to intimates. It is unguessable from her lightly inflected Viennese accent, though it might be deduced from her unusual openness and directness.

She was born (at Kladruby in Czechoslovakia) into the crumbling remnant of the Central European aristocracy during the last months of the Second World War. Her German father, Baron Gunther von Reibnitz, had inherited an ancient but impoverished Prussian title. He joined the Nazi Party in 1930 and the SS in 1933, and served with the 31st Panzer Regiment in Poland during the war.

Her mother, Maria Anna Szapary, comes from a distinguished Austro-Hungarian family who served the Habsburgs as courtiers, politicians (Princess Michael's great-great-grandfather was a Prime Minister under Franz Josef I) and diplomats.

With the Red Army approaching, the couple fled westward with their three-year-old son Fred and the infant Marie Christine. At about this time, according to a family friend, the Baroness discovered that her husband had been previously married and divorced. Her bishop told her that the Church could not recognise her marriage and that she and her husband must live henceforward 'as brother and sister'. (The ruling did not, of course, affect the legitimacy of the children under Canon Law.)

The couple parted and divorced. The Baron went to the Portuguese colony of Mozambique, where land and labour were cheap, to become a citrus farmer. The Baroness, who must be a remarkable woman, took the children off to Australia, where she worked as a beautician in Sydney. She, too, remarried (as she was free to do in the eyes of the Church, her first marriage having been invalid). Her husband was an emigré Polish count, Thaddeus Rogala-Koczorowska, who was working as a municipal clerk.

The family lived in a suburban bungalow, spoke French at home, rode and swam. Princess Michael attended a fashionable convent school, Kincoppal. Her mother told her stories of the past and spoke of how sweet life has been before the fall. The child was brought up to think of herself not as a New Australian, but as a European with a distinctive past and a negotiable future.

After a visit to the Baron in Mozambique when she was 20, she spent a year back in Sydney designing clothes during the late 1960s' flowering of the boutique industry, before taking off for Europe to seek her fortune. In London, she took a diploma in design at the V&A, specialising in the English eighteenth century, and became apprenticed to the interior designer Mrs Evelyn Chance, in whose Belgravia home she had a small flat.

Her first marriage at 26 to Tom Troubridge, a merchant banker, fell apart after he was posted to Bahrein. She was bored by the limiting society of Anglo-American bankers and oilmen, and returned to London alone to form her own successful firm, Szapary Designs. One of her commissions was the Iranian Embassy that was gutted in the 1980 siege.

The marriage was dissolved, and the Vatican eventually granted an annulment. When she and Prince Michael decided to marry, Lord Mountbatten acted as their adviser and intermediary with the Queen, whose approval of the match was required (Prince Michael renounced his place in the succession to the throne.) They married at a civil ceremony in Vienna Town Hall, Paul VI having refused a dispensation to marry in church because of their declared intention to bring up their children in the Church of England. The dispensation was granted by John Paul II in 1983.

Prince Michael was a major in the Royal Hussars. Besides his pay, he had a private income large enough to sustain a cavalry officer in considerable style. Princess Michael was a successful West End design consultant. But by the standards of the international café society in which they moved, peopled by men with great inherited wealth or newly minted fortunes, they were not well-off.

In 1980, Prince Michael resigned his commission to go into the City, where he is a director of STC, Walbrook Investments and London United Investment, as well as Aitken Hume. He was a good soldier and a happy one. He is a conscientious businessman. But in the professionalised world of the corporations he inevitably plays what is primarily a plenipotentiary role. His four directorships probably bring in about £100,000 a year.

Princess Michael gave up designing professionally five years ago. She has an income from unidentified 'business interests' and is beginning a career as a lecturer and author. Weidenfeld will be publishing her collection of short stories of historical princesses. She carries out public engagements for numerous charities, particularly those concerned with the arts and medical research.

By the quietish, horsey and doggy canons of the Queen's life, the couple lead a rather glamorous existence. Skiing at St Moritz, scuba-diving in the Caribbean, hunting with the Beaufort or the Cotswold. Their Queen Anne manor house, Nether Lypiatt in Gloucestershire, is within a few miles of Charles and Diana and the Mark Phillipses. Princess Michael redesigned the interior. They have two children, Fred (five) and Gabriella (three) and numerous Burmese cats (brown).

The Countess of Dudley and the biographer Fleur Cowles have acted as her companions and guides in the still surprisingly protocol-conscious ambience of the Royal Family and their circle. Inevitably, there is social skirmishing on the fringes of any court. Princess Michael has some critics within that circle as well as many admirers. Not long ago, Lord Dudley was diverting dinner parties with readings of his verse satire on her social life.

The difficulty is that she is in the royal circle, but not of it. Had she chosen to lead a purely private life, that would not have been an obstacle. But, like the Duke and Duchess of Windsor, she has allowed herself to be courted by the international set, among whom extravagant gifts and favours returned are acceptable currency.

Since Prince Michael is not in the Civil List, there is no impropriety in his wife mixing pleasure with advantage. But there is, of course, a contradiction between the mores of the old landed society, of which the Royal Family is one of the last relics, and the free-wheeling style of the super-rich. It seems snobbish in 1985 to be endorsing those antique social values, yet it is hard not to feel a sneaking sympathy with those of her circle who complain that the dashing princess is trying to have it both ways.

HRH The Duchess of York

6 March 1988

It is the burning question in saloon bars all over the country. It is a question so sensitive, one touching on so many national emblems and taboos, that it should perhaps be spoken, as well as written, with a capital letter at the beginning of each word: Has the Duchess of York Gone Too Far?

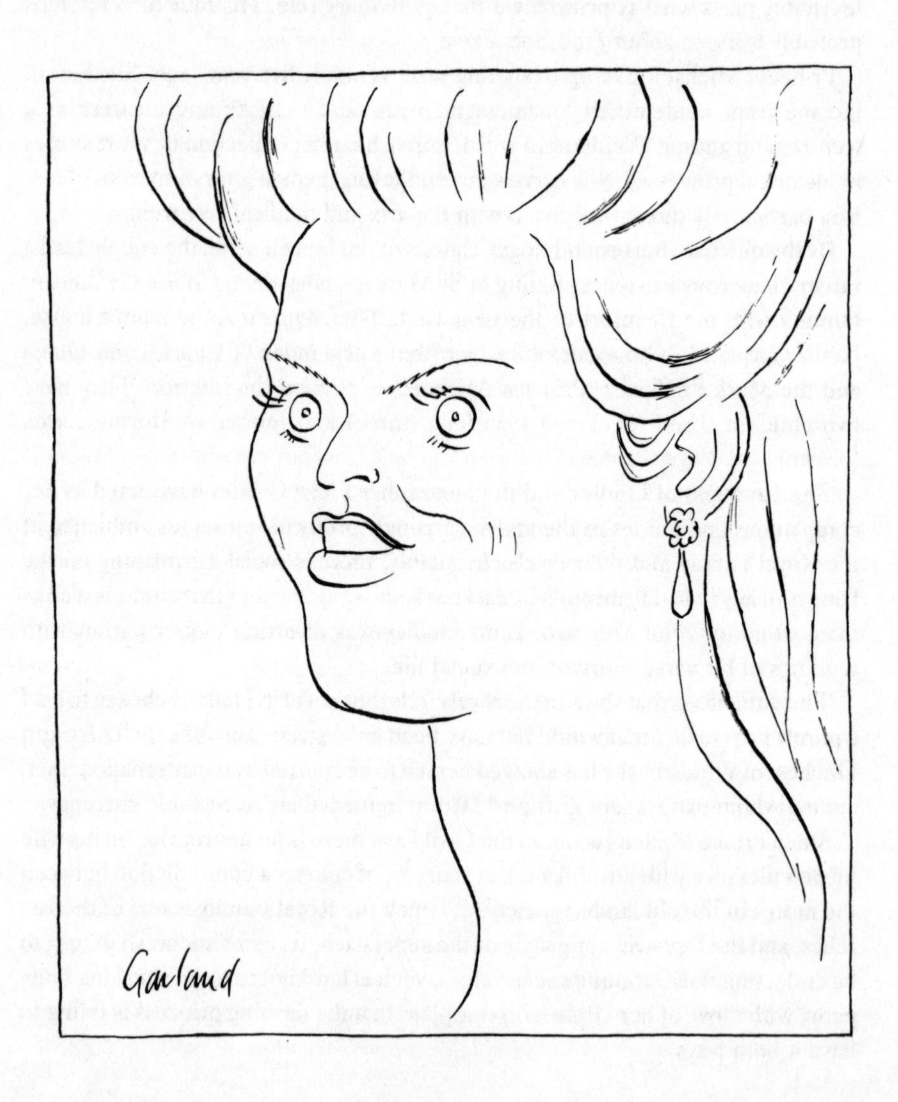

It is one thing to joke with children who present bouquets about your love of sweets; quite another to engage in sexually suggestive banter with a nutty heckler in Hollywood – 'I love you', 'I'll see you later', 'Promises, Promises' – (the man was a foreigner, to boot). Her revelation that the Royal Family pull their lavatory handles upwards, and not down like the rest of us, may be of academic interest to plumbing historians, but it does destroy the mystique somewhat. Her disclosure in America that her sister-in-law's most treasured memory is a dance she once shared with John Travolta must have come as a bitter disappointment to all those dedicated public officials who thought the Princess of Wales was happiest opening a new National Grid switching station at Didcot.

Something appears to have gone awry with the Royal Fairy Story. Even in this day and age, it is easily possible for the noblesse to be too obliging. With her behaviour in Los Angeles, the Duchess of York has marched her family to the top of the hill, then marched them down again. And when they were half-way up . . .

If you drive down the Mall, at any time of the day or night, you will always see two lights burning on the top floor of Buckingham Palace. It is the office of the Royal Scriptwriters, the anonymous but dedicated men intent on turning Buckingham Palace into our own Southfork Ranch, 'Dallas' into 'Palace'. Until now, barring the occasional regrettable moment to which even the best-run families are prone, they have got it unerringly right, composing a plot with a fearful symmetry and structural rhythm, ever since the Queen herself starred in the first televised episode doing a spot of washing-up at a Balmoral picnic. The dramatic high spot was when Prince Charles's cello string snapped and hit young Andrew in the eye.

Charles grew up to become Action Man, an apparently carefree bachelor until family responsibilities required him to settle down. His role was then taken over by Andrew, Hero of the Falklands War, dashing escorter of starlets, until marriage claimed him too. Then – a neat touch, this – we had Edward, the Failed Action Man with a desire to be Really Useful. Anne developed from petulant, horsy daughter into a dedicated, courageous, universally respected charity worker. Margaret and Michael occasionally star as attendant princesses, there to swell a scene or two or steal the odd episode within the matriarchal family presided over by Miss Elizabeth.

There seemed, at first, the same symmetry, the same care to create subtle yet essential differences in the choice of Royal Brides. Diana was the virginal, shy young thing who wouldn't use one word where none would do, a size-10 dedicated follower of fashion, with a temper as short as her skirts and a patience as thin as her silk ball gowns. She would be seen on royal occasions, not waving but frowning.

It was not long before several episodes were taken up with the thrilling rumours of trouble at the Palace. Things, according to the curious and unnamed legions of 'close friends of the couple,' ordinary 'friends of the couple' and a multitude of 'Royal aides' who supposedly contact the tabloids at moments like this, were wrong with the marriage. Charles was talking to plants because they understood him better than his wife. The Nation held its breath. All good knockabout stuff, and the ratings soared.

Onto this scene and into the script came Sarah Ferguson, a touch of brilliance, an evidently inspired invention. Bubbly, extrovert, talkative, bigger, older, with a past (and an O-level), even a job – her experience working for a publisher enabled her to correct a spelling mistake last week when David Hockney presented her with his book inscribed 'Dutchess'. She appears to have kept up her interest in books – she recently asked for a signed copy of Tom Wolfe's best-selling 'The Bonfire of The Vanities'. Another neat contrast with Diana, who you feel would rather open an exhibition than a book.

She was a compliment to Andrew and a complement to the Complete Family. Sarah and Diana became the royal twin-set and the pearls.

The Duchess of York has become the favourite of the Queen – she finds her easier to understand and fathom than Diana. The Duke of Edinburgh is much taken with her rather raunchy sense of humour. Some of her favourite jokes are a little difficult to print in a family newspaper, and others that are – 'What smells worse than an anchovy fillet? An anchovy's bottom' – are best accompanied by the sound of bread rolls being thrown.

She was, and is, not so much a Sloane Ranger – Diana's role – as that slightly lesser social breed of girls known as 'Soanly Rangers' – these are Sloanes who find it cheaper to live in places like Clapham and Stockwell (they got their name because they explain their location by saying, 'It's only ten minutes from Sloane Square'). Indeed, many of her old friends, the ones from school that she used to go with on hitchhiking trips to Brazil, live in these places and she and Andrew are frequent guests at dinner parties in that part of London. Most of their friends, the real ones who don't ring the tabloids, seem to have originally been hers rather than his, with the exception, perhaps, of Mr and Mrs Elton John.

The marriage of the fourth in line to the throne began well, according to the script seemingly mapped out in that tiny room in Buckingham Palace. Sarah Ferguson made a rather hopeful, if slightly naive, statement that 'Andrew and I are marrying each other, not the whole world' and meritocracy gained a foothold in the aristocracy with her declaration that she intended to carry on as a 'working woman,' keeping her publishing job while her husband continued his job in the navy. Then there was Action Woman with her intrepid flying lessons (during the courtship period Fleet Street, as it was then called, had already found her a pretty action-packed car-driver). In a few short months, she was being described as one of the country's best dressers – in courtship days she was criticised as being 'dowdy' at worst, and 'eccentric' at best (the last accusation did surface again last week when she wore the family curtains to a Los Angeles ball). A national poll, sample size unknown, decided that her shape was preferable to that of Diana. A more recent survey claimed that the majority of the nation preferred her legs as well.

It's clear that everyone thought that Sarah Ferguson would be the opposite, even the antidote at times, to Diana. She would be a royal personage, and not a royal character. Since then, however, things have changed – the sweet smell of success seems to be being replaced by one of excess. The Duchess of York's dedication to her publishing job diminished drastically – since the book she was working on before her marriage came out she has resigned.

Her husband has had an exceptionally large amount of leave from his ship, and at times it has seemed as if the couple did marry the world, to judge from the large parts of it in which they have taken their holidays. The ease with which the couple got their controversial planning application for a new house past the authorities quashed any fanciful notions about meritocracy. The number of free gifts, right from the flying lessons and assorted travel 'freebies' that the Duchess has felt able to accept, has raised eyebrows even among people who appreciate the problems of having to exist on a mere £50,000 a year (plus free accommodation and an officer's salary). A member of the Balmoral staff has recently told a French magazine that the Duchess has become 'off-hand'.

And a friend of the couple, actually a close friend who is also an aide, says that there has been a cooling off lately between the two sisters-in-law, because Diana has become jealous of the attention her new relation is getting from the media. Even the Queen has had occasion to remind the Duchess of certain aspects of *lèse-majesté*, such as the fact that you don't wave when someone wolf-whistles at you.

This was not how it was meant to be. Sarah Ferguson was made a Top Person when she married Prince Andrew, but she wasn't meant to go over the top; was meant to be in the limelight, not to hog it. If, as is often said, the Royal Family are our greatest ambassadors, then should our ambassadors really hit their husbands over the head with wine bottles, even if they are papier-mache film props (especially when it's a gimmick that's already been done once before)? What do the people who come to watch the Changing of the Guard outside Buckingham Palace make of the even more strange spectacle of the new guard changing things inside the Palace?

Of course, all this might have been anticipated by those script writers. It is no bad idea to have a few months of critical and censorious comment in the saloon bars – only to be silenced instantly by the unalloyed joy when the Duchess of York becomes nappy and glorious with a bouncing royal baby.

HM QUEEN ELIZABETH THE QUEEN MOTHER

5 August 1990

In 1969 the age of the talkies arrived for the British Monarchy. At last the Royal Family were heard to converse in other than the formal phrases and brief courtesies of their public engagements.

It was the greatest revolution in popular perception of the insitution since Lord Esher's invention of modern royal ceremonial at the end of the nineteenth century. The effect, like *Alice in Wonderland*, was to transform heraldic playing-card figures into occupants of the same physical and intellectual universe as the rest of us, making them much more attractive as individuals.

But the Queen Mother, like her elder daughter, is a star of the silent age. She dwells on the far side of that portentous divide, remaining adamantly in the pre-talkie era. Privately, she counselled against the change. Publicly, she is still as mute as Marcel Marceau. What is she really like?

She looks a good sort. The strong chin suggests a less ferocious version of the Red Queen in *Through the Looking Glass*, the sympathetic smile a non-dithery White Queen. Perhaps it's precisely this combination of grit and gentleness that has always enchanted her companions. But since all information about her is filtered through a protective screen of friends and courtiers, who can be sure?

The cataract of sentimental drivel in the media that prefigured her ninetieth birthday yesterday has been no help. The gawping housemaids on the staff of the *Sun* ('the Darling of the Nation') have done their highly profesional best, but have discovered nothing of consequence. In the *Sunday Times* Sir Alastair Burnet has given us his much-loved impersonation of Mr Collins in *Pride and Prejudice* praising Lady Catherine de Bourgh ('Her poise, her gestures . . .'). The *Independent on Sunday*'s nerve has cracked and, bucking the house rule (which is to pretend that the Royal Family isn't really there), it has published an irreproachable *laudatio*.

One turns to the standard hagiographies compiled by numerous indefatigable ladies. They do their best, too, but they are fatally impeded by their exclusion from the principal sources of truthful biography: the personal correspondence of the subject and the candid testimony of family and friends. They are obliged to rely, like the tabloids, on anecdotes of microscopic triviality.

What is unhealthy about all this, indeed insulting to the intelligence, is the tone of veneration. The Queen Mother is popular in a healthy, hearty way, but she is not revered. No Englishman of the eighteenth or early nineteenth century, moved though he may have been by an uncomplicated deference to royalty, would have countenanced such nonsense, and her own ancestors would have thought it grotesque.

They were the hard-drinking Scottish Earls of Strathmore, at whose dinner parties a pageboy was kept under the table to loosen the gentlemen's collars as they fell from their chairs. She was the ninth of ten children of the fourteeth Earl, and grew up in one of those great Edwardian households that seem to have existed to facilitate the mass slaughter of game and consumption of amazing quantities of protein – a ceaseless intake from the groaning sideboard at breakfast to the last plate of ptarmigan sandwiches in the billiard-room late at night. It was said of Edward VII that 'he did not toy with his food', and the Queen Mother has enjoyed a good appetite for food and drink.

She has lived all her life amid great wealth. When she was four her father inherited £250,000 on the death of the thirteenth Earl, making him a multi-millionare at today's values. It is reasonable to assume that, besides her Civil List annual allowance (due to increase from £439,000 to £640,000 next year) and a generous provision under George VI's will, her old age has been comfortably buttressed by Strathmore family trusts, despite the many stories around London that she perpetually complains about her 'overdraft'.

Her happy childhood was spent at St Paul's Walden Bury in Hertfordshire. Every May the Earl would transport his vast menage to a handsome Adam house, 20 St James's Square, for the London season. Every August they would move on to Glamis Castle in Scotland for the shooting. She was educated by governesses and tutors, apart from two shorts spells at private day schools in central London.

Even allowing for the romantic predilections of country house photographers of the period, it is obvious that she was an exceptionally lovely girl with an intelligence and sensibility absent from many vapid society beauties. She was blessed with an equable temperament and a natural gaiety that help to explain her subsequent popularity. 'The only completely unselfconscious sitter I ever had,' said the portrait painter John Singer Sargent.

Public who warm to her presence at public engagements or on the racecourse are responding to a simple gift for projecting what one must assume to be genuine feeling. Presumably, like anyone continuously engaged in official ceremonies, she has learned to dissemble boredom. Mostly, one seems to be looking at a woman unselfconsciously enjoying herself.

Among older people affection for her is enhanced by three episodes in her life: her well-documented sense of injury when Edward VIII's abdication in 1936 thrust the succession on her utterly unprepared husband; George VI's decision to remain in London during the Blitz and their wartime visits together to meet bombed East Enders; and her premature widowhood in 1952.

As the Scottish radical Tom Nairn has pointed out in *The Enchanted Glass*, the distinctive cut of her pastel-shaded clothes is totemic, not chic. You could sit all day in the lobby of the Connaught or the ice-cream parlour at Fortnum's and not see a single woman dressed remotely like the Queen Mother. Long before Sir Gordon Reece remade Mrs Thatcher's image or Peter Mandelson Neil Kinnock's, the old pros in the Royal Household had grasped the laws of telegenesis. The common jokes about her – the Pearly Queen, Gordon's gin, etc., all doubtless apocryphal – at least show how the public *want* her to be.

What the conventions of the silent era have mostly obscured, of course, is her intelligence. She is a cultivated woman within the somewhat insular boundaries of her class and generation. She recommended Arthur Koestler's novel about the Stalinist terror, *Darkness at Noon*, to Winston Churchill, who read it and insisted that his Cabinet did so too. Nowadays she is more likely to be reading detective stories by P. D. James or Dorothy L. Sayers.

Her three homes – Clarence House next to St James's Palace, the Royal Lodge in Windsor Great Park, and the Castle of Mey in Caithness which she bought and renovated – contain her well-chosen collection of twentieth-century paintings, started under Kenneth Clark's tutelage, which includes Monet's *The Rock*, Sisley's *The Seine near St Cloud*, and works by Sickert, Paul Nash, Graham Sutherland and Augustus John.

Her main recreations have been National Hunt racing (as an owner she has had nearly 400 winners in the past 40 years) and fishing. She owns a herd of Aberdeen Angus cattle and a flock of Cheviot sheep.

As a member of the Royal Family she inhabits and endorses a socially fortified coterie governed by an archaic protocol that would seem utterly alien to most of her admirers if they ever experienced it. Kindly as the Queen Mother is, she is really not very like anybody's grandma.

Does popular affection for her and the other Royals have any political significance? Radical intellectuals, desperately trying to get the old republican jalopy back on the highway, have tried to argue that it has – to our detriment as a modernising society. As a dowager queen, does she embody some of the sacral magic of kingship? Homespun constitutional romantics like Enoch Powell might perhaps claim so.

A serious case can be made that the Queen Mother has done more than any other individual in this century, with the possible exception of King George V, to give the Royal Family its present distinctive character. She made her husband a King and her daughter a Queen – neither of whom had been born to the task. These are good enough reasons for most people to join the weekend's celebrations, not to mention the affection and respect that even a hardened old republican would be loath to deny her this weekend.

DIVINES

The first name in this section will probably be the least familiar. I have included the Reverend Michael Scott because he was a personal friend of Astor's whose selfless devotion of his life to the oppressed people of the Third World represented much of what Astor's *Observer* stood for. Scott's championing of such causes as the Nagas became familiar to *Observer* journalists in the 1950s and '60s. He died in 1983.

The other religious leaders are more mainstream. Martin Luther King is portrayed at the height of the civil rights fight in the USA but at a time when he was still relatively unknown to British readers. Both Cardinal Hume and Dr Robert Runcie were profiled in 1982, the year of the Falklands War, which caught both prelates in its crossfire. It nearly led to the postponement of Pope John Paul II's visit to Britain, which Cardinal Hume was instrumental in saving; and Dr Runcie's sermon at the Falklands memorial service, urging compassion for the defeated Argentines, brought a storm of protest from some quarters and could be seen as the beginning of Mrs Thatcher's disenchantment with him.

The 'peg' for Terry Waite's profile in January 1985 was his visit to Libya to attempt to persuade Colonel Gadaffi (or Qadhafi as the paper then quaintly styled him) to release four British missionaries being held hostage. He was successful in securing their freedom. Nobody dreamt that before long Waite himself was to be taken hostage in Beirut, during another similar mission. At the time of writing he is still held captive.

THE REVEREND MICHAEL SCOTT

4 December 1949

It was a dramatic moment when a tall, delicate-looking Anglican parson stood up last week before the United Nations Trusteeship Council to plead the cause of the Negro population of South-West Africa.

He spoke as the accredited representative of some 50,000 peasant tribesmen who were liberated from German rule after the First World War, but who now live uneasily and anxiously under the mandatory rule of the Union of South Africa.

The Revd Michael Scott is one of the few Europeans who have ever succeeded in crossing the barrier of suspicion that separates Black from White in Africa. Among contemporaries, only Albert Schweitzer – philosopher, musician, surgeon, scientist and humanist, whose hospital at Lambarene in French Equatorial Africa is known to thousands of Africans as a haven for the sick and the needy – has won such confidence and prestige. And before him, there was the great David Livingstone.

Between him and Michael Scott there is at least one striking parallel. While Livingstone was working at his remote mission station in the Northern Transvaal, he was accused by the leaders of the Boer Republic of sheltering behind the sanctity of the cloth to spread mischievous propaganda and to incite Africans against the Europeans. Much the same accusations are levelled by the descendents of those Boer Republicans against Michael Scott, who, like Livingstone, has waged a lonely fight against a tide of White antagonism.

Michael Scott was born 42 years ago, the son of an English country parson. He was educated at King's College, Taunton, and intended to go on to Cambridge University but ill-health made this impossible. His doctor advised going to a warmer climate, so, at the age of nineteen, Scott made his first visit to Africa. His temper is at once revealed by his choice of work in a missionary leper colony for natives, where he remained for a year. He decided to make the Church his career, and he returned to England in 1930 to be ordained at Chichester two years later.

At first his work in the Church followed conventional lines. From a small Sussex vicarage he went on to a living in Kensington; thence to the less genteel surroundings of Clapton, and, finally, in 1935, to India.

Among the poor of London and, even more, among the squalid millions of Bombay and Calcutta, Scott found the opportunities that his nature demanded. Compassion for the weak, the oppressed, the infirm, the underdogs of the world, soon developed into a settled purpose to live with and for those who most needed his help. He was to identify himself with the needy, uncompromisingly.

On the outbreak of war he left India and returned to join the RAF. Characteristically, he joined as an aircraftman, not as a chaplain. But he was invalided out of the Service early on, and decided to return to South Africa. This decision to make Africa the scene of his self-imposed labours was to have major consequences.

In Johannesburg, where Michael Scott now came to work, he found the same squalor, dirt, poverty, and malnutrition as in India. He also found racial discrimination. From then on, single-mindedly and without tactical compromise, he has fought for the interests of the African population.

The war against Nazi Germany had encouraged among some of the European community a spirit of liberalism and racial tolerance; there was talk of a New Deal for the native peoples. But this new spirit did not long survive the end of the war. Increasingly, Michael Scott came to be regarded as a nuisance and a crank. Increasingly, as his reputation for fearless championship of the Africans spread throughout the Union, his name became associated with trouble of every kind.

One night in Durban he saw some European hooligans beating up Indian passive resisters. Scott's reaction was to join the passive resistance movement himself. He was arrested and sentenced to three months' imprisonment. His prison experiences were turned into a vivid and forceful document which he submitted to the South African Penal Reform Commission.

Soon after leaving gaol, he received an appeal from a group of African ex-servicemen who were squatting in abject misery on a site they had named 'Tobruk'. The camp was in chaos, owing to corrupt and inefficient leadership. Scott decided to stay and reorganise it: settling down in a shack beside a little canvas church he had built – which was later burnt down by a hostile African mob which disapproved of some of his reforms – he introduced some order and sanitation to the camp, used the whole of his savings to pay overdue wages, and arranged finally for an improvised 'civic' authority to take over – though not before he had again been arrested for living in a non-European area.

Scott next went to the Transvaal, where his investigations into the near-slavery conditions among farm labourers in the Bethal district aroused violent opposition. Angry European farmers publicly threatened to lynch him should he ever set foot in the district again. So he returned alone to face his critics at a public meeting. He was met by a howling mob that refused him a hearing, and police had to intervene to prevent violence. His calm on this occasion, and his lack of bitterness, deeply impressed those who witnessed it.

Finally, his three-year struggle to help the Africans of the former German colonies, culminating in his travels to the United Nations, has won for Michael Scott a unique position among the peoples of Southern Africa. They have also earned him the opprobrium of many Europeans, who accuse him of being a dangerous crank, a misinformed fanatic, an irresponsible trouble-maker.

The impression that this controversial figure makes on those who know him best is one of diffidence and reserve. He is hesitant in speech, temperate and restrained in argument and respectful of other people's views. But he is totally uncompromising where he believes that principles of justice and humanity are involved, and he is unmoved by considerations of what may or may not be regarded as practical, even by his well-wishers. In appearance he is still youthful, with a strikingly handsome face that has something of the saint and something of the rebel. He is careless of food, clothes, and all material pleasures. For some years now, since he resigned from his Johannesburg parish, he has had no regular income, and has lived and travelled on the alms of those who wish him well: he has lived exiguously.

Whether Michael Scott's exploit at Lake Success will have any immediate effect on the fate of his protégés may be doubted. Nor can the influence of his actions on the ultimate outcome of the African story, fraught as it is with alarming and incalculable possibilities, be foreseen.

What is certain is that the Africans in their millions will be watching and listening to what he says and does. The simpler tribes will probably make up chants recording his existence and efforts. There is one such chant amongst the Zulus mocking the activities of a committee of Christian ladies that Michael Scott often quotes as an example of the consequences of what he regards as an inadequate kind of Christianity:

The Committee
Is at the School.
We are plagued
By Christians.

It is not likely that the chants on Michael Scott will be in this vein.

DR MARTIN LUTHER KING

29 October 1961

A new spirt is abroad among southern Negroes in America, and the man who embodies it is a clergyman of 32, the Reverend Martin Luther King, who is in London to appear on *Face to Face* tonight, to preach in Bloomsbury, and to speak at the Central Hall, Westminster.

Anyone who enquires into what is happening in the southern states finds areas of vagueness and evasion, as if it were an underground operation in an occupied land. Even when it goes into action, who is leading what is not easily determined. But the involvement of Dr King is never in doubt.

Such formal organisation as the new movement has is to be found in the Southern Christian Leadership Conference, of which Dr King is founder and president. But he also has humbler duties as associate preacher in a back street of Atlanta, the capital of Georgia. The white cab-driver who takes you to King's address says doubtfully: 'You know that's a Nigger quarter?'

The church faces a row of derelict frame houses, and the street is busy with black people. After this, King's own setting is surprisingly rich. His office has none of the varnished bleakness found in the chapel halls of England, but is comfortably opulent. American Negro leaders have learnt the value of an impressive front.

Yet the well-dressed black man who rises from behind the big desk to receive a white visitor is neither arrogant nor effusively friendly. A white man who admires him very much says that King 'has a hard time loving us white folks', but perseveres because love is essential not only to his religious philosophy but also to his techniques of social action.

King is uncommonly small, but sturdy and compact. Those who from time to time have roughly arrested him and thrown him into gaol probably have reason to be thankful that he was eager to go. He is handsome, wears a black pencil moustache on his wide upper lip, and would look as much at home in one of the healthier jazz combos of New Orleans as he does in the Ebenezer pulpit. Like President Kennedy – with whom, to the astonishment of white southeners, he has the most friendly relations – he looks even younger than his age.

Most of the driving spirits in the New Southern Movement are young, and most are Negro ministers of religion. There are, of course, other and older Negro bodies, notably the National Association for the Advancement of Coloured People, founded in 1909, with which the new movement is often said to be in conflict. As if to contradict this, Dr King has his own NAACP certificate of life-membership framed on his office wall. But the NAACP has always battled for Negro rights through the courts, and is mainly northern-based.

In the south it is traditional for preachers to lead the Negro community, if only because the church was originally the one tolerated institution for blacks. But although a few brave old men strove to lead their people 'out of this Egypt of segregation', many more of them preached a simple and emotional gospel which helped, often by design, to reconcile the black folk to their lot.

Now Negro preachers of an entirely new kind have begun to appear. Most are highly educated, and all reject the fundamentalist belief that a minister's duty is to preach nothing but the gospel. They take it to be their religious duty to lead their people out of inferiority, injustice and affliction now, here on earth, and by the shortest, most dramatic route.

The Negro church has not accepted this internal revolution calmly. There is real conflict between men of the older tradition and the new young militants. There have been vain attempts to limit King's influence. At the last annual meeting of King's own church body, the National Baptist Convention, USA, Inc., which has five million members, factions fought for microphones on the platform, and one man who was knocked off the edge died of injuries. The battle was not really between the Old Guard and the New Wave, but the president, who was struggling to retain his office, did accuse the platform-invaders of being 'King's men'.

There are men of the Old Guard – not all of them old – who genuinely disapprove of King's methods. The chances are that many of them do not properly understand King's aims or his philosophy – which is not surprising, since King himself doesn't seem wholly free of doubt, and often wears a melancholy look.

The steps by which he came to southern leadership are logical enough. Like other sensitive Negroes born in the south, he bitterly resented the indignities imposed on him. His father was a stubborn individual resister. (He is head of the Ebenezer Church in Atlanta, and is also called Martin Luther King. So is the elder of Dr King's two sons – a confusing dynasty of Kings.) As a theological student in the north, King sought a means of using Christian love to eliminate social evil. He came across Gandhi's philosophy of non-violence and was enraptured by it.

King could have stayed safely and profitably in the north, but chose instead to return south, as a Baptist minister in Montgomery, Alabama. Here, in 1955, he had the chance to use Gandhian techniques when other Negroes who decided on a total boycott of segregated buses made the virtually unknown newcomer their spokesman.

Segregation on the Montgomery buses was not ended by the boycott, though it became a world-wide sensation and made King the most celebrated of all American Negro leaders. What ended the boycott was just another old-fashioned court action by the NAACP. People who think King is interested in his own aggrandisement say that this has somehow been 'glossed over', though, in fact, it does little to detract from his astonishing achievement.

For the first time in American Negro history, a city of black people persisted in organised resistance for a year. By so doing they confounded the southern whites who believed that 'Niggers couldn't organise anything but a crap game'. They proved that humble Negroes really cared about the condition of their lives, and that resentment in the south was not simply aroused by a few agitators. King was under intolerable strain. But under his guidance, and in spite of much provocation, the whole thing was carried through without violence, and began the great stirring throughout the south.

It is said by those who wish to diminish King that his Southern Christian Leadership Conference has never started anything. In a literal sense this is probably true. The lunch-counter sit-ins that followed the Montgomery boycott, and spread through the south like wildfire, were started by 'a coupla black college kids' in Greensboro, North Carolina. The sensational Freedom Ride this year was started by the northern-based Council on Racial Equality, and when this first drive was brought to a bloodstained halt in Alabama, was at once picked up by a group of students from Nashville, Tennessee. Each time King appeared only in Act Two, as it were, and seemed to have been taken by surprise.

It could be that King's share in these actions has been deliberately hidden. The new movement is disciplined and avoids careless talk, especially to white reporters. The action groups certainly get training in non-violent techniques, and, where they need it, finance from a central source. But the movement has many parts, with each unit recognising a separate duty to act promptly and without consulting the Atlanta office.

Anyway, King is not a leader in any conventional sense. For thousands of young southern Negroes he is 'the Man', a source of ideas and strength even for those who have never seen him in the flesh. When things start to roll, the young people have no need to summon him. He simply arrives, talks to them in a curiously intellectual version of the old southern preaching style, and joins them on the happy road to gaol.

The white supremacy groups in the south see his hand in all their misfortunes. The young ministers speak of his 'charism' – a favourite word of theirs – and believe he has a grace specially vouchsafed by God. He may also be seen as an ordinary young man, delighted by his pretty wife and their three small children, wishing he had more time to stay at home reading books. Whatever the truth, King and his young clergymen have changed the whole spirit of the generation pressing at their heels.

CARDINAL BASIL HUME

30 May 1982

The Pope's visit, after weeks of on-off-on-again anxieties, has been a diplomatic and personal triumph for Cardinal Hume – a triumph all the more dramatic for being seemingly out of character.

Since he was conjured out of the mists of the North Yorkshire moors six years ago to become Archbishop of Westminster, Basil Hume's warmth, simplicity and

directness have made him the most popular Catholic prelate in Britain since the Reformation. But nobody has ever thought of this unassuming intellectual, with his long Plantagenet face and diffident smile, as a Prince of the Church, versed in the labyrinthine politics of the Curia.

John Paul himself was always predisposed to come. It was his Vatican advisers who worried about the effect on the Church in Latin America. Hume clinched it by persuading the two Argentine Cardinals Aramburu and Primatesta in Rome nine days ago. It was a victory not for statecraft but for sincerity.

Hume, 59, is the son and grandson of medical men on his (agnostic) Protestant father's side and of army officers on his French Catholic mother's. He grew up in a solid, cultivated middle-class family in Newcastle where his father Sir William

Hume was a heart specialist. One of his sisters is married to Lord Hunt, the former Cabinet Secretary.

As a boy, accompanying a Dominican friend of his mother's, Fr Alfred Pike, on his rounds in the poorer parts of the economically stricken city, he gazed appalled at ill-nourished, barefoot children of his own age. The experience turned his thoughts to the priesthood.

At Ampleforth, the fashionable Benedictine school, he was good at games (fast bowler, captain of the first XV), bright but not intellectually outstanding, a natural leader. In September 1941 he entered the monastery there as a novice after wavering between the social commitment of the Dominicans and the contemplative life of the Benedictines. The war was going badly. He agonised over the decision. He says now that, given the choice again, he would have joined the Army.

In 1944 he went up to St Benet's Hall, the Benedictine house at Oxford. He played rugby for the Greyhounds and for a cup-winning college side composed of Benedictines from St Benet's, Jesuits from Campion Hall and Welsh Methodists from Jesus: an awesome array of the forces of righteousness. He got a second in history.

Sant' Anselmo, the Benedictine seminary at Rome, was then under the influence of German theologians, who were regarded by their English brethren as narrow, authoritarian and much too Rome-oriented. Hume was sent instead to read theology at the liberal University of Fribourg, developing a breadth of sympathy that was to contribute to his choice as Archbishop 25 years later.

Back at Ampleforth, he became head of languages and a housemaster. It was the happiest period of his adult life. He is a man uncomfortable amid the complex manoeuvrings of hierarchies. In the relaxed and friendly school atmosphere, he could operate directly through one-to-one relationships, and experience the close comradeship that he misses in his present busy but lonely eminence.

In 1963 the Ampleforth monks elected a successor to Abbot Herbert Byrne, who had served 24 years. The contest lay between Hume and Patrick Barry (later to become headmaster of Ampleforth and a prominent figure in public school politics). Hume had been chosen six years earlier to instruct the young monks in theology. It turned out to be a key appointment. He is one of those gifted teachers who inspire lifelong gratitude. 'His students were deeply impressed by him,' says a friend.

'They all became Basil's men and eventually voted for him. It was an involuntary exercise in vote-catching.'

Hume was 40 when he became Abbot. It was a difficult time. His first years coincided with the Second Vatican Council. The monastery was divided. There was disappointment that he failed to give a stronger lead.

When he was chosen as Archbishop thirteen years later, many grammar-school-educated London priests, grappling with the poverty of inner city parishes, were dismayed at the appointment of a monk from a remote monastery and a smart school. It is true that he had no direct experience of parish work and of the frustrations of the lower reaches of the Church's bureaucracy. But he had been responsible for administering a community of 150 argumentative monks, half of them scattered in twenty parishes throughout Wales and the North. A third of his time was spent travelling on business outside Ampleforth. It was certainly not a life of meditative seclusion.

The choice to succeed Cardinal Heenan in 1976 lay between Hume, Derek Worlock (then Bishop of Portsmouth), a first class administrator, and Michael Hollings of St Mary's, Bayswater, a widely respected radical whose support was organised by the Duke of Norfolk.

Heenan had risen – like most of his predecessors since the restoration of the Catholic bishops in 1850 – through the hierarchy of the Church. He was a prelate of the old school: commanding, paternal, exacting obedience, intolerant of waywardness. There was broad consensus about the need for a successor who would reflect post-war change in the Catholic population.

At the beginning of the nineteenth century, on the eve of Emancipation, there were only 80,000–90,000 Catholics in Britain, mostly descended from scattered communities that survived the Reformation. The majority of Britain's 5.5 million Catholics today have sprung from the successive waves of Irish immigration since the 1840s.

About 1.3 million are first- or second-generation Irish; 670,000 are immigrants from other countries. But the other two-thirds – 2.5 million assimilated descendants of nineteenth-century immigrants, 500,000 converts, and 500,000 old English Catholics – have no sense of ethnic separateness. At the same time, education has carried many of them into professional and managerial jobs.

The old duality between a recusant élite (viz., *Brideshead Revisited*) and an Irish proletariat is out of date. There is still a slightly higher proportion of manual workers among Catholics than in British society as a whole, and the immigrant tradition survives in the heavy Catholic Labour vote. But there is now a substantial and growing English Catholic middle-class: independent, questioning, impatient of authority. That middle-class has led the intense doctrinal debate of the past fifteen years, and its interests and attitudes dominated Hume's selection in 1976.

It desired two things: a leader who would embody simple Christian values in an age of declining congregations and theological confusion; and one who would clearly identify English Catholicism with English culture.

In both respects, the Cardinal has succeeded beyond expectation. He is a man of manifest spirituality and humanity; and his Englishness has been displayed in his reasonableness and tolerance, and in his courageous alliance with Canterbury. He and Dr Runcie have remained close throughout the Falklands crisis, neither saying anything without reference to the other. 'It would never occur to him to insist that the Catholic Church must not be seen not to take the lead,' says a Jesuit. 'He has absolutely no side.'

In the sombre surroundings of Archbishop's House – which the late Patrick O'Donovan used to describe as looking like 'a nursing-home for upper-class alcoholics' – Hume installed an ex-directory hot-line on which any priest in his diocese can call him for advice at any time. He was the first English Catholic bishop to publish full accounts of his diocese. He has taken time to help many priests and laymen through personal crises.

Yet the enormous affection he inspires is often strongly coloured by exasperation. He possesses the defects of his virtues. He is sometimes ineffective, partly because he is too kind-hearted to coerce people, partly because he is too intellectually honest to pretend to certainty he doesn't feel. He is by temperament a cautious conciliator who loathes conflict.

On secular issues, like arms control and race relations, and on doctrinal ones, his critics say he speaks in liberal language but doesn't act in the same spirit. 'He makes splendid speeches at international congresses about ecumenical relations,' says a parish priest, 'but when we want to know whether we can share communion with the Anglicans down the street, the answer's No. He's where the vocal Catholics are, but is he where the people are?'

His friends argue that he would like to be more radical than the Pope allows him to be. Critics reply that this has not impeded Cardinal Suenens in Brussels or Bishop Elchinger in Strasbourg.

Not all the criticism is fair. Hume personally intervened to persuade the Callaghan Government to stop arms sales to El Salvador. He authorised the sale of the diocese's shares in South African gold-mines. He lobbied against the British Nationality Bill. On the doctrinal front, he worked with great skill behind the scenes to bring initially hostile English and Welsh bishops behind the National Pastoral Congress at Liverpool in 1980, ensuring that it was a genuinely open, not a managed debate on the future of English Catholicism. On the other flank, of course, he is criticised by those conservatives who wish the Church to remain primarily an instrument for individual sanctification.

In any case, the old style of hierarchial leadership – whether conservative or radical – is perhaps less important. The new Catholicism is more a matter of local decision and personal conscience.

If the Catholic community is less anguished, though not less disputatious, than it was a decade ago, it is at least partly due to its new self-confidence, which Basil Hume has inspired and cherished. The Pope's historic visit fittingly crowns that achievement.

DR ROBERT RUNCIE

12 September 1982

Looking back at the row over the Falkland Islands service in St Paul's, when the Prime Minister was said to be 'livid' because a more triumphal note was not struck by the Archbishop of Canterbury, a thoughtful Church of England cleric remarked the other day that the Archbishop himself had been delighted by the uproar.

It had made Dr Runcie visible. Until then, the cleric said wittily, what with the popularity of Cardinal Hume, the Pope's visit, and the TV success of *Brideshead Revisited*, it had begun to look as though Hume was the nation's leading churchman and the Roman Catholics the Established Church. At least now everyone knew it was Dr Runcie who was head of the national Church.

Since his appointment as Archbishop in 1980, Dr Runcie had in fact by no means been silent. He had criticised the Government's overseas aid programme, and its Nationality Bill, he had praised the Brandt Commission; he had condemned the H-block hunger strikes. He had figured prominently on television screens during the royal wedding and the visit of the Pope.

But his refusal to bow to pressure over the St Paul's commemoration service was the first sign to reach the lay public that the new archbishop might turn out to be a formidable character, despite appearances. He had, before St Paul's, stated his belief that an Archbishop of Canterbury should not necessarily always act as the cement of society, but should sometimes be the grit. Judging by the letters that poured into Lambeth Palace after the service, his stand met with wide approval from church people, since the mail ran 95 per cent in his favour. Dr Runcie is a self-critical man, and sensitive to what others think of his performance. It would not be surprising if he, like the thoughtful cleric, felt he had passed successfully his first serious test since he became the 102nd archbishop.

Dr Runcie is not a natural prince of the church. In person, with his spectacles and frown, his voice with its hints of Malcolm Muggeridge, and his gentle, modest, and approachable manner, he lacks some of the physical advantages that used to be a boon to the beetle-browed Archbishop Ramsey, and are at present a boon to the monkish Cardinal Hume and the electrifying Pope John Paul II. (The theatre and the Church have much in common.)

Nor is Dr Runcie a conventional prelate who finds it easy to lay down the law. He likes to tell the story of the American philosophy professor who asks his class at the end of a seminar whether they have got it clear and, when they chorus 'yes', groans that in that case they have got it wrong again. Over simplification he regards as a vice, not a virtue.

His temper, one might say, is academic and intellectual, though his career has also shown him to be someone who instinctively questions the ecclesiastical status quo and is ready, sometimes eager, to promote reforms. The Church of England is often accused of complacency; but that is the last word that could be applied to Dr Runcie.

His family background is modest. His father was an electrical engineer in Liverpool, and Robert, born in October 1921, was educated locally before he won a scholarship to the least intellectual of Oxford colleges, Brasenose. He served during World War Two as a successful officer in the Scots Guards, winning, as is well-known, the Military Cross for pulling one of his men out of a blazing tank under enemy fire – a proof of physical courage that must have given pause, if only briefly, to some of his recent warlike critics.

Becoming a clergyman after Oxford, he has said, seemed the obvious thing to do. He got a first in Greats, which showed him to be clever as well as brave. He underwent his theological training in Cambridge (Oxbridge has been a large part of his life) and spent two years as a curate on Tyneside, where he and his vicar formed a mutual regard for each other – invariably a good sign. It was this former mentor, John Turnbull, later Archdeacon of Ripon, whom Dr Runcie consulted when he was asked to become Archbishop. Turnbull was on his deathbed and advised Runcie to take the job, saying that if one was asked to do such a thing it was normally right to accept.

After Tyneside, Runcie went back to Cambridge for seven years, first to his old theological college, successively as chaplain and vice-principal, and then as fellow and dean of an ordinary college, Trinity Hall.

Here he met his wife, who stimulates as much gentle Barbara Pym-like gossip in the Church of England, a gossipy organisation, as all her predecessors combined. Her father was a Trinity Hall law don, and she acted as the dean's secretary. Since then, she has made her own career in music as a teacher and performer, and shown an up-to-date wish not to live merely as an appendage of her husband.

A former member of her husband's theological staff still recalls the blast Mrs Runcie gave him more than a decade ago for allowing his children to use her children's slide. 'Too much religion makes me go off pop,' she told a radio audience. When her predecessor took her round Lambeth Palace, she remarked, on being shown the drawing-room, that it would be a splendid place for disco parties.

As a devoted friend remarked of her not long ago, 'she is like a puppy who tumbles into mistakes'. There are two children, a boy and a girl, both sent to traditional public schools.

It was when Dr Runcie was appointed principal of Cuddesdon theological college, seven miles from Oxford, that he began to make his mark. Cuddesdon, a nineteenth-century Gothic pile in a quiet village, has been a positive nest of bishops, with a tradition of what might be called 'liberal orthodoxy'.

Dr Runcie opened up the place both to women (here Mrs Runcie played crucial role) and to outside thinking (those were the years of radical theology, with 'God is Dead' in the United States and 'Honest to God' in England). He improved the college buildings, and became well-liked as the Cuddesdon parish priest (a post that goes with the principalship and one that Dr Runcie took very seriously).

The sudent unrest of the 1960s did not leave even Cuddesdon unaffected, and he introduced some timely democratic reforms. 'But he always kept the reins firmly in his own hands,' says one of his staff.

A bishopric duly followed the nine years at Cuddesdon, the see of St Alban's, where Runcie's most significant innovation was probably his scheme of ministerial training. This insistence that priests must be theologically competent relates to the heart of what Runcie is trying to do as Archbishop.

From his high-ceilinged study at Lambeth Palace, with its big window looking on to trees, the Archbishop observes a national community conscious of nuclear threats, distrustful of promises of technological or political utopias, yet anxious for something to live by.

He used to tell his Cuddesdon ordinands that the mark of a good priest was the moral strength to ask the right questions. 'Today I think, yes, that's OK, but now it's time for a few answers.' What does the Church stand for?

The question is readily asked. But Church of England members are often peculiarly unemphatic (compare, for instance, Polish Roman Catholics). And the hierarchy and theologians are not providing convincing answers. Inside the palace, they abhor what often seems to be the blur of the modern C of E, and refer to Jung to make their point for them: 'An ethical fraternity with its mythical nothing is a pure vacuum and can never evoke in man the slightest trace of that age-old animal power which draws the migrating bird across the sea.'

Traditional clergyman's language, says Dr Runcie, when it is employed these days, often seems to disappear into symbolism. We live in a 'verbal ice-age'. 'It is not the moment for *summas*,' for comprehensive, dogmatic compendia of Christian belief. 'It is more a time for putting together stones in the wasteland' (Dr Runcie knew T. S. Eliot).

As for 'the answers,' and his prime concern that the Church must engage much more positively in 'serious religion' – and demonstrate that Christianity has more guts than vague humanism – he has told (politely) the Church's Doctrine Commission to set to work on producing, with the House of Bishops, a series of precise and authoritative doctrinal statements. 'Instead of that litter of books on the parish bookstall – behold instead a line of paperbacks in ice-blue covers on everything from euthanasia to the Virgin birth.' He is determined to produce a theological ferment.

Christian or not, most people would agree with him that the nation is ready for some rigorous thinking about the mysteries of life. Dr Runcie may well be the man to promote it.

BISHOP DESMOND TUTU

8 May 1983

If the line between politics and religion is always blurred, nowhere is this more so than in South Africa, where the deadly sparring between white and black nationalists is taking on the dimensions of a theological civil war.

Both sides claim biblical justification for their cause: the Dutch Reformed Church on the one hand, with an Old Testament argument that a God-fearing nation – in this case the Afrikaner 'nation' – has a divine right to its own separate existence; the proponents of a black theology of liberation, on the other hand, claiming that Christ's mission on earth was to identify with the poor and the oppressed.

From Dr Daniel Malan, an ordained minister in the Dutch Reformed Church who became the first Prime Minister to propound the doctrine of apartheid, and from Chief Albert Luthuli, a lay preacher in the Methodist Church who led the African National Congress in the 1950s, there is also a long line of preacher politicians on both sides.

In this context, it is hardly surprising that the voice which now wins broadest acceptance in South Africa's black community is that of a churchman, Bishop Desmond Tutu.

As general secretary of the South African Council of Churches, Tutu is the putative spokesman for the country's 13 million non-DRC Christians, 80 per cent of whom are black. The Dutch Reformed Church withdrew from the council even before Tutu took over in 1978.

Many whites in Tutu's own Anglican Church see him as a troublemaker. When there was a move two years ago to make him Archbishop of Cape Town, the titular head of the Anglican Church throughout southern Africa, the Church council was unable to agree, for the first time in its history, and a compromise candidate was chosen. A white clergyman, who is one of Tutu's admirers, admits there are members of his congregation who say openly that they hate the man.

For the Government, it is more than just a matter of hate. To them Tutu is sinister. They are given to conspiracy theories to explain what to them is the abiding mystery of South Africa's pariah status in the world, and they see Tutu as the pivotal figure in a vast and shadowy network of subversion that includes the Soviet Union, the World Council of Churches, the United Nations, Western liberals and the whole Third World.

It is probably only Tutu's bishop's mitre and his growing status abroad, particularly in Britain and the United States, that has prevented the Government thus far from banning him.

They have limited themselves to preventing his travelling abroad, as they did again recently when they refused him a passport to accept an invitation to preach in St Paul's Cathedral last Sunday.

What the whites fail to see in their blinkered world is that in black terms Tutu is a moderate. He stands in the vulnerable centre of a rapidly polarising society, still preaching racial reconciliation to two sides who seem to be moving inexorably towards violent confrontation.

He has a sense of mission rather than of strategy, and if a thing seems right to him in biblical terms, then he does it. This led him a few years ago to meet with Prime Minister P. W. Botha, which brought sharp criticism from black radicals. There were dark mutterings about his possibly being sucked into the system and becoming another Bishop Abel Muzorewa.

The meeting itself proved futile, with the two men talking past each other: Tutu about the need to abolish apartheid, Botha about the threat of terrorism. Despite this and the criticism, Tutu is reluctant to say he would not see Botha again, if the opportunity arose.

'Who are we to prejudge the grace of God?' he says. 'It's very difficult for me, as a church leader, to say: "Go to hell!" To say God's grace cannot operate on P. W. Botha.'

'That's the trouble with Desmond,' observes one young radical. 'He believes in the Gospel literally. Love thine enemy, he keeps saying. At his age he should learn to hate a little.'

If hate is alien to the man's nature, anger is not, nor militancy. He has turned a defiant face towards the authorities many times, well knowing their reputation for ruthlessness. He marched through Soweto at the head of a column of protesters during the 1976 riots, during which more than 600 blacks were shot dead.

For all his sense of mission and his intensity, Desmond Tutu is not dull company. He has what is often called an impish sense of humour.

It is his voice more than anything that reveals his personality. Its range is extraordinary, from deeply sonorous, as when he chants the Eucharist service in the small Soweto church where he serves as parish priest, to sudden high-pitched yelps and giggles; when he is excited. It can move through all these registers in a single sentence, as it responds to his mercurial spirit. But it is never bland and pious.

Desmond Mpilo Tutu was born 51 years ago in the West Rand town of Klerksdorp. His second name means 'life' and his grandmother gave it to him because he was a delicate baby who was not expected to survive. 'That was my first commitment to faith,' he says with one of those delighted giggles.

It is one of the great ironies of South Africa that this turbulent black priest, who so disturbs the White Government, arrived where he is because of the apartheid system.

The Church was his third choice as a career. He wanted first to be a doctor, and was actually accepted by medical school, but his parents could not afford the fees. So he became a teacher and worked contentedly in several schools until he was 25 and already married.

Then in 1957 the Government introduced its system of state-run 'Bantu education,' and along with many other black teachers Tutu quit. Only then did he consider the ministry as a career.

'I was not moved by very high ideals,' he recalls. 'It just seemed that if the Church would accept me, this might be a likely means of service.'

The seeds of idealism had been sown at an earlier stage, however. Tutu recalls that his mother was the dominant influence in his childhood: a simple but compassionate soul with little education who worked as a washerwoman and cook.

His father, a teacher, was strict and quick with the strap. Mother was always the one to intervene. 'She was always taking the side of underdogs in all kinds of situations, even when they were in the wrong,' says Tutu. 'I suppose I either inherited or copied that.'

When Tutu was twelve, the family moved to Johannesburg, where his mother took a job as cook in a school for the blind. Life at the school was a salutary experience, as the lad found himself surrounded by compassion and dedication to the deprived.

It was there, too, that he first saw the man who was to have the biggest single influence on his life. Father Trevor Huddleston, a parish priest in the black slum of Sophiatown whose magnetism and commitment made him the best known and most controversial churchman in South Africa's history.

'I was standing with my mother one day, when this white man in a cassock walked past and doffed his big black hat to her,' Tutu recalls. 'I couldn't believe it – a white man raising his hat to a simple black labouring woman.'

Later Tutu received his training for the priesthood in Huddleston's Community of the Resurrection. When asked why he does not hate whites after all the racial suffering they have inflicted, Tutu is disposed to say it is because he was fortunate in those he met during his formative years.

After he was ordained, he went to King's College, London, and later spent three years in England.

When finally he returned to South Africa, it was as a man who had freed himself from the emotional and intellectual shackles of second-class citizenship.

Tutu risked his life to try to save a security policeman at a political funeral in the Ciskei 'homeland' eighteen months ago. He flung himself across the man's body, when the angry crowd of 15,000 set upon him with stones.

When he thought he had saved him, Tutu returned to his rostrum, his clerical robes soaked with the policeman's blood. But later the crowd dragged the policeman away and beat him to death.

The oncoming struggle in South Africa could be something like that, Tutu reflects: 'People holding off a little, because you say so, then, when you turn your back, they continue.'

Terry Waite

13 January 1985

At a critical moment in Terry Waite's two-hour interview with Colonel Qadhafi a note was passed to the mercurial Libyan leader. Recalling that mail is said to take about six months to reach its destination in Libya, Waite made a wary joke. 'You have an efficient postal service here, I see.' Qadhafi paused, then laughed, and by the end of the interview a good rapport had been established between the two very different men.

Humour is one of the secrets of Waite's success. His colleagues guarantee that if you put him in a room with any group of people, however unpromising, they will soon be chuckling together. His size – he is six foot eight inches and weighs sixteen stone – is another asset. 'Very difficult people defer to him because he is so tall. He has a natural authority. That and his directness are an unbeatable combination,' says a Lambeth Palace colleague.

His style of negotiation has a warmth and openness about it which contrasts sharply with the subtler ways of politicians and diplomats. He is a good listener and can focus attention on the human beings involved in a diplomatic contest. His manner inspires trust. When Qadhafi enquired about Libyans being tortured in British jails, Waite replied: 'Do you believe I am telling you the truth? Libyans are not being tortured in jail.' Waite, aged 44, will not say much about the interview which secured the recommendation that the British hostages should be freed. Discretion is a vital part of his valour and he is scrupulously fair about people with different views from himself.

He argues that Qadhafi should not be written off and that the man who was once asked by an American journalist 'Colonel Qadhafi, are you mad?', is well aware of what the world thinks of him.

But it wasn't only his genial manner and the quiet, measured tones of a man of faith that won him through to the Libyan leader. He has an astute brain, a powerful grasp of theology and philosophy, and enough foxy cunning to make him a first-class negotiator, the Church's answer to Henry Kissinger. He thinks on his feet. He had not realised until his meeting with Qadhafi in a Bedouin tent that the harassment of Libyans in this country was a major stumbling block to good relations. Fears had to be allayed or the mission would falter. 'The idea that the Church should set up a telephone service for Libyans was thought up on the spot,' he says.

Yet the preparations for his visit left nothing to chance. Months of patient work preceded it and he did not go until the signs were favourable. He has a diplomat's coolness in a crisis but admits to a temper. He lost it when he reached the airport with the Iranian hostages four years ago and was told at the eleventh hour that their departure would be delayed.

The Foreign Office, while keeping a careful public distance from the Archbishop's special envoy, is privately enthusiastic about his talents. They would have liked to use him to serve his country had he not already decided to serve his God.

Terry Waite grew up in Styal, Cheshire, son of a village policeman and, as a boy, dreamed of travel. He joined the Grenadier Guards but had to leave because he found himself allergic to the khaki dye in his uniform. He then studied theology at the Church Army College in London because he was attracted by the army's 'passionate coolness'. Later he studied in the United States, Louvain and Rome. He worked for the Anglican Church at home before becoming adviser to the first African Archbishop of the province of Uganda, Ruanda and Burundi. He and his wife, who was eight months pregnant at the time, were held at gunpoint during Idi Amin's expulsion of the Ugandan Asians.

For a time he was attracted by Catholicism. He worked for the Roman Catholic Church as a consultant on missionary work in Africa and then for the Vatican itself. Shortly after Dr Runcie's arrival at Lambeth, he showed his usual talent-spotting skill by appointing Waite as his secretary for Anglican Communion affairs.

His absence from home during two of the last four Christmases has involved real sacrifice. He is a devoted family man, telephoning them regularly from distant parts of the world. His wife, Frances, a Belfast solicitor's daughter, is as ill-at-ease as her husband is comfortable in the limelight. He has four children, nineteen-year-old twin girls, an eighteen-year-old daughter and a thirteen-year-old son. They live in a terraced house in Blackheath, where he campaigns for preservation of the old locality. He is a member of the Travellers Club and the Left-Handed Society. He likes music, reads Jung, and often rides to work on a bicycle.

During the past three months, since his first, secret visit in November, his bulky presence has become familiar to the Libyans – first to a small élite of foreign liaison bureau officials, now through television and the newspapers to a wider public. His huge frame fits uneasily into the low-slung Bedouin tent with carpets on the floor that Qadhafi keeps pitched inside his heavily fortified barracks headquarters in the centre of Tripoli for receiving important guests. But Terry Waite is now accepted there as Britain's most trusted envoy since Ambassador Oliver Miles left town with his staff last May.

The Libyans refer to him sometimes as 'deputy Archbishop', but Terry Waite simply smiles at the mistake. He feels his true vocation is to work as a lay member of the Church of England. He has never felt a desire to be ordained, though most people still wrongly assume he is a priest.

On his return to London after his last visit, Waite felt he needed an extra lever to persuade Qadhafi that it might be in his own interests to release the hostages. Church contacts in Africa suggested a private approach to the Colonel through President Julius Nyerere of Tanzania, a practising Roman Catholic and current chairman of the Organisation of African Unity.

Archbishop Runcie telephoned Dr Nyerere in Dar es Salaam and Terry Waite was despatched immediately to the Tanzanian capital. Nyerere promised he would write a letter to Qadhafi recommending that he receive the Archbishop's envoy to discuss release of the hostages.

Now Waite is on his third visit to Libya. Last week he spoke to a People's Congress meeting in a circus tent in Tripoli.

He has avoided any contentiously political statements, has listened carefully to the complaints of relatives of Libyans in jail in Britain, and has stressed the virtues of compassion, which are understood by readers of the Koran as much as by those of the Bible. All seems set for a successful conclusion of the 'deputy Archbishop's' delicate diplomatic mission. And yet, until the hostages are firmly back on British soil, a tiny suspicion must remain that he might have been the victim of a Libyan propaganda exercise.

Waite fully realises that, but remains an optimist. 'What both sides are interested in is fairness and justice,' he says. 'I like to think we have achieved a little bit of mutual respect beyond the actual politics of the hostage situation. The ability to establish personal relationships is crucial to solving problems in many parts of the world that seem beyond solution. All you need is common sense.'

There has been banter as well as common sense during the political marathon in Tripoli. His interlocutors asked him, when he arrived last week on a Libyan airline flight from London, if he had had a comfortable journey. The Archbishop of Canterbury's envoy said he had found it difficult to cram his six foot eight inches inside an economy class seat.

'But our People's Society tries to make everyone equal, so we have no first-class seats,' replied Dr Slitni, Libya's deputy Foreign Minister, who has led the negotiations with Waite.

'That may be man's intention, but it is certainly not God's design,' remarked Mr Waite. 'Ah! But didn't you observe the plane was made in America?' said Dr Slitni. It says something about Terry Waite's ability to disarm that it is he himself who tells the story.

But then, no one who actually works with Waite will say a harsh word about him. In the ranks of the churchwardens' brigade of course there have been grumbles that it is he, a layman – not the Archbishop – who now runs Lambeth Palace; and, even more dangerously, outside the Church, rude demands as to why the two men do not simply change places. That is not wholly fair, for the well-orchestrated publicity surrounding his missions has had far more to do with a media-conscious Archbishop than with Waite himself. He is a pressman's delight – not least because he actually looks like a Russian Orthodox patriarch.

He may yet fail in his attempt to free the Libyan hostages; but he will still have come nearer than anybody else to success. Maybe that explains why no voice has yet ventured to complain that a man of religion is meddling in politics.

POPE JOHN PAUL II

28 December 1986

The Renaissance Pope Julius II went down in history as the warrior pontiff, defending the interests of his Church with cannon. His successor, John Paul II, will be remembered as the public relations Pope who has chosen jet travel and the media as his weapons.

In the eight years since his election, the Pope, now aged 66, has travelled half-a-million miles outside Italy and visited 70 countries – some of them, like his native Poland, more than once. In 1986 alone, he has been all over India, spent a week in Latin America, and has just completed his longest and most punishing pastoral journey yet: a 31,000-mile swing through six former British territories in Asia and the South Pacific.

In 1987, there will be a gruelling fortnight in Chile, Argentina and Uruguay, a tour of the industrial areas of the Ruhr, a third visit to Poland, and a journey through the southern United States from Miami to Los Angeles.

No previous Pope has placed such emphasis on the unifying message that John Paul has proclaimed as the reason for his travels, though sometimes travel seems to be its own reward. When *Observer* correspondent David Willey asked him on the overnight flight to Bangladesh last month why he wished to visit this overwhelmingly Muslim country in which Catholics are a tiny minority, he replied: 'They are simple, religious people, and they want to see the Pope.'

The expense, of course, is enormous. The bill for his Australian trip was about £1 million a day. Part was paid by the Canberra Government, but most had to be found by the local Catholic Church. As the Australian press pointed out, the Pope's visit cost ten times as much as the Queen's. On the flight home, he told correspondents that, in his opinion, money was no object when you were dealing with transcendental values.

This ceaseless travelling defines John Paul's pontificate and, at the same time, obscures its essential character. He has become the world's most popular religious leader, with the presence of a superstar but possessing an infrangible dignity that effortlessly surmounts the destructive vulgarities of mass communication. He is respected for his courage, his humanity, and his assertion of principle in an age of relativism, by millions of people who are not Catholics, not religious and, in many cases, deeply critical of Catholic doctrine. Yet his travels are an expression of his belief that the unity of the Church can be maintained only by strict papal authority. Notwithstanding appearances, he is a deeply conservative man.

This conservatism derives partly from temperament, no doubt, partly from the character of Polish Catholicism, partly from his experiences as a priest, academic theologian (at the universities of Cracow and Lublin) and prelate (Archbishop of Cracow) in a Communist state. He worked in a factory before turning to the priesthood, and part of his appeal is a down-to-earth quality that he has never lost. The early skills he acquired as actor, playwright and poet have also been useful.

He is certainly a less isolated figure than any of his recent predecessors have been, and by temperament a more convivial one than most of them. Unlike Paul VI, he does not like to take meals in the company only of his secretary. There are normally guests at his table for both luncheon and dinner. Bishops visiting Rome are often invited for a personal chat over a meal.

Outside the public gaze, he likes to relax in informal clothes and to unfasten his clerical collar. A Polish priest he had invited to lunch changed from his everyday suit into a cassock for the occasion.

The Pope broke into laughter when he saw him. 'Why are you in disguise, my old friend?' he asked. 'I thought the cassock was obligatory,' the priest replied. 'You didn't understand,' said the Pope. 'All I said was that priests should be immediately recognisable when they go out in public.'

There is a small video theatre in the papal apartments for screening movies, but the Pope does not watch much television apart from TV news bulletins. His main recreations are reading, swimming in the pool he installed at the papal villa at Castelgandolfo, and – on the rare occasions when he can make an incognito trip into the mountains – walking.

On tour, he has little time for relaxation. On the Australian Air Force plane that carried him twice across the Australian continent in a single day, he barely bothered to look out of the window. While Cardinal Agostino Casaroli, the Vatican Secretary of State, used the flying time to brush up his English by listening to language tapes, or reading a Freddie Forsyth thriller, John Paul buried his head in a German work of theology.

While travelling, he eats little and drinks neither tea nor coffee. His main meal of the day is a cooked breakfast. He never used the curtained bed set aside for him in the plane, telling his staff that, if there were not beds for everyone, he didn't wish to be singled out.

Tensions between the Pope and many of his flock have been expressed in well-publicised disagreements about abortion, artificial birth control, the admission of women to the priesthood and the participation in communion of divorced Catholics. The central issue underlying them is obedience to Rome – that it must be left to the Pope to decide what is Catholic and what is not. Many Catholics believe that the unity and durability of the Church would, in the long run, be strengthened by a less authoritarian approach.

Many – particularly (but not exclusively) priests working in ravaged inner-city neighbourhoods – also wish that he would identify the Church, much more specifically than he has done, with opposition to the social forces that create poverty. The Pope argues that the Church has always preached in favour of the poor.

There is no prospect of change in John Paul's attitude to birth control or to second marriage in church. He believes firmly in the efficacy of natural birth control methods, despite scientific evidence to the contrary, particularly in the Third World.

But it is fair to say that his view of local Churches and their needs has been conditioned by his experiences during his travels. For example, he treats the flourishing young Church in Africa quite differently from that of the robust and wealthy Catholics of North America, approving liturgical experiments with African music and rhythms in the mass, and gently chiding them, not hectoring them, for polygamy. ('Pope Says One Man One Wife' ran a headline in the *East African Standard* during his visit to Nairobi.) He has carefully avoided a showdown with Archbishop Emmanuel Milingo, former head of the Church in Zambia, who is now carrying on his faith-healing activities in Rome under the watchful eye of the Vatican.

John Paul personally directs Vatican policy on the most important conflicts. He oversees all matters referring to errant theologians like Leonardo Boff, the liberation theologian from Brazil, and Fr Charles Curran, the American university teacher whose views on sexuality have been heavily criticised by the Vatican. And national bishops' conferences are nowadays packed with the Pope's own men. When a synod was held in Rome last year to reassess the consequences of the Second Vatican Council twenty years after, there was little divisiveness.

But the issue of 'collegiality' – the extent to which the hierarchies of national churches should be democratised – has not been resolved, and will be an important topic in John Paul's private discussions with American bishops on his US tour.

Two years ago, the Pope cracked down on liberation theology with a Vatican document that described Communist regimes as 'the shame of humanity'. Fr Boff was hauled off to Rome and forbidden to publish for a year. John Paul simply doesn't understand what is going on in Latin America, Boff has argued.

The Pope frequently condemns economic injustice, but his condemnation is inevitably a generalised one, usually detached from specific programmes and policies, certainly from revolutionary ones. This makes his possible trip to Moscow such a talked-about subject.

When Mikhail Gorbachov visits Italy in the spring, he will be received in audience by the Pope. An invitation to Moscow is on the cards. John Paul has made his conditions clear: no Moscow without a pastoral visit to Catholic Lithuania, where the Church survives in a hostile environment. Until now, the Russians have ruled Lithuania out of bounds. A compromise is possible. However, the Pope has always distinguished between the spiritual needs of his small Baltic flock and the great political implications of an eventual visit to Moscow.

Such a visit would be the most momentous act of papal diplomacy since World War II.

ACADEMICS AND INTELLECTUALS

As a simple introduction to the work and the personality of Professor A. J. Ayer, the 1957 profile reprinted here could hardly be bettered. His passion for soccer in general and Tottenham Hotspur in particular are mentioned. The newspaper for which he wrote soccer reports was the *Observer*. Bertrand Russell had become known to a whole new generation in the late 1950s and early 1960s for his passionate espousal of the cause of nuclear disarmament. He received the ultimate *Observer* Profile accolade: he was 'a great man', though the profile admits difficulty in explaining why. (Charles Chaplin was another to have greatness thrust upon him, as will be seen in another section.)

In 1976, the name of Milton Friedman was an unfamiliar one in Britain outside university economics faculties. His theories were to become well known in this country after Mrs Thatcher came to power in 1979 and put many of them into practice, without quite the same zeal as the Chileans and, fortunately, British democracy survived. (So, by the way, did Chile's, being restored in 1990.)

Malcolm Muggeridge was profiled just before his eightieth birthday, a frequent excuse for a profile, the *Observer*'s long-service award; Sir Isaiah Berlin is an example. But the reason for Muggeridge's profile was his reception into the Roman Catholic Church. (Incidentally, Muggeridge's early novel *Picture Palace*, based on the old *Manchester Guardian*, whose suppression for fear of libel is mentioned, was reissued in the 1980s.) The 'peg' for Jonathan Miller's profile turned out to be a false alarm. He announced his retirement from the theatre and the opera to dedicate himself once more to medicine but in 1990 he was still as active as ever as a director.

PROFESSOR A. J. AYER

15 September 1957

In the current series of BBC television *Brains Trusts*, a sprightly and eloquent figure has begun to attract the eye and the curiosity of the public – partly, perhaps, because he neither talks nor looks much like the popular conception of a philosopher. Who is Professor A. J. Ayer, and what is the 'revolution in philosophy' with which he is associated?

Roughly speaking, the revolution derives from a conviction that many philosophical problems of the past are rooted in a vague or muddled use of language and tend to disappear if they are examined severely from this point of view. The revolutionaries therefore believe in analysing strictly the use and abuse of words, instead of using them as magical and semi-poetic talismans which deliberately allow a variety of meanings. This movement, which ranges widely between the ideas of Bertrand Russell and those of Wittgenstein, involves a recognition that language must be pruned and pared and redefined if there is to be any possibility of using it as an intelligible means of logical argument. One of the pioneers of this new philosophical development in England was A. J. Ayer.

Now Grote Professor of the Philosophy of Mind and Logic in the University of London, Ayer has none of the pomposity which his present title suggests. Twenty years ago he was the *enfant terrible* of Oxford philosophy, the introducer and populariser of severe Viennese attitudes at a time when Oxford philosophy was still vague, ill-directed and explanatory rather than opinionated. The chief function of a philosophy don, then, was to explain what had been said by his philosophical predecessors rather than to suggest a revealing opinion of his own. Philosophy tended to be a dead subject, not a living issue on which it was possible to take violent sides.

Ayer was one among several others of his time at Oxford who, by deliberate and stimulating acts of didactic provocation, made it clear that there was a current school of philosophy which actually opposed, rather than being resigned merely to explaining, the schools of the past. Whether Ayer knew it at the time or not, he wished to persuade his pupils that his own fresh point of view was the right one, rather than to make them, for the purposes of their examinations, adequately informed about the views of Plato and Aristotle.

Ayer had most of the personal qualifications which were necessary for achieving this difficult change of emphasis. Physically lithe, small, and with the pale, mobile face of a nervous fawn, he had, and retains, an immense personal charm. Even the rich and idle undergraduates of Christ Church condescended

to take rather more interest than usual in the work they did for their philosophy tutor.

The concept of 'Professor Ayer' is indeed a difficult one for his friends to accept. Since childhood he has been known as 'Freddy', and this is a case in which a nickname is vitally apt. There is something cocksparrow-like about this outwardly self-confident man; and one has to know him well before recognising that the apparent assurance conceals a real modesty and inner nervousness. His characteristic and constant juggling with a watch-chain, the quick sideways glancing of his brown eyes, the tenseness of his frame – all these reveal an alert uneasiness.

Ayer has no great interest in the higher flights of art, and no religious sense in any of the many meanings of that obscure word; yet he has the intelligence and sensitivity to recognise these gaps in his understanding. In fact his intelligence is immense, even if it chooses a rather limited field for its normal operations. An editor who gave him books to review remarked that Ayer's bacon-slicing machine was a beautiful instrument, but not always appropriate to the books which were thus sliced into segments. His mind is fundamentally commonsensical, but capable of carrying the implications of common sense into far, obscure and almost dreamlike regions.

Ayer was the only child of a French-Swiss father and a Dutch-Jewish mother, but the father, a timber merchant, became a naturalised British subject before the birth of his son. The mother was a Miss Citroen, whose father built not Citroen but Minerva cars. Ayer went to Eton as a King's Scholar in 1923, and his career there was as distinguished as its opening. He was never the traditional 'clever boy' whose nose is glued only to his books. Indeed, he played occasionally for his school at both rugby and association football, and was awarded his school colours for the Wall game. He has, incidentally, retained a keen interest in competitive sport, and has written newspaper accounts of football games in which his admired Tottenham Hotspurs have participated.

He won an open Classical Scholarship at Christ Church and a first-class degree in Greats three years later. He then spent a few months in Vienna, where he attended meetings of the *Wiener Kreis*, that school of Austrian philosophers, dominated by Wittgenstein and Carnap, which was to have so enduring an influence on him. He was a lecturer and research student at Christ Church from 1933 to 1944, Fellow and Dean of Wadham from 1944 to 1946, and has been Professor at London since the last date. During his lively wartime career in the Welsh Guards and Military Intelligence, he thoroughly displayed his famous gift for adapting himself to new surroundings. His popularity, even in the most apparently alien company, was almost legendary.

Ayer has contested two unsuccessful local elections as Labour candidate for the Westminster City Council, and has visited China on a delegation which included Sir Hugh Casson, Rex Warner and Stanley Spencer. By no means a fellow-traveller with Communism, he is a radical in the old and best sense of the word – a natural iconoclast and a man of deep though by no means ostentatious compassion. In fact, the extreme dryness of his philosophy seems to be in odd contrast to the warmth of his heart.

In 1936 Ayer published his first book *Language, Truth and Logic*. It was a young and arrogant assault on 'much of what has passed for philosophy', and it created an immediate stir in academic circles. The metaphor is suitable, for a cartoonist of the time might have depicted the youthful Ayer stirring a bubbling cauldron in which the indignant metaphysicians waved their fists. This result could not have been achieved unless the book had been a good one, and indeed it exhibited all that lucid passion which has distinguished Ayer's philosophical writing ever since.

It was largely a labour of exposition, and its author was greatly and gratefully in debt to such empiricist elders as Moore, Russell and Carnap. Yet this rigorous little work had an influence far outside academic circles, and it succeeded in bringing the term 'logical positivist' to the idle attention of the educated British public.

The two most important Viennese principles which Ayer expounded were the view that all philosophy can be reduced to linguistic analysis, and the insistence that any proposition which cannot be, in principle, verified by the senses is literally nonsensical. The claim was gigantic: 'I maintain,' wrote Ayer, 'that there is nothing in the nature of philosophy to warrant the existence of conflicting philosophical "schools". And I attempt to substantiate this by providing a definitive solution of the problems which have been the chief sources of controversy between philosophers in the past.' It is a measure of the writer's skill that this vast claim was given a plausible appearance of fulfilment.

There were, in fact, many logical loopholes in this structure. Ayer himself has perceived and admitted some of them, while attempting to fortify others. His *The Problem of Knowledge*, which appeared last year, was every bit as brilliant and lucid as the earlier book, but a great deal more mature. Younger members of the school have marched out to left and right, some of them adopting standards of meaning which are even drier and more severe than those propounded in *Language, Truth and Logic*; others becoming more indulgent and allowing that there may be more than one meaning of the word 'meaning'. Yet the philosophical school of linguistic analysts now dominates the British and many of the American universities, and few Anglo-Saxon philosophers stand altogether outside the movement.

It may be felt that the claims of the school are still much too high and too wide, and that there are many fields of legitimate philosophical speculation where the method of linguistic analysis is inapt and, in the literal sense of the word, impertinent. It may be felt that metaphysics are a proper study for man which cannot be 'eliminated' by the waving of a logical wand. But none of this can alter the immense value of Ayer's contribution to the recent clearing of philosophical decks. If a new school of philosophers were to arise, in the teeth of Ayer's deprecation, it would not be able to disregard the caustic labours of the linguistic analysts.

It is likely that the combative and high-spirited Grote Professor would secretly welcome such a development. For the moment he has to be content with stropping his cut throat razors on colleagues and disciples who differ from him only in inessentials. But this David would surely be delighted if a new metaphisical Goliath were to stride on to the field of battle.

BERTRAND RUSSELL

19 February 1961

No doubt some people, on reading that Bertrand Russell is willing to spend his time like this, will think that it merely proves how silly a clever man can be. Others, more charitable, will murmur 'Senility,' and turn to the sports pages. Yet millions more, including many who are not nuclear disarmers and who disagree profoundly with his policy, will feel proud that an old man of 88, who has long enjoyed every honour which men can give, should feel so concerned about the future of humanity that he is prepared to risk abuse, imprisonment and even death – for it is not the kind of thing usually recommended for men of 88 by their doctors – in order to draw attention to the dangers which threaten it.

Abuse, imprisonment and death are not things which have ever greatly troubled the third Earl Russell. He has been in prison before for publicly denouncing conscription during the First World War. He has been abused at different times for advocating pacifism, rights for women, free love, trial marriage, new methods of education, preventive war and unilateral disarmament.

Death he has not yet experienced, though he was very close to it when a plane in which he was travelling to Norway crashed and deposited him – at the age of 76 – in the icy sea; but as a consistent atheist who believes firmly that there is no God and no life after death, he regards it with the scientific detachment of a man who is about to see the proof of one of his favourite theories.

It is easy to recognise Bertrand Russell as a great man – perhaps, after Sir Winston Churchill, the greatest living Englishman. It is much more difficult to explain exactly why he is a great man. Certainly his *Principles of Mathematics* and *Principia Mathematica*, both published before the First World War, helped determine the direction in which modern philosophy was going to move; but how many people in this country today have read the *Principia* and can understand it? And of that handful, how many are competent to judge Russell's contribution compared, say, with that of Frege or Whitehead or Wittgenstein?

Nor would Russell himself wish to be judged purely as a philosopher. He has always expressed a certain dissatisfaction with philosophy, and especially with modern philosophy, which he feels is often niggling and petty. He has always sought some reality which would transcend humanity. Though it may sound an odd thing to say of so determined a sceptic, there is something almost religious in his search for impersonal, objective truth. As he once said: 'I wanted certainty in the kind of way in which people want religious faith.'

But Russell is also a humanist, with a humanist's passionate concern for human beings. He has written many books on politics and sociology. All of them have that dazzling lucidity which won him a Nobel Prize for Literature and which makes it almost impossible to disagree with his arguments while reading them; yet few have lasted well and only one, his essay on power, could be called a classic. He has left no body of political writing to compare with that of his godfather, John Stuart Mill, or even with that of his own contemporaries, Croce and Ortega y Gasset.

The truth is, perhaps, that Russell has never wholly understood politics. He inherited from his Whig ancestors – his grandfather was Lord John Russell of the Reform Bill – a superb intellect, a passion for freedom and that independence of mind which is aristocracy's greatest gift. He also inherited a certain temperamental aloofness and lack of understanding of the way in which men and women behave.

The tendencies were no doubt exaggerated by his upbringing. His parents died when he was a child and he was brought up by his grandmother, who had him educated privately at home. She intended him for politics, but from the age of fifteen the shy and lonely boy found himself bored by this prospect and more interested in mathematical and philosophical speculation.

At Cambridge he got a first in Mathematics and was elected a Fellow of Trinity College. He soon found himself a leader of that brilliant circle of intellectual young men which Keynes described so well and D. H. Lawrence disliked so much.

Well-to-do, superior, breathing the optimistic air of Edwardian England, they believed firmly that human nature was essentially reasonable and that human beings had only to be freed from restraints and superstitions to be happy. They repudiated all versions of the doctrine of original sin, of there being insane and irrational springs of wickedness in most men. They were pre-Freud as well as pre-Hitler.

Almost everything that has happened since 1914 has been a fatal blow to these comfortable beliefs. Bertrand Russell, a passionately honest man as well as a brilliantly perceptive one, has continually tried to adjust his theories to events. A visit to Russia in 1920 greatly modified his views on Socialism, and he was one of the first to see the corruption inherent in the Communist system. (He didn't wear the rose-tinted spectacles of the Webbs.)

Stalin's oppression of the Kulaks and the rise of Hitler converted him from the pacifism which he had preached – and practised – during the First World War. But he has never fully overcome this ineradicable tendency to think that politics are much simpler than they are.

As Keynes put it: 'Bertie in particular sustained simultaneously a pair of opinions ludicrously incompatible. He held that in fact human affairs were carried on after a most irrational fashion, but that the remedy was quite simple and easy, since all we had to do was to carry them on rationally.'

The same tendency to overrate the intellectual side of men and women has infected his personal relationships and made him an unreliable – though always exciting – guide on such subjects as marriage and the education of children.

It is not that Russell himself is inhuman, for few men are personally more attractive or more charming – even now at a party his white hair and bird-like head will always be surrounded by the prettiest women – but simply that, like Plato, he expects human beings to behave like philosophers, whereas in reality it is philosophers who behave like human beings.

Then why is Russell a great man? There are, perhaps, two reasons. In an age when the emotional side of man has been dominant, an age when cruelty, intolerance and hysteria have been rampant throughout the world, he has continued to expound the great truths of eighteenth-century rationalism and nineteenth-century liberalism in a clear and unmistakable voice.

The fact that these doctrines were not the whole truth about humanity doesn't mean they were false. It has been Russell's great contribution to preach the virtues of tolerance and to denounce the vices of cruelty and bigotry when other men forgot and lost heart.

He has also revived the role of the philosopher as public figure. At a time when academic philosophy was becoming increasingly abstruse and remote, he deliberately left the study in order to nag, excite and interest ordinary men about the great questions facing humanity.

Like Voltaire (whom he resembles a little, except that he has no malice), he has been a kind of intellectual gadfly on the rump of the affluent society, continually asking awkward questions, often answering them wrongly himself, but always forcing men and women to think harder by his own disinterested passion for truth. He hasn't hesitated to use journalism and television to do the kind of thing Socrates did by walking and talking in the streets of Athens.

Some have sneered at Russell because he opposed the First World War and supported the Second; because at one moment he advocated using the American advantage in nuclear weapons to impose disarmament on Russia, and now advocates unilateral disarmament. He would reply that always he was convinced as to the rightness of his own theories, that a man must act on what he believes to be true, and that there was something to be said for each of these positions at the time.

He is now convinced that humanity will be destroyed unless the Great Powers get rid of nuclear weapons, and that they can be shocked into doing this only by the protests of ordinary men and women, even if it means breaking the law.

These views may be wrong. They certainly underrate the immense difficulties of comprehensive disarmament. Perhaps sitting down on the road is not the best way to secure peace. Yet Russell's campaign during the last five years to awaken the world to the perils of nuclear war is certainly one of the most impressive and unselfish political actions ever undertaken by a private citizen, and has already had one momentous and beneficial result.

Russell in England and Einstein in America were together the founders of the 'Pugwash Conference' of Western and Russian scientists, which meets each year in private to discuss the problems of nuclear war. Its importance is now recognised by Presidents and Premiers. If Mr Kennedy and Mr Khrushchev reach some agreement on how to control nuclear weapons, they will owe something to Pugwash and to the frail old man with the tough mind who doesn't think himself too old or too busy, too important or too clever, to lead a protest in the streets.

MILTON FRIEDMAN

12 December 1976

Two years ago, Milton Friedman, the brilliant American economic theorist who received the £98,000 1976 Nobel Prize for Economics in Stockholm on Friday, was invited to Chile to advise on curing the country's inflation, then around 350 per cent a year.

Friedman prescribed his celebrated 'shock treatment': a sudden and heavy cut in the growth of the money supply and in Government spending. His advice was accepted. Two United States-trained monetarists of the Friedmanite school were appointed to head the economic Ministries. The inflation rate has now fallen to 180 per cent.

Inevitably, there have been regrettable side-effects. By the beginning of the year, nearly one in four manual workers in Greater Santiago, the country's main industrial region, were unemployed. Mass bankruptcies have pauperised a large section of the Chilean middle class, while what remains of the country's wealth is being concentrated in the hands of a small group with the financial resources to command credit.

Withdrawal of Government support for farmers has led to a big drop in food production. Malnutrition has reached alarming levels. More than 60 per cent of Santiago children examined recently were chronically under-nourished. The Church has been feeding 50,000 people from soup-kitchens in the capital alone in a struggle to prevent children from starving to death in what was one of the most developed countries in Latin America.

The only economic activity that continues to show remarkable profits is speculation by finance companies, which borrow abroad at eleven per cent and relend the money on a 30-day basis at three or four per cent above the inflation rate.

In the absence of Government credits, industry is compelled to rely on such loans and pass on the cost to consumers. To combat the rise in consumer prices, the Government has removed tariffs against foreign goods, thereby striking an even more savage blow against domestic producers.

Chile has become a laboratory for achieving the economic 'freedom' to which Friedmanite theory aspires, though Friedman has stressed that his role has been that of adviser not policy-maker, and that his advice assumed the existence of effective welfare programmes.

A leading Santiago businessman told the *New York Times* correspondent last week: 'You are witnessing the dismantling of Chilean industry by people who are trying to prove that they can run an economy on theories alone.'

But Friedman has never pretended that the social cost of his prescription would not be harsh. 'My only concern,' he has said of the Chilean Government's policy, 'is that they push it long enough and hard enough.'

Friedman is the most influential economist since Keynes. As the leading exponent of the monetarist school, which maintains that the economic cycle is determined more by the money supply and interest rates than by taxation policy, he has helped to create the intellectual climate in which the crisis of the industrialised nations has been argued since the autumn of 1973.

In Britain, his ideas have influenced Sir Keith Joseph, Enoch Powell and other Tory thinkers, including the editor of *The Times*. He is also, as *Panorama* and *Money Programme* viewers were able to judge last week, an engaging and spirited controversialist. In a science largely inaccessible to the ordinary people whose lives it governs, who are baffled by the way the experts constantly hedge their bets, Friedman's iron certainty is extraordinarily persuasive. Even his cheerful prediction of the destruction of British democracy if his radical remedies are not adopted is taken seriously.

His Nobel Prize, which has provoked bitter criticism among third world economists as well as within the Swedish Royal Academy of Science itself, was awarded for his research-based theoretical studies at Chicago University, where he has been Professor of Economics since 1948, not for the doubtful benefits bestowed on the children of Santiago. The danger is that it will be seen as international sanction for the good professor's wilder excursions into the theology of *laissez-faire*.

Friedman, 64, is the son of an immigrant draper from Eastern Europe who died when the boy was fifteen. He grew up in a working-class neighbourhood in Rahway, New Jersey, and worked his way through Rutgers University as a waiter and shop assistant. He was introduced to economics by a young professor, Arthur Burns, now chairman of the United States Federal Reserve Board, who remains a close friend as well as a critic.

His course was set at Chicago University, where Frank Knight had made the 'Chicago School' a powerful force in economics. After ten years in the government service, he returned at the end of the war to assume leadership of the school. His Tuesday afternoon workshop on money is legendary for its intellectual rigour.

He is a slight, bespectacled man of five feet three inches, whose dress tends towards frayed Ivy League tweeds and slim 1950s ties. He and his wife, Rose, also an economist, have a hilltop home at Ely, Vermont, above the Connecticut River Valley, from which a seemingly endless flow of books, scholarly papers and popular articles issues forth. Their son David is an economist in Virginia, and their daughter Janet a lawyer in San Francisco.

Friedman owes his popular reputation as an economic wizard to two correct predictions in America in the late 1960s. In 1967, after nine months of an expansionary fiscal policy coupled with a static money supply, Keynesian economists expected rapid economic growth. Friedman predicted the opposite, and was proved right. The following year the US Government imposed a tax surcharge of ten per cent to fight inflation, but rapidly increased the money supply. Friedman correctly predicted that this would increase economic activity, which only slowed down when the Federal Reserve Board reduced the growth in the money supply, as Friedman had advocated.

His monetary ideas are still far from being universally accepted. He is accused of having produced a 'black box' theory, arguing that A produces B without demonstrating how it actually happens. His critics say that he has given undue importance to only one of several causes of inflation, thereby distorting the true picture. But he won an important victory last year when Congress ordered the Fed to set growth-targets for the US money supply.

Friedman's ultimate political value is freedom from government coercion. He advocates this with an uncompromising thoroughness that exhilarates the conservative-minded as much as it appals almost everyone else. He advocates not only the end of public ownership of industry and of government intervention in the form of tariffs, import quotas, foreign exchange restrictions, farm price supports, pollution control, rent control and minimum wages, but also the dismantling of state provision for health and education.

It is a nineteenth-century concept of freedom. The only country that has so far been able to pursue it in its full rigour is one of the most brutal police states in the world, and in Chile the major economic catastrophe it has produced has aroused opposition to it even within the ruling Junta itself.

His idealisation of the market as the most economically efficient and most politically acceptable way of satisfying social needs ignores the obvious practical imperfections of the system. Logically, but ridiculously, Friedman is hostile even to government efforts to promote economic competition.

Much of Friedman's detailed critique of the failures of British economic management is now common ground: for example, the need to switch resources from the public to the private sector, to reform the tax structure to encourage incentive, and to shift emphasis in welfare programmes from bureaucratised services to cash payments.

But in his argument in favour of a drastic change of direction, the public debate seems to be swinging against him.

His familiar medical analogy – that the doctor's duty is to prescribe the remedy and not to worry about the unpleasantness for the patient – is hardly reassuring. The cold-turkey cure has killed many an addict. The future of British democracy would be as much at hazard from a Chilean-style deflation as it is from continued high inflation.

MALCOLM MUGGERIDGE

28 November 1982

'Of course, history is all lies.' It is one of Malcolm Muggeridge's favourite themes. Like all he says and much he writes it is a joke, but meant seriously at the same time. He loves paradox, and antithesis: between the Will and the Imagination (his friend Hugh Kingsmill's concept), between power and love, between 'history' and reality, and – variation on the same theme – between the facts and the truth. He often quotes his old friend A. T. Cholerton, a correspondent in Moscow during the 1930s, who was asked what was the truth behind the great show trials: 'Everything is true except the facts.'

We know the facts about Muggeridge – all too many of them, indeed, and often self-contradictory. He is a broadcaster and a recluse, a journalist who hates journalism, a retiring self-publicist.

On the telly (which he affects to despise but yet so clearly loves) he is a superb, acidulated comic, with his magnificent gargoyle's face and his extraordinary voice pulling and kneading the words as he mocks the world. Perhaps he is best of all in conversation, talking with that permanent grin that isn't quite a grin, describing as it might be the husband of a formidable literary lady: 'Well of *course*,' (swooping noise) 'he did the only thing you *could* do if you were married to her.' (Pause.) 'He went deaf.' And now at last, after all his other incarnations he finds himself a member of – 'The Catholic Church . . . which has a special niche today for twentieth-century lost souls who, in the empty caverns they inhabit, take comfort from the echoing of sanctus bells and benedictions, and absolutions. Rome

Sweet Rome! Be you never so sinful, there's no place like Rome.' Thus, once, Malcolm Muggeridge. Has the Pilgrim's Progress ended at last? Has he found his Home – and the Truth?

Malcolm Muggeridge was born 80 years ago next March into the lower middle class and into the Fabian religion of progress, both of which he left before long. His father was a City clerk, and an energetic Labour councillor. From the local school he won a scholarship to Cambridge and read natural sciences, for no good reason. His few friends at university had religious rather than political interests: at Selwyn he lived on the fringe of the Anglo-Catholic set and one man training for the clergy, Alec Vidler, became a lifelong close friend.

After Cambridge Muggeridge pottered aimlessly, working as a schoolteacher in Birmingham and making his first overseas forays to teach in Ceylon, and then for three years in Cairo. Before that, in 1927, he had made a more important departure than any professional appointment by marrying Kitty Dobbs; he was 'marrying up' in terms of left-wing society. This enchanting girl was the niece of Beatrice Webb. Mugggeridge did not ask his parents to the wedding. Despite many and severe strains put on it, mostly by Muggeridge himself, the marriage has remained the sustaining centre of his life. Kitty, his children and grandchildren are his greatest solace.

A connection formed with the *Manchester Guardian* when he was in Cairo led to a staff job in Manchester, leader-writing from a stuffy little room in the famous Cross Street 'corridor'. In Manchester he made more friends, including A. J. P. Taylor; he formed an aversion both to C. P. Scott, then at the end of his 50-year career as editor-proprietor, and to Kingsley Martin, then another leader-writer and afterwards editor of the *New Statesman*; and he began his disenchantment with 'liberalism' – ever after a somewhat amorphous hate-object.

More important than the Manchester years was his time in Moscow in 1932–3 as the *Manchester Guardian's* correspondent. Half a generation before the God Failed for so many others, before Stalin's purges began in earnest, Muggeridge saw not only the horrors of tyranny and famine but the whole underlying fraud of Communism. Moscow was then full of doting fellow-travellers of every hue. The experience left him with a contempt for such people, for all 'Dawnists' who thought that some secular millennium was just around the corner – a contempt all the stronger because he had been one such when he arrived in Moscow. He described, and exorcised, his experiences in a novel, *Winter in Moscow*. Although suffused with a bitterness and even, to a later generation, spotted with anti-Semitism it is a very good book. It earned him the perennial hostility of the Left without doing him much good elsewhere.

During the mid-1930s he enjoyed a period of journalistic prosperity, earning £20 a week – good pay then – on the *Evening Standard*, but then removed to the country with his family to live by hack-work (novel reviews at five guineas a column, 30 shillings a thousand as a 'ghost') and to write books. There had been two other novels, one of which was too obviously about the *Guardian* and was suppressed by threat of libel; there was a debunking life of Samuel Butler; and, written in the first months of the war, there was *The Thirties*, an admirable piece of 'quicky' journalism.

But before that was another and more remarkable book, *In a Valley of this Restless Mind*. Commissioned in quite different guise, it appeared as a 'novel' about a young man, worldly, hard-bitten, hard-drinking, lecherous, apparently wandering around London, in fact in search of God. The book went unlauded except by one reviewer, Evelyn Waugh.

The war found Muggeridge in Intelligence. He wrote about this later in farcical vein, not least of his time as a British secret agent in Lourenço Marques. One of Muggeridge's salient characteristics as a nian and as a writer is scorn. Without a conscious wish to do so he has written sneeringly of all those from his father on who had wished him well; he has bitten every hand that fed him and mocked all those who helped him; he laughs at everything that he has seen or done.

In this he is unfair not only to others but to himself. The war was a good example. His post in Africa was, in fact, a very important one, overlooking the Mozambique Channel through which all Allied shipping passed on its way to the Middle East and where much of it was sunk by U-boats. Muggeridge played a notable part in the capture of a U-boat and a supply ship, but it was all grist to the satiric mill – as too was a suicide attempt he may or may not have made at the time.

At the end of the war he was in Paris where he did his 'only worthwhile thing' in saving several Frenchmen from the not always discriminating vengeance of the *épuration* and in rescuing P. G. Wodehouse from further persecution. He then demobilised himself and went to work for the *Daily Telegraph*. His last 'staff' job was an unsatisfactory five-year stint as editor of *Punch*. Higher rungs in Fleet Street might have come his way, but it was with understandable relief that he retired to be a freelance jester, a contemplative and a *vieillard terrible*.

In his later years Muggeridge has not only achieved national fame through television but acquired a band of devotees, including two younger jesters from *Private Eye*, Christopher Booker and Richard Ingrams, who see the hermit in his grotto at Robertsbridge as little short of a saint.

He has also made a good many more enemies, who see him as a posturing hypocrite, a jaded voluptuary who rails in old age against the vices he practised so vigorously for much of his life. Certainly it is not hard to call the Older Mugg a humbug, and sometimes even a bit of a bore. He continues to back into the limelight and to live off the publicity which he pretends to hate. Living now off yoghurt and fruit, and in ostentatiously self-proclaimed celibacy, does he not reprobate the sins he can no longer enjoy himself?

When a man in his eightieth year has just finished his spiritual Aeneid it is probably not the moment to accuse him of simply striking attitudes. But for all that Muggeridge has held and holds sincere and deep beliefs, it may be that the most characteristic thing about him is his love of performance. As a young man he had a play produced. He still loves to tread the boards, literally as well as in the broader sense. He once played a clergyman in a Peter Sellers movie, and he was even more memorable as the Gryphon in Dr Jonathan Miller's television *Alice*. He could have been a greater character actor.

Come to that, he *is* one. However much he may long for the catacombs, Malcolm Muggeridge cannot keep away from the footlights. Whether he is a saint is fortunately for Someone Else to judge. For sure he is a trouper, a great entertainer, a card.

SIR ISAIAH BERLIN

11 June 1989

'I understand you're only doing your duty,' Sir Isaiah Berlin tells his interviewer gravely, '. . . *as Eichmann put it.*' His diffidence towards the media is legendary. It possibly springs from an emigré's fear of the English distrust of cleverness. But, once bagged in a Wimpole Street consulting room, he is full of warmth and charmth (as Sam Goldwyn used to say).

His 80th birthday last Tuesday was celebrated with a dinner at Corpus, his old Oxford college, by 90 representatives of academia, diplomacy and the *Haute Bohème*. Many of his readers must be toasting him in gratitude for the originality and luminous clarity of his essays.

He is widely loved and widely *enjoyed*. The thing about Isaiah is that he is all of a piece. His intuitive sensibility towards his friends is matched by the intuitive power with which he puts his finger on the animating principle inside the personal view of a philosopher. The breadth of his sympathetic exposition of incompatible theories reflects his humane tolerance in daily life.

He talks very fast in a growly bass as if trying to keep up with the speed of his mind, sometimes swallowing his words. 'It used to be said of Isaiah that he was unintelligible in several languages,' says the historian A. L. Rowse. He is the embodiment of the Oxford spirit: dispassionate, eclectic, undogmatic, elegant in expression, and with a sense of fun that can spiral into comic fantasy.

He was born in Riga, the only child of an anglophile Jewish timber merchant, and can remember during the Revolution seeing a man being overpowered by police and dragged away. 'I've never forgotten the sight of him struggling,' he says. 'It left me with a horror of violence.' He has remained a resolute, though never clamorous, anti-Communist.

In 1919, the family migrated to England. At home in Kensington, they spoke English. But, from the age of twelve, he read his way through his father's library of Russian classics. At St Paul's, he discovered Joyce, Eliot, Pound, Huxley and the literary magazine *transition*, and won a scholarship to Corpus to read Greats and PPE, specialising in philosophy. He became one of Auden's successors as editor of *Oxford Outlook*, got a double first and was elected to All Souls.

In his speech at Tuesday's dinner, he likened Oxford in the 1930s to Europe. Christ Church was like France: grand, autocratic and cosmopolitan. New College was like England: solid, unimaginative and governed by Wykehamists. Balliol was like America: brash, ambitious and multi-racial. And Corpus – ah, Corpus! – was like Denmark: small, quiet, orderly and admired by everyone. 'I've always thought,' murmured his friend Sir William Hayter, 'that All Souls was rather like the Vatican: it has no subjects and claims a close relationship with another world.'

In the 1930s that other, metropolitan, world was a powerful presence in the debates on appeasement inside the graduates-only college. Several members of the Chamberlain Government were Fellows of All Souls. So was the Editor of *The Times*, Geoffrey Dawson. So was a group of elderly Liberal Imperialists led by Lionel Curtis, of whom it was said that, if you wanted two archbishops to sign your letter to *The Times* next day, he could arrange it. Isaiah was one of the younger Fellows who argued with them. There was little hope of denting the belief that Hitler, however *outré*, was a useful bulwark against Bolshevism. But, as he says, 'if you wanted to know the British governing class, All Souls was the place to be'.

His anti-Fascist credentials were not in doubt. He was a member of the 'Pink Lunch', a leftish group organised by G. D. H. Cole that included Richard Crossman, the economist Roy Harrod, the philosophers Stuart Hampshire and John Austin, and historians like Christopher Hill and E. H. M. Jones. In Maurice Bowra's words, they 'helped to create a new seriousness at Oxford without impairing its traditional relaxations or its intellectual detachment'. But he has never been a man for campaigns and platforms, still less for sectarian obsessions.

Philip Toynbee, in *Friends Apart*, recalled that 'Isaiah's disapprovals were modified, even counteracted, by his unlimited curiosity in every kind of human being: he was as interested in "the bad" as he was in "the good" – indeed felt for the bad a sort of gratified admiration. He liked behaviour'. It is a striking phrase. Behaviour – intellectual, moral and political – has been his life's work. He presents ideas not as impersonal systems but in the context of the individuals who held them, like Tolstoy, Turgenev and his hero, Herzen. That is one reason why he is so readable. He talks about them intimately as if they were friends whose virtues and foibles he knew from personal contact.

In 1939, his short book on Marx was published. It remains one of the most readable on that cloudly subject. Since then, he has found the essay his natural form, preferring specific topics rather than the comprehensive treatises publishers have pressed him to write.

During the war, he served in the British Embassy in Washington, writing a staggeringly well-informed weekly summary of US opinion which is said to have been Churchill's favourite reading. He was employed at the San Francisco Conference checking the Russian version of the UN Charter, but was vetoed for Potsdam by Anthony Eden, miffed that Isaiah referred to him as 'the Sleeping Beauty'.

In 1945 he was seconded to the Moscow Embassy. His most moving essay, included in *Personal Impressions*, describes his meetings with the poet and novelist Boris Pasternak and the poet Anna Akhmatova, the last great survivors on the ravaged slopes of the Russian Parnassus. Mandelshtam had perished in the

Stalinist camps. Mayakovsky and Tsvetaeva had taken their own lives. Eisenstein was beleaguered. Other great artists had died or fled to the West.

In the middle of a clandestine visit to Akhmatova, he heard an unmistakable English voice bellowing, 'Isaiah! *Isaiah!*' Out of the window he saw Randolph Churchill, 'looking like a tipsy undergraduate'. Randolph explained that he had just arrived in Moscow, heard that Isaiah was in town, and was merely employing a method of locating his friends he had found serviceable at Christ Church. Inevitably, he had been followed by secret police. Rumours circulated that a British delegation had arrived to persuade Akhmatova to leave Russia and that Winston Churchill, a lifelong lover of Russian poetry, was sending a special aircraft.

On a later visit, Pasternak's wife Zinaida begged Isaiah to persuade Pasternak not to have *Doctor Zhivago* published outside Russia, fearing reprisals against their children. Moved by this plea, Isaiah told the writer that he would have the novel microfilmed and buried in different continents so that it would survive even nuclear war.

For Pasternak, of course, *Doctor Zhivago* was his last testament. He replied with anger. 'He had spoken to his sons; they were prepared to suffer; I was not to mention the matter again – I had read the book, I surely realised what it, above all its dissemination, meant to him. I was shamed into silence.'

Back in Oxford, he switched from pure philosophy to the history of ideas, becoming Chichele Professor of Social and Political Theory, and later President of Wolfson College. He also revived the British Academy, transforming it into a useful research council for the humanities. At 47, he married Aline de Gunzbourg, the French-born daughter of a Russian Jewish banker. (He has three stepsons.) They have homes in London, Oxford, New York and Parraggi on the Ligurian coast, where Isaiah can be sighted striding along listening to Verdi on his Walkman. He pursues rare opera performances all over Europe. His friends Alfred Brendel and Ronald Grierson, chairman of the South Bank Board, have organised an all-Mozart birthday concert for him at the Festival Hall on 17 July.

Everybody knows the story of Irving Berlin's wartime invitation to Downing Street. The semi-staged version (all parts played by Isaiah) is wonderful. Clemmie wanted Winston to thank the composer for a large charitable gift. Winston, absently connecting the name with the Washington Embassy, suggested a lunch invitation. A richly confused conversation ensued, Churchill becoming increasingly mystified by Berlin's Lower East Side accent:

'What's the most important thing you've done for us lately, Mr Berlin?'

'White Christmas.'

'Do you think Roosevelt will be re-elected?'

'Well, I've voted for him myself in the past, but this time I'm not so sure.'

'When do you think the war will end?'

'Mr Churchill, when I get home I'm going to tell my children and my grandchildren that the Prime Minister of Great Britain asked *me* when the war would end.'

Winston closed the lunch brusquely. Later, Clemmie explained, and Churchill told the War Cabinet the story that afternoon. Berlin was sharing a suite at the Savoy with Alexander Korda. 'It's a funny thing, Alex,' he said. 'Somehow, we just didn't seem to click.'

INTERNATIONAL

With the *Observer*'s reputation for internationalism, it would be easy enough to produce a book of *Observer* Profiles consisting entirely of international political figures, which makes it extremely difficult to whittle the number down to a representative sample. Some excluded themselves by being written in a stodgy, lifeless style, which gave more prominence to the world situation reigning at the time of writing than to the subject's personality.

Nelson Mandela was profiled at the time of his arrest in 1962. He was sentenced to life imprisonment in 1963 and released in 1989. In 1959, Fidel Castro, who had just overthrown the Batista regime, was virtually unknown to the British public and most of the *Observer* Profile, presumably written by the paper's Latin American specialist Jock Halcrow Ferguson, provided an admirable biography of the man. His conclusions turned out to be entirely wrong – 'He believes in democracy and plans to give it to Cuba for the first time in its history' – but the holding of such a view at the time is an interesting example of the high hopes that Western liberals then held of Castro. The profile of John Kennedy, who, however liberal, did not share the *Observer*'s view of Castro when he in turn came to power the following year, falls some way short of idolatry, scrutinising for example his record on McCarthyism, but by and large gets him right.

The profile of Mao Tse-tung betrays the brilliant insights of the paper's then China expert, Dennis Bloodworth, accurately sensing the imminent upheavals of the Cultural Revolution. I have included Mark Frankland's by-lined portrait of Jimmy Carter after his 1976 election victory because it too accurately pinpointed what would be one of Carter's chief weaknesses: his poor relations with Congress, which were to help him lose to Ronald Reagan in 1980.

Neal Ascherson's wisdom is evident in the Lech Walesa portrait, written just after his release from detention a year after Solidarity had been banned in 1981. His conclusion, about Walesa's lasting legend, turned out to be spot on. The interest in re-reading George Bush and Mikhail Gorbachov, both coming men at the time, lies in seeing whether their profiles read their future right. In the case of Bush, the answer is No; in that of Gorbachov, Yes. François Mitterrand was clearly going through a rough patch in 1984 yet bounced back, as the profile thought he might, to win a second term as President of France in 1988. Yasser Arafat (by Colin Smith) is included because of that quality of survival which the profile emphasises. And Helmut Kohl's 1990 portrait marks the year of German reunification.

FIDEL CASTRO

11 January 1959

The word Youth, with a capital letter, has a slightly sinister significance in Europe – the Hitler Youth is an example. It conjures up ideas either of uniforms and uniformity or of indifference and irresponsibility.

In Latin America it has a very different significance. It means rebellion, private enthusiasm, political precocity. Older Latin Americans equate it with students who embarrass Mexico City bus-drivers by organising, unasked, riots on their behalf. To these older people the sometimes fanatical enthusiasms of the young educated class represent nothing more than growing pains.

They tend to forget that it was such young people who were largely responsible for freeing their countries from Spain over a century ago; that, while their elders cowered and prevaricated, it was the university students of Argentina who first acted against Perón, at the risk of their futures, and sometimes of their lives; that, in Latin America, the young people of this generation, whatever their class or background, are almost inevitably better educated than their parents, less cynical, and more energetic.

Fidel Castro, who now, if he wanted, could be the master of Cuba, is a member of this younger generation – he is still 31 – and, at the same time of the ever-growing middle class that is changing the face of Latin American society.

He was born in rural Cuba on 13 August 1927. His father had started his working life as a labourer for the United Fruit Company of Boston, but by the time Fidel was born had become the prosperous proprietor of a sugar estate. His mother belonged from birth to Cuba's old-established landed gentry.

Fidel himself was brought up on the farm. He grew up in a difficult period of Cuba's history. Unlike the mainland Latin American countries, Cuba had remained a colony of Spain until 1898, in the lifetime of Castro's parents, when it was freed by the Spanish-American war.

But the freedom was relative. It came to Cuba during the presidency of Theodore Roosevelt in the United States, the days of Manifest Destiny and the Big Stick, when the United States was an unacknowledged imperialist Power. And United States involvement in Cuba was largely the responsibility of a capitalist *yanqui* newspaper proprietor called William Randolph Hearst.

The Cubans, like the Filipinos, were to Teddy Roosevelt 'little brown brothers'. Having never been allowed by the Spaniards to run their own affairs since Columbus discovered their country in 1492, they understandably made a mess of it, and let opportunists take over the government. The United States occupied the newly freed country almost immediately, on the grounds that it couldn't look after itself, and remained in virtual charge until 1923.

Young Fidel therefore grew up in an atmosphere of anti-United States feeling, in a country whose whole economy – based on sugar – depended on the United States market. He also grew up during a dictatorship, that of General Gerardo Machado y Morales, who had been in power for two years when Castro was born.

When Castro was a child, therefore, imperialism (Spanish or North American) was hated, professional politicians were despised, and dictatorship was detested. The respectable middle classes felt, in a contemporary word, 'Bolshie'.

Castro, instead of being sent to an inadequate state school, went to Jesuit colleges in Santiago de Cuba and the capital, Havana. Santiago is the capital of Oriente Province, from which the rebellion against Spain was launched. Havana was even then a centre of political and social corruption. The contrast and the lesson must have made their impact on the growing boy.

Like the majority of his class and generation in Latin America, Castro became an idealist early. At the University of Havana, where he collected the equivalent of an MA and an LLB, he was already involved in politics more seriously than English undergraduates ever were, even during the Spanish civil war. He was in fact arrested for joining a group who intended to mount an expedition against Trujillo, the dictator of the Dominican Republic.

Machado had been overthrown in 1933 and replaced by a new government under Colonel Carlos Mendieta. But the power behind the throne was Fulgencio Batista, a former army sergeant-clerk who had realised that an army is run, in the last instance, by its NCOs, and, seeing the way the wind was blowing, had organised a sergeants' revolt in aid of the 1933 revolution, and in 1940 (by then self-promoted colonel) got himself elected President.

After that Batista occasionally allowed professional politicians to replace him, but took over, by military coup, whenever it suited him, on the grounds that they were corrupt, which they were. In 1952 he removed Dr Carlos Prío Socarrás, who was busily bringing charges of corruption against his predecessor of the same Auténtico Party, while allegedly feathering his own nest. Batista, having made himself President again, immediately showed himself more corrupt than either of them.

Fidel Castro was by this time a post-graduate student at the University of Havana. He was sickened by what was happening to his country. The vast majority of the people, white, Negro, mulatto, mestizo, were sugar-workers or urban poor, and had never known the democracy, freedom, or equality that all political parties – and Batista himself – claimed to stand for. The middle class and the intelligentsia were browbeaten and muzzled. The only people who were doing nicely were pampered army officers, high-class prostitutes, crooked politicians, businessmen who paid graft to the regime, and big-time gamblers who had left the United States for their own good.

On 26 July 1953 the tall, brown-eyed, ascetic-looking young man, whose name means Faithful, led an angry, crazy revolt against the Batista barracks in Santiago de Cuba, which failed, as it was bound to do. So complete was the failure that Batista treated the whole thing as a childish joke, and refrained from torturing or executing Castro: he merely imprisoned him. But, despite Batista's contempt and his own failure, Castro's abortive revolution became a symbol to Cubans who believed in freedom and deplored dictatorship and corruption.

In 1955, Castro was released under a general amnesty and went into exile, first in the United States and then in Mexico. In both places he met plotters against the regime, comfortable exiles living in such places as Miami, forming shadow governments, and having *émigré* squabbles amongst themselves. He realised that these were not the types to fire the inspiration of a people and set up a new Cuba. The only way to do that was to fight, and to show by one's own example that dedication could pay off against cynical odds.

On 26 December 1956 he landed from a yacht on the coast of Oriente with 80-odd like-minded young men. The weather was against them; their arrival was delayed for two days, and they landed in a swamp. The word had been passed to Batista, and his trained professional troops moved in and wiped out all but twelve of the would-be revolutionaries. But the remainder, amazingly, were not disheartened. They took to the mountains and gradually gathered a core of guerilla fighters around them, of all classes and both sexes.

They trained them on the lines of the Yugoslav partisans and the French *maquis*. The men disappeared by day and attacked by night. They ran rings round Batista's heavily armoured troops – who had United States-supplied weapons, and later the promise of British ones.

They built up their force from twelve to 500, to 1,000, to an eventual estimated 3,000, with countless quiet local supporters and fifth-columnists in Havana and elsewhere. To embarrass Batista they burned sugar estates (starting with Castro's own), blew up power-stations, cut railway lines, and carried out hazardous stunts such as the polite kidnapping of Juan Fangio, the motor-racing world champion from Argentina.

Their sympathisers all over Latin America smuggled them arms and whipped up support. In Venezuela, which overthrew its own dictorship a year ago, the Sección Venezuela of the 26 de Julio movement took space in the newspapers to advertise for Cuban and Venezuelan volunteers, and got them. Now, all this has paid off, and Batista's troops have capitulated before what Batista once described as a 'small bunch of amateurs'.

Castro's political ideas were still to some extent obscure. A Socialist – though nowadays a more moderate one than in his student days – he believes in democracy, and he plans to give Cuba just that, for the first time in its history.

More important, he knows he stands for something much bigger – a new Latin America: democratic, Catholic and stable. He is part of a movement that has in the last few years overthrown dictatorships in Brazil, Argentina, Colombia and Venezuela, and maintained democracy elsewhere.

There are only three tiny dictatorships left in Latin America today, and the new democracy elsewhere owes its existence largely to the courage of young idealists. But few have had their courage and idealism put to the test as Castro's has been. His bearded, youthful figure has become a symbol of a continent's rejection of brutality and lying and shoddiness. Castro knows it, and every sign is that he will reject personal rule and give his country the opportunity to show by its example that it can run its own affairs as seriously as any other nation.

JOHN KENNEDY

1 January 1961

People in many countries are still feeling as they have done since Mr Kennedy's election: at once unusually hopeful and exceptionally unsure. If they withhold their full enthusiasm they cannot on that account be thought unfriendly towards America, or unduly sceptical. Their uncertainties are shared by too many Americans.

The full depth of the uncertainty is not disclosed by that phenomenally close shave at the polls. Kennedy went into the election with unusually severe handicaps – his youthfulness, his parentage, his Roman Catholic faith. He took a campaign line which Adlai Stevenson had twice shown to be disastrously unpopular. Kennedy's opponent repeatedly accused him of an immature recklessness in foreign affairs that might land America in war. Finally, at Roman triumphs in Philadelphia and New York close to election day, President Eisenhower – still deeply respected by most Americans – publicly turned his thumbs down on Kennedy's candidacy. What is remarkable is not that he won so narrowly but that he won at all.

Yet few of those who voted for Kennedy did so with cheerful assurance. Among Americans who most ardently wish him to succeed are many who don't know what to make of him, who are afraid he may let them down. The slightest hint – as when the President-elect played nine holes of golf one day in Florida – is dolefully exhibited as evidence that no exhilarating change is to be expected in United States leadership.

There are, of course, certain superficial grounds for uneasiness. In a world of elderly rulers, no one could appear less like a statesman than Kennedy. He still looks impossibly young. With that square, handsome face, the untidy hair and obsessional dislike of hats, that enormous natural smile, and the tall, careless elegance of an Ivy Leaguer, the President-elect is a prince among young American males. But knowing the unique dignity of his office, one looks at Kennedy with surprise.

He has tried hard to diminish his physical assets. His hair has been cut as close as he could get it to the skull-cap pattern now favoured by tribal custom in the States. The ovation other politicians do their best to provoke, with arms outflung, he has received diffidently. His first concern has always been to plunge into another of those desperately earnest speeches.

Kennedy is dedicated to seriousness and probably knows that his startling charm, though not in the least bogus, is misleading. In spite of his sincerely friendly ways, he can easily become aloof. There is, indeed, something a little unnerving about the droop of his eyelids that suggests an inner personality, isolated and severe.

Americans have been wondering out loud if it can be safe for them to have as their leader in a cold-war world a young man whom even the Soviets may find it almost impossible to dislike. But those who know him intimately don't suppose themselves to be enchanted. They say Kennedy can sometimes make it clear that a group of Irish immigrants who fled across the Atlantic from the famine of the 1840s didn't produce what is now one of the nation's richest and most powerful families without ruthlessness.

In Kennedy's exotic family background there is much that Americans find delightfully consistent with the American Dream, but also some cause for uneasiness. Few people seem inclined to condemn Kennedy for his grandfathers. Both of them were Irish-American political bosses in Boston, ruling their wards from saloon bars and rarely above a little fiddling with the vote. Yet affectionate admiration seems to dominate the public view of 'Honey Fitz', the celebrated Mayor of Boston who was Kennedy's maternal grandsire, given to dancing an Irish jig in his frequent moments of political triumph.

The skeleton in the cupboard is Kennedy's father. It was Mr Joseph Kennedy who made the massive family fortune, mainly by skilful manipulation of the stock market. Though it is often alleged that 'Joe used his money to buy the White House for his son', what really leads some Americans to doubt the President-elect's inherent quality is the political reputation his father acquired as Ambassador to London before the last war. He is thought to have been an appeaser, faintly pro-Nazi, somewhat anti-British. And many suppose him to be a domineering man who still has a firm grip on his son's political conduct.

It is true that John Kennedy is rooted among men who saw politics as a series of manoeuvres. But this is a fairly common American view of the electoral process. An American politician would no more go into a campaign equipped only with ideals than a lady burglar would go housebreaking in a hooped skirt.

The fact is that Kennedy fought his election as a rational idealist. He took a great and known risk by summoning the people to the pains of an American Revival, and by making his own devotion to social justice abundantly clear. At the same time he worked with his younger brother, Bobby, who as campaign manager patiently laid down a foundation of bloc votes as the firmest guarantee of victory.

No one denies that Kennedy has a political intelligence of the highest order and in the American sense. But if a prudent manipulation of the vote is thought to be bad, then at least one should recall that the late Franklin D. Roosevelt used a similar strategy and did not, like Kennedy, make his aims and intentions as President clear.

Equally, there can be little doubt that in his early days the President-elect was influenced in world affairs by what his father thought. In his first book, *Why England Slept*, published in 1940, John Kennedy certainly reflected his father's basic opinion, which was simply that Britain was almost certain to lose the war. But the book didn't preach appeasement and was not anti-British. What was most remarkable about this immature work was its almost total lack of emotion. It showed a cold detachment, remarkable in one so young, and barely credible in a young American writing about Britain at that highly emotional hour.

In any event, Kennedy has said that his political disagreement with his father is now 'total', and there seems to be no reason to disbelieve him. The father–son relationship is plainly complex, though deeply affectionate. No doubt Dad still tries to exert the old domination. But when the son takes a course directly opposite to the one recommended, this commonly brings a paternal telephone call saying: 'Best dam' thing you ever did.'

Perhaps the most damaging thing being said about the new man in the White House is not that he adopted his father's beliefs, but that he has no deep-rooted convictions of his own. One American writer of Kennedy's generation has said that when his fellows 'got drunk and wept as the Spanish Republic went down', Kennedy was missing. The implication has been accepted by Kennedy as true. He has said, sadly: 'Some people have their liberalism made by the time they reach their late twenties. I didn't. I was caught in cross-currents and eddies. It was only later that I got into the stream of things.'

What these cross-currents were is set out most clearly in the biography by Professor James MacGregor Burns. From this it appears that Kennedy's father was indeed domineering, perhaps of necessity since he had a quiet and deeply religious wife and nine vigorous and variously gifted children. But he often had to be away from home and the dominant function was then assumed by his eldest son, Joseph. It may be that he took special care to impose his will on John, who came next in the family line and was therefore most likely to dispute a delegated authority.

At the same time it was Joseph who succeeded brilliantly at most things. Though the two brothers went briefly to the London School of Economics, it was

Joseph whom Laski identified as a future President of the United States. If as a result John became a bit withdrawn, unwilling to take any positive stand, it can't be thought surprising.

But Joseph died, heroically, in the last war, and the common assumption is that John had the family's devout obligation to succeed thrust upon him. Some people use this to explain what they suppose to be his lack of passion, the fact that he shows no burning zeal for a cause. He has been pursuing, they say, someone else's destiny.

But Kennedy has always been interested in politics and world affairs. He may have taken up these pursuits because he had to do something: his father made all his children millionaires when they came of age and openly challenged them to earn his contempt by being 'rich, idle bums'. The President-elect began before the war those journeys of political enquiry through the world which he has since continued, not bothering much with official circles but subjecting such experts as a far-flung correspondent of the *New York Times* to 'hours of searching inquisition'.

There is nothing in the record to suggest that Kennedy had any dazzling flash of enlightenment along his road to Damascus. He has been through at least two major experiences which might be thought traumatic. As a naval lieutenant in the Pacific he became famous when, in charge of a torpedo boat that was sunk by the Japanese, he rescued two men; he injured his back and later contracted malaria. In 1954 he went through a long and painful illness and 'drifted close to death'. But if either of these affairs did more than edge him closer to 'the stream of things', he has never admitted it.

As a congressman he learnt to prefer 'a somewhat crippled Bill' to none at all, and so, step by step, advanced through fourteen years of politics based on congressional life in Washington. His method has been to acquire facts insatiably, to consider any situation in their light alone and then to form a judgment impartially. A procedure which may sound pedestrian and prudent has been in his case nothing of the sort. It led him when he was still a novice to make an abrupt and politically hair-raising attack on the leadership of the American Legion; it led him to make a startling Senate speech on Indo-China and a stunning one on Algeria.

Kennedy plainly dislikes even the milder displays of public emotion; conceivably he is by nature unemotional. But it would be absurd to think that he has not been driven along by some compelling force. He made up his mind long ago to seek the Presidency. Since then he has pursued it with fabulous energy.

Apart from the help he has had from the glamorous Kennedy Clan – his three sisters and two brothers, with their husbands and wives, all of them unusually attractive people – there has been nothing exceptional in the nature of his campaigning methods. But whatever anyone else has done, Mr Kennedy has done at least ten times as much.

There are black marks on the Kennedy record, none darker than his failure in 1954 to join the majority in the United States Senate in censuring Senator McCarthy. He was in hospital at the time, but few liberal Americans have ever been willing to accept this as sufficient excuse. He has since given the censure his modified support, but whenever he is pressed to be more emphatic he replies: 'First give me back that year.' This may be mere evasion; equally he might be taken to mean that whatever he said now could bring him no real absolution.

Those who suppose that no one could decently be loyal to McCarthy should read the definitive account of him written by Richard Rovere, in which this appears: 'There were Roman Catholics, particularly those of Irish descent, who saw in his aggressive Hibernian the flaming avenger of their own humiliations and who could not believe that the criticism he provoked was based on anything but hatred of his Church and his name. To these and many others he was a symbol of rebellion.'

It is difficult to believe that this was ever Kennedy's view. But he must have known that this was how many of his friends felt about McCarthy. And as he once put it himself, how could he 'holler' against a man whom his father had supported and with whom his brother had worked? Yet it remains a disturbing fact about Kennedy that he doesn't seem to have been alarmed into throwing off the restraints of loyalty by what many people took to be a national obsession with evil.

Any good president of the United States takes the stand at his inauguration as an enigma of sorts. Certainly Kennedy intends to be the boss. 'The President,' he has said, 'cannot share his power, cannot delegate. He alone is the Chief of State.' To some it may appear that this notion of his office is reflected in Kennedy's choice of a government, and especially in his rejection of Adlai Stevenson as Secretary of State. Just as certainly, whatever confronts him, Kennedy will take it on with zest. When he describes what lies before him as 'the hell of a revolutionary time', one may suppose him to be tacitly rubbing his hands.

Most people predict for the new era an initial period of adjustment at home, seeking to reduce – perhaps sensationally – such social ills as discrimination against the Negroes and the unfair share of hardship now being endured in America's depressed areas, due mainly to automation. These won't be the acts of a nationally introverted reformer: they will be an essential part of President Kennedy's vision of the continuing conflict between American capitalism and Soviet Communism.

'If we lack compassion for those who are sick or poor or aged here,' he has said, 'we cannot convincingly show compassion abroad. If human dignity and human rights are not shared here by every American, then those in other lands of other races will treat our pleas for democracy with suspicion and indifference.'

It will also be a first concern of the new president to bolster American military power and to make its nuclear deterrent invulnerable, so that any Soviet use of nuclear weapons may become 'irrational'. And there is no doubt that Kennedy intends to sponsor a revival of the Western alliance's sense of unity and common purpose.

There are some political issues – such as how much to use United Nations channels, or whom to back in Algeria and in South Africa, or, most difficult of all at present, how to cope with the Congo – where United States policy is bound eventually to make a choice that will put a strain either on her relations with some powerful European interests, or with powerful Afro-Asian sentiments. On other issues – such as whether West German troops shall have nuclear equipment – there is another awkward choice to be made: on the one hand there are certain West European sentiments to be satisfied, on the other there is the need to seek overall Soviet-American arms agreement.

So far, Kennedy has not made it clear how he will resolve these difficult dilemmas; and prediction would be rash. Many leading American Democrats, including intellectuals, supported Sir Anthony Eden over Suez; they believe that President Eisenhower's armaments policies were wrong only because too weak, and think that to accept United Nations Assembly verdicts is an abdication of responsibility. Whose advice will Kennedy take?

We have yet to learn much about him, as a statesman and as a man. That he is in many ways enigmatic should be counted neither against him nor for him. But every living person must share the hope that he will reveal himself to be as wise as he has already shown himself to be dynamically active – and he might.

NELSON MANDELA

19 August 1962

Whoever betrayed Nelson Mandela to the South African police has given them an impressive victim. As an underground commander he had become a figure of unusual importance on the African scene. He directed the stay-at-home strike which, in spite of its limited success, certainly disrupted and discoloured the celebrations laid on by the Afrikaner Nationalists to mark the achievement last year of their new Republic. He compelled them to expose the armed strength with which they intended to subdue non-white resistance.

For fifteen months since then, he skilfully – even impudently – evaded arrest, so that people now call him the Black Pimpernel. A few days ago he was captured at last and on Thursday was brought before a court in Johannesburg.

Mandela himself would probably reject his popular title as too romantic. He is a responsible, intelligent and resourceful man, a lawyer who in any free society would surely have won the utmost distinction. He is in fact the closest equivalent yet produced by the liberation movement to a true leader of the Resistance in Occupied France.

He is a huge and strikingly handsome man of 44, with a broad, formidable face.

His natural elegance and nonchalantly royal bearing are enhanced by a passion for good clothes. He talks in a booming, carrying voice which he rarely tries to modify, sometimes exciting apprehension in those who had secret meetings with him in Johannesburg.

Nelson Rolihlahla Mandela was born to be Chief of the Tembu, the biggest single tribe in the Transkei. His father died when Nelson was twelve. He was trained thereafter for the chieftainship, under rigid discipline, by his uncle and under the austere rules of Methodism by his mother.

It seems that Nelson was by nature rebellious, unhappy even as a boy about the settled pattern of his life. He wanted to 'do something out of the way'. His vague discontent hardened into firm purpose when he went to Fort Hare, the college for Africans, and got friendly with Oliver Tambo, a quiet and modest young man with surprisingly resolute political ideas. The two became involved in a college row with political implications and were suspended.

This crisis forced a decision from Mandela about the pattern of his future. His uncle ordered him to accept the principal's conditions and return to Fort Hare. But after two years of political discussion in the college dormitories, Nelson was determined 'never to rule as chief over an oppressed people'.

For the young heir this was a grim decision, tearing at the nerve-ends of tradition, bewildering and painful to his people. But he fled, first to the gold mines of Johannesburg, then into hiding among the unemployed in the African township of Alexandra on the outskirts of the city. Here began his remarkable friendship with Walter Sisulu – also arrested by the Nationalist police a few days ago – a self-educated man of the people then deeply embittered by the constant ill-treatment of Africans and his own feeling of helplessness.

Sisulu gave Mandela extraordinary aid. When he heard that Nelson wanted to be a lawyer, he persuaded a white, Jewish firm of attorneys to take him on, and in many other ways nurtured him like a brother. No doubt Sisulu behaved as he did partly because he himself is a Tembu. But it also appears that Sisulu thought he saw in this vital, intelligent fugitive from the Transkei the makings of a great African leader.

Nelson finished his degree course by correspondence and went on to the University of the Witwatersrand to study law. He found the place in a political ferment, with the young Africans planning their Youth League, designed to inject a new militancy into the ANC. It is now assumed that Mandela was then a racialist, opposed to such 'foreign' concepts as Communism, as most of the Youth Leaguers were. Certainly his break with African tradition had been limited. He was not against the idea of chieftaincy, only against the notion that he himself should serve as a chief. One may imagine that he listened with a natural sympathy to his fellows who proclaimed a semi-mystical nationalism.

But he seems in fact to have listened with equal attention to all those conflicting voices. His closest friend was a young Indian Communist called Ismail Meer.

Nelson practically lived in his flat, always crowded with young 'resisters', sharing the endless cups of tea, the curry at all hours, the jazz sessions, the banishment of sleep, the orgy of talk.

But Nelson is remembered as having been 'rather aloof' and already by far the best-dressed rebel. He did not neglect his studies quite so much as others did and in due course was launched on a legal career. He married a girl who was herself 'political' but was not eager to see Nelson ruin his practice for the cause.

When the first real test came, Mandela showed how much he had been influenced by those lively voices at 'Wits'. He and his old friend Oliver Tambo had just set up in partnership as attorneys, in offices on the shabby side of Johannesburg. But this was 1952 – the year of the Defiance Campaign Against Unjust Laws. Chosen as Volunteer-in-Chief, Mandela left the office, allowed his marriaged to break up and went off to travel the country.

Africans now speak with awe of Mandela's achievement. He prepared and disciplined many of the 8,500 who ended up in gaol. And as he was helping to train the army of volunteers, Mandela was also evolving a scheme of more enduring value, one which now reduces a little the damage done to the liberation movement by his arrest.

This was the M Plan, dividing the whole black part of the country into cells under the care of Congress activists. Its aim was to allow all Africans to feel themselves involved in the freedom struggle. It has still to be fully implemented, but where it really got going the bans of the Government have had markedly less effect on Congress vitality. And when the iron will of the Afrikaner Nationalists forced Congress to go underground, there was at least the nucleus of an organisation that could carry on.

From 1952 onwards Mandela followed the inevitable course of a recognised freedom fighter. In 1956 he was arrested for treason along with all the others; he was one of the minority obliged to endure the full four years of trial. At one point he took over the defence and was also one of the Africans called to give evidence.

Then last year an All-In African Conference was called at Pietermaritzburg to marshal one last peaceful protest before the white-dominated Republic became a repressive reality. By chance the current ban on Mandela had just expired. Before the authorities were fully awake, he hurried to Natal, risking instant arrest, and there delivered a rallying speech that still inspires Africans walled in by the long silence.

It was said of Mandela then that he had at last 'emerged' as a true leader of his people. Oddly enough, the same thing had been said of him at least twice before – when he showed his quality as Volunteer-in-Chief and when he helped to destroy the Government's case at the treason trial. But between these peaks he seemed to fade quietly away from greatness.

There can be little doubt that Mandela is self-effacing by nature. Perhaps, too, he has found it useful to exploit his elegance as a disguise, sometimes embellishing it with an air of indolent detachment. But he also genuinely believes in collective leadership and does not wish to stand out as a hero. His real faith rests on organisation – coldly planned, tough, tempered, ready for rough action in the 'war' he is sure has already been declared by the Nationalists.

Mandela had been underground since April 1961. Everyone knows about the debonair role he played a month later, under the noses of the police and with the whole armed might of the Government turned out against him, in organising the stay-at-home. Everyone knows how he ran his press relations from call-boxes, how he made appointments in the heart of Afrikanerdom and kept them all, on the dot.

What he has done since then is something for his prosecutors to prove. It is no secret that several times he has slipped out of South Africa, visited many countries, and slipped back again. He popped up in Addis Ababa last February at a Pan-African conference, and made a sensationally moving speech. In this, as in pamphlets that appeared in South Africa after the partial failure of the stay-at-home, Mandela began to ask whether a government bent on using the utmost force to crush the freedom struggle could for ever be countered by peaceful and non-violent means.

One may only imagine how much self-denial there has been in Mandela's life over the past fifteen months. In 1958 he married again. His second wife, Winnie, is a child-welfare worker in Johannesburg and keeps going, in Orlando township, the little brick house where the books, the record-player and the pictures still reflect her absent husband's tastes.

Nobody knows how often Nelson contrived to see his wife and their two youngsters – or the three children of the first marriage now at school in Swaziland. But we may be sure that the courage with which he has faced these denials will be seen again when the Nationalists bring him, with his old friend Sisulu, once more into court. For Mandela is a brave man who can induce bravery in others. As one of the self-exiled Congress leaders said in London the other day: 'I have never worked with anyone who did more to banish my fear.'

MAO TSE-TUNG

6 January 1963

One of the world's most powerful men, poised now to influence the course of global events in 1963, yet remains for most of us a remote and legendary figure. Even Genghis Khan is probably less blurred in the general imagination than the man who could order an invasion of India when this winter's snows have melted in the Himalayan passes. He is one of the two that make the Sino-Soviet quarrel, which has never been so bitter as it is today and which might deny us all hope of coexisting peacefully with Communism.

Mao Tse-tung, Chairman of the Chinese Communist Party, says nothing publicly. He holds himself in reserve like the main body of an army. His reticence, made all the more possible by his retirement from the position of Head of State in 1958, enables him to maintain the legend of his oracular infallability. It also fosters the alarming mystery that surrounds him.

The Chairman's genius has been inspired by his vision of Chinese history. In this the main heroes are men like Sun Wu, the revered strategist who laid down for Mao the laws of guerrilla warfare fully 2,500 years ago. With him stand the peasant leaders of popular uprisings who overthrew tyrannical emperors and foreign usurpers. And Mao's vision has been further coloured by the great historical romances of Chinese literature, in which peasant outlaws outwit unjust authority, and craft scholar-tacticians confound the generals of despots.

From these influences have come the principles on which Mao's success is founded. He has consistently believed that any victorious rebellion in China must be based upon the ubiquitous peasant. And he has taken his revolutionary strategy, military and political, from the bandit and the guerrilla, who exploit weakness but fade away when strength confronts them, whose enemies dispose of greater forces but may be outnumbered locally and destroyed piecemeal.

Mao Tse-tung was born in December 1892 in Shao Shan village, Hunan Province, the son of a successful rice-trading peasant. Eldest of four children, a would-be scholar greedy for books, Mao flouted the wishes of a father he despised, refused to become a farmer and set off for elementary school – a lanky, broad-shouldered, but almost penniless gawk in his teens.

China was then ruled by alien Manchus, dismembered and exploited by foreign powers. Even when, in 1911, the republican revolution came at last, the country was soon carved up once more, among the rival warlords.

His schooling over, Mao took a humble post in the library of Peking University. But his master there was Li Ta-chao, the future founder of the Chinese

Communisty Party. Mao began the serious reading for which he had hungered. He read and absorbed Darwin and Spencer. He also imbibed Dr Sun Yat-sen's dictum that the individual must sacrifice his freedom for the greater good of the group. Then he discovered Marx. When the Chinese Communist Party held its first congress in 1921 Mao was among the few people present.

But in the years that followed the Communist leadership in Russia pinned its faith to the Nationalist Kuomintang (KMT) and to Chiang Kai-shek as the most effective revolutionary and anti-imperialist forces in China. Chinese Communists were instructed by Comintern delegates to join the KMT and to work on the principle that revolution must be spearheaded by the urban industrial proletariat. This policy, a farcical failure in agrarian China, was finally sabotaged when in 1927 Chiang ruthlessly suppressed the Communists in Shanghai.

Now contemptuously xenophobic, Mao set out to fulfil what he believed to be his obvious destiny. He had already fomented one uprising among the rent-racked peasants of Hunan, a province of tough, pepper-chewing bucolics who make outstanding soldiers and brigands. Starting with 1,000 ragged rebels in Chingkangshan in 1927, Mao built up his famous Peasant Soviet in the mountains of neighbouring Kiangsi.

In the five campaigns launched against him by the enormously superior forces of Chiang, he put his treasured principles of guerrilla strategy into practice with brilliant results. Only in 1934 was he finally forced out of his southern stronghold and began his historic Long March, with 100,000 followers on a fighting detour of 6,000 miles through the whole of KMT China. Precisely one year later he reached Yenan in the North – with 20,000 survivors.

From the Yenan hills the Communists were destined first to play their part in defeating the Japanese and thereafter in sweeping Chiang Kai-shek from the mainland. The cave-dwelling Mao of the Yenan period was not, as might be supposed, a grim and single-minded ascetic but a man of diverse interests. Thin, stooped, a chainsmoker and none too clean in his habits, he married his third wife – a Communist film actress – leaving his loyal second to find some other cave.

In his lopsided, sprawling Chinese script, he penned those vigorous and pungent verses in classical metre which his admirers call scholarly poetry and his detractors doggerel. He plunged into the intricacies of land reform. He toyed with a simplified Romanised script for Chinese. Nor was he politically idle. He planned ahead. A man whose romanticism is firmly anchored in respect for facts, he has always emphasised that one must 'conceive the campaign as a whole', keep the long-term object in view and acquiesce in the exigencies of the present.

So, in spite of everything, Mao was ready for an alliance with Chiang in 1937, when he was needed in order to achieve the destruction of the Japanese. So again in 1945, Mao advocated coalition with the KMT even though in 1940 one of Chiang's generals had lured Mao's new Fourth Army across the Yangtse and then butchered it. Mao needed the co-operation of capital and calculated that the KMT could easily be taken over by the Communists later.

This was to be the prelude of a typical example of Mao's military strategy applied to the political revolution – the introduction of his New Democracy in which not only workers, peasants and intellectuals would play their part, but also the petty and national bourgeoisie, until their 'revolutionary usefulness' was exhausted.

The bourgeois revolution that should in theory precede the socialist revolution could thus be skipped without any disruption of the economy. Mao soothed the shopkeeper while attacking the monopolist. In 1950 he reassured the rich and middle peasants while eliminating the big landlords. Once more he was destroying his opponents piecemeal. Like a good guerrilla leader, Mao has always believed in well-timed violence. He has said 'Revolution is not a dinner party' and 'Communism is not love, but a hammer for destroying the enemy.'

There has never been much love lost between Mao and Moscow. The Russians condemned the peasant revolution and the New Democracy as unorthodox, accorded no recognition to Mao and steadily backed the KMT, even when Chiang was attacking the Communists. In 1948 Stalin was still advising Mao not to attempt to take over China. Mao ignored him and in the ensuing months duly wrested the whole country from the KMT. Stalin was furious.

Mao distrusted Stalin but recognised his stature as a revolutionary and an ideologist. He has no such regard for Khrushchev. For the man who was already being called 'the world's greatest theoretician,' the final betrayal by Moscow came when Khrushchev championed the theory of peaceful coexistence with imperialists powers and of the 'evitability of war'.

In Mao's view, the principles that applied to the problem of 'liberating' and unifying China yesterday apply to liberating and unifying the world today. And the solution to the problem lies in armed struggle.

Chiang's treachery against the Shanghai Communists in 1927 taught Mao that national bourgeois revolutionaries are not to be trusted but to be fought. A tactical alliance may be made with them only if there is a greater enemy, like Japan, to be overcome. This not only disposes of the world's Nehrus. It also means that to contemplate coexistence with the Americans is an unforgivable error of strategy, since it is not sanctioned by the existence of an even greater enemy. Mao's consistent cultivation of Soviet friendship and of solidarity within the Communist *bloc* does, of course, have this sanction.

Mao should still be trimming and compromising as he did when his target was China. The lean Mao of Yenan was not only cautious but patient, a man who faced facts and warned sternly against dogma, saying that 'even cow-dung is more useful as a panacea'.

Thickened and bowed, this Cassius has now in theory become Caesar. His eyes gaze out remotely from beneath the strong, curving brow; the hair is thick but greying and receding. The low voice, the expressive hands can still charm, but the face is often heavy, brooding.

Mao the tactician has continued to bend from time to time before the wind – before the Russians outside and 'go-slow' technocrats within the Chinese politburo. But Mao the strategist now seems to be corner-cutting for glory.

Khrushchev's denunciation of the Stalin cult in 1956 directly challenged Mao who, depicted in his simple, grey buttoned-up uniform and black cotton shoes, was already being represented to the masses as a national father, the almost god-like 'Stalin of China'.

By 1958 he was making an open bid for the leadership of international Communism. He called for the Great Leap Forward, the concentration on local back-yard iron and steel production at the expense of agriculture, which was expected to provide China with a short-cut to industrial strength and independence from foreign aid. He masterminded the hasty regimentation of hundreds of millions into people's communes in a race to bring China to the final stage of Communism ahead of any other Socialist country.

The consequent economic chaos and administrative muddle disclosed another Mao – a leader who pushed ahead with impractical and over-simple national plans in order to justify his political dogma in the face of all economic objections and who was ready utterly to destroy the way of life of the man he had so long championed – the Chinese peasant.

Yet Mao, like China, absorbs and adapts rather than innovates. In the past his brilliance has lain in his very flexibility, his sense of the possible, his ringcraft. In a steam age these attributes made him formidable enough. In a nuclear age terrified of one fatal miscalculation, their eclipse could make him even more dangerous. For Mao's eyes are fixed on that point at which the traditional concept of China as mistress of the world, the cosmic unity expounded in all Chinese philosophy and the Communist theory of world revolution intersect – to prove that peace depends on oneness and oneness on the ruthless elimination of all opposition.

He is a chauvinist who has hardly travelled abroad and is said to be disconcertingly ignorant and suspicious of the outside world. He is not daunted (he would have us believe) by the fear of nuclear war. Men count more than material – and there are 700 million Chinese.

Never did a man wield so much power over so many – and Mao Tse-tung is a man who believes in the necessity of using force against his adversary. He still gives reassuring exhibitions of tactical patience. But now behind these shows there looms the shadow of a vast impatience. Mao Tse-tung was 70 years old on Boxing Day and Sun Wu could teach him no guerrilla footwork capable of defeating Time itself.

Jimmy Carter

7 November 1976

The day after Jimmy Carter's election I shared a taxi with a girl who had just left the Republicans' election night party. She was carrying a smart little black dress on a clothes hanger and must have looked very pretty wearing it, but now she was plainly miserable about Gerald Ford's defeat. 'Such a good man,' she said.

When she got out, the taxi-driver said: 'Poor kid. These young people always take it too hard,' and then explained why he had voted for Carter. A few years back, he had had in his cab Jimmy Hoffa, the Teamsters' Union boss, who not long ago was kidnapped and probably murdered. Hoffa had warned about the coming inflation, and he was certainly right. Now Carter might do something about it, the driver said, because he seemed to feel for the ordinary people, while Ford was a real Republican, a friend of big business.

Anyway, the day before the election he made up his mind to vote. (In 1972 he couldn't bring himself to vote for Nixon or McGovern.) He chose Carter, but it wasn't easy, he said. 'Because I still feel I don't know anything about this guy. I don't know where he's come from.'

And that seems to be how many Americans felt about the election. The less well off, the people who live in the troubled big cities, the factory workers and, overwhelmingly, the blacks voted for Carter, but without obvious enthusiasm. Except in the south, where regional pride apparently moved people to vote for a fellow southerner, the turnout was even less than four years ago.

For the odd thing was that the sense of Carter as an enigma grew during the campaign. He started with a tremendous lead over President Ford, yet somehow his character ended up as one of the main issues. Most Americans seemed to agree with the tired and sad girl in the taxi that Ford was a good man, in no way mean, and not likely to snap under pressure. But Carter – didn't he seem to contradict himself, to show a mean streak, and to get bad tempered when things went wrong?

The last thing Americans wanted was to have to worry once more about the man in the White House, and Carter was for many of them shaping up as a worry. From the moment he entered the Democratic primaries up till election day last Tuesday, Carter had one great disadvantage. He was a southerner. Southerners, and especially little-known southern politicians who want to be president, still cannot expect much understanding in the rest of America.

In Carter's case there was also suspicion about his attitude to the race question.

He became Governor of Georgia in 1970, partly by seeming to go along with white prejudices. His slogan was: 'Isn't it time somebody spoke up for you?' Implying, like George Wallace, that liberals were forcing change on helpless ordinary folk.

Carter's behaviour on race is, in fact, impeccable. Even black politicians in Atlanta, who did not support him this year because they think him insufficiently liberal, have never suggested he is bad on racial problems. Liberals, nevertheless, have persisted in suspecting him of not being quite so clean on the race issue as his record as Governor of Georgia suggests. Conservatives, on the other hand, believed he deceived the white Georgians in the 1970 election.

So from the start of this year's campaign, there were people on both halves of the political spectrum who were saying that Carter could not be trusted, that he was peculiarly double-faced even for a politician. And it was his bad luck that, as the campaign developed, the chief issues were of the tricky sort where a firm position risked losing as many votes as it gained.

On the economy, Carter could not simply attack unemployment. He also had to say he would cope with inflation, even though that was not entirely reconcilable with his stand on unemployment. He continued to attack established politicians, but at the same time he needed their help to get out the vote in the big cities of the north-east. He suffered much more than President Ford for his somewhat blurred statements on abortion. Carter's hedging was given a lot of attention in the media, although when Catholics came to vote very few were apparently influenced by anything said on the subject.

As the campaign developed, and Carter kept sliding in the opinion polls, journalists suspected they had found other flaws in him. He seemed to be not very steady under strain. He was short tempered. He gave the impression that he had to win at all costs. People recalled uneasily what he had written about his first unsuccessful attempt to be Governor of Georgia in 1966. 'I remember the admonition: "You show me a good loser, and I will show you a loser." I did not intend to lose again.'

At dawn on Wednesday, when Carter got back to his home village of Plains after a victory celebration in Atlanta, he told the waiting crowds: 'The only reason we were close last night was because the candidate wasn't quite good enough as a campaigner.' It was an admission of what had, in fact, been obvious: towards the end of the campaign, Carter had lost some of his usual self-assurance.

There was no innocent explanation for this. Apart from the tricky nature of the campaign, it had, for Carter, been exceptionally long, and he was tired. He was also (by his own choice) somewhat beleagured, because he relied chiefly on his small personal staff, and far less than is usual on the Democratic Party and its famous names.

In fact, the more one examines this fascinating man, the harder it is to interpret his troubles in recent weeks as a hint of something awful that he has so far managed to hide – that deep down in Jimmy Carter there is some new variant of Lyndon Johnson at his most monstrous or Richard Nixon at his most devious.

In the first place, Carter's childhood and youth, unlike Nixon's or Johnson's, were both remarkably secure and successful. He loved his mother, respected his father. He worked hard on the family farm at Plains, accepted thrashings from his father, when his high spirits got out of hand, and was recognised as a promising pupil at the local school.

In 1937, when he was twelve years old, he produced an intriguing document called 'Jimmy Carter's Health Report'. It contained thoughts such as: 'The healthy boy is clean . . . bathing gets rid of germs. A clean mouth is necessary . . . breathe through the nose and not through the mouth.' He also produced a list of 'Healthy Mental Habits'. Number One was 'the habit of expecting to accomplish what you attempt'. Number Four was 'the habit of sticking to it'.

Carter said not long ago that he and his wife Rosalynn had grown up in what, by comparison with today, were simple times. There is something of the storybook in this childhood, with its loving but disciplined family life, the pine forests and red clay fields, in which the boy played with black and white friends, and the ambition that he'd had since he was five to go to the Naval Academy at Annapolis.

The ambition came true (Mental Habit Number One). By all accounts, he was an ordinarily lighthearted cadet. His seniors criticised him for smiling too much. But at Annapolis and afterwards in the Navy, Carter said later, 'I stretched my mind'. His mind, by the account of people who have tested it, is today an extremely effective machine: thorough, retentive and curious.

Carter's successful naval career, which included working under the formidable Admiral Rickover on the development of the first nuclear submarines, his retirement to look after the family farm and business when his father died, and his early political career in the Georgia State Legislature all seemed evidence of a successful young southerner of the new generation.

The certainty and security of his early life were broken in 1966, when he lost the election for Governor of Georgia. The solidity of his life till then offers no clues to any flaw in Jimmy Carter, to any minute crack in his mental or spiritual structure that might suddenly show under the strain of the presidency.

It is not altogether clear what he went through after the 1966 defeat. Members of his family tell different stories about it. His mother says she noticed nothing. But Carter has described it in terms that recall the spiritual despair of a seventeenth-century Puritan. 'Nothing I did was gratifying. When I succeeded in something, I got no pleasure out of it.'

Shortly after that, after a long talk with his sister Ruth, who is a well-known evangelist and Christian faith healer, Carter was, as southern Baptists say, born again. Carter re-examined his religious belief, found it wanting, and vowed to put his belief in Christ above all else.

Many Americans find talk about religion as distasteful as their nineteenth-century ancestors found mention of sex. Carter's experience of being 'born again', his willingness to discuss his religious beliefs, if asked (though no one could say he flaunts them), has been associated by many people with his self-assurance. Their conclusion: Carter may be dangerously self-righteous, the sort of man to take on the rest of the world, because he believes God is on his side.

The self-assurance is there, all right. Norman Mailer went down to Plains a few weeks ago to talk to Carter, and decided that 'he had the silvery reserve only the most confident astronauts ever showed'. Mailer also decided that Carter felt he possessed 'an inner directive that he was not conventional but unique'.

Carter himself admits to an unusual self-assurance 'that I'm doing the right thing', that God wants him to do the best he can with his life. 'I have a constant drive to do just the best I can.' Norman Mailer found this attractive and it's noticeable that many of the people who don't are those who fear that a Carter presidency will not give them the respect or influence they believe they deserve.

The issue here is Carter's populism, his belief that America is not a just society, that government should work for the poor and unprivileged, and that it should be open to the ordinary people, and not the private preserve of the powerful in Washington.

These are powerful instincts in him, though they are disguised to some extent by his conservative liking for balanced budgets. They can best be summed up by a phrase in the speech he made after winning the Democratic nomination, that love must be aggressively translated into simple justice.

Carter has already made enemies by not chumming up with famous old Democrats either of the political or intellectual sort. His offhand refusal of help from J. K. Galbraith, the Harvard economist, is still being gossiped about. He has also not admitted famous journalists into his inner circle. One of them has just written that while usually one hopes presidents will grow in office, 'with Jimmy Carter, the hope has to be that he will shrink'.

Sally Quinn, a writer for the *Washington Post* who has a malicious and agile eye for Washington's obsession with power, says that the city is waiting for the arrival of the Carterites with as much trepidation as Phnom Penh awaited the entry of the Khmers Rouges.

What Washington and the leaders of the Democratic Party want from Carter is an invitation to share power with him. At the moment they are scared they will not get it, or that it will go to the wrong people.

A Carter administration is almost sure to be stormy. He says he means to be an aggressive president. He expects Congress to follow him, not to double guess his leadership. He admits he will not rush to compromise. Civil servants may well find him literally breathing down their necks, for one of the first things he will do is to try to reform the bureaucracy. This is in tune with everything we know about his personality.

About Washington's suspicion that that personality hides something worse, something dangerous, one must suspend judgment. Carter said last week that he intends to be a better President than he was a candidate. Once in the White House, he is obviously going to try quickly to clear up the doubts about him.

Habit Number Three of his boyhood's healthy mental habits was 'deciding quickly what you want to do, and doing it'.

LECH WALESA

21 November 1982

Last year, two Polish journalists asked Lech Walesa: 'Are you strong enough to continue being your own man, not allowing yourself to be bamboozled by anybody, not letting anyone set you up?'

Nettled, Walesa shot back: 'I am strong enough to be myself always and not to be set up by anyone – not my wife, not my children, not anyone.'

Now comes the real test of this independence. Since he was so unexpectedly bounced into liberty a week ago, every power-group in Poland has plans to use him, many of which blatantly amount to setting him up. The Church has schemes, the Government (at the moment affecting lofty indifference) is probably cooking something up, those of his friends who are free will be bombarding him with canny or crack-brained ideas thought up in their internment camps.

The underground Solidarity resistance leaders also have their own designs for him. And with mobs of photographers and well-wishers babbling round the Walesas every time the door opens in Gdansk, it is not hard to imagine what his exasperated wife, Danuta, wants; that everybody should shove off and leave the family in peace.

Liberation can be trauma as well as joy. Unlike most of the other Solidarity internees, Walesa has had no contact with his comrades for almost a year. He has been alone – torment for such a gregarious, extroverted man. He has grown fatter, smoked too much and worried. Now he has to learn the complicated and discouraging reality of Poland eleven months into martial law, which is probably quite unlike his own guesswork while he was confined.

That he remains a popular hero is beyond doubt. It is also pretty clear that most Poles still regard him as the leader of Solidarity, even though the union has been formally dissolved. Yet, although Walesa is not a modest man, mass adoration has never made him lose his head. His influence, he thinks, is a sort of loan. Those who gave him their trust could take it away again.

As he says, 'I was at the bottom, and I will be at the bottom'. He is a genuine trade unionist who knows that he cannot act alone, and his first priority now will almost certainly be to demand the release of his colleagues who remain interned.

Walesa became mighty through oratory. That is already a limit on him, as nobody is going to let him loose on a packed hall in the near future. Before the Gdansk strike of August 1980, the little committee which prepared it – the Free Trade Union of the Coast – did not think too highly of him. He niggled about details, while the intellectuals wanted to debate vast ideas. It was only when he was pulled over the shipyard fence and began to speak that his talents emerged.

Yet his hold over his fellow-workers was more complex than it seemed at first. He was a real workers' tribune, who dominated as much through his patter and wit as through any big words. The workers saw him not just as a hero but also as a card, even a chancer, who hinted that he was as much at home with foul means as fair (in places where 'They' frame the rules so that nobody at the bottom of the heap can win, the whiff of lawlessness is always welcome).

He was also a consummate manipulator. Walesa could make a mass meeting change its mind three times within ten minutes, and could snatch the microphone away from a rival in mid-sentence. At the same time, his power was conditional – and he knew it. The workers did not follow him blindly, even while they were mobbing him for his autograph. When he made a mistake, they would oppose him loudly and at once.

As time went by, Walesa developed a perfect lust for the process of negotiation itself. He will have to watch himself carefully now; in 1981, he showed how proud he was of his genius at striking deals, argued out until opponents became accomplices. 'Pole must talk things out with Pole,' he used to repeat. Sometimes these handsome new compromises fell apart, and a widening rift appeared between Walesa's 'moderates' and the radicals in Solidarity. Since his release, he has already spoken eagerly of the need for a 'national understanding'. But the situation is far more polarised now than it was last year, the chances for durable or genuine deals between government and people far trickier.

Lech Walesa is a thoroughly crafty man, as his long nose and foxy, russet eyes suggest. At times, especially in the intoxicating days of 1980 after the strike succeeded and Solidarity emerged, it looked as if he would dissolve morally in the blaze of fawning publicity, the luscious offers, the invitations from worthies who had been chasing him through prisons and police stations for the previous ten years. This did not happen. Neither did he regard as a paradise the West, which so often in history has abandoned the Poles to their fate. The main thing about the West for him was that the Pope lived in it.

Walesa is often spoken of as if he were little more than a Catholic puppet, whether it is the Pope or Archbishop Glemp or Father Jankowski, his confessor, who pulls the strings. But, like most Poles, Walesa is at once pious and insubordinate, a vivid sinner whose contritions are always real. The truth is more that Walesa has dragged the Church along behind him. Between them, the late Cardinal Wyszynski and the Pope managed to slow him up, insisting that if he did not try to reach common ground with the Communist regime, the outcome might be slaughter, invasion, even the loss of Polish independence.

That mixture of piety and rebellion is very Polish, but then Walesa is not for export. He was born on a small farm 39 years ago, in the middle of the Nazi occupation. His father died from the effects of forced labour. His mother married her husband's brother and eventually went to America, where she was killed in a car crash (the man paraded around Republican platforms in 1980 as Walesa's father was actually his uncle).

Lech went to school at Lipno, only otherwise famous as the birthplace of Pola Negri, the silent-movie actress. In 1967, he joined the Lenin Shipyard at Gdansk as an electrician. He married Danuta, an assistant in a flower-shop, and there are now seven children. In December 1970, he was involved in the bloody Baltic strikes which overthrew the regime of Edward Gierek, and his career as a rebel began.

As it leads up to 1980, the Walesa story becomes a chain of arrests, sackings, attempts to organise workmates, more arrests and more sackings. (It is worth saying that in any other country in the Soviet bloc, bar Hungary, a man with such a record would have been crushed with a sentence of at least ten years.) Anger at the helplessness of the Polish workers drove him on; so did nationalism; so did a sense of moral suffocation in years when everyone in authority lied as a matter of course. And yet the deepest of all his motives was a concern – an obsession, even – which is at once very Polish and pre-Christian. He wanted to avenge the honour of the dead.

Year after year, he and his friends went to the shipyard gate to commemorate the dead of 1970. Sometimes they brought stones in briefcases, to start building a monument. Always they were chased away or arrested. Always, Walesa came back the following December until, in December 1980, he helped to dedicate the three towering steel crosses which still stand there. He was the Polish Antigone.

What happens to Lech Walesa now? The Government suggests that he no longer matters; his release has served its purpose as a chess-move to persuade the Church, the population and above all the West, that General Jaruzelski is working towards the lifting of martial law and that Poland is returning to 'normality'. He might be given some Church job, on one of the lay advisory committees in Gdansk or Warsaw.

But the regime may still nurse plans for him, even though an album of secret photographs of his alleged sins has apparently been compiled to dismay the Church. One rumour suggests that he will be approached to lead a tightly bridled system of Christian trade unions, to run parallel with the new official structures and give at least the impression that trade union pluralism has been restored.

He has always said that he yearns to retire, to become a private person again. In the long run, that could be the most dangerous option for the regime. Polish heroes of the past – Kosciuszko, Pilsudski – frequently bowed out and cultivated their gardens, only to surge back to leadership at the next national crisis. It may be that the less Walesa does in the next few years, the more potent his legend will become.

GEORGE BUSH

6 February 1983

There is no real English equivalent of the American term 'preppy', though it carries overtones of a Hooray Henry, a landed gent, a silly ass, and even *noblesse oblige*. Preppies have lots of money and went to private schools before going on to Yale or Harvard. Their clothing is expensively casual. They are from the East Coast and believe in playing a loyal game along with the rest of the team. They tend to use faintly dated slang, like 'Fantastic' and 'Jillions'. But however you define them, George Bush is one.

He arrives in London this week on the last stage of his European tour, which has been designed to impress America's allies with the sincerity of Ronald Reagan's commitment to disamament. Bush has had ten splendid days; he has been handed the golden chance to appear every night on the nationally networked news programmes. Until this year he could have taught Jeeves a few lessons about remaining discreetly unnoticed in the background.

The job of vice-president has always been a frustrating one for an ambitious politician. Since the war only two elected ones, Truman and Johnson, have succeeded directly, both times following the president's death. While he was campaigning for the Republican nomination in 1980, Bush made his contempt for Reagan plainer even than the demands of electioneering required: he harped on his rival's age and called his fiscal programme 'voodoo economics'. He declared 'unequivocally' that he would not accept the vice-presidential nomination. Reagan certainly didn't want to offer him the place; he drafted Bush only after he had failed to persuade Gerald Ford. Even when the Republicans won, Bush had few illusions about the job. 'If I'm not up to the President's liking, I guess I'll be going to a lot of funerals – in Ecuador,' he said.

He is not even trusted by the ultra-Right who helped to get Reagan elected and who now have such profound anxieties about their former hero. Bush is seen as a late convert to conservatism, with a suspicious record of support for causes such as equal rights for women and abortion. Yet it is hard to see why the Right is so troubled: Bush remained loyal to Richard Nixon to the end and to an extent still is. In 1980 he produced an extraordinary and chilling definition of how one side might win a nuclear exchange: 'You have a survivability of command and control, a survivability of industrial potential, protection of a percentage of your citizens, and you have a capability that inflicts more damage on the opposition than it can inflict on you. That's the way you have a winner.' He never did get round to explaining exactly what percentage of citizens might hope to be protected.

His father was Prescott Bush, a stockbroker and Republican senator, a severe man who brought up his children according to Victorian precepts. There would be a Bible reading at breakfast each day with a particular moral, supposed to fashion the day's behaviour. He went to the right private schools on the East Coast, and left in 1942 to become the youngest pilot in the US Navy. With a flair for good publicity which has perhaps recently deserted him, he was filmed while being plucked from the Pacific after being shot down by the Japanese. He won the Distinguished Flying Cross.

When he was twenty he married an equally top-drawer wife, Barbara Pierce, the daughter of a rich magazine publisher. They have five children.

He read economics at Yale and was something of a baseball star. He keeps up an interest in athletics and is obsessed by his own fitness. When he plays tennis, four Secret Service men have to stand around him, one in each corner of the court. When he does his daily jog of three miles or so, two more bodyguards follow him and another, even fitter than the rest, has to run the course facing him, jogging backwards.

Well-born Americans destined for a life of public service generally earn their pot of money first, and Bush took off for the oil fields of Texas. He began by working an 84-hour week, sweeping up and painting the oil drums. He founded his own company, went into offshore drilling, and became a semi-millionaire when he sold out in 1966. His success in this harsh business makes him resent the label of effete Eastener which is often pinned on him. Texas is his political base and he enjoys pretending to be J.R. without the props: one cynical Washington observer says that he 'talks like he's from Connecticut, wears a French watch, and doesn't even own a working cowboy hat'. When he campaigns in the west he blends sharp, East Coast wisecracks with a malevolent Texan drawl. 'Listen,' he says of William Loeb, the notorious newspaper publisher, 'he's a real hard guy. On a scale of one to ten he gave Bo Derek three.'

But he fails as a hard man himself. In 1980 in the actual campaign against the Democrats he was supposed to do Reagan's hatchet work while the presidential candidate remained the amiable nice guy. Bush simply wasn't up to it.

In 1964 he ran unsuccessfully for the Senate and two years later was elected to the House of Representatives for a Houston district. In 1970 he gave up his seat to try for the Senate (unsuccessfully) but was, by then, sufficiently well-established for Nixon to make him US Ambassador to the UN. At the height of Watergate he became chairman of the Republican National Committee.

He opposed civil rights legislation in the early 1960s. He has since become a convert, but remains a fiscal conservative and hard-liner on foreign affairs. Under President Ford he headed the US mission to Peking, and then became Director of the CIA. His anti-Soviet instincts, always present, were fully confirmed. He said later: 'I see the world as it really is . . . I had the job of preparing the national intelligence estimates for the President. I had to tell him what the Russians were up to, and believe me, from that experience I have no illusions about Soviet intentions.'

By this time Bush had done almost everything, and yet it was hard to see exactly why he was where he was. 'He is the David Frost of American politics,' says one British observer who has followed him round the States, 'he rose without trace.' Another says: 'Bush has never failed in any job, but he has never left a mark in one either.'

When, in 1980, it was clear that he had lost the nomination he surrendered with good grace and good breeding. Having been put on the ticket, though he shrank from taking the low road, he campaigned for Reagan with as much vigour as he had earlier campaigned against him. This established his reputation as a loyal team player, and he has held it since.

It is difficult to measure his influence accurately, since he advises Reagan only at their private weekly lunch. He has, like all vice-presidents, travelled a great deal abroad, but at home he has saved the President from at least a few of his terrible blunders, such as when the President sought tax exemptions for racially segregated colleges. He also acts as a link with groups such as blacks and the labour (trade) unions, for whom Reagan has little time or liking.

When Reagan was shot in March 1981, Bush, unlike Alexander Haig, who appeared to be near panic, behaved with a degree of dignity and restraint, neither leaving a power vacuum nor muscling in too obviously and ambitiously. Reagan from then on liked his unchallenging style even more. He had already asked Barbara Bush: 'Is George happy? Does he feel that what he's doing is worthwhile? I just want to be sure he's doing enough. If the awful, awful should happen, George should know everything.'

Bush has made his own appalling gaffes, such as when he toasted President Marcos of the Philippines by speaking of the 'love' Americans had for 'your adherence to democratic principles and democratic processes'.

It is not easy to see precisely why he is in public office. His beliefs, while doubtless sincere, are scarcely burning convictions. Even Reagan himself has an identifiable vision, though it is of a distant and perhaps non-existent past.

Bush has already flown some 314,000 miles in the service of his boss, and this present tour is indubitably his most important commission. If he fails to convince Europe of the President's sincerity, the cohesion of the Western alliance may be fatally wounded.

He would certainly like to be president, largely, one surmises, because it is one of the few jobs in American politics which he has not yet tried. He would, he says, be a 'crackerjack' president – another giveaway preppy phrase. He has admirers (our own Norman Tebbit is one) but not too many followers. In the harsh world of Washington politics he is not, currently, thought the man most likely to succeed, unless of course something 'awful, awful' should happen. As the cynical joke has it: 'George is only a brain-scan away from the presidency.'

FRANÇOIS MITTERRAND

21 October 1984

The young French Resistance leader known as Morland, who spent a few winter weeks on a mission to London 41 years ago and whose habit of travelling on British military aircraft so scandalised General de Gaulle, will be back on a State visit on Tuesday as President François Mitterrand.

The bombed, embattled London of the winter of 1943 will be much on the President's mind: he has asked to meet old friends in British Intelligence and to revisit Dartmouth, whence he embarked on the dangerous night crossing home to occupied France.

A State visit, with its emphasis on symbol and ceremonial, is no time for deep political discussions. But when 'François' meets 'Margaret' – he and Mrs Thatcher are now on these terms – and he congratulates her again on her escape at Brighton, it will occur to both of them that they are, in very different ways, in a state of siege.

While Margaret is weathering the attacks of the IRA and the defiance of striking miners, François is suffering from a political wasting disease. He has dropped lower in the popularity charts than any President of the Fifth Republic, and nothing he has yet been able to do can persuade the public to look more kindly on him. He is halfway through his seven-year reign, and time is running short; his Socialist followers are disoriented; his Communist allies have deserted him; and the country is faced with a period of constitutional turmoil, if some way can't be found of preventing the right-wing opposition from winning the general election in 1986.

It is strange to look back now on the victorious François Mitterrand twirling a long-stemmed rose in his fingers as he walked alone across the Place du Panthéon on the first day of his presidency. In those early weeks of what Mitterrand calls, with an ironic shadow of foreboding, his 'state of grace', an Elysée Palace footman was quoted as saying: 'It's good to see him – he looks so happy.'

No one could describe as happy the face that the French President, who will celebrate his 68th birthday in London, has been turning to the public recently. Stoical, withdrawn, perhaps forlorn, are words that might come to mind.

During his visit to Aquitaine a few days ago, the pale Mitterrand mask became briefly animated for the required set pieces of cordiality, determination and patriotic zest; then the light was switched off, and the President was alone with thoughts that seemed far from comfortable.

Looking back at half-time in a term of office which seemed so spacious when he set out, Mitterrand is not short of reasons for melancholy. The period of reforms the Socialists are proud of – abolition of capital punishment, shortening of working hours, higher basic pay, earlier retirement, decentralisation – lasted only a year.

Then the Socialist economic policy of giving more money to the workers to create the growth that would provide jobs for the unemployed – putting on sail, while France's neighbours were battening down hatches against the storm – this central ambition of the French Left collapsed in three devaluations of the franc, a giant trade deficit and a desert of austerity which is still not crossed.

Now the language of out-of-power Socialism has had to be turned inside out. Unemployment has increased under the rule of the Left and must be admitted to spring from deeper causes than right-wing heartlessness. Inexorable market forces have been allowed to dismember the steel and coal industries, which the incoming Socialists swore to preserve. The 'wall of money' and the 'logic of profitability' against which Mitterrand fought in the old days must now be seen as the indispensable foundation of workers' prosperity, the creators of the safe jobs of the future.

'How happy the Left would be today in opposition!' wrote Jean Daniel, the editor of the left-wing *Le Nouvel Observateur* last week. And Daniel guessed that Mitterrand in his 'bitter solitude' sometimes imagines himself still in opposition, eloquently scourging the policy of a government which is, alas, his own.

The private landscape of the President's life has changed little over the years. He and his wife Danielle – they met in the Resistance and have two grown-up sons – still live in their small house in the narrow Rue de Bièvre in the Latin Quarter and use the Elysée Palace as an office and state banqueting hall. It is no secret that she is further to the Left than he is. He still bears traces of his Catholic upbringing in a country stationmaster's family of eight children. One of his brothers is a general, another is a leading industrialist.

Danielle's family were Freemasons, left-wing and anti-clerical. It has been a wrench for her to conform to the role she will play in London: the silent, smiling consort and shop-window model for French *haute couture*. But she has managed to tame her initial rebellion.

Their country house at Latché, near Bordeaux, is under even heavier police guard now that the Basque country just to the south of them is shaken by France's decision to extradite Spanish Basques wanted for terrorism on the other side of the frontier.

At Latché, Mitterrand, wearing a large floppy peasant beret or a broad-brimmed gardener's hat, is apt to sink into moods of deep rural abstraction. His house guests have to be careful to make themselves scarce at these moments. This is the side of Mitterrand which produced his journals and made him say after his greatest defeat, in the presidential election against Giscard d'Estaing ten years ago, that pursuing the political contest seemed to him less interesting than 'three oak trees in a field or a good novel'.

At the Elysée, the President keeps his door open to a wide variety of people including opposition leaders and Brigitte Bardot, ambassadress extraordinary of the animal world. But he moves increasingly among advisers who belong to his camp in the Socialist Party and are more or less under his spell. He has never made and kept friends easily among his contemporaries, but he has been quick to sponsor the careers of younger men, and they have remained strongly attached to him.

His protégés are now appearing in senior positions all over the establishment, and in the summer he made the most prominent of them, 37-year-old Laurent Fabius, Prime Minister. But for the moment, Fabius's sudden popularity has done nothing for Mitterrand's image. It is even suggested that the new Prime Minister's youth may have had the cruelly unexpected effect of making the man who raised him to high office seem old and out of date.

Mitterrand's break with the Communists and his abrupt abandonment of his government's struggle with the Catholic schools have not helped him either. It is not surprising, therefore, that he has seemed to turn with relief from his intractable domestic problems towards international statesmanship. One foreign journey has followed another. In his long experience of international affairs he has been forced into no major renunciations. His insistence that one can be both a nuclear warrior of the West and a Socialist champion of the Third World has caused some puzzlement but won him overall respect.

Now he can see only eighteen months ahead to the elections which could land the country with the 'cohabitation' problem of a right-wing Government and a Socialist President still with two years to serve.

Who will attend summit conferences? Who will speak for France? Two leaders of the Right – Giscard and Chirac – are prepared to 'cohabit', that is, to serve as Prime Minister under Mitterrand. The third, Raymond Barre, is not.

Gaullists point out that de Gaulle would certainly have resigned in such a situation, but there is every sign that Mitterrand intends to cling on. If he stepped down, he would invite the electorate – almost coerce it – into voting for a right-wing President. The alternative would be a seven-year rift in the state, a constant incitement to chaos. He is not prepared to close the Socialist experiment, inevitably for a very long time to come, on its present disappointing record.

Someone who watches Mitterrand from close quarters said last week: 'He reminds me of a boxer who is taking it quietly for a round or two, before slugging back hard in the later stages.'

Already in Aquitaine Mitterrand was speaking of himself as an arbiter above the struggle, whose role it was to intervene when political passions became overheated. His experience in the short-lived governments of the Fourth Republic, when he was a Minister eleven times, has taught him that in French politics the most beleaguered causes can be saved at the last moment.

The right-wing leaders also have their problems. They have dropped low in the opinion polls and are quarrelling among themselves and are threatened by the rise of the extreme Right.

French Socialism is certainly losing height rapidly, but it still has the country's most adroit pilot at the controls.

MIKHAIL GORBACHOV

11 November 1984

The announcement that Soviet Politburo member Mikhail Gorbachov is to head a Soviet parliamentary delegation to London next month has touched off a quite unusual flutter of interest.

The reason is only partly that he is a key member of the Soviet leadership, as close to being the number two in the Soviet Communist Party as it's possible to get, and therefore a strong candidate to succeed the 73-year-old President Chernenko. But there is interest, too, because he appears to represent a new generation of leaders, far better educated than the Brezhnevs and Khrushchevs, and perhaps less likely to have a chip on the shoulder when dealing with the outside world.

Gorbachov was only just in his teens when the Red Army cut up Hitler's *Wehrmacht* and laid the foundations for the Soviet claim to superpower status.

His youth was punctuated with triumphs of Soviet power – the Soviet atom bomb, the Soviet hydrogen bomb, the first Sputnik satellite that overnight knocked the complacency out of an America that had believed itself infinitely more advanced.

This is a man whose career has coincided with a growth of Russian power undreamed of by the tsars or even by Stalin. It is not unrealistic to suppose that it has bred in him a maturity and sense of responsibility that was denied to earlier generations in the Communist Kremlin that felt they'd only survived by a whisker.

It must be said that there's little in Gorbachov's appearance to mark him out as a new Kremlin man. He is burly, with far-gone baldness revealing a birthmark that runs back from the top of his forehead (it is airbrushed out in official photographs). On public occasions he wears the same dark suits, gaberdine macs and soft hats with the brim turned up all round that his colleagues do. He looks what he is – the offspring of Russian peasants.

But particularly since the death of Leonid Brezhnev in 1982, when he emerged as right-hand man and confidant of the new Soviet leader Yuri Andropov, Gorbachov has been very generally perceived in Moscow as the man you pin your hopes on, if you want change in Soviet society. His comparative youth – he is younger than Chernenko by twenty years – has something but not all to do with it. His public statements are certainly not the reason. Unlike most of his Politburo colleagues, he has not published a collection of his speeches, perhaps for the good reason that they would remind everyone of how limited his experience at the top has been. Until Brezhnev's death he was running the country's farms, and you don't attract attention even in Moscow with speeches on sugar beet and combine harvesters.

The feeling that Gorbachov is sympathetic to new ideas and change has been built up by gossip, some of it very likely inaccurate, and by more informed talk that has leaked out of the one place where real politics are conducted in the Soviet Union – the Central Committee.

The impression has emerged, cloudily, perhaps, but no less compellingly for that, that Mikhail Gorbachov is a man who wants to get the Soviet Union moving.

Mikhail Sergeyevich Gorbachov (accent on the last syllable) was born on 2 March 1931 in the village of Privolnoye, in Stavropol region, rich farming land north of the Caucasus mountains. According to his official biography, he began farm work while still at school but then in 1950, aged nineteen, made the dramatic jump into Moscow University, where he joined the law faculty. He is the only Moscow University graduate in the present leadership, and its only trained lawyer, too. (Most of the Politburo had at best a higher technical education.) There's no doubt that this has added to his standing among educated party members and the intelligentsia as a whole.

Gorbachov was at university at a peculiarly interesting and difficult time. Stalin died in 1953 and his death and the pressures and discontent it released were to find authoritative expression in Khrushchev's secret speech attacking the old dictator, delivered in 1956. Russians who knew, or knew of, Gorbachov at university say he was critical of Stalin's crimes even before Khrushchev's speech. Nevertheless, the record shows that he was an active Komsomol youth organiser at university, joined the party one year before Stalin's death, and on graduation returned to Stavropol to party, not legal, work.

The odd, and potentially damaging, thing about Gorbachov's career is its lack of diversity. He worked in the Stavropol party machine from 1956 to 1978, starting as a youth leader and ending up as the region's boss when only 39. Although he scored eye-catching successes in farming, he doesn't seem to have made any vivid mark as a leader. One Russian with an unusual knowledge of Soviet politics has argued that Gorbachov has yet to show in his career the toughness, the 'killer instinct', needed to get to and stay at the very top. (A rival for the leadership, Grigori Romanov, the ex-Leningrad leader who now supervises the defence industry, seems by contrast a most lethal politician.)

It's possible that Gorbachov didn't even really have to fight his way to power in Moscow. In 1978, Fyodor Kulakov, the party secretary running agriculture, died and Gorbachov was picked to replace him. Kulakov was an ex-Stavropol man. So was the powerful Mikhail Suslov, keeper of the Kremlin's ideological treasures. Perhaps Suslov wanted his own protégé to balance Brezhnev's men. In any case, the job was as dangerous as it was enticing. Farming was the country's Achilles' heel. Significantly there had been talk that a desperate Kulakov had suggested radical changes provoking an almighty row in the Politburo and the heart attack that killed him.

In the event, Gorbachov managed a programme of massive farm investment, sponsored personally by Brezhnev, that brought some but not sufficient results. He pushed some new ideas such as giving a group of workers full responsibility for an area of land and rewarding them by results. The thrust was significant – to increase the peasant's tie to the land, a tie that Stalin laboured mightily to cut. But neither this nor any other experiment has worked magic.

What did work magic for Gorbachov was the short rule of Yuri Andropov. This clever, tough-minded and austere Communist found in Gorbachov the ideal right-hand man in his effort to clear up the murk and muddle left by Brezhnev. Gorbachov saw to the details of Andropov's campaign (frustrated by the latter's illness) to purge the party and government leadership. As Andropov weakened, Gorbachov stood in for him, liaising between the sickroom and the Politburo.

There is no unchallengeable evidence that Andropov himself believed that Gorbachov should succeed him. But many party members who supported Andropov hoped he would and did not hide their disappointment when he did not. He was the sort of leader they could be proud of: educated, with a strikingly good-looking auburn haired wife, the two of them genuinely cultured even to the point of going to the Bolshoi for pleasure. Gorbachov had been more visible under Andropov. He had led a parliamentary delegation to Canada, where he handled tough questions coolly and lucidly (though in no way giving unexpected answers). In rare encounters with foreign diplomats, he had impressed both by his knowledge and his courtesy – the louring manner thought *de rigeur* in formal Politburo appearances is clearly in his case misleading.

Today, Gorbachov has almost certainly surrendered his agricultural brief (surely with a relieved sigh) and now oversees the economy generally, as well as the party and key appointments. He is gathering the experience which older Politburo members, like Foreign Minister Gromyko and the now sickly Defence Minister Marshal Ustinov, thought he lacked at Andropov's death. He is also in a position to build up his strength against younger rivals, notably the abrasive, and in some intellectual quarters feared, Romanov.

It is already being put about that he is soliciting all sorts of new ideas to get both Soviet economy and society moving again. And this is significant, for few intelligent Russians doubt that their country has reached a point where the old methods no longer work and that new ones – not just economic experiments but social and political ones needed to support them – must be found if the country is not to remain in outmoded isolation.

The hopes for this kind of change, which might slowly modify the world's perception of the Soviet Union, have been pinned on this clever farmer's boy from the rich Black Earth grainlands. They may be misplaced. Gorbachov may be more apparatchik than apostle of change. Or, as some fear, he may lack the cutting edge to win the battle to succeed Chernenko. But it remains a matter of interest to us all that the Soviet Union should have at least a potential leader waiting in the wings who has become the repository of hopes of this kind.

YASSER ARAFAT

18 December 1988

Exactly five years ago this weekend Yasser Arafat was engaged in some fracticidal strife in a shrinking enclave he and his men were trying to hold around the northern Lebanese port of Tripoli. As the Syrian-backed Palestinian rebels under Abu Mousa closed in, things could not have looked worse either for himself or the Palestinian cause.

For the second time in fifteen months the chairman of the PLO was about to lead his tattered battalions into a ship-borne evacuation of Lebanon.

On the first occasion defeat had been turned into a huge propaganda victory. The devastating fire-power the Israelis had inflicted on West Beirut had brought world condemnation and confirmed the Palestinians as underdogs. In the end, the PLO's infantry had swaggered out of the rubble into the waiting evacuation fleet under the protection of an international force and a mostly admiring world's Press.

Tripoli was different – the awful sight of a stateless people indulging in the ultimate wickedness of civil war. A few days after Arafat departed on a Greek ship

– appropriately named, it seemed them, *Odysseus* – an *Observer* reporter attended his last Tripoli press conference. It was held in a sandbagged apartment block while his men tried to dispose of a colony of rats which had taken up residence in the piles of festering rubbish outside, for the chairman is a fastidious man.

Would he take up the Italians' offer of a helicopter ride out of Tripoli over the Israeli patrol boats to one of their frigates waiting offshore?

He would leave, he said, when he thought the situation was right. How could he go when his volunteers were facing death daily? Would that be the honourable thing to do? What would we think of him? The eyes, watery, seemed to plead, 'Give me a break,' but this may have been because the room was full of cigarette smoke. (Arafat does not smoke.)

In the week of his greatest triumph it seems only proper to point out that the most enduring quality of Rahman Abdel Raoud Arafat al-Qudwa al-Husseini, also known as Abu Ammar which means 'the builder', and al-Ikhtyar, which means 'the old man', is his grit.

He never gave up, he never surrendered. He is the Palestinians' Churchill. On the West Bank and in Gaza the children of the *Intifada* play deadly games taunting the Israelis with his portrait.

Yet had Robert Bruce experienced this leader's list of setbacks, one feels the fugitive Scot might well have trod on that spider and crept further into his cave.

Arafat has known defeat all his adult life. He first tasted it at the age of nineteen in 1948 when the new State of Israel won its first war and the first of the Palestinian refugees came to Gaza.

How active a part he played in that war is unclear. But in 1956, by then a recent graduate of the Faculty of Engineering at Cairo University, he was a lieutenant commanding an Egyptian demolition platoon when the Israelis stormed into the Gaza Strip in collusion with the Anglo-French adventure at Suez.

Three years later, while he was working as an engineer in Kuwait, Arafat founded al-Fatah. At the time it was one of many offshoots in the region of Nasser's vibrant Pan-Arabia and a very minor one at that. Gradually, the new powers in the Third World began to show an interest. In December 1962 Arafat visited Algiers and obtained the blessing of President Ben Bella who took him along on a visit to China.

Then came the ignominious Arab defeat of June 1967, which led to the occupation of the Jordanian territory west of the River Jordan, the West Bank, and again the Gaza Strip which the Israelis had withdrawn from after the 1956 campaign.

Arafat's guerrillas, the fedayeen, set themselves up in bases in Jordan and began to make such a nuisance of themselves that the Israelis started to launch retaliatory raids on Jordan itself. At the same time the PLO began to embrace the revolutionary theatre of the hijack. In February 1969 Arafat was elected the PLO's chairman, a position he has held ever since.

By September 1970 King Hussein had decided that the Palestinians were out of control and unleashed his Arab Legion on their refugee camps which had become armed citadels. Outnumbered and outgunned, it was a foregone conclusion.

Desperate fedayeen swam the Jordan and gave themselves up to Israeli patrols. This was Black September. The PLO rebased in Lebanon and rapidly turned their areas into a state within a state.

The south of the country became known as 'Fatahland'. The resulting shift in Lebanon's demographic balance played its part in detonating the civil war which would ultimately see the PLO headquarters being exiled to Tunis.

It was here, in September 1985, that the Israelis made their last confirmed attempt to assassinate Arafat with a pinpoint bombing raid that killed 60 PLO men. The chairman, increasingly conscious of his weight, was out jogging at the time.

In Geneva last week there was a brief moment of panic on the part of the Swiss police when Arafat's car was caught up in a traffic jam. Journalists who witnessed the scene were struck by the fear visible in Abu Ammar's face.

Certainly, he has a right to be frightened. There have been numerous attempts on his life, mostly from enemies within the Arab camp. As a result, he leads a peripatetic life, rarely sleeping in the same bed two nights running. Despite this lucifugous existence his followers put his survival down to something else. They call it *baraka*, a kind of sixth sense.

Arafat was born in Gaza in December 1929, the fifth of seven children. His father was a wealthy merchant with business interests in Cairo as well as Gaza. His mother was a prominent member of the al-Husseini clan and was connected with the Mufti of Jerusalem, a thorn in the side of the British Mandate.

As a member of a bourgeois family with some connections, however tenuous, with the old aristocracy of Ottoman Palestine, Arafat was brought up in a houseful of servants in what was then part of British occupied Egypt.

He was an unprepossessing teenager, short in stature, with blubbery lips, slightly hyperthyroid eyes and bad acne. But he was already demonstrating that power of oratory Arabs so admire. While a pupil at Gaza's Zeitoun secondary school, where a teacher gave him the nickname Yasser, he became leader of the Gaza section of the anti-Zionist organisation called al-Futuwwa. He still speaks Egyptian Arabic, as it happens the language of the region's film stars.

The Yasser Arafat the world knows today began to emerge in the early 1960s, when the headway he was making with Third World leaders persuaded him to adopt a style more befitting a representative of the struggling masses.

The Keffiyeh head-dress of the Palestinian peasant, the very symbol of his revolution, now covers an entirely bald pate. His pioneering of the fashion for nail-scissor stubble is said to owe much to the fact that a shave brings on a rash. He eschews tobacco, alcohol and coffee and tends to offer visitors herbal teas which he himself sometimes sweetens with honey. But this appears to be for dietary rather than religious reasons.

Like most Palestinians he is a Sunni Muslim, but he never seemed to make much public fuss about religion until fundamentalism – and perhaps the prospect of Iranian dollars – was at its height. Then word was put out that the chairman prayed five times a day.

He has never married and when asked about it normally says that he is 'betrothed to the revolution'. This has led to prurient speculation about his private life, some of it probably whipped up by the Israeli secret service.

In fact, he is said to have had a relationship with an Egyptian woman for many years now. The lady in question is thought to be a friend of one of his sisters. Until recently this sibling lived a quiet life in the Cairo suburb of Heliopolis. Then, earlier this year, some men broke into her apartment, bound and gagged her, and went through her address book. They were presumed to be Israeli agents.

To an extent Arafat has always represented the moderate, he would prefer to say 'realistic', wing of the PLO. If one charts his progress from when he first made the cover of *Time* magazine in 1968 to his 'Gun and the olive branch' speech at the UN in 1974, it is possible to see how his emphasis on minimalist policies has increased.

But until now he has invariably drawn the line at recognising Israel, explaining that it was the PLO's last card. The *Intifada* has undoubtedly changed all that. Israel has never been so isolated. At last, he feels strong enough to play it.

HELMUT KOHL

11 March 1990

One of Helmut Kohl's friends said to him early this year: 'Helmut, you have the chance to be the Chancellor of all the Germans.' Kohl leaned forward and hissed passionately, 'I want to be. I want to be, I want to be'.

Last week, the passion got the better of him. In a lonely and inexplicable attempt to avoid accepting the finality of Germany's eastern frontier with Poland, Kohl looked like a horse which had torn loose and run amok and was now being hauled back into its stall by the stable lads.

The wild ride of Helmut Kohl ended in defeat but he was not yet prepared to

admit it. He reared his chin above the circle of TV cameras and his voice grew truculent as he felt thc world's incomprehension strike at him through the reporters' questions.

Next day, after he had been roughly harnessed in long sessions with his Foreign Minister, Hans-Dietrich Genscher, Kohl would only concede that German foreign policy had been through a period of not clearly explicable turbulence. 'Mistakes were made on all sides,' he said grandly, 'including by me.'

Those mistakes were hardly Kohl's first in his eight years of office as West German Chancellor. But they did for the first time create real alarm among his Western allies, and in Poland. Has Kohl forgotten Europe and become a nationalist? Almost certainly not. 'His basic political creed,' says the editor of a newspaper which supports the Kohl government, 'remains the binding of Germany to the West, in a collective economic and security partnership. He is European to a fault – but also German to a fault.'

Like all peoples, the Germans have their faults and most of them are personified in the pipe-smoking 'genial giant' (he is six feet four inches and puts on weight easily) from the Rhenish provinces. All agree he is arrogant and impatient, totally convinced he is right and unable to tolerate criticism – one reason he has virtually no friends in the news media. Polite biographies mention his 'instinct for power' – others say he is simply power-hungry. One aide in the Bonn Chancellery says brutally: 'He really has no political vision, except to stay in power.'

Such a judgment is common, but tells only part of the story. His entry in the authoritative *Munzinger-Archiv* of international biography speaks of an 'almost unshakeable . . . sense of mission' which propelled him into full-time politics at the age of 29 as a member of parliament in his home state of Rhineland-Palatinate. At 39 he was state premier, at 43 federal chairman of the Christian Democratic Union (CDU), and at 52 Chancellor – in each case the youngest person to hold the office.

Helmut Kohl was born the son of a civil servant in the Rhineside city of Ludwigshafen on 3 April 1930. His family, he says, was 'Catholic but at the same time liberal, and moderate nationalists'. His formative years were spent under the Nazi dictatorship. It gave him a horror of extremism – which for him includes socialism in all its forms – but above all a driving desire for 'normality'.

As he put it in an interview last year, the Germans 'want to live in peace. They want to live in freedom. They want social justice. They want to find happiness in life. They want to be glad'. He sees himself as the man who can provide them all that, following in the footsteps of the Federal Republic's first Chancellor, Konrad Adenauer. Kohl frequently refers to Adenauer in conversation, and sees himself as his political grandson.

The absolute pre-condition for achieving these objectives is external stability for Germany, which is why Kohl is, and remains, a convinced European and Atlanticist. Defeated in the Second World War, West Germany has no great power illusions left, unlike Britain or France, and Kohl has no objections to giving up elements of German sovereignty, so long as it is for the good of the Germans. He is certainly no nationalist in the Thatcher sense.

Despite that, in the exciting weeks since the revolution in East Germany overthrew Communist rule, Kohl has broken loose from some of the old tethers that used to guide West German policy. 'In the past we took no single important step without previously agreeing it with Paris,' Kohl's predecessor Helmut Schmidt wrote last week. That old shibboleth has been brutally cast aside by the Chancellor, causing considerable anxiety in Paris.

There are various explanations for Kohl's un-German behaviour. According to one long-time observer, he is 'as unforgetting and unforgiving as an elephant', something those who have tried to oppose him within the CDU know only too well. Added to that is his very German love of playing the offended party. Kohl is piqued at the hypocrisy of allies who supported German unity only as long as it appeared impossible – a common attitude – and now is taking his revenge by presenting them with a *fait accompli*.

At the same time, he believes the allies take it as read that Germany is anchored firmly in the West. 'But he's wrong,' says a conservative newspaper editor. 'He can't grasp that despite our having served 40 years' probation, the rest of the world is still suspicious of Germany. He's far too well-informed to think we can do without Europe, but he acts on the assumption that the whole world knows that too. He expects them to understand why he feels he has to play domestic politics on issues like German recognition of Poland's western border.

Kohl knows there can be no question of regaining the eastern territories lost to Poland and the Soviet Union at end of the Second World War. But because he knows the world knows it too, he believes he can give right-wing German voters the impression, which would last perhaps until the West German elections at the end of the year, that some doubt could still be cast on the question.

Similar reasoning underlies his bizarre assertion last week that the reparations question was as important for the Germans as the border question for Poland. That statement, said a former close aide in the party, 'was made out of pure political calculation'. There is a widespread feeling that Germany has 'paid enough' and Kohl is tapping the stream, quite apart from believing it himself.

Despite his attempts to win favour, the Germans do not greatly love their Chancellor, the first West German leader regularly to stand lower in the opinion pools than his party. He is also the first to be a figure of malicious jokes, made easier by his provincial accent and horribly convoluted manner of speech: 'I answer the question affirmatively all around with yes,' is a typical example.

The media likes to portray him as a *Dummkopf*, which is unfair; while he is certainly no intellectual – one Bonn thinker says he distrusts intellectuals as 'godless creatures' who try to disturb his certainties – he is one of the most cunning politicians Germany has ever seen.

Many Christian Democrats would like to get rid of him, but nobody will risk a challenge, knowing they cannot break his iron grip on the party. His secret is simple, says one insider: 'Kohl's knowledge of the party, right down to the smallest official in the smallest branch, is immense. He has an uncanny memory for how each one of them got their posts, what skeletons there are in what closets, and he knows every IOU there is to be called in. He never feels that an evening spent drinking with a party functionary is wasted.'

No detail in the life of the party is too small for Kohl to concern himself with, which is not the case in government. According to a Chancellery official, he 'hates having to deal with facts and doesn't have the patience to read long briefs. What he really prefers is an oral presentation. He operates almost entirely on the personal level, which you can see in the Chancellery staff: the great majority are friends, relatives of friends or friends of friends.'

His former aide goes further. 'Kohl has problems with people who have authority in their own right,' he says. 'He tolerates no gods alongside him, and those who don't praise him get persecuted.' That gives his kitchen cabinet – presided over by Julianne Weber, the secretary he brought to Bonn with him from the provincial capital of Mainz when he became Opposition Leader in 1976 – a tremendous power.

His wife Hannelore, whom he married in 1960, spends more time in their home in the Ludwigshafen suburb of Oggersheim – Kohl feels great ties to the region, which is probably why he retains an accent most other Germans regard as abominable – when she is not travelling to raise funds for her favourite charity, helping brain-damaged accident victims.

Although an interpreter before the birth of their two sons, Walter and Peter, she was seemingly unable to teach Kohl more than small-talk English and French. It was as if he knew his real destiny lay only in Germany, his truly beloved Fatherland.

WRITERS, ARTISTS, MUSICIANS

The *Observer*'s literary and arts pages have long been regarded as two of its strongest features and their influence on profile selection and writing can be seen to good advantage here. The tone of some of the early ones is didactic, weaving a portrait of the artist or writer into an essay on the state of art or literature at the time. The profile of Henry Moore in 1951 is a perfect example. It is the sort of tone later adopted on television by Huw Wheldon's 'Monitor': a determined effort to explain culture in simple language to the masses, which doubtless worked well at the time but seems dated nowadays. That particular tone is wearing away by the late 1950s (Auden, Betjeman) and has disappeared entirely by the 1960s (Amis, Bacon).

The literary profiles of the 1980s were enormously enhanced by Mark Boxer's drawings. They were among the very best he did for the series, which is very good indeed, perhaps because his subjects came from the world he knew best: literary and artistic London. Sadly, the last article in this section is an appreciation of Boxer himself (by his friend Anthony Howard) which occupied the profile slot he had so often adorned the Sunday after his untimely death in 1988, at the age of 57.

T. S. ELIOT

7 March 1948

Andrew Eliot, a cordwainer, born in 1627, left the Somerset village of East Coker in middle age to go to America. Thomas Stearns Eliot returned to that spot (via Messrs Faber and Faber) in 1940.

The poem 'East Coker' begins with the words 'In my beginning is my end': it ends with the words 'in my end is my beginning'. But in between? In between were generations in Boston and an unbroken communication with learning and with heaven which may have infringed even the supposed celestial monopoly of the Lowells or the Cabots.

The Eliot family had a dignified and austere ecclesiastical and academic tradition. (The grandfather of 'T. S.' established Washington University.) His mother, descendant of Isaac Stearns, an original settler of 1630, composed a dramatic poem, 'Savonarola', to which Thomas, her seventh and youngest, has written a pious filial preface. He has regained for the family, if they had ever lost it, an impeccable English – a new English – accent. The official assumption of English nationality in 1927 was redundant by exactly 300 years – the precise date is, surely, not by chance: and exactly 21 years later, he has the OM.

Whether the honour is exclusively literary – as fellow poets would prefer – is problematical: it might also be political, a gesture to America, since this heir of a Bostonian tradition was born at St Louis and had part of his peripatetic education at Harvard as well as in Oxford and Paris. It might also be ecclesiastical – as fellow bishops should not deny. For Eliot, who, unlike most natives of St Louis, proclaims himself Royalist and High Church, is naturally an arch-poet and temperamentally a major bishop. The extent to which his style is founded upon the Authorised Version has been overlooked by his critics.

No poet and critic of his standing before him has been more rigidly careful to let out nothing unauthorised. There has been no hint of rashness or scandal in his judgment of contemporaries. This gives weight to his critical authority. At the same time he has been radical in his assessment of classics. He has impugned Milton, which made him liable to some stinging rebukes, and he has said of *Hamlet*: 'So far from being Shakespeare's masterpiece the play is an artistic failure.' At the same time Eliot has founded a new poetic tradition in the theatre, a feat of genius, and his two plays, *Murder in the Cathedral* and *The Family Reunion*, have raised the temperature of more theatres than the Mercury almost to fever point. (Incidentally, the title *Murder in the Cathedral*, obviously good box-office, was not his own invention.) It is interesting to notice that his first book of poems,

Prufrock and Other Observations, was published in 1917 in the same year as 'Tradition and the Individual Talent', perhaps his most important critical statement, was delivered. Both came early: both are middle-aged, finished, original work. Mr Eliot has indeed relied upon being upper-middle-aged, and upper-middle-class, all his life.

Having, as a travelling scholar, known pre-1914 Europe and having consumed its tradition with exquisite greed, he returned briefly to America – and then returned to a Europe in apocalyptic ruin. Wavering between the profit of America and the loss of Europe, he chose Europe, if positive choice it were: Europe already had chosen him. He saw this European world from abundant angles, as bank official, schoolmaster, and editor. His command of the literary review, *The Criterion*, never failed the proud claim of its title.

He had arrived back with the seventeenth-century style which Andrew Eliot had taken with him. But it was a style revealing a profound sea-change. Here was something as new to language as the application of electricity; and this impact upon the vocabulary of poetry was immense, and increases. Eliot created the poetic style of the twentieth century; again, a feat of genius. And it is, one might say, personal and ancestral. This he did here, in England, almost by instinct. For his means of expression, poetry is wholly natural to him; his rhythms are original and innate, as the rhythms of all true poets are. He is often so allusive as to be elusive, but the essential quality of the poetry transcends the intellectual snobbishness of his method and the elephantine tip-toeing of his expositors.

There is no monotony about him. In the same year he produced books on *The Idea of a Christian Society* and *Practical Cats*. In a comic poem he describes himself with his

> . . . brow so grim
> And his mouth so prim
> And his conversation so nicely
> Restricted to What Precisely
> And If and Perhaps and But—

'How unpleasant', he says, 'to meet Mr Eliot.' But the opposite is the case. For it is enchanting to meet this self-doubtful, modest person, so gloriously ready to laugh with a most unexpected kind of yaffling sound. He is not so much a don as a college – where on any staircase Professor Channing-Cheetah may have the room below Sweeney, and where a bell called Medium Tom tolls precisely and with a dead stroke on the sound of 49. But he has created a new respect for the mystery of poetry; he has done for words what he would do for The Word – and in *The Four Quartets*, these two aims are triumphantly brought together.

It is possible to divide his work into two. The unfinished 'Sweeney Agonistes' – perhaps his masterpiece had he finished it – is the turning point in his development as a poet: it is his last look back at the Waste Land of the world he was leaving; yet it is as near as he has ever got to humanity. For an instant the Edgware Road in which he lived escapes, becomes unauthorised, impolitic, at first-hand.

Mr Eliot is eminently – one can use the word without a hint of cliché – eminently respectable. He has made no literary enemies but many unseen opponents; a few unseen friends but many public worshippers. Through his influence he has been the occasion of a mass of appalling verse and the cause of a portion of true poetry. In his capacity as publisher he has been able to exclude and to accept; there may be a hint of bias for his fellow churchmen, but that is a welcome sign of human frailty. Father Eliot has indeed heard confession of contemporary poetry more often than any other, and must have discovered some pretty odd things in the process. Whether his influence as a poet will be as lasting as the present imitation of him tends to suggest, none of us can live to see. Lacking the self-confidence of Enoch Soames or the professional skill of Madame Sosostris one cannot attempt to 'haruspicate or scry'. Every one has his own idea of the greatest living poet, but that Eliot is the most famous living poet perhaps only he himself would be found to doubt.

GRAHAM GREENE

27 November 1949

One day in 1930 a young man, whose first novel had been a great success, sat down to write for a newspaper what he hoped and desired from life. Amongst the usual list of good things to which most young men aspire, he inserted one odd item. He hoped to have time in the future 'to become thoroughly acquainted with such strange and slightly sinister suburbs as Brixton and Streatham Hill'.

Nineteen years later, most of Graham Greene's youthful dreams have been fulfilled. His success has been enormous. The sale of his last novel, *The Heart of the Matter*, has already exceeded 100,000 copies in this country alone. And the 'Harry Lime' theme of his film, *The Third Man*, is discussed over the sherry of highbrows and the tea of Lyons Corner House.

This immense success has grown in large part from his exploration of 'sinister suburbs', from his discovery of monstrous flowers of evil behind conventional facades. Mr Greene has the most sensitive nose of all contemporary writers for the odour of spiritual decay. He smells it wherever he goes, whether in the jungle of English bed-sitting-rooms or in the streets of Africa and Mexico.

To point out that the action in many of his stories resembles that of ordinary thrillers is too easy an explanation of this cultured writer's vast success. It is also too superficial, for, although they have in common the main themes of violence and pursuit, Graham Greene's characters, and particularly his heroes, are usually without the glamour that surrounds the fugitive from justice of the popular novel. They are seedy, down-at-heel, weak, rather stupid individuals, and essentially failures. Seldom able to control the external world, they are buffeted about by it and caught up in events like plaintive puppets: all they have to rescue themselves with is a soul and a sense of its purpose.

Mr Greene's books, even those he labels 'Entertainment', are discussions of moral problems, and the success and failure of the characters he describes come from their spiritual strength or weakness. The well-known fact of his Catholicism is often advanced as the reason and explanation of this, but a closer examination shows that his Catholicism is not always the same as that believed by the great majority of his co-religionists. If he has a strong belief in sin, he has a more dubious one in salvation. In most of his books, the Church and her laws appear more as the enemy than the friend of her members, and seem to be ranged on the side of the police and the pursuers to bring them down. This makes his heroes into lonely figures who have to come to terms with their conscience and work out their salvation in their own way.

His fellow-Catholic and fellow-novelist, Evelyn Waugh, who shares with Greene a taste for violence, but prides himself on the strictness of his religious orthodoxy, angrily condemned some theological aspect of *The Heart of the Matter* as 'very loose poetical expression or a mad blasphemy'. Mr Greene, writing of the distinguished Catholic novelist, François Mauriac, has remarked: 'If my conscience were as acute as M. Mauriac's showed itself to be in his essay, *God and Mammon*, I could not write a line.' And he has said that membership of the Catholic Church 'would present me with grave problems as a writer if I were not saved by my disloyalty'.

Graham Greene's slant on Catholicism has always had its exponents, the greatest of whom, Pascal, wrote 'In spite of all our miseries which assail us and have us by the throat, there is an instinct in us which we cannot repress and which raises us up'. All Mr Greene's characters could, in the opinion of his friends, be used as illustrations of this principle. Perhaps his wide appeal comes not only from the mystery, excitement and terror he discovers behind the drably familiar landscape, but because he offers all its anonymous, down-trodden inhabitants the chance to see themselves as pathetic martyrs.

The films bearing his name generally put forward only one aspect of his work. Evidently, the film industry considers that the glamour of wickedness, rather than the struggle for redemption, is the heart of the matter. Certainly, it is only Mr Greene's imaginary world without his message that appears on the screen.

The writer of these books and film stories is tall, slim, long-fingered, reticent; a man of 45, slightly worn looking, and with pale eyes that seem to be contemplating an inner joke. He dresses demurely, speaks quietly, enjoys such refined sports as winning under another name the *New Statesman* competition for a parody of his own style. In outward form, he certainly belongs to a world of private rooms and gardens, rather than to the hired basements and gay promenades of crime.

The course of his outward life has been as untroubled as his appearance would suggest. He grew up as the headmaster's son at Berkhamsted School, and passed quietly through Balliol into the least adventurous type of journalism – sub-editing on the *Nottingham Guardian* and, later, on *The Times*. He published a fugitive book of poems; became converted to Catholicism while in Nottingham; married at 23, and settled down in a Queen Anne house on Clapham Common. All the time, he studied and practised the art of novel writing, in which he has had an almost uninterrupted success without undue labour. During the war, he was employed by the Foreign Office, and when his house on Clapham Common was bombed, withdrew his wife and children to Oxford, where they still live. Since the war, he has moved about Europe, spent much time in London, where for a while he held a directorship in a well-established publishing house, and produced the books and films that have brought him such fame and fortune.

There is nothing in his gentle progression through a harsh world to indicate why this shy and aesthetic man should have been fascinated by the cruelty, wickedness, and self-destructive capacity of man. Nothing, except in his writings themselves. Here the fascination is present from the start. He describes how he noticed in his father's school that 'appalling cruelties could be practised without a second thought,' and observed that 'one met for the first time characters, adult and adolescent, who bore about them the genuine quality of evil'. The lack of satisfaction which the central characters in his novels find in their own sins and the horrible fates that usually befall them after sinning complete the picture.

Whatever the spiritual or psychological reasons for Graham Greene's popular appeal, the literary merit of his work requires no comment and, being authentic, deserves no explanation. He has mastered the art of story-telling and brought to contemporary letters a natural talent for vivid imagery; and, although he has been highly rewarded, the reading public remains in his debt.

Sir Malcolm Sargent

30 July 1950

Romantic symphonies are apt to make the ordinary listener feel ten times the man he normally is. Sir Malcolm Sargent, who has been giving people this kind of stimulus for years and who has just extended his field of force by becoming permanent conductor of the BBC Symphony Orchestra, seems to be stimulated in this way all the time.

The powerful motor which he starts up in his audience only for short bursts has, one might suppose, reached perpetual motion in Sir Malcolm himself. This is a happy state of affairs for him and for the listening public. He hurries about the world, making music at all points between the Antipodes and Stoke-on-Trent. By conducting orchestras he first produces for himself an abnormal liveliness, and then ploughs almost the whole of the spiritual profit back into the business.

Malcolm Sargent was born in 1895 into a background of tuning forks and paper-backed scores. His father, who had a small business in Stamford, was an amateur organist and choirmaster. Young Sargent himself conducted his own orchestra at a local pageant when he was fourteen. He became an Associate of the Royal College of Organists when he was still at school and a Bachelor of Music before he came of age.

The young man who in time became organist at the parish church in Melton Mowbray is now described by Sir Malcolm as someone without musical ambition. It was, he says, only a chance meeting with Moiseiwitsch which made him into a concert pianist; it was an encounter with Henry Wood in Leicester which led him to take up conducting. In each case the operative phrase was 'You're wasting your time'.

Even though Sir Malcolm's achievement since then has been an enlargement upon the usual form of progress to distinction, it would be quite wrong to think of him as one for whom making music is the sole, or even the dominant, aim. His real purpose, which he readily declares, is to have an enjoyable life. What gives him his delight in music is the whole process of making it. The results – memorable performances, a growing fame, people telling him that his concerts have put them in touch with 'eternal values' – are a part of the process, but for Sir Malcolm only a part. He sees the life of a conductor as a vivid and multifarious end in itself.

The technique he finds fascinating. But while Sir Malcolm enjoys a conductor's normal encounters, they are by no means enough for him. He goes on, sleek, elegant and assured, to absorb wider and more varied experiences. He rejoices in the whole adventure of an itinerant musician's life. He likes meeting people, and likes travel, and he is always vividly curious about minor oddities and wonders.

It is significant that Sir Malcolm remembers no dominating *musical* experience. His life is so busy, he says, that the recollection of any one performance is quickly engulfed. The only concert that seriously interests him is the next. Rather than any particularly good Beethoven finale (which has its unique importance for him at the time), he remembers climbing Vesuvius or watching an elephant catch, pluck and eat a pigeon. ('Surely they're vegetarian? I must ring up the zoo.')

One might be forgiven for supposing that in extra-auditorium encounters he favours a Personage. *Debrett's Peerage* stands among other useful works of reference in his living room and signed photographs of royalty and viceroyalty are everywhere. But he gets along equally well with the men who with such serious zeal blow the brass instruments of a works band.

Sir Malcolm certainly enjoys the impression his vitality makes on other and less dynamic folk. He delights in showing people the crowded pages of his engagement diary, on which at intervals is printed DAY OFF ESSENTIAL. When they say 'You'll kill yourself,' he replies 'What fun!' The full exploitation of life certainly acquired a new meaning for him some years ago, when he almost died and had to spend two years in idleness. His days now are more carefully planned than his own attitude of gay heedlessness would seem to imply.

His London flat is at the very hub; the terracotta frieze round the Albert Hall bulges past his windows. It is an operational headquarters. His personal staff works with him on the premises, preparing his scores, planning the Diary, and the whole regimen is a matter of strict timing. It is a comfortable, even an opulent, flat, efficiently planned for living as a cultivated art. What one misses is any sign of relaxed domesticity; Sir Malcolm does not care for the aimless inactivity often practised at home.

Of his part in the making of music, Sir Malcolm has a clear and modest notion. He is the Interpreter, without whom no composer can give his Message to the world. He 'produces' a symphony of Mozart as another produces a Shakespeare play; the whole art lies in recognising that there are a dozen *good* ways of saying 'To be, or not to be'. To this he brings a quick and penetrating imagination and a really strong sense of duty. His integrity appealed in particular to Elgar, who invited Sargent to meet him, took him through all his major works and became his friend. Elgar once said: 'So long as Sargent is living I shall not worry about the interpretation of my works.'

Audiences love Sir Malcolm's visible glamour; he is dark, slim, always immaculate, always wearing a red carnation; his conducting technique has its own clear-cut artistry. But he also satisfies those critics who are not easily misled by glamour – the professionals in the orchestra. In England they may be seen earnestly tapping the stems of their music stands. In Madrid, after one rehearsal and as he came in for the next, they gave him the full exuberant fanfare normally reserved for the most popular matador. It is magnificently typical of Sir Malcolm that he knew the correct riposte; he threw his hat across the arena.

This is the kind of encounter for which Sir Malcolm lives and for which he travels the world. He devotes himself with a restless zeal to the enjoyment of life. And he does it in such a way that all kinds of people, many of them utterly unknown to him, get a share.

HENRY MOORE

24 June 1961

There have been times when the artist's work held a central place in the life of the community – indeed, taking a long view, this has been the normal situation. In all primitive communities and in every civilisation before the present one, artists (and particularly sculptors) were employed to make works that must have been communally treasured or they would not have survived to fill our museums.

In those days, art was what it should be – a dialogue between its maker and the community, with the community knowing what it wanted said. The relationship was – on an epic scale – that which exists between children and toymakers. Today, art has largely become an enforced monologue. Nobody really knows what they want of artists: as for sculpture, we scarcely know what to do with it, no matter what its shape or character.

Hence the extraordinary position of Mr Henry Moore. He has won the chief international award for sculpture, been proclaimed by an Arts Council official 'Britain's greatest living artist'; his work is eagerly bought by museums and private collectors here and in the USA for the highest prices; and he has been selected for a one-man show at the Tate Gallery in Festival year. Yet his figures in the South Bank Exhibition and at Battersea probably earn more unappreciative comments from the average onlooker than do those of less successful sculptors. This combination of official, academic and private support with public neglect seems likely to become the classic position of a leading artist in our day.

How this distorted position has come about is a very long story covering hundreds, even thousands, of years, but the broad facts seem to be these. As the organisation of human society became more complex, so the artist became further removed from the multitude. Then, with the advent of machinery and its profoundly bewildering effects on human society, a sort of cultural Ice Age set in. The artists have survived – by sheltering in various ways from the blighting effect of social indifference. But in the course, they have become dependent on a new type of protector – dealers, critics, pundits and a few isolated individuals, with, quite recently, the powerful addition of the directors of state galleries and officials of other art-promoting bodies (like the Arts and British Councils).

The primary difference between these new protectors and the communal bosses (lay or spiritual) on whom artists heretofore depended is this: the new protectors give opportunities, but no orders. Whereas the artist was formerly the servant – often the most favoured servant – of a demanding community or king,

he is now left in ghastly solitude to think up his own ideas like a mystic, to demonstrate 'genius', to speak to an imaginary listener. His patrons are today his sycophants or exploiters – and this is neither their fault nor his: it is the fault of the evolution (or bewilderment) of society.

Although society and patronage have been thus transformed, the artist himself remains the same animal that he always was. Henry Moore is an example of all of this – a simple, straightforward, sensible man with an urge to make things, who has had to exist by teaching in academies and impressing a few well-placed people. He is, in all probability, the same stone-hewing, wood-carving, clay-modelling sort of man who made the sculpture of all the ages represented in the British Museum. But, unlike his predecessors, nobody tells him what is wanted, because nobody knows the answer; the modern convention is that the artist must decide this question for himself. From his patrons he can get only passive admiration or their priest-like assumption of the role of interpreters. What he must lack is the warmth, excitement and demands of a communal culture.

Henry Moore was born some 50 years ago in the small town of Castleford in Yorkshire, the seventh son of a coal miner. It was the art mistress at the local school who noticed his talent and first encouraged him to model and draw. Then came the war of 1914–18, in which he served as a private and was gassed at Cambrai. Being a gentle and studious type, he returned to Castleford as a schoolteacher, but then obtained an ex-serviceman's educational grant and went to Leeds as an art student.

He showed exceptional gifts and won a scholarship to the Royal College of Art in London. Here he lived the hard-working life of the serious art student – Moore was always a very serious fellow – spent much time in the British Museum, and fell in love (for life) with the primitive Mexican 'reclining' figures – head held high and turned, weight on elbows and lower spine, and knees up – of which he has produced countless variations over a long period of hard work.

A travelling scholarship took him to France and Italy, where he reacted to the work of primitives, and modern-primitives. On returning, he showed the capacity essential to big success in modern art. He tenaciously produced his own style, with sufficient variations to maintain a repute for originality (the quality not demanded in previous ages) and with enough proximity to the work of other modern artists, notably Picassó, to be identifiable as a member of their movement.

Moore soon evolved a personal speciality – the making of holes in his figures. Although all sculpture that departed from the solid block contained holes or air spaces of some kind, his systematic use of holes undoubtedly gave his work identification. He gained support from Herbert Read, an important writer on art who was greatly elated by his discovery of Moore, the late Sir Michael Sadler, a notable collector of new art forms, and others. The Leicester Galleries, an enterprising West End art shop, presented three exhibitions of his work during the 1930s. And the most valuable of contemporary patrons, the connoisseurs turned directors of public galleries, Philip Hendy, Kenneth Clark and John Rothenstein, who shared the same ideas as Read and Sadler, weighed in with their massive support. Moore was made.

It is comon to hear the workings of this process, with its tendency to 'star' creation, referred to in artistic circles as 'the racket' – sometimes as 'the other racket', a reference to the older and parallel system of advancement via the trade union or artists themselves, the Royal Academy. The two processes, it should be noted, are not only different but mutually exclusive, and Moore has evaded suggestions that he might exhibit at the RA; quite rightly, from a practical viewpoint. But the activities of neither of these sets of men deserve any such term (with the possible exception of the operations of some dealers). They are merely the necessary answers to a situation of cultural void.

The characteristics of Moore's work – on which a mass of writing has been expended, usually eulogistic and couched in the fantastic jargon of the professional 'authority on art' – are highly interesting. He has, with much seriousness, attempted to rediscover the fundamental qualities of sculpture as an artistic medium – and succeeded in so far as his work cannot be mistaken for anything but three-dimensional form (the holes prohibit two-dimensional viewing). He has, in common with most other modern artists, become absorbingly preoccupied in the materials of his trade – this can easily be understood, if it is accepted that our cultural vacuum has robbed art of its usual content or meaning, which was previously conferred by the social beliefs and popular appetites of the time. And he has discovered new models by turning to Nature's own sculpture – pebbles washed into strange shapes by the sea, bones, rock formations and tree trunks.

Undoubtedly a master craftsman with a strong sense of organic form, he has, by these means, made contact with one deep need of the more sensitive spirts of our distressing days – the need to regain touch with the earth (which some gratify through the Soil Association, others by archaeology, and many by living in the country or dreaming of so doing). In this, he has in some degree fulfilled one of the strange new roles inflicted on the artist, that of producing a *Weltanschauung* or view of life (instead of reflecting one, as any primitive or even coherent community would have demanded).

But there is another aspect of some of his work that strikes the eye of the beholder, yet is seldom mentioned by the interpreting priests – its touch of sedate horror or positive ugliness. This he achieves by putting tiny heads, oval or split, on a quasi-human form; by adorning a mechanistic lump with nipples or the suggestion of an eye; or, most simply, by labelling an abstract form, that looks like nothing in particular, 'Mother and Child'.

There is a justification of this use of horror (which he practises more soberly than many others) that is never made, because the phenomenon itself is never admitted. Horror is to beauty what tragedy is to comedy, or dissonance is to harmony, or heat is to cold – an opposite in one scale of values. That a taste for the grotesque or the horrifying exists in human nature scarcely needs to be argued. It is not to an artist's discredit if he uses it; and indeed it could be argued that by so doing he expresses the malaise, or assaults the indifference, of our age more effectively than he could by any other means.

Whatever the reason, Henry Moore has certainly made his impact on the upper strata of our intellectual life. If we have no common culture, that is not his fault. Yet he might well be envious of those who practise such a social art as architecture, which *cannot* be practised in isolation. It is almost impossible to visit the South Bank Exhibition without contrasting the gaiety and confidence of its architecture with the solemn and self-conscious air of its more advanced sculptural exhibits. What a pity that sculptors do not need to work with other people, such as constructional engineers, to seek buyers before they start work, to contend with genuinely functional problems! But they do not; and commissioning would provide no substitute for a place in the social fabric. They must struggle on, speaking chiefly to themselves, until the rest of us feel as much at home in our human and material surroundings as did our forbears in theirs, and produce a culture – which may take centuries.

EVELYN WAUGH

31 July 1955

Sometimes an investigation into the life and character of a writer reveals a personality disturbingly at variance with the impression given by his books. It is somehow reassuring to find that Evelyn Waugh, the country gentleman and clubman, does not conflict at all with Evelyn Waugh, the novelist – author of last month's *Officers and Gentlemen*.

Though by no means an introspective writer, he reveals in his books a very great deal about his values, his habits and his overt personality. His best books are extremely funny, and he himself is a humorist both in word and conduct. His books show a respect for noble birth and physical courage, and so does he. His books are often rude and arrogant, and he himself delights in the same qualities.

Unlike most popular novelists, Waugh's popularity is based on a caustic, even brutal attitude to the kind of people who make up the great majority of his readers. He does not treat his readers with the gruff affection of a Priestley or with the solemn and mystical respect displayed by Charles Morgan. Most 'ordinary' characters in Waugh's novels – that is to say, most members of the middle or working classes – are either ridiculous or odious or dull, and it is reserved for a

small minority of his many aristocrats to bear the serious burden which his novels have increasingly demanded.

In almost any other age than our own there would be nothing odd in this, for it is in the grand tradition of Shakespeare and Molière that the 'lower orders' are either comic or dislikeable, while real and potentially tragic life is reserved for those of royal or noble blood. But since early in the nineteeth century this attitude has become an eccentric one, and Waugh's very deliberate return to the old literary convention is a phenomenon which seems to demand attention.

It soon becomes clear that it is not only in literary convention that Evelyn Waugh has made a deliberate return to the past. Both in his life and in his books he reveals himself as a passionate and romantic admirer of a vague and vanished age in which life was both more savage and more glorious than he finds it to be today. It is no disparagement of his obvious religious sincerity to see in his conversion to Roman Catholicism – 'the old religion' – another aspect of his nostalgia. His deep respect for the *potentialities* of the aristocracy is as undisguised in his life as it is in his books: to call it snobbery is not to analyse it more profoundly. If snobbery implies sycophancy, the word is absurdly misapplied in this case, for Evelyn Waugh has never bowed his knee in humility to anyone not ordained by the Catholic Church.

This squat, broad-shouldered man is pugnacious, brave and unyielding, and many of the semi-legendary stories which have grown up like ivy all round him tell of the truculent reproofs he has delivered to his noble friends for their failure to keep up the high romantic standards which Waugh's nostalgia demands of them. It is reported, for example, that a *grande dame* who arrived to spend a weekend at Waugh's Gloucestershire house was turned away at the door because she had failed to bring a lady's maid with her.

Similarly Evelyn Waugh's high respect for physical courage has led him, and particularly in the two volumes of his most recent novel, to speak of the army in almost amorous terms; yet it seems that he himself was continually at odds with those both above and below him in rank during his wartime military career. His brave, prickly, witty personality found it impossible to like or respect the military colleagues whom he had set out to admire. In fact, his desire to admire is so strong that any given object of this tentative admiration is bound to crumple under the heavy burden of his expectation.

It has sometimes been scornfully pointed out that Evelyn Waugh is not himself an aristocrat – is in fact, most solidly, a member of those solid middle classes for whom he expresses such disdain. But it is also true that he has never indulged in that last infirmity of romantic minds, the invention of an imaginary and blue-blooded pedigree. His Romantic predecessors, Alfred de Musset and Victor Hugo, were both guilty of this absurdity, but Waugh has scornfully avoided it. He is, almost self-confessedly, a fellow-traveller of the nobility's stately and imperceptible progress, and has never made any pretence of party-membership.

He was born in Hampstead in 1903, second son of the publisher and literary critic, Arthur Waugh. He was educated at Lancing and Hertford College, Oxford, where he read modern history. After going down from the university he studied for a time at Heatherly's Art School (the first edition of *Decline and Fall* was admirably illustrated by its author); and then became a master at a private school.

It was this last experience which gave him the idea, if not the material, for writing his first novel, *Decline and Fall*, which was published in 1928. This book was an immediate and most well-deserved success. It disclosed a new young writer who was both boisterous and sophisticated, and who took a marvelling delight in the preposterous creatures of his own fruitful imagination. The book is neither satirical nor 'significant'; it is a *jeu d'esprit* of pure humour, and perhaps the funniest novel to have been written in English during the twentieth century.

Evelyn Waugh showed, and has never ceased to show, that he belongs firmly to the English twenties of this century, a colourful but sad period from which many young people turned away in disgust to search for salvation in extravagant acts of faith. Some became Communists, but more took refuge in extreme traditionalism. When *Vile Bodies* followed, a slightly uneasy note had already been introduced, and it was never quite to disappear from Waugh's subsequent novels. Why did he love and hate these smart young people so much? It became apparent that he was unable to let them play out their absurdities without his heavily unspoken comment.

Even in his last two-volume novel, though a tame and rather long-winded labour, there are brief passages of pure humour which bitterly remind us of his half-buried talents. Here he has done his best to be socially broad-minded – a languid aristocrat deserts his men in action – many of the middle-class officers are brave and likeable despite their bizarre vocabulary – but the two books are still riddled with romantic social nonsense. If Waugh shows from this work that he has tamed some of his prejudices, he shows also that he has tamed his capricious talent.

His youth was adventurous. After a brief period as a schoolmaster he embarked on nine peripatetic years, travelling in many parts of Europe and the Near East, and making more strenuous expeditions to the Arctic and tropical America. He has been three times to Abyssinia (which has provided him with a background for two of his funniest books), once as *Daily Mail* correspondent with the Italian armies in 1935. This was a typical example of Waugh's almost childish desire to shock. Because most of Protestant England believed that the Abyssinians were in the right, and that the Italians were behaving not only badly but boringly badly, Evelyn Waugh thought it interesting to support the 'catholic' and 'civilising' crusade of white man against 'wog'.

In 1937 Waugh married Laura, youngest daughter of the late Aubrey Herbert, and he now has six children. The large and happy family live in Gloucestershire on the considerable and well-earned income which Evelyn Waugh derives from his highly successful novels.

In 1939 he was commissioned in the Royal Marines, and served as a company commander. Later he joined VIII Commando, went with them to the Middle East and fought gallantly in the evacuation of Crete. He was on General Laycock's staff and subsequently transferred from the Marines to the Blues. In 1944 he went to Yugoslavia as a member of the British military mission to Marshal Tito. If he saw little action in the war, it was perhaps his over-zealous pugnacity which led to this most unwished-for result. For nobody has ever doubted his fanatical courage, both physical and moral, or his admiration for the military virtues.

In our time it is hard indeed for the romantic to breathe, and Waugh's robust ability to endure is not the least admirable of his many fine qualities. Inevitably he has been led into absurdities. Here, for example, is the clubman's picture, in *Men and Arms*, of England newly embattled in 1939: 'Everywhere houses were being closed, furniture stored, children transported, servants dismissed, lawns ploughed, dower houses and shooting lodges crammed to capacity; mothers-in-law and nannies were everywhere gaining control.' One does not feel that this faintly caricatured panorama deviates very far from the author's own impression. Something is missing in this vision, but blindness is perhaps the first penalty which romantics must pay for their self-indulgence.

Waugh is a man of great, if rather tigerish, personal charm. The pleasure of his company is partly due to relief and gratification at finding that his claws are temporarily drawn in. When they are out, it is no fun at all for his victim. He is a great comedian, but his serious values, of which he becomes increasingly aware, are not very different from those of G. A. Henty. Embittered romantic, over-deliberate squire and recluse, popular comedian, catholic father of a family, Evelyn Waugh is one of the oddest figures of our time.

MARIA CALLAS

15 June 1958

The visit to London of Maria Moneghini Callas comes as the climax of the centenary celebrations at the Royal Opera House. Last Tuesday the Queen attended a gala at which Callas's appearance in a scene from Bellini's *I Puritani* was the high point of the evening. On Friday the Greek-American soprano is to sing for the first time in London one of her greatest roles: Violetta in Verdi's *La Traviata*.

That Callas should crown these celebrations is as it should be, for in recent years she has established herself as the *prima donna assoluta* of the decade.

No other singer of the day challenges her supremacy; none can match her ability to win frenzied acclaim from the most critical and even hostile audience, none commands her huge fees (at the New York Metropolitan last year she received over £1,000 a night), or the fantastic attention that the world's press devotes to her slightest move; and none can match the astonishing series of scenes, scandals and triumphs that have marked her progress to the top.

The odd thing is that all this should happen in the middle of the twentieth century, rather as though W. G. Grace were to reappear at Lord's. For just as the age of liberal individualism was the heyday of the prima donna, so the growing egalitarianism of the modern world marked her decline. With the increasing complexity of the orchestral writing in the later works of Verdi and Wagner the balance of power in the opera house began to shift away from the stage to the orchestral pit, and the turn of the century saw the arrival of the conductor-despot. Under the collectivist banner of 'ensemble', men like Mahler and Toscanini waged unceasing war against singers' prerogatives. They did so with such success that fabulous creatures like Patti, who always travelled in her own railway coach, became as extinct as dodos.

But Callas is far removed from the sort of nineteenth-century diva who sang her role with sublime indifference to any dramatic considerations and regarded the mere suggestion of a rehearsal as an impertinence. On the contrary, she is acutely aware of every dramatic detail and nuance, and meticulous in the preparation of every role. Whereas the old-style prima donna was often ludicrous in her stage behaviour, Callas's performances have an extraordinary musico-dramatic unity: she is at once a great actress and a great singer.

Yet her basic vocal material is by no means exceptional. She has a big voice but it is not conventionally beautiful. She is, for instance, unable to pour out a stream of full, golden tone in the manner of Milanov, and many people hearing her for the first time are disconcerted by the flawed and rancid notes she from time to time emits.

What is so remarkable is the use to which she has put this unpromising material, by sheer tenacity and willpower and musical intelligence. She has developed a phenomenal control over every inflection and shade of tone and expression, an ability to throw off the most elaborate *fioriture* with fluency and ease and to unfold a line of wonderful eloquence, purity and formal beauty. Her perception of style is acute, her knowledge of early nineteenth-century vocal ornamentation is profound and detailed; what she has to say about music and singing is full of insight and mature understanding. With Callas music and drama, sensibility and technique go hand in hand.

Maria Anna Sofia Cecilia Kalogeropoulos was born on 3 December 1923, in New York of Greek immigrants who had arrived from Athens only four months previously. Her childhood was not a happy one and the family were far from well off. Callas has bitter memories of those day. She is reported as saying 'My sister was slim and beautiful and friendly, and my mother adored her – I was the ugly duckling, fat and clumsy and unpopular.' She wore thick glasses (she still does when not in public) and ate compulsively. 'I hated school. I hated everybody. I got fatter and fatter.' At the age of eight she took up music and then voice lessons, and won one or two amateur contests. She discovered that 'when I sang, I was really loved'.

But serious musical training began when the family returned to Athens in 1936, and she won a scholarship to the National Conservatory. In 1942, aged nineteen, she made her début and sang a number of roles at the Athens opera. At the end of the war she returned to New York, where she continued her rigorous studies, was offered the role of Madam Butterfly, but refused it because of her size. In 1947 she sailed for Italy, was auditioned at the Scala and rejected as an imperfect vocalist, but finally got an engagement at Verona.

Here she met two men who were to play a large part in her career. One was a wealthy, white-haired Veronese businessman called Battista Meneghini, whom she married in 1949. The other was the venerable Italian conductor, Tullio Serafin. It was Serafin who coached Callas and took her to Venice, where she sang heavy roles like Isolde, Turandot and Brünnhilde. But the turning point in her career came at the end of 1948 when Carosio, who was due to sing Elvira in *I Puritani*, fell sick. Serafin proposed Callas. At first the idea seemed crazy, for not since the days of Lilli Lehmann had sopranos tackled both heavy Wagnerian parts and the florid roles written by Bellini, which demand, not dramatic vehemence, but purity of line and agility of voice.

It was in the title role of Bellini's *Norma* that London first saw her in 1953, a large Junoesque figure striding about the stage with a curious loping roll. Callas was by this time already one of the outstanding singers of the day. But she was not happy either with herself or with her voice. The effort of employing this heavyweight instrument in roles demanding extreme agility was terribly taxing. In addition to this she felt tired and miserable and ashamed of her bulk. Invited to go shopping (a pastime in which she now indulges with passionate intensity) she replied mournfully, 'What, and drag all this round with me?'

In this originated the much-publicised Callas slimming course, which landed her among other things in a libel action against a pasta factory, owned by the Pope's nephew, who claimed that the 44 lb. she had lost were due to 'the physiological macaroni produced by the Pantanella mills at Rome'. Great publicity was also given to a highly questionable statement by a Milan doctor who claimed that Callas's phenomenal drop in weight was due to success, which had stilled her anxiety and need for love and thus brought an end to her compulsive eating. Be that as it may, the fact remains that in 1955 a new Callas emerged, svelte, elegant, mondaine. Relieved of its double chin, her face took on a new life. Her huge dark eyes under their thick black brows are arresting. And with her considerable height her slim figure (too slim for a singer, said many a knowing voice with evident *Schadenfreude*) is both commanding and graceful. The ugly duckling has become a swan.

This was the new Callas, the Callas whose qualities enticed Luchino Visconti to the Scala where his productions brought the theatre to a new height of brilliance. For the first time her physical self was not a shame and a mortification. Her interest in clothes and society grew. More than this, the voice gained in agility and brilliance, which matched the growing dramatic mastery this natural actress had acquired through new confidence in her physical appearance and through her association with Visconti.

But fame has not brought Callas assurance. The last two years have seen a series of scandals and quarrels that have resounded across the world, and given the impression of a fierce, wilful tigress. There have been scandals in Chicago and in Edinburgh, in San Francisco and Athens. Then in January there was the uproar in Rome, when Callas felt unable to continue a performance of *Norma* before President Gronchi, and, more recently, a break with the Scala, where she has enjoyed her finest productions and greatest triumphs, and which lies at the heart of the city in which she and her husband have made their home.

Obviously she has made her own contribution to turning every molehill of trouble into a mountain. But because these quarrels are in part a reflexion of her character, it would be an error to suppose that she relishes them. Her troubles lie deeper than the prima donna's conventional tantrums; they can, perhaps, be traced to the psychological insecurity of her early years. In one way this insecurity has been the making of her as an artist; for her perfectionism has an almost obsessive quality, and a more comfortable woman would be a lesser singer. On the other hand her insecurity makes her acutely sensitive to anything she takes to be an affront or a manifestation of hostility. To this she adds a devastatingly direct turn of speech (there is now litle trace of her New York origins in her pungent use of English) which is liable to inflame the situation still further.

Like most public personalities Callas can put forward a formidable array of charm. Yet basically she is the least brittle of women, the least contrived of personalities. She is, to her own detriment, incapable of maintaining a smooth façade – at least for long. Sooner or later the lid pops off, and out streams that character, forthright, spontaneous, combative, intelligent, prickly, dedicated, and tremendously wholehearted. Buried inside the slim and hugely successful singer is a fat little girl still desperately compensating for an unhappy childhood; and the fruit of this compensation has been the metamorphosis of an unloved child into the greatest prima donna of today.

JOHN BETJEMAN

8 February 1959

To many people it had long been gloomily evident that in our time good poetry could never be popular poetry. Mr Eliot's plays are written in a kind of verse which the public can easily mistake for prose, and Dylan Thomas's *Under Milk Wood* was written for radio with a large audience deliberately in mind. They provide no exception to what had seemed to be the rule. It has taken John Betjeman to upset the rule, and his *Collected Poems*, which was published last December, has now sold more than 30,000 copies. It is a success which must have surprised, perhaps even unnerved, this modest and privacy-loving man.

It is true that Betjeman's pale, chubby face, balding head and enthusiastic voice are known to television viewers, who have often heard him defending the rights of single-line railways and Victorian architecture. But this public figure is in many ways misleading. Because he is an excellent clown it would be easy to mistake him for one of those harmless English eccentrics whose prophetic utterances can be dismissed as an elaborate joke.

There isn't the least doubt that he is English, in spite of the name, which some distant Dutch forebear bequeathed to him. And he *is* eccentric, both in his manner and in the waywardness of his nostalgic affections. He wears a terrible, battered, round felt hat and owns some clothes which used to belong to Henry James. His chief interests are class, sex, religion and architecture, not necessarily in that order. He shows considerable expertise in the English social system: he knows whether Mavis is a higher class name than Doreen, and what it means if you shop at the Home and Colonial. But he does not look down on people, and has quite unforced friendships with waitresses and vergers and museum custodians.

The Church of England is to Betjeman a kind of super club whose eccentricities help to give it meaning and catholicity. He is as alert and amused about ecclesiastical distinctions – High Middle Stump, etc. – as about class distinctions. He takes a great delight in the obscure: nineteenth-century clerics who published one book of verse, small museums, odd views of London seen from eccentric branches of public transport systems. Many of his poems were first printed in little local magazines, and the kind of class *coup* which gives him most fun would be the discovery of, for instance, a Hapsburg living in Tottenham.

For all this, Betjeman is a man of serious passion, and a man whose declared outlook on modern life deserves to be taken seriously. In the most literal and careful sense of the word he is a reactionary. This does not mean simply that he is a conservative – though he is; it certainly doesn't mean that he is blindly and stupidly opposed to everything new. Betjeman is a reactionary in believing that most of the social and physical changes he has witnessed in England have been changes in the wrong direction. A devout High-Church Anglican, he is probably less offended by the general loss of faith in his time than by the substitute faiths and fetishes that have crowded in to fill the vacuum.

He dislikes the cult of psychology and sociology; he intensely dislikes the barbarous modern spirit of utilitarianism at any price, and nothing has excited him to so many public actions as the threatened destruction of old buildings. Though he first became widely known as a pioneering defender of certain railway stations and Victorian churches, his architectural tastes for the architecture *of the past* are catholic, and his architectural scholarship is unquestioned. Of course, there is something whimsical about his love of Victoriana, an element of patronising sentimentality, like the attitude some people adopt towards a scruffy and 'lovable' dog. But in his case self-mockery is always liable to rear its disarming head.

Betjeman has always been aware of the important part association plays in our aesthetic appreciations. He is a very English Englishman – no traveller and not much interested in foreign countries. And the England that he loves and praises most intimately is the England that he knew as a boy. It might seem that this particular England is a comparatively esoteric one, and it is certainly true that the reader who has shared something of Betjeman's background is likely to be more intimately moved than the reader whose origins are very different from the poet's.

But further reflection on these poems may show that their appeal is much wider than it at first seems. The private jokes and references stand out, but there is a whole Betjeman world – of suburbia and English churches, of railways and the country, of motor-cars, advertisements and schoolgirls – that is perfectly accessible to a majority of Englishmen.

Finally, in this effort to explain the phenomenon of Betjeman's popular success, he is by nature a compassionate man with sympathies extending far beyond his range of moral and aesthetic approval. He *can* be superior, in a most un-Christian way, but normally his contempt is reserved for types and tendencies, not for individuals. There is genuine human sympathy as well as comedy in this poem, for example:

> 'Let us not speak, for the love we bear one another—
> Let us hold hands and look.'
> She, such a very ordinary little woman;
> He, such a thumping crook;
> But both, for a moment, little lower than the angels
> In the teashop's inglenook.

Nostalgia for one's childhood does not necessarily mean that the childhood was a happy one. Betjeman was the only child of a powerful and rather alarming father, towards whom his feelings were a mixture of affection and guilty insufficiency. It was not an uncultured home – the father was an amateur painter and a collector of prints – but the business atmosphere of North London was never congenial to the young Betjeman. It was a sad and divisive experience for both Betjemans when the son refused to join the father's long-established family firm of glass and woodworkers.

He spent two terms at Highgate Junior School – a typical Betjeman story tells how he presented to a master called T. S. Eliot a paper handwritten volume of verse entitled *The Best Works of Betjeman* – and then went on to the Dragon school, Marlborough and Oxford. At the Dragon school he was happy; at Marlborough, where he was regarded as somewhat below the required social level, he was less so (his idea of hell would be a perpetual rugger scrum). At Oxford he did not get on with his tutor, C. S. Lewis, to whom he makes minute comic and derogatory references in his books.

In 1933, at the age of 27, John Betjeman married a daughter of Field-Marshal Lord Chetwode ('Well, Betjeman, if you're going to be my son-in-law you needn't go on calling me Sir. Call me Field-Marshal'). They now have a son of 21, and a daughter of sixteen. Mrs Betjeman is very much a character in her own right; she is an expert on animals and Indian architecture and runs a teashop in Wantage, near where they live.

Betjeman spends a certain amount of time in a very small flat in the City of London with handblocked William Morris wallpaper and a lot of second-hand books. He entertains his friends in a City chophouse, where he orders champagne in tankards, and he takes them on informative scrambles across bomb sites or round obscure churches.

Betjeman is a man of passion and sensibility and even those who do not share his specific views on contemporary Britain will rejoice that his poetry is now being widely read. It might be said of him that his prophetic attitude is too negative and despairing. It might be said that he is too romantic and emotional a character to deal with the serious social issues which he sometimes tackles in his verse. Britain would certainly be a poorer place without her brilliant reactionaries, but they might serve their country better if they didn't elevate a private nostalgia into a public policy.

Betjeman's weapon sometimes seems like a broom against the ocean; change can perhaps be directed but it cannot be avoided. Yet no one who looks about him in modern Britain can feel complacent about the direction which our lives and our surroundings seem to be taking. John Betjeman has helped to preserve in us a love and respect for our past that no civilisation can dispense with.

KINGSLEY AMIS

14 January 1962

Judged by his own definition of success – to succeed in one's chosen career – Kingsley William Amis has no reason to feel sorry for himself. As a novelist he commands both critical respect and best-seller sales; as an academic he left Swansea last summer after eleven satisfactory years there as an English lecturer and he has now gone to Cambridge as the first Director of Studies in English at Peterhouse who is also a Fellow of the College. Financially he has little cause for regret: besides his salary and literary earnings, the film of his second novel had its first showing last week.

But any serious writer wants his books to be read as he intended, and here Amis has less reason for satisfaction. His first novel *Lucky Jim* (which has also been filmed), had an immediate welcome when it appeared in January 1954; it also became the symbol of an ill-defined movement of revolt whose members, whether or not they admitted membership, were lumped together under the much-misused label, Angry Young Men.

Even more annoying for Amis, the novel was widely misread. Because its hero, Jim Dixon, was appalled by the tediousness and falseness of much of academic life, he was interpreted as a symbol of anti-intellectualism. Because he taught at a provincial university, he became a symbol of contempt for Oxford and Cambridge. And because Amis himself taught at a provincial university, he and Dixon became associated in people's minds.

In fact, Amis resembles Dixon chiefly in his ability and readiness to make funny faces (his features, thanks to an almost imperceptibly drooping left eyelid, give the faintest impression of lop-sidedness). Dixon is a hopeless lecturer who detests his job: Amis enjoys his work. Dixon is aggressively conscious of his social, cultural and intellectual shortcomings: Amis, now 39, charming and socially assured, is in no apparent doubt of his cultural and intellectual qualifications.

Perhaps he is confident because he had an uncomplicated background. He was an only child. His father was an export clerk with a manufacturing firm, earning just enough to provide his family with a comfortable home in Norbury, SW16. His mother, he remembers, had a maid when he was small, and he himself never lacked 'any reasonable luxury'. He won a scholarship to the City of London School, a day boys' public school where Asquith had been educated, and won an open exhibition to St John's College, Oxford. In 1942 he went into the Army (Royal Signals), which he disliked, mainly because of his fellow officers, especially majors and above; but is glad to have had the experience.

In October 1945 he went back to Oxford, took a First in English, but, somewhat to his surprise, failed to get his B.Lit. In 1949 he went to Swansea, where, except for a year at Princeton as visiting lecturer in creative writing, he remained until last year.

While never really poor, he has been too close to poverty for comfort; the near-squalid conditions of *That Uncertain Feeling* were largely taken from personal experience. But in 1951 his wife (he married in 1947 and has two sons, aged thirteen and twelve, and a daughter of eight) came into enough money for them to buy a house, furnish it properly and buy a car. It was now that *Lucky Jim*, on which he had been working for years, really got under way, and its appearance in 1954 put him well into the upper income group. (So far the book has had 21 impressions besides paperback editions. Translations include: *Jim Il Fortunato*, *Jim-la-Chance*, *Glück für Jim* and the Polish *Jim Szszesciarz*. Amis lives a few miles outside Cambridge in an old cottage, large, warm and convenient enough for comfort; this month he hopes to move into a house he has bought in the town. His oldest and youngest children go to local private schools; the younger boy is at Cambridge Grammar School (he would like to see the great public schools abolished, except that 'governments which abolish bad things tend to abolish good things, like liberty'; he would not send his children to one). He eats and drinks well – studying drink is the nearest he has to a hobby (perhaps this was why he had no objection to sponsoring a beer advertisement: 'I thought it would be fun, and it was'). He collects recipes for powerful mixtures such as Mr Sutton's Gin Blind: four parts gin, two parts brandy, one part orange curaçao. He dresses smartly: in *Take a Girl Like You*, Patrick's interest in clothes 'is a bit of me'.

It is not clear just how seriously he takes his politics, especially in view of his Fabian pamphlet, *Socialism and the Intellectuals*, which appeared in 1957 and contained the remark that the best and most trustworthy political motive was self-interest. It was unwise not to amplify the apparent paradox: what he dislikes, as he made clear in a radio talk last sumer, is unquestioning enthusiasm for immediately popular, emotion-rousing causes. The implication is that the better way is steady support of less spectacular, even unpopular causes. This is a valid argument; it is also true that it is easier to note causes that Amis thinks should not be supported than causes he thinks should.

The pamphlet gave rise to another mistaken idea about Amis, that he is frightened of being thought an intellectual. What he is frightened of (and this comes through in some of his poems) is intellectual pretentiousness, which may help to explain his advocacy of science fiction as a legitimate form of literature – his *New Maps of Hell* is the first serious appreciation of science fiction – and his advocacy of jazz as a legitimate form of music.

Sweeping statements about Society are not really Amis's line, however. He is more at home as a critic of Eng. Lit., where his 'revaluations' are controversial and highly readable: he has called *Beowulf* the only long poem in the language more boring than *The Owl and the Nightingale*, and he dismissed most of Dylan Thomas as 'a blend of answerless riddle, outworn poeticism and careful linguistic folly'.

Most of all, he is at home as a novelist, where he has provided some wonderfully funny writing and some of the most pointed observation of contemporary society. Above all, there is the Amis Figure, not necessarily the 'great English comic invention' hailed by some critics, but certainly developing from his first appearance as Jim Dixon, who was a bit of a caricature, to his latest as Patrick Standish, who is far more carefully observed.

As a novelist, Amis's greatest weakness is construction. In *Lucky Jim* the characters appeared when the plot needed them rather than when circumstances did. *That Uncertain Feeling* (published in 1955; its film title is: *Only Two Can Play*) was more tightly written and technically a big advance, but it had a sentimental ending tacked on, quite out of key with the rest of the book. *I Like it Here* (1958), his weakest book, had a slight element of mystery, perfunctorily married to an account of a trip to Portugal. The ending of the latest, *Take a Girl Like You* (1960), was indeed implicit in its beginning – too implicit, perhaps. It was so inevitable that some people ceased to care just how it was reached.

He writes slowly, making notes on the back of cheque books, old envelopes and other scraps of paper. Then, when he has time, they go into a 1*s* 3*d* exercise book. For his next novel, set mainly in America (which he admires, somewhat uncritically), the exercise book has such jottings as:

> Ernst stickler for accuracy. Impression of having done fair amount of stickling in other fields.
>
> Irving to Roger: 'I'm your unsteadying influence.'
>
> The Bangs quarrel in Danish at party. H. challenges E. to remember her history. – You were born in Kalundborg. – You see! K! That fish market! Later about religion.

Finally, when enough of the plot is clear, he starts writing, straight on to a typewriter.

Amis claims that 'I try to write good books,' and his unvarying text is that it takes a serious writer to be a really funny writer. Bad reviews hurt, but 'although they spoil breakfast; they don't spoil lunch'. It is not that he is arrogant. Moments of feeling inadequate come only too often, as a writer, as a teacher ('there is nothing more depressing than to come out of a tutorial and think, My God, I've taught that girl nothing') or as anything else. He tries to be thankful for such moments – he believes they help him to be a better writer and a better person.

Some people complain that he harps on sex. Others try to read his novels as social commentaries. He finds such judgments irrelevant, though the fact that they are made at all is evidence of incomplete communication on his part. but such critics have a clue. Amis is a man of his time who writes good comedy and incidentally produces a disconcertingly accurate picture of the world around him. Never before has society examined itself so closely and constantly. And if some of Amis's characters are immoral and frank about it, they are not very different from the world they mirror.

FRANCIS BACON

27 May 1962

In a back-street behind Piccadilly, a man may sometimes be encountered wearing a huge pair of sunglasses, grey flannel coat, tight trousers, grey flannel shirt, and black tie. He walks rapidly into the darkness. He has cropped hair, a round puffy face and he looks about 35. He is in fact in his early fifties – his conquest of age at once gives him a slightly spooky, Dorian Gray quality – and he is the painter, Francis Bacon.

For the next five weeks, the Tate Gallery is paying Bacon the tribute of a big retrospective exhibition of his work. Bacon may remain in London for the occasion, or he may not. He is a man of whom most people, his friends included, catch only occasional glimpses.

In the past few years, there has been a Bacon boom. His pictures have changed hands for £3,000. In this country he is about the only English painter who excites art students. Abroad, there is more interest in Bacon than in any other British artist.

His paintings, even when they are simply lampoons, are unlike those of anyone else alive. He is, indeed, a freak. He uses the back of the canvas; he is wholly untaught. His best-known series – the outcome of an obsession with Velasquez – features a richly dressed prelate whose mouth is opened in a soundless scream.

Bacon once said he was trying to paint the track left by human beings – like the slime left by a snail. The shapes appear transient and out of focus, like the figures in a dream remembered at the moment of awakening.

The human beings in Bacon pictures seem half animal, or half reptilian. Sometimes they have the whiteness of death; sometimes they are white and red, like joints of meat. Some seem to be dying, or liquefying. Almost all of them display people at moments of extreme stress, whether of passion, isolation, or despair. One senses Bacon's fascinated interest in corruption.

During the last Bacon show one visitor remarked that he had never felt so close to the presence of evil. Evil or not, few people will visit the Tate without being stunned by Bacon's really tremendous power to convey the underworld of tension and suffering – humanity with the lid off.

Bacon paints without reference to any current convention and he lives as he paints. He dresses anyhow and lives anywhere. He has largely dodged all the usual institutions – school, marriage, community, family, armed forces, job. He has no interest in money, except for gambling and champagne.

Yet if he does not fit into ordinary society he is by no means a rebel. He finds the world of criminals more interesting than the world of normal people – but nevertheless, on his best behaviour, he would give no hostess anxiety about his performance at her dinner table. His manner is unformidable, gentle and unaffected. He is a good talker, bubbling, funny, friendly, gesticulating elegantly with strong, plump forearms.

One of Bacon's strong points, arising from his isolation, is that he could never be corrupted by success. The Tate exhibition will leave him cold. If he were rich, he says, he would not only never show his pictures, he would very rarely even bother to finish them. As it is, using a razor, he often destroys them.

Bacon is an articulate, sophisticated highbrow character, but he does not think there is much point in talking about his work, on the principle enunciated by Pavlova that 'if I knew why I danced I wouldn't dance'. He says, however, that his starting point is always his own nervous system: 'I always want to *record* a face or body, and I want to do it as near my own feelings as possible. It's the exact opposite of abstract painting.'

There are two central things he is trying to do. First, he is trying to catch the grin without the cat – to catch the sensation of a human presence and its flavour, whether menacing or desperate, without having to create the full physical density of the body. Secondly, he wants to show people in extreme situations. He would say that day-to-day behaviour is of no importance; the real test is what happens in situations of crisis.

These two ideas are pure Bacon. His other aims are more usual. He wants to make the animal come through the human being; and he wants the paint itself to carry its own implications (in the same way that a poem can produce meanings that the poet did not expect).

'Oil painting is incredibly strange and difficult,' he says. 'There's an enormous element of chance about just the turn of the brush. In the actual process of painting, the thing you really want to do slips through.'

In the seedier Mediterranean countries, Bacon has noticed how Arab children, left to fend for themselves without any rules imposed from above, become miraculously uninhibited and adept at getting by. Bacon is an English Arab.

His father, when Francis was born in 1909, had retired from the army and gone to Ireland to train racehorses on his wife's money. A bad asthmatic as a child, Francis was allergic to horses. His father was allegic to education. Francis, so far as he can recall, had only one year's formal education in his life – at Dean Close, Cheltenham, where his father, having abandoned Ireland, was enjoying his second retirement.

At sixteen, with his family's consent, and on a minute allowance, Bacon left home and moved to London. He spent the next years travelling and getting by with a string of odd jobs. He worked in a Lyons restaurant, as a valet and as an interior decorator. He started to paint occasionally and, with the coming of the war, regularly. Whereas most people found the war reasonably occupying, Bacon had more time on his hands than ever before. He was unfit for the army, so he joined civil defence. But living in dormitories did not suit his asthma and he eventually left.

So he painted. He met Graham Sutherland, who generously helped and encouraged him, and by the end of the war he had acquired a small following. Since then, his reputation has steadily expanded.

In middle-age, neither fame nor money has caused Bacon to change his unsettled way of life. He moves constantly, often in the direction of the Mediterranean, where he especially likes the cities by the sea, and especially those with facilities for gambling.

Other painters gamble, but none so seriously as Bacon. The two activities are not so separate as one might think. Both (for Bacon) are matters of chance and both stretch his nervous system to the limit. At Monte Carlo not long ago he had some big wins, then lost everything. Afterwards he said the same thing sometimes happened with his painting – greed caused him to take a risk beyond his powers.

The spasmodic disarray of Bacon's way of life is reflected in his studios. One of his longest stays recently was in a Battersea flat. The Bacon workshop there was what the architect had intended as a smallish front bedroom. The place looked as though a dustman had stacked a lorry with oddments – canvases, easels, bunches of old paintbrushes, broken crockery, an abandoned chest of drawers, a heap of books, torn newspapers and a pile of old copies of *Paris-Match* – and dumped the lot into the room through the roof. Bacon uses saucers to mix his paints, and wipes his hands on the curtains.

Most of his pictures are big, and he often does not see them properly until someone else hangs them up in a much larger room. By that time he has long since lost interest.

One might say even that Francis Bacon is not fundamentally interested in art at all, though he greatly admires some of the old masters, such as Velasquez and Rembrandt. He prefers life to art – especially, he once said, the life of the gutter. Yet he sees life itself, now that his religion is dead, as nothing but a brief, empty interval between birth and death. So for Bacon the only thing that has any permanent value at all, the only thing that can last, are the marks made by the artist. In his painting, Bacon is trying to catch and hold for a moment the image of man, because that is the only way he can conceive of reflecting and preserving the terrible reality of life.

Harold Pinter

27 April 1975

Harold Pinter, whose new play *No Man's Land* opened last week at the National Theatre, has sometimes seemed as enigmatic as one of his own characters. Since he first arrived as a dramatist seventeen years ago, people have been trying to decode his work in a literal way that misunderstands the nature of

poetic symbolism. His life has been ransacked for clues. A picture has emerged of a secretive, haunted man: it is a picture that surprises his friends.

Pinter himself, by nature reticent but not obsessively so, has responded by becoming increasingly wary of personal revelation, to the point where he now appears to distrust even his own quoted remarks. This caution can lend a misleading air to his conversation that some interviewers have readily identified as 'Pinterish'. Perhaps it's best to leave his inner life where it belongs, and stick to more easily verifiable facts.

He was born in the East London borough of Hackney in 1930, close to the marshland of the River Lea, the only child of Jewish parents. His father was a ladies' tailor in a small way of business. In 1939, shortly before his ninth birthday, he was evacuated to Cornwall with a party of boys in the care of a local schoolmaster and his wife. They were billeted in one of John Nash's fanciful essays in Gothic architecture, a castle standing in woodlands on the coast near Mevagissey. The boys attended the village school.

But he was very homesick. A year or so later, during a lull in the Blitz, he was reclaimed by his mother. He was evacuated two more times before going to Hackney Downs Grammar School at fourteen on an LCC scholarship.

The dislocation and occasional loneliness of these five school years turned him to adult reading. He was mature, highly competitive, good at games (he was an outstanding schoolboy sprinter) and at acting. He wrote romantic verse and short stories. 'I had two brilliant boys; John Bloom [the former washing-machine millionaire] and Harold Pinter,' one master has recalled. 'Neither did a stroke of work.'

He played Macbeth and Romeo in school productions. ('Pinter . . . excelled where strong action reinforces words, as where he flung himself on the floor of the Friar's cell in passionate histrionic abandon,' the school magazine reported.)

He obtained a place at RADA, but felt out of his depth among more assured students. After two terms, he feigned a mental breakdown and spent the next year mooching round London with his friends, living off his LCC grant.

He was a conscientious objector, spent three terms at the Central School of Speech and Drama, and two or three years barnstorming in Ireland as repertory actor (starting at £6 a week) in Anew McMaster's touring company.

He then spent another three years in provincial rep (under the name David Baron), during which he married the highly talented and appealing actress Vivien Merchant. In May 1958, his first full-length play, *The Birthday Party*, was given its first London performance. It folded after a week, under irritable and sometimes derisive notices from the critics.

'The first act,' said *The Times*, 'sounds an offbeat note of madness; in the second the note has risen to a sort of delirium; and the third act studiously refrains from the slightest hint of what the other two may have been about.' The *Manchester Guardian* grumbled: 'What all this means, only Mr Pinter knows, for as his characters speak in non-sequiturs, half-gibberish and lunatic ravings, they are unable to explain their actions, thoughts or feelings.'

Pinter was in fact brilliantly pushing forward frontiers that had already been explored by Kafka and Beckett. It is a measure of his success in widening the horizons of British theatre that such mystified comments by leading London critics now sound so strangely out of touch.

Two years later, *The Caretaker* established him firmly as an important British dramatist. No English play has had quite the same impact. It was *The Caretaker* that established Pinter and the enclosed and peculiar world of his plays.

Today, a successful screen writer and film and stage director as well, he lives in a cheerful Nash house overlooking the boating lake in Regent's Park, with a library of twentieth-century literature on the top floor and a tiny, angular study on a level with the area basement. His son, Daniel, seventeen, is at St Paul's.

To meet, Pinter is a mild-mannered, good-humoured man, rather modishly dressed, with an actor's slightly formal habits of speech and movement. In conversation, one has the impression of a tough, disciplined, practical mind with an ironic, but not pessimistic, way of looking at the world. (It was Noël Coward who wrote of *The Caretaker*: 'Above all, its basic premise is victory rather than defeat.')

Pinter takes an amused view of attempts to load his work with unintended significance. Christopher Morahan, head of plays at BBC Television, remembers him suddenly discovering in the published edition of *A Slight Ache* that the stage direction *A slight pause* had been misprinted as *A silent pause*. 'God!' said Pinter. 'All over the bloody world there are people trying to act out a "silent pause".'

'He is very spare in his appraisal of his own work,' says another friend, the actor Donald Pleasance. 'Before one production, he simply remarked to us: "I'd just like to say that there is no character in either of these two plays that I particularly admire."'

He has largely resisted the temptation to imitate himself. His success as a screen writer (*Accident* and *The Go-Between* among many) has relieved him of the need to write plays to make a living. (He spent the whole of 1972 adapting Proust's *A la Recherche du Temps Perdu* for a film that has yet to be made.) He has been able to limit his truly personal writing to work for which he feels a real creative need.

His passion is cricket. Throughout the winter, he practises on Saturday mornings in the indoor nets at the Middlesex Cricket School. During the season, he captains the Gaieties, a club side with a strong fixture list in and around Surrey. He is a moderately aggressive batsman and in-fieldsman (physically, he is tallish and well-built); better at facing fast bowling than slow, according to actor Robert East, a member of the side; and a ruthless tactician. He has a collection of 100 Wisdens and an ancient, almost fossilised early cricket bat, which he keeps in his study. (A critic has remarked that cricket resembles his plays – people standing around in obscure relationship to one another, making sudden unexplained, sometimes menacing movements between long silent pauses.)

Pinter's dramatic method – the unsettling contrast between the naturalism of the characters' speech and the dream-like sequences of situations in which they are presented – has become familiar enough to have been parodied and copied a great deal.

His authorial objectivity as a dramatist has been compared with that of Shakespeare and of Chekhov. He has explicitly abrogated the author's right to get inside his characters and claim to know what makes them act and how they feel – a right that, as Martin Esslin has pointed out in his critical study of Pinter, was given up long ago in the novel.

Pinter's relationship with his audiences has described a curve. At first, he was taken to be wholly obscure. *The Birthday Party* appeared at a time when the English stage was flooded with dotty plays (theatrical equivalents of *The Goon Show*). Pinter was suspected of emulating them without having the grace to be equally funny.

The Caretaker, on the other hand, told a perfectly comprehensible story with a full complement of believable characters.

Early in Pinter's career, much was made by critics of the essential incomprehensibility of character and events in real life, and therefore of the truthfulness-to-life of plays that refused to explain anything. Esslin uses the analogy of a crowd gathering in a street to watch an argument between two men that develops into a fight. It is unlikely that the spectators will ever get a clear idea of what the issues in the quarrel are, let alone the antecedents and personalities of the participants. Yet the fight has a meaning.

'A bystander sensitive enough to react to the emotional climate of the incident,' he writes, 'could gain a deep insight into life, a greater awareness of its true nature than if all the facts and motivations had been explained.'

It is true that our days are full of unanswered questions – but do they only remain unanswered because they are unasked? By the time we have got ourselves together to examine the parade of events, it has marched on. But we could follow it if we had the time and ask the participants what had happened and why. It does not follow, of course, that we would tell the truth – or that we could if we would.

Following *The Caretaker* Pinter's work was largely devoted to exploring this phenomenon. It was given classic expression in the television play *The Collection*, in which an attempt by the two participants and their respective partners to discover (or to conceal?) the truth about a rape/seduction/fantasy/slander (all possibilities that could, at various points of the evening, be crossed out and then reinstated) became a metaphor for the defensive isolation of every one of us.

He has also shown his famous 'ear' to be far more than a built-in tape-recorder. After *The Caretaker*, he largely abandoned the working-class settings and speech-patterns which had made him famous (though he returned to them for his next full-length stage play, *The Homecoming*) in favour of middle-class comedy of manners. The change no doubt reflects his own altered circumstances;

but in both worlds it is less the realistic accuracy of his dialogue than its rhythmic potency that sweeps one away.

He has been praised for respecting the hesitancy of ordinary speech (the famous 'Pinter pauses' are as likely to occur within speeches as between them) instead of producing an artificial fluency. But he can be as powerful a rhetorician as Osborne. The anatomy of the 'slum slug' in *The Collection* (with which one character vituperates another) is carried out in short, dry periods, rather than rolling paragraphs. But the words are carefully organised to hurt.

Pinter's objectivity towards his own characters has been well summed up by the American critic Harol Clurman, reviewing the prize-winning Broadway production of *The Homecoming* in the *Nation* in 1967:

'Pinter's manner is icy: he does not declare himself. He leaves interpretation to the audience. (This is most brave.) He has a keen ear for dramatic speech, he writes with superb control: there is hardly a wasted world. At first one is inclined to think that he must be either wickedly unfeeling or perhaps that he has no convictions. But no! Only a prophet or a fanatic, fiercely moral, can be so damning.

'But Pinter is wholly of our moment: we refuse to be hortatory, to cry out, plead, condemn or call to account. Since we do not permit ourselves to "take sides" overtly, we grin to keep our jaws so tightly clamped that it becomes hard to tell whether we are kidding or repressing pain. The mask is one of horror subdued in glacial irony . . .

'He is an artist, one of the most astute to have entered upon the world stage in the past ten years. Those who do not respect and appreciate his talent understand little of our times or its theatre.'

TOM STOPPARD

14 November 1982

Tom Stoppard, whose new comedy *The Real Thing* opens at the Strand Theatre in London on Tuesday, is the most consistently popular serious dramatist writing in English. His plays commend themselves to audiences for three reasons: they are funny, and they are good-natured and they are bewitchingly clever. These qualities, of course, are intimately connected.

A critic described *Jumpers* as 'genuinely benevolent,' and it is indeed filled with a *joie de vivre* that expresses itself both in affection towards the characters and in an apparently inexhaustible gusher of jokes.

His last play, *On the Razzle*, was made up almost entirely of jokes (one-liners, sight gags, elaborate structures of misinterpretation) and qualifies on these grounds as one of the most experimental ever written.

It caused one reviewer to worry that Stoppard might be squandering a precious resource. The concern was surely misplaced. The appeal of his plays lies not in individual laughs but in the spirit that keeps the laughs coming. If that spirit ever gives out, it will avail him nothing to have saved up a few prize chuckles from earlier and happier days. He will either have to stop writing or become a different dramatist altogether.

This light-heartedness has aroused considerable critical resentment. At first it was thought that someone who wrote so amusingly could not possibly be serious. Now it is accepted that he is – and that, in some eyes, only makes it worse.

His work has been subjected to a gigantic decoding enterprise on both sides of the Atlantic. For a time Stoppard responded by offering his own amused, ambiguous, sometimes perverse commentary, dissociating himself from programmatic interpretations.

'For me,' he has said, 'the particular use of a particular word in the right place, or a group of words in the right order, to create a particular effect is important: it gives me more pleasure than to make a point which I might consider to be profound.'

More recently he has shown signs of wishing to back away from critical controversy altogether. He has just turned down a proposal by Faber, his publishers, to bring out a collection of his literary journalism.

Stoppard, 45, was born in Czechoslovakia, where his father, Eugene Straussler, worked for the Bata shoe company. In 1939, the company transferred the family to Singapore. Stoppard, with his Czech mother and elder brother Peter, were evacuated to India just before the colony fell to the Japanese in 1942. His father, who remained behind, died in enemy hands. When, in 1946, his mother married a British army officer Kenneth Stoppard, the boys took his name.

Stoppard rejects the theory that, like Conrad and Nabokov, he owes his distinctive handling of the language to having acquired it as a foreigner. He spoke Czech until he was six, when he learned English at an American school in Darjeeling.

A slightly more persuasive suggestion is that an early boyhood spent listening to expatriate English gave him that heightened awareness of idiom that some Indian writers possess. But wit and paradox scarcely require such factitious explanations.

After the war, the family came to England. Stoppard was a boarder at the Dolphin School (a prep school) in Newark and at Pocklington School (a sixteenth-century foundation) in York, where he was a leading member of the debating society. 'I remember being completely indifferent as to which side of any proposition I should debate on,' he told the late Kenneth Tynan.

He left at seventeen and a half, after taking A levels, to work as a reporter – and eventually reviewer and humorous columnist – on the *Western Daily Press* and the *Evening World* in Bristol.

In the early 1960s that graceful city was a nursery of future artistic talent in the overlapping coteries of the theatre and journalism: the playwrights Charles Wood and Peter Nichols, the novelists A. C. H. Smith and John Hale, the film director John Boorman and the actor Peter O'Toole.

Stoppard made two fortunate friendships. The first was with Smith, who hired him to contribute to a sophisticated weekly arts page he edited on the *Western Daily Press*. Stoppard still thought of himself as a newspaperman. 'He was an absolute sucker for the romance of journalism,' Smith recalls. But being published alongside more mature writers, like David Holbrook and the late B. S. Johnson, gave him critical confidence.

At about the same time, he became a beneficiary of the legendary kindness of the actress Val Lorraine and her husband, Bob, who befriended (and, in effect, subsidised) more than one struggling artist. Stoppard stayed with them for nearly three years, becoming part of the family, freelancing for a pittance while he worked at nights on his first full-length play, *A Walk on the Water*, which was produced on TV in 1963.

His literary interest in those days was less in the absurd (though he admired Beckett) than in a variety of conscious stylists: Wilde, Nabokov, Hemingway, Mailer.

Three years of frustration followed before an Edinburgh fringe production of *Rosencrantz and Guildenstern are Dead* was spotted and praised by Ronald Bryden in *The Observer* in 1966. A telegram from Tynan led to it being presented at the National Theatre the following year. Stoppard awoke and found himself famous. He also found himself rich: the play, which was also a hit on Broadway, brought him well over £300,000 in the first few years.

Some critics muttered about existentialism (a philosophy he has said he didn't know then and doesn't like now), but it was generally enjoyed as an ingeniously prolonged conceit on the off-stage existences of two Shakespearian nonentities: one that established its own rules and kept to them with fanatical integrity.

It was a dazzling demonstration of comic talent, reinforced in succeeding years by such self-defining mechanisms, small and elegant, as *The Real Inspector Hound*. These pieces played with words, ideas, situations and characters (usually outrageous variations on stock types) mainly for their own sake.

He opened out with *Jumpers* in 1972 about a professor of moral philosophy married to a former musical-comedy star. That union says a lot about Stoppard's plays. For the philosopher philosophises and the singer sings, but there is a lot of hilarity in his role and a lot of pain in hers.

She is seen between her husband, perhaps the last man alive to believe in moral absolutes and trying to come up with a religious system to support them, and a cynically pragmatic Vice-Chancellor who is good at everything including acrobatics. He is called Jumper, and the puns that bounce off that name into every corner of the play are characteristic Stoppard: both fun and functional.

In the background of *Jumpers* lurked what Stoppard has called 'a joke-Fascist outfit' – though they seem more like electorally victorious Socialists. Political themes and their relation to morality became explicit in subsequent plays, starting with *Travesties* (1974), another intellectual vaudeville that showed Lenin preparing for the Bolshevik revolution while a refugee in Zurich: a status also enjoyed by James Joyce and Tristan Tzara, who stood in the play for, respectively, art and the 'fashionable magic' of anti-art.

More recent plays have been influenced by Stoppard's growing involvement with dissent in Eastern Europe. The TV play *Professional Foul* (1977) was set in Czechoslovakia, and the play with music *Every Good Boy Deserves Favour* (in the same year) in Russia. In both, anger was mediated through the usual qualities of wit and meticulous organisation.

Neither was controversial. Stoppard had picked the one issue on which most shades of opinion in Britain were united. But in *Night and Day* (1978) he chose the thornier subject of press freedom and its vulnerability to political or industrial pressure. For the first time, the incipient tensions between himself and the dominant theatrical Left became manifest.

To meet, Stoppard is a relaxed, amusing man with a sharp wit and the casual dandyism of a successful actor. Only the ghost of an inflexion and a mid-European instinct for *gemütlichkeit* perhaps betray his provenance.

His first marriage to a nurse, Jose Ingle, was dissolved ten years ago. He and his second wife Miriam, a former managing director of a pharmaceutical firm and now a writer and frequent TV broadcaster on popular science, live in a handsome Vanbrugh house in Iver, Buckinghamshire, with his four sons, two from each marriage. His summer garden parties there – complete with caterers and a marquee – have become one of the more glamorous social events in the theatrical calendar.

He is a keen cricketer – a decent club standard wicketkeeper – and collects English watercolours and modern first editions. He is also a generous contributor to both theatrical and libertarian causes, working unobtrusively for Amnesty and Writers and Scholars International.

Although he is still exploring the boundaries of radio drama – his new pastiche le Carré-type thriller, *The Dog it was that Died*, will be broadcast by Radio 3 on 9 December – his recent work for the theatre seems to be turning towards naturalism.

The intellectual fireworks are still in evidence, however, and they reinforce his advantage over most of his contemporaries. He is one of the few who can make an audience feel, through the texture of his work, that the human condition, social or metaphysical, is really worth bothering about – or, in plainer terms, that life might actually be worth living.

JONATHAN MILLER

9 January 1983

In the middle of last year Jonathan Miller announced his retirement from the theatre and the opera house. He promptly unveiled two of his best productions to date: *Hamlet* in the small London Warehouse, and *Rigoletto* at the Coliseum. He was awarded the CBE in the New Year's Honours and is now putting the finishing touches to one of his final opera commitments, *The Magic Flute*, which opens in Glasgow on Wednesday. In a few months he says goodbye to all that and takes off to McMaster University in Canada as a visiting professor in medicine.

It is just over twenty years since Miller burst on the public in *Beyond the Fringe*. Since then he has enjoyed success as a TV producer (*Alice in Wonderland* and the BBC Shakespeare series he rescued from a disastrous start); as a theatre director; and, following in the footsteps of Kenneth Clark, Bronowski and Galbraith, as a popular intellectual pundit with his own series, *The Body in Question*. He has failed only as a cinema director.

He was, briefly, an associate director of the National Theatre before falling out with Peter Hall in 1975. He lectures in America, addresses the Royal College of Physicians, and has just completed a new BBC series (to go out next month) in which he interviews psychologists. It is hardly an empty life but Miller, as usual, is racked with doubts and misgivings, even a sense of having wasted a large part of his allotted time on earth.

Miller's problem is how to husband his quite extraordinary talents. One of his first heroes was Danny Kaye, whom he saw at the Palladium after the war. At Cambridge he blossomed as a revue performer of grace and aplomb and could quite easily have become an outstanding actor. But apart from on the occasional TV chat show he has renounced performing. As a director he has an instinctive gift for finding resonant visual and historical analogues and for itemising psychological and behavioural detail. But the range of his interests almost forbids concentrating on any one of them. For all that, the time has come, he feels, to return to medicine and, in particular, to his first love, neurology.

After *The Magic Flute* there is *The Beggar's Opera* to be done for BBC TV; then a revival of his 1979 English National Opera production of *The Turn of the Screw*, and *The School for Scandal* (one of his favourite plays, along with *Hamlet*, *King Lear* and *The Seagull*) for Robert Brustein's American Repertory Theatre in

Harvard. His agent says this really does seem to be the farewell tour. But no one is going to object if he creeps back to the theatre in a few years' time.

There was a strange idea some years ago that Miller mucks about with plays and operas. Very few of his productions, in fact, have been treated anachronistically. Notorious exceptions were *The Merchant of Venice*, transposed to a mercantile Rialto of the late nineteenth century, and a *Measure for Measure* set in the Vienna of Freud and Schoenberg inspired by a book of August Sander's photographs. And, of course, *Rigoletto*, with its direct quotation of Edward Hopper's *Nighthawks* and 1950s New York mafia setting.

The curious, very English, ambivalence about Miller arises chiefly from a suspicion (not unmixed with envy) of anyone who refuses to draw demarcation lines between intellectual disciplines. It is all right, perhaps, for someone respectably dull like C. P. Snow. But a C. P. Snow in corduroy trousers is something else. The most obvious symptom of this distrust is the *Private Eye* saga of Doctor Jonathan, a pretentious Johnsonian figure holding forth in NW1 in an interminable tirade structured on absurd leaps between literary, medical and painterly references. Thus the predominant view of Miller in this country is that of a 'pseud'. By contrast, the American critic, Susan Sontag, has described him as 'one of the most valuable people in the United Kingdom'.

Miller read natural sciences at Cambridge before qualifying as a doctor. The success of *Beyond the Fringe* made him financially secure: he bought the house in Camden Town where he still lives with his wife, Rachel, a GP, and their three grown-up children. He worked in various London hospitals before drifting into the theatre. His first directing job was a short play by John Osborne at the Royal Court, but contemporary drama is not one of his preoccupations. Not because he is against it but because it does not suit his temperament or his particular obsessions.

His life could be viewed as a sustained process of making connections between painting, literature, the social sciences (the late Erving Goffman was a key influence), anthropology, photography, physiology and philosophy. But he is also utterly unstuffy. Actors and singers relish the relaxed playground atmosphere he creates in rehearsal. He sets them free with the tumultuous force of his comic invention.

The flood of his enthusiasm makes him a marvellous teacher. He communicates his ideas in a stream of articulated explanations and analogies and is incapable of tailoring this performance to differing conditions. Once in Scotland (where Miller has a cottage retreat), he and Nicholas Garland, the cartoonist, happened across an old weaver. In five minutes Miller had begun an intense conversation with the old man on the history of looms and weaving. Garland says he could just as easily have been in full flight in his home in London.

Miller's father was the distinguished child psychologist Emanuel Miller and his mother, Betty Miller, the biographer of Browning. When Jonathan directed

Hamlet, *Ghosts* and *The Seagull* at the Greenwich Theatre in 1974, under the Freudian sub-title *Family Romances*, he viewed the trilogy as a related look at the notion of an absentee father. The poet and critic James Fenton, who knows Miller well, suggests that much of his anxiety about wasting time stems from the hovering admonitory presence of his late father asking when he intends to get on with the serious work. Perhaps this explains why he is a superb interpreter of the supernatural elements in Shakespeare. His ghosts are always worth catching.

The actress Penelope Wilton is one of what might be termed the loose-knit Miller repertory company (others include Michael Hordern, whose New Year knighthood delighted Miller, Peter Eyre, John Shrapnel and Susan Engel). She sees Miller's departure from the theatre as a sign of the times in the arts. Outside the big national companies, it has become increasingly difficult at a time of recession and grim retrenchment to sustain congenial, improvised conditions of work. The crises at the Riverside Studios and the Round House illustrate this. Miller has never wanted long rehearsal periods or laboratory conditions on the Eastern European scale. He is completely pragmatic in his approach to directing. But he cannot be contained in concrete bunkers or routine schedules. On the other hand, Nicholas Garland suggests that maybe he has directed all the plays and operas that he feels are worth doing.

With his intellectual rigour goes a great generosity of spirit. Practically everyone who has met Miller has unqualified affection for him. But he also has a great capacity for violent hatred: of critics and malevolent snipers. He is subject, too, to black depressions and his family has had to learn to cope with these. He is almost pathologically vulnerable to adverse comment. Edmund Wilson once said that he would get up in the middle of the night and pore over the bad reviews his books had received 30 or 40 years earlier. Like Wilson, Miller never forgets or forgives.

Jonathan Miller is 48. Tall and gangling, he favours expensive but comfortable clothes: shirts and ties from Brooks Brothers in New York, heavy duty corduroy trousers, wedge-soled casual shoes; a friend has noted his predilection for 'lovely socks'. He lives well. His recreation, he has noted enigmatically in *Who's Who*, is 'deep sleep'.

Now that he has made his categorical statement of farewell to the theatre, it remains to be seen what more he can achieve in a career that, so far, would have exhausted and satisfied a dozen lesser humans. One thing is certain: the cultural landscape of the past two decades would have been much poorer without him. In his recent autobiography, Laurence Olivier recalled working with him at the National: 'Jonathan excited us beyond measure by the limitless variety, the orginality and the fascinating colour in the expression of his ideas. He was the only man; we were thrilled by him and remain so.'

SIR RICHARD ATTENBOROUGH

17 April 1983

Nobody who knows Dickie Attenborough well was surprised when he announced on Friday, after a day's reflection, that he would not after all be attending the racially segregated première of *Gandhi*, in South Africa. It had always seemed probable that his decision to go had been made while he had his mind on other matters in the run-up to the Academy Awards. But many men, having committed themselves, publicly, would have found it hard to muster the largeness of spirit needed to confess such an error of judgment. After 40 years in the film industry, Sir Richard Attenborough is a national institution. All those war and adventure movies have embedded him in our consciousness as an anxious but dogged survivor of a peculiarly British type.

He is admired as well for the personal doggedness with which he has pursued certain liberal ideals as a film-maker in the face of formidable obstacles: with *The Angry Silence*, *Oh What a Lovely War!* and his twenty-year obsession with *Gandhi*.

He is, of course, a shameless show-business romantic. *Macho* Hollywood executives are sometimes startled to be apostrophised *fortissimo* as 'Darling!' in the laid-back ambience of the Beverly Hills Hotel. (The earnest chartered accountants and investment bankers with whom he sits on boards of directors in London have grown accustomed to it.)

Despite his initial lapse over South Africa, he is not, like many entertainers, a political innocent. He was in the Labour Party for 36 years before quitting to join the Social Democrats (his wife, the former actress Sheila Sim, was still campaigning for Labour at the Darlington by-election last month) and both his parents were lifelong members of the party, active in the movement to help refugees from Franco and Hitler. He and his younger brothers – David (the naturalist) and John – grew up amid talk of trade unionism, the Slump and the approaching European war.

He was born, 59 years ago, in Cambridge, where his father was an English don at Emmanuel, moving soon afterwards to become Principal of Leicester University College. It was a happy, extrovert household, joined in 1939 by two refugee half-Jewish daughters of the chief medical officer of Berlin.

Dickie, the family comedian, had wanted to become an actor since early childhood. From Wyggeston Grammar School, he went to RADA on a Leverhulme Scholarship, winning the Bancroft Prize and quickly graduating to the West End stage, where his unusual mixture of boyish charm and inner tension established him as a potential star.

After a cameo role as the panic-stricken stoker in *In Which We Serve* (his first film), he joined the RAF and qualified as a pilot. He was about to complete his training in Canada when he was seconded to the RAF film unit to play the lead in *Journey Together*, a morale-booster made by the Boulting Brothers.

By the time it was finished in 1944, the demand for pilots was easing. Rather than be transferred to the army, he volunteered for the operational side of the film unit, flying in Bomber Command Mosquitos and Halifaxes over Germany as a flight-sergeant air-gunner, with cameras mounted in place of guns. Those celebrated roles as other ranks under stress were based on direct observation.

When the Boultings cast him as Pinkie, the sadistic teenage gang-leader in *Brighton Rock*, Graham Greene complained that he lacked the necessary aura of evil. In the event, he turned in a subtle and sensitive performance. Greene, as honest a man as he is an artist, wrote a generous letter saying how pleased he was.

He was good in comedy, too: as a smart operator in *Private's Progress* and *I'm All Right, Jack* and, later, as RSM Lauderdale in *Guns at Batasi*, compressing a century of military tradition into a single quivering performance of real comic stature, perfect to the last speck of blanco.

The transition from Stoker Attenborough RN to Dickieji was a direct consequence of his determination to escape from type-casting in run-of-the-mill war films. In the late 1950s, he decided to give up acting for a few years until he matured, forming a production company with the actor, writer and director Bryan Forbes.

The Angry Silence (about a strike and its aftermath) was their first film together – and the first of Attenborough's famous battles to raise money for non-formula pictures. The Boultings, by now in charge of British Lion, agreed to put up £100,000 if the budget was cut to that figure. Attenborough persuaded the principal players and technicians to give up their salaries and gamble on a cut of the profits, taking the lead himself to save money. It was a commercial success.

They also made *Whistle Down the Wind*, *The League of Gentlemen* and *Seance on a Wet Afternoon* together in the early 1960s before Forbes left for Hollywood and Attenborough began his now legendary entanglement with *Gandhi*.

There were two big obstacles: it was a highly sensitive subject which could not be filmed without the help of India's notoriously pettifogging bureaucracy; and it needed a gigantic act of faith by investors (the eventual budget was £14.6 million) after another Gandhi film, *Nine Hours to Rama*, had flopped.

That kind of challenge is not unique. Film-makers are constantly engaged in trying to raise money for wildly impractical film projects, most of which turn to dust. Attenborough has a talent for wrestling with angels and pulled it off with a combination of charm, drive and unending patience, making allies and ultimately friends of Mountbatten, Nehru and Indira Gandhi.

Meanwhile, Attenborough limbered up by directing Joan Littlewood's *Oh What A Lovely War!* (a *succès d'estime* but a commercial failure), *Young Winston* (his first attempt at big crowd scenes) and *A Bridge Too Far*, whose confused narrative of the 1944 battle for the Rhine bridges betrayed Cornelius Ryan's lucidly constructed book, but was enormously successful at the box office. Attenborough had ten per cent of the profits.

He is a formidable businessman. As chairman of Capital Radio, he led the syndicate that won the franchise from the IBA. Then, when its revenues collapsed during the three-day week not long after starting up, and the station came close to disaster, he devoted most of his time to saving it, pledging part of his impressive art collection (since redeemed) against additional financing.

As a director of Goldcrest, his shrewd commercial judgment (not least on *Gandhi* itself) is helping to parlay Pearson Longman's wary initial stake into a profitable enterprise. He is also Edmund Dell's deputy chairman at Channel Four.

His flamboyant, slightly absent-minded green room manner disguises an unflappable temperament. John Whitney, director-general of the IBA, recalls seeing him in India two years ago – a calm, plump, immobile figure in a broad-brimmed straw hat nearly submerged by the citizenry of Bombay, who were restaging the 1947 riots all too enthusiastically, and settling some personal scores in the process. 'Darlings!' Attenborough was remonstrating, 'we're supposed to be making a film about *love and peace!*'

The Attenboroughs – they have a son and two daughters – have lived for more than 30 years in a handsome Queen Anne mansion on Richmond Green. In a cynical and piratical business, he is known for numerous unself-regarding acts of personal generosity to actors, technicians and their families who have fallen on hard times.

His success with an expensive international blockbuster doesn't really solve the basic problem of reviving a healthy, moderately budgeted British film industry. This is how to tap television for investment, either by extending the producers' levy to TV showings or by direct BBC and ITV financing of film production. However, Goldcrest's achievement in bringing pension-fund money into a high-risk business – with Attenborough's reputation as security – is an encouraging portent.

As for critical doubts about *Gandhi*, many of them seem beside the point. One doesn't go to a miracle play for political analysis or psychological conflict. It is, of course, a very English picture in its dramatic perspective on imperial decline, as well as in the visual vocabulary of its magnificent photography of the Indian landscape.

But it is above all a marvellously conceived vehicle for a legend. Dickie Attenborough may have been a little carried away by natural afflatus at the Academy Awards ceremony last week, but by his imagination and his grit he has earned the right to present the film in the way he chooses to: as an exemplary argument for an alternative to the political violence of the 1980s.

MICHAEL FRAYN

1 April 1984

Michael Frayn walked into Sardi's restaurant in New York on the night *Noises Off* opened on Broadway: and everybody clapped. He wasn't expecting this, and blinked and peered through his spectacles in the blaze of the television lights. Frayn is (on his own admission) an ambitious and competitive character, but there is a diffidence and donnishness in his bearing that sit smilingly on a man now enjoying a massive popular success on both sides of the Atlantic. Though he concedes that *Noises Off has* made him money – enough to replace his old Audi – he insists it is far from the reputed million. He has only bought another Audi.

He now awaits the opening of three new productions on the London stage. His latest play, *Benefactors*, has its first night at the Vaudeville on Wednesday; his translation of Anouilh's latest play, *Number One*, transfers from Windsor to the Queen's later this month; his translation and adaptation of Chekhov's unseen first play, which Frayn has called *Wild Honey*, opens at the National in July. And on 8 April a film about Jerusalem, written and presented by Frayn, goes out on BBC1.

Frayn at 50 is cool, dry, contained, detached. Behind him, a track record apparently crowned with constant success. In his time he has been a notable journalist, a prizewinning novelist, the writer of several well-received and well-attended plays, a few documentary films, and a philosophical work called *Constructions*.

He began life in Mill Hill, in a flat above a Victoria Wine Stores. His father was salesman for Turners' Asbestos Cement. The family soon moved to pebbledash suburbia in Ewell, a source of embarrassment in Frayn's struggling youth, but later of celebration in film. Frayn remembers his childhood as happy – he thinks of much of his life as happy – but his mother died when he was twelve, and there were some bleak years.

His father's consequent engagement of a housekeeper meant that Michael left his barbaric private school, where each day some twenty boys queued to be beaten by the clergyman head after morning prayers. Kingston Grammar School proved a haven of civilisation after that. He had a brief religious phase, when he got himself baptised. Then at about fifteen he read Shelley, and became militantly atheistical, Communist, and 'more and more culturally snobbish'. He wrote poetry, stories, plays; and 'my centre of gravity shifted to the centre of London'.

His national service was ('apart from basic training') another good time: he

learnt Russian at Cambridge and got his eye in for his undergraduate years. When he arrived at Emmanuel College he knew exactly what he wanted to do there – write for *Varsity*, *Granta*, and the Footlights – and he did them all. The May Week Footlights revue he wrote in his last year 'fell into the stalls like unrisen sponge cake' and (shamingly) was not brought to London. But he 'passionately enjoyed' Cambridge, and despite his busyness achieved a respectable 2.1 in moral sciences, to which he had switched from modern languages. He retains an admiration for Wittgenstein and an aptitude for tough philosophical argument.

He always wanted to be a writer, but said he wanted to be a journalist, which 'seemed more plausible'. In those days the editor of the *Manchester Guardian* made recruitment visits to the older universities and in 1957 Alastair Hetherington offered Michael Frayn a job in the Manchester newsroom, then furnished with roll-top desks, down which a typewriter would irritatingly slide.

Frayn did not like Manchester. Another reporter recalls the innocent optimism of his arrival, declaring his intention of living in 'the artists' quarter'. Persuaded that Manchester did not have a Left Bank, he combed the city for his next thought, a Gropius-inspired flat overlooking the river (another chimera). 'Among the flat-capped Mancunians, with that strange hair – like Julius Caesar's – and that bizarre way of talking, throwing his arms about – he was certainly an exotic,' recalls his old news editor.

A less affectionate ex-colleague recalls his 'ferocious' desire to be famous – 'and perhaps for a better class of fame than he's had' – and his outspoken ambition to send his (yet unborn) children to Eton. Frayn admits that at Cambridge he had been 'dazzled by the style' of his Etonian friends, clever collegers like Bamber Gascoigne, 'and I don't suppose I've ever completely shaken that off'. Nevertheless, he was a Labour supporter at this time (now he is SDP), though he has never joined any political party.

After two years, he was given a plum, the old Miscellany column, which meant he could go to London. Miscellany was supposed to be serious, but it was thrice-weekly, and Frayn found he could never get enough leg-work done to fill it up. So he began writing about a cast of invented people like Rollo Swavely the PR man and the upwardly-aspirant Horace and Doris Morris; and they went down very well for the next three years.

Then he moved to *The Observer*, where he wrote a column for six years, did 40 *What The Papers Say* programmes on television, and five novels as well. *The Russian Interpreter* won the Hawthornden Prize; *Towards the End of the Morning* is most journalists' second favourite Fleet Street novel. Then, he says, he lost the knack of novel-writing; and, feeling his column was getting predictable, 'thought I should stop before other people began to notice this, too'.

His first play, *Jamie*, produced on television in 1968, came to him in its entirety in a single sleepness night. The others have taken longer. A friend recalls Frayn's wife Jill complaining, about this time, of innumerable visits to dreadful plays in the West End while Michael learnt his next craft. Frayn recorded his incarnation as dramatist through the production of his first piece of theatre, *The Two of Us*, in 1970. 'All right, they laughed,' he growled, of a cheerful audience in the pre-London run. 'But why didn't they laugh until they fell helpless on the floor?'

Now – as near as dammit – they do. But now he wants them to do something else. He has alarmed the cast of *Benefactors* by saying he hopes they don't get a single laugh. This is to him an entirely serious play. And, as an old friend says, 'Michael is a very serious man, and he takes life very seriously'.

In the now considerable body of his work in several media, Frayn has given almost nothing of himself away.

The observations of his friends reflect his caution and reserve and what one called Frayn's 'inaccessibility in his deepest recesses'. People who have known him for 30 years will falter, after a few reminiscences, and say perhaps they never knew him that well after all. 'Anyway, why shouldn't he be a private man, represented only by his work?' protested one, after the usual pause for thought.

In his work – and perhaps also in his life – Michael Frayn has been preoccupied with people's impulse to order chaos and to structure their worlds; and with the division in their lives between their public personae and what these conceal. *Noises Off*, while it reduces its audiences to helpless mirth, is showing them the mess and panic hidden behind the stage of our public lives.

Frayn's own public persona is immaculate, co-operative, tactful, and courteous. He is noted for (naturally) doing the right thing: buying the first round of drinks; offering help to stranded drivers. 'He has a strong sense of social duty: he would see a blind man over a zebra crossing even if he were already late for the most important appointment of his life,' said a friend. 'This is admirable. But it is not the end of morality. Good behaviour can only achieve so much. It doesn't see you through everything.'

Frayn's marriage ended in 1981, after 21 years: he now lives with Claire Tomalin, the literary editor of the *Sunday Times*. The breakdown of his own private world structure seems to have been the most disturbed and disturbing element of Frayn's orderly life; and he admits it has changed him. 'The certainties seem less certain. When I was a young man everything seemed obvious, in terms of how one should live. There do seem to me now great problems in how to live one's life.' His wife, a social worker, still lives in the house in Blackheath designed and built as part of a small community by the Frayns and their friends in the early 1960s. Two of their daughters are at college, the youngest still at school.

At the highest peak of his public achievement (so far), Frayn is temporarily stumped when asked if he is still as ambitious as he admits he has been. Then he says: 'I suppose every writer feels there is something they would like to say – that's on the tip of one's tongue – about one's experience and understanding of the world. Then you finish something, and realise it's still there – unsaid, waiting to be said. In that way, I am just as ambitious: to get it said.'

ALAN BENNETT

12 August 1984

A double nostalgia surrounds the reopening of *Forty Years On* in London this week. Alan Bennett's celebration of the ideals and idiocies of an England now past has itself become a theatrical legend, wrapped in golden memories of John Gielgud's incandescent evocation, as Albion House's retiring headmaster, of that lost Edwardian world. Paul Eddington, Gielgud's deputy in the 1968 production, now succeeds Sir John to play the head himself; but Alan Bennett will not, this time, play Tempest, the junior master who flaps about with the school play to salvage something from the Wreck of Time.

Alan Bennett has himself salvaged quite a lot. At 50, he retains the thick fair hair, pink cheeks and impenetrable owlishness that first became publicly visible in *Beyond the Fringe* 25 years ago. It is the face a bespectacled schoolboy wears when pretending to be doing nothing while up to something for which permission would be unlikely. Bennett is a difficult man to fathom, and does not encourage an attempt to do so. He dislikes interviews, as he has made clear in the (quite numerous) interviews he has given over the years.

An Englishman Abroad, his television play about Guy Burgess, has this year brought Bennett wider recognition (and more awards) than any other of his plays. He notes wryly that the great and good who shape opinion are more interested in spies than north-country life, the subject of most of his work in the past decade.

He is himself a Yorkshireman, and often retreats to the cottage in the village of Clapham that was his parents' retirement home. (His father is now dead; his mother lives in a home near his married brother in Bristol.) But since 1969 he has lived in a house in London NW1 (a postal district he was the first to make famous), full of good paintings and dark shadows, and veiled by Venetian blinds and (just now) swathes of scaffolding, from the inside of which he has a surprisingly good view of his neighbours off their guard and his workmen not doing any work. He also goes to New York a bit. Some years ago he invested money in the Odeon restaurant when it was acquired by a former boy actor in the first *Forty Years On*, though 'I don't get anything out of it now except free meals'. He rides a bike around London, and drives north and south in a big Volkswagen.

Bennett's father was a butcher with his own shop in Headingley, Leeds, over which the family lived. He was a clever boy. 'Shy, competitive and charmless,' he believes. 'A censorious Christian Tory.' His famous sardine-tin sermon owes something to a Headingley vicar with 'a characteristically upper-class way of preaching'; there was also, in his adolescence, a strong personal faith. He has renounced it now, though he still loves hymns, knows the Book of Common Prayer by heart, and goes to church in Clapham, when they use the old service. He denies the toughness of moral judgment that other people still find in him. 'I don't think I get as far as judgment now. I think one just watches, without coming to any decision.'

He got on to the Russian course in Cambridge for his National Service, where he began doing clerical and military monologues in revues. Though he had a place at Sidney Sussex, he worked 'under my desk' for a history scholarship at Exeter College, Oxford, which he took up in 1954; later achieving a first and an academic job. At Oxford he also acquired a subterranean reputation for being funny. He was occasionally persuaded to do his monologues in college, but (in the memory of Patrick Garland, then president of OUDS) 'adamantly' refused to join the mainstream of university theatre. Bennett just says he was scared stiff.

Nevertheless, as a postgraduate he joined Oxford's Edinburgh Festival revue, though its director wouldn't include his sermon. One night Bennett conspired with his cronies to smuggle it into the show; the next year (1960) he was back in Edinburgh, performing it in the most successful revue ever to come out of the festival. The impresario Donald Albery was heard to mutter (against the noise of a Brighton audience leaving in droves), 'The blonde one'll have to go'. But the show (and Bennett) played the West End and Broadway for the next four years.

Beyond the Fringe was the first and last collaboration of its four creators who, Bennett admits, 'didn't really get on all that well' (though they have remained part of each other's lives). The received view of the quartet's offstage lives in the two-year American run was that while Peter Cook was dabbling with Kennedys, Jonathan Miller joining the New York Jewish intelligentsia, and Dudley Moore setting off for megastardom amid starlets, Alan Bennett was sitting in New York public library writing home to his parents in Leeds.

Bennett agrees that he turned down two invitations from Adlai Stevenson to a dinner for Mrs Kennedy, because he was afraid he would be sick with shyness over the table. 'Monstrous behaviour,' he says now: though he still dislikes posh do's.

He had a thin time after *Beyond the Fringe*, aware of how well the other three were doing. Then in 1966 came his television series, *On the Margin*, where *Life and Times in NW1* began.

Bennett's life as a performer has continued through his writing, notably as the son in *Intensive Care*, a work drawn from his experience of his own father's death, and one of a series of television plays remarkable for their courage, compassion and humour in confronting the horrors of life – illness, exile, senility, death.

Bennett says he always thinks he wants to write a silly stage play, but finds that it soon 'plunges into gloom. I suppose I am a pessimistic person'. He spent two Oxford vacations working at Leeds crematorium. ('Only cutting the grass,' he points out hastily, 'nothing to do with the bodies.')

'When Alan is working terminally,' said a colleague, 'then he can find sources of joy.' But he has worried about his use of the horrors as material: 'because in the most awful circumstances, there's a bit of you that is not committed to the suffering.' His mother has now lost her memory for objects, which makes her say things which are very funny as well as distressing, and he writes them down.

Bennett is a complicated and contradictory man: reticent and forthright, gentle and sharp, generous and unforgiving. He is modest and diffident in manner, though. 'I think he knows when he's written something amusing,' murmurs Sir John Gielgud. But while harshly self-critical, he has (in one friend's view) a 'violent, but not resilient' response to criticism. 'Humour is what keeps him sane,' said another: 'so there is always humour. But he does get angry and upset about things, and – though I haven't seen it myself – I gather his anger is awesome.' Bennett himself says, 'Most of it stops inside'.

He is a loyal but demanding friend. 'There is a weight of emotion, blackness, hurt, that one senses and walks round,' said a colleague. Even close companions seem a little afraid of him. 'There is a demon, that can get out of hand,' said one: 'and unless you're going to play the same game, you're sunk.'

Recently he published an account of the turbulence between himself and the late Kenneth More during the pre-London run of his play *Getting On*, when More banned him from rehearsals. Bennett never saw More, or the play (which later won an award) again. 'Alan's nuclear weapon,' said a friend, 'is withdrawal of himself. He can simply disappear from people's lives.'

He is equally good at turning up, and (partly as a result of *Getting On*) is a constant presence when a work is in progress. He says he has spent most of this year 'titting about' on the shooting of *A Private Function*, his first feature film, set in Yorkshire in 1947, with a chiropodist hero played by Michael Palin.

In the glare of publicity and the expansive warmth of success, Alan Bennett remains a shadowy figure behind the blinds of his house, where (his friends believe) he lives alone. Much has been made of his melancholia, his solitude: the truth is probably another Chinese box inside that neat and acceptable image. 'Look – he's turned himself from a Leeds lad into a West End playwright,' said one friend. 'He's well off; he reads a lot, buys good pictures, eats good food, spends a lot of time in New York, and has complicated relationships with interesting people. I think he has a good time: though I think he'd be very cross to hear me say that.'

Alan Bennett will himself allow that while he gets fed up with the way people seem to see him, the misconception has its usefulness. 'I'd rather the public have an image, and not quite fit it. It'll do to play with. That way, you're free.'

TED HUGHES

23 December 1984

They took their time over the decision but in the end the timing was perfect. Less than a week before Christmas, it was announced that a carpenter's son, Ted Hughes, had been appointed the new Poet Laureate. The powers that be, it seems, are not above a sly religious joke.

Ted Hughes is no Messiah, but his poetry has a messianic intensity which marks the end of an era. The old dispensation, the cosy sociable world of John Betjeman and his teddy bear, has been left behind. The new Laureate is a stern, uncompromising poet who speaks of 'the Muse', 'inspiration' and of negotiation with the dark forces, and who has written much about the bleakness and brutality of the natural world.

One of his best poems, for example, part of a verse-journal he kept while working on a farm, describes the poet's harrowing experience with a lamb that 'could not get born'. The poet feels inside the mother 'into the slippery, muscled tunnel, fingering for a hoof', but still cannot get the dead lamb free. In the end he has to slice its head off and work the headless body out until it lies finally 'in a smoking slither of oils and soups and syrups'.

It is an astonishingly powerful poem, authentic and gripping when Hughes reads it, but not a poem for weak stomachs. And there is bound to be some trepidation in high places about any forthcoming odes on royal occasions.

Yet those, like Lord Gowrie, the Arts Minister, who have had a strong say in the appointment, will not be let down. Hughes is a shrewd man, well aware of his responsibilities, and will know when to do the decent expected thing and when to follow the dictates of his own vision. He is a safer choice, in this respect, than someone like Gavin Ewart, who might have proved more politically embarassing.

Philip Larkin was the favourite to be Laureate because he promised, in his own special downbeat way, to continue the Betjeman tradition. But though Larkin may have talked himself out of the running by reminding everyone of his lack of productivity, he did not, as has been suggested, actually turn the post down. Hughes, in the end, was the first choice: he is Laureate by right, not by default.

Certainly in the country at large there will be less surprise about his appointment than in London's literary circles. A poll of poetry readers some years ago showed Hughes to be the most popular contemporary British poet, ahead of Larkin, Ewart, Charles Causley and the rest.

In schools and colleges he has been part of the syllabus for some twenty years.

A marvellous performer of his work, solemnly intoning in a strong Yorkshire accent, he is much in demand for readings. And on the rare occasions he does perform, his tall craggy presence and rapt concentration exert a hypnotic effect on audiences.

Nor is it surprising that Hughes should have said yes. Though his England is not Betjeman's – it is more moorland than metroland, more Gothic than Victorian, more pre-Christian than C of E – he is a staunch patriot with a strong sense of cultural tradition. His book *Remains of Elmet*, for example, a commemoration of the mills and chapels of the dying Calder Valley, is a lament for a lost bit of England every bit as nostalgic as Betjeman could be. And a deep feeling for the nation's history lies behind what is probably his best known poem, 'Pike'.

Hughes was born in 1930, at Mytholmroyd, in the West Riding of Yorkshire, and grew up under a huge rock face, towering over the valley, which seemed to block out all light and hope: 'I lived under it as under the presence of a war, or an occupying army' he has written, 'the oppression cast by that rock was a force in the minds of everyone'. But the moors above, which he began to walk to at the age of three or four, were an exciting escape. And at Mexborough Grammar School, encouraged by an excellent English teacher, he started to write.

At Pembroke College, Cambridge, to which he went after two years' National Service, he began by studying English but later changed to archaeology and anthropology. He was soon taken up as the Cambridge poet of his generation and after graduating worked towards his first volume of poems, supporting himself through odd jobs as a rose-gardener, night-watchman and script reader for J. Arthur Rank.

When his first book, *The Hawk in The Rain*, appeared in 1957, it won him the New York Poetry Centre Award and instant acclaim on both sides of the Atlantic. It also established him as a new sort of 'nature poet', anti-Georgian, anti-pastoral, much possessed by death and violence. 'My manners are tearing off heads,' says the hawk in the title poem of his second book, *Lupercal*. 'Terrifying are the attent sleek thrushes on the lawn' goes another, verging on self-parody.

The summer before his poetic début, Hughes had met and married Sylvia Plath. For six years they travelled, taught and wrote together – in Spain, North America, London and Devon – as well as producing two children. But in 1962 they separated. The following year Plath committed suicide. Further private tragedy was to follow for Hughes shortly afterwards.

The 1960s were a traumatic time for him and the traumas left their mark on his most controversial collection, *Crow*, published in 1973, an agonised and nihilistic book in which words like *death*, *blood*, *black*, *bone*, and *burn* recur as a kind of incantation. Some critics praised the book, others denounced Hughes's 'skimped and shallow dealings with the human world'. But many of the poems have a knock-about verve, a cartoon-strip comedy, which hint at the poet's reserves of humour. *Crow* wears a grin; there is a grim laughter in the face of adversity.

In 1970 Hughes married Carol Orchard, the daughter of a Devon farmer, a hospitable and likeable woman who, friends say, has given Hughes a new stability. They live comfortably in a rambling old house near Exeter. In 1977 Hughes was awarded the OBE. His poetry of recent years has lost some of its earlier tightness but he remains a marvellous observer of the natural world.

A celebrator too, increasingly attentive to the gentler, more delicate face of nature. Apple trees, salmon, swifts, kingfishers, heather, harebell, calves, heron, craneflies – all these have received his loving attention in poems that outdo D. H. Lawrence in their insight and spontaneity.

Hughes is a naturally private man, and the intrusion of American academics, digging over his life with Sylvia Plath and treating him as a kind of fossil, have hardened him in his privacy. He remains understandably reticent about those years, but has been scrupulous in editing and publishing not only Plath's poems but generous selections of her letters, excruciating though some of these must be to him.

Though private, he has already shown himself willing to play a public role on behalf of poetry, particularly with the young. Some years ago he leased his old Yorkshire home Lumb Bank to the Arvon Foundation, which puts on residential courses there for aspiring writers, and he remains the driving force behind the organisation. He is a great believer in the importance of poetry in schools and has written a great deal for children himself, including one classic, *The Iron Man*.

In person Hughes is far from being the bardic, seer-like 'possessed' poet that popular stereotypes suggest. Although he is knowledgeable about such occult topics as eskimo myths and witchcraft, conversation is just as likely to turn to his cousin's splendid make of corduroy trousers or the evils of modern farming methods. The desecration of the countryside is something he feels strongly about, and he may use his post, as Betjeman did, for conservationists' ends. Unlike Betjeman, he will keep his distance from the capital. Though not someone who could happily be called a 'provincial writer' (he has more guile and sophistication than that label would allow), he has little liking for the city.

'Do not pick up the telephone' runs one of Hughes recent poems, about the menace lurking down the line. It is an injunction he will do well to remember in coming months, pestered as he will be with requests and invitations. But Hughes, a man of great integrity, will resist the blandishments, staying true to his own art without reneging on his new public responsibilities – which is why his appointment is such an inspired choice.

IRIS MURDOCH

11 May 1986

Iris Murdoch is still a philosopher as well as a novelist. Every day she gets up early and attends to the major philosophical work she has been writing for some years. As a taster, she recently published *Acastos*, a slim volume of two Platonic dialogues, to the approval of her critics.

No one pretends that *Acastos* will sell many copies, but that concerns its author as little as the fact that *The Good Apprentice*, her most recent novel (published last autumn) has sold better than any of its 21 predecessors in the United States. (Its sales here are higher than all the others' except *The Sea, The Sea*, which won the Booker Prize in 1978.)

Iris Murdoch is 66, a woman who has found international recognition for her creative intelligence, and who defends her privacy with strategy and vigour. She shamelessly turns the tables on anyone who might try to ask her personal questions, particularly visiting journalists.

She once thrilled a Christian group in Oxford by agreeing to come to talk to them: only to settle down, on her arrival, to interrogate them on their experiences of belief. Her publisher and agent spend whole lunchtimes in London speculating about the book she might currently be writing, of which she tells them nothing, and about which they do not dare to ask.

Her face shifts between acuity and sadness when it is not cheered by a smile. She dresses (and likes dressing up) in clothes predictable chiefly for their element of surprise: encouraged by her husband, John Bayley, the literary critic and Warton Professor of English at Oxford. Both the Bayleys, while praised for the generosity of their friendship, are acknowledged to be misers over personal information. When they recently moved from a large stone country house to a small suburban brick one in north Oxford they did so without telling many of their friends or their neighbours in Steeple Aston, the village where they had spent the 30 years of their married lives.

Iris Murdoch was the only child of Anglo-Irish parents. Her father came from the north of Ireland, her mother from the south; they met in a Protestant church in Dublin, where her father heard her mother's 'very high, pure soprano' (she was training to be an opera singer). Her father fought through the First World War 'from day one' in a cavalry regiment; the family left Ireland when Iris was one.

Her father was 'very anxious that I should have a tip-top education': she received it at Froebel, Badminton and Somerville, where she took a first in

Greats in 1942. Then she followed her father into the civil service; left it to work for UNRRA in Austria and Belgium; and spent some time in Paris, encountering existentialism and Jean-Paul Sartre. In 1947 she went to Cambridge to study philosophy, and in 1948 back to Oxford to teach it at St Anne's.

An SCR colleague remembers this as 'a rather original, unusual appointment' by the college's rather conservative principal; and Iris Murdoch quickly distinguished herself by the brilliance of her mind and unorthodoxy of her appearance. She published her first book, *Sartre, Romantic Rationalist*, in 1953; and her first novel (after 'a number of false starts') *Under the Net* in 1954. Both were acclaimed.

A former undergraduate recalls her feeling of privilege and bafflement in their tutorials. 'You were aware that you were in the presence of someone who had made her mark on Thought, who was being as nice and kind as she possibly could be to someone who didn't understand what she was talking about.'

Iris Murdoch found Oxford teaching 'a great strain', and gave it up in 1963. But her kindness is still legendary; and her intellect and will still drive her through a sequence of unremitting pressures and deadlines – all self-imposed. 'One's life is so crammed with work.'

No one knows much about it, of course: she guards the routines and rituals of her day as jealously as her deeper secrets. She is deliberately vague about the philosophy work which is her first task, and which she does not intend to complete for several years. Indeed, 'it may never emerge. Philosophy is almost impossibly difficult. I think we might begin to have some glimmerings if we had a different lifespan – if one could live 100 or 200 years'. (For an interview, she offers 45 minutes.)

She writes her novels on the grandest scale, building their structures from 'erotic mysteries and deep dark struggles between good and evil'. Her models, companions and colleagues are Tolstoy and Dostoevsky, Proust and Dickens and Henry James. (This did not prevent a now-famous howler in *The Good Apprentice*, when she misquoted the first line of *A la Recherche du Temps Perdu.*)

Her manner is unpretentious, yet her confidence is absolute. 'Nothing is ever changed by anything I say – or anything anyone else says,' reports John Bayley. She refuses editorial intervention, even over a comma. At the suggestion that the sheer size of her recent fiction (never fewer than 500 pages) may deter some readers, she shrugs. 'I scorn such readers.'

Both professionally and personally she is a moralist. Her concern is with goodness, its struggle and its triumph; and with reality, truth-seeking and truth-telling. 'She once said, "I don't think I could tell a lie any more",' says a friend. 'And she's had that effect on me.' Yet her books are full of the dark areas of human experience: crime, violence, guilt, deception, magic, sensuality, death. She explores murder and incest with gusto (as it occurs within the confines of the London-based middle classes); and adultery is an omnipresent force in her books – though we see it in her characters' heads more than their beds.

Religion fascinates her, though she does not believe in God. She is 'very attached' to the Christian Church (also to St Augustine); she has 'thought about' becoming a Buddhist. But her real god is Plato. 'I feel absolutely at home with his thoughts.' She became a Marxist in her teens, and later an active member of the Communist Party. But though she went on to join CND and the Labour Party, she voted for Margaret Thatcher at the last election, and is vehemently right-wing on such subjects as trade union reform, Chinese Communism, and private education.

Very few people have seen Iris Murdoch's composure ruffled. Only occasionally does she become impatient. And she can show and receive strong emotion. The memory of her parents (her mother died last year) can move her to tears. One friend recalls that Iris Murdoch was the only person with whom she could share the worst of her grief over the death of a child.

The Bayleys have no children, though Iris Murdoch is noted for her patronage of young writers and artists, and her rapport with the young. 'She takes one very seriously, which is comforting when you're a child,' said a godson: 'because most people don't.' By her seriousness and her silences she also commands deference and forbids foolishness in her chosen circle. 'I'd never gossip to Iris, though I would to John,' said one member. 'And I wouldn't gossip to John in front of Iris.'

Yet Iris Murdoch is also (like her husband) sociable and convivial – 'friendly to *everybody*,' said an observer. 'They almost *like* bores.' They have no television, and 'there is no embarrassment about tackling Wittgenstein or getting into Sartre over breakfast,' reports a guest. But they are also excellent dancers and fiendish poker-players, and know by heart the popular songs of the 1920s and 1930s. They travel a lot, rarely sending a postcard; they like jokes, pubs and swimming, and good food and drink. (John Bayley does all their cooking.) Iris Murdoch maintains a London flat: 'but they're always together, like two peas in a pod.'

John Bayley notes that, unlike many literary giants who were notoriously difficult to live with, his wife 'doesn't have a demon. Creation is for her a quiet, still, mysterious activity; and as a book is going on she becomes more and more tranquil'.

Yet there is a compulsion in the quietude. 'She *must* be writing,' said one friend. 'The books are her lifeblood. If she wasn't writing them, I think she'd curl up.' Iris Murdoch says: 'If there were not another book to write, I'd feel like a beaver not allowed to build its den, or the bird its nest.' She admits that she has 'moments of blackness and despair: times when no life comes, when one thinks one would never think of anything again.' But they do not last long. Pretty soon, 'the life comes'. She can write on. Her publisher and agent can relax over their coffee cups.

MARGARET DRABBLE

19 April 1987

A new novel by Margaret Drabble appears later this month, the first for seven years. In the meantime, she has edited the *Oxford Companion to English Literature* – a huge task, which she completed at record speed. She then (uncharacteristically) suffered 'deep anxiety and distress' because she could not get another novel going. Then, characteristically, she did.

'If a problem comes up, at which anyone else would shy away, Maggie does the opposite,' said an intimate. 'She *goes* at it.' More carelessly, Margaret Drabble recalls: 'I just carried on bashing out beginnings.' The result is *The Radiant Way*, which she is now publicising in a whistle-stop tour across Canada. The schedule looked a little tiring, as she admitted before she left: but Mrs Thatcher seemed to manage these things. And anything that Maggie can do, this one can surely do better.

Margaret Drabble has achieved much in her 47 years. At Cambridge (she was a scholar at Newnham) she won fame as an actress and a double first. All her books have been bestsellers. She has taught English literature in an adult education college; lectured about it all over the world; demonstrated in public on political issues; and was twice a star witness in Old Bailey obscenity trials. She has made two marriages, brought up three children, and nurtured many friendships.

No one knows how she does it. A lot is (thought to be) known about her and she says she would cheerfully tell an interviewer intimate details of her underwear if asked. But in her open, honest and direct public persona there is the containment of a transparent mask. She keeps whole tracts of her life and character private; but does so with such friendliness and frankness that it is easy not to spot that there is a silence, a barrier, a defended territory there.

She was born in Sheffield in 1939 into a family of high achievers. Her father, whom she calls a self-made man, moved from Mexborough Grammar School and a job in his father's sweet-making business to Cambridge, thence to become a barrister and later a circuit judge. He met her mother at school; Mrs Drabble, like her two elder daughters, read English at Newnham, and later read a book a day. The first Drabble daughter became the novelist and critic Antonia Byatt; the third, Helen, is an art historian; Richard Drabble, born when Margaret was eleven, is a barrister. He remembers his middle sister as 'very energetic and authoritative'. On what subject? 'On *any* subject.'

She remembers being dogged by a bad stammer: 'When I was little I did anything to avoid attention.' But later, 'I wanted people to notice I was there.' At The

Mount, her Quaker boarding school in York, she played the lead in *St Joan*: it became legendary not only as a piece of acting, but because in it she did not stammer once.

At Cambridge, the actor, Clive Swift, was on the Amateur Dramatic Club's audition committee. He recalls the 'fierce emotional intensity' of her acting and the 'surprising lower register' to her voice. He also fell in love with her at first sight. Professor David Daiches, who taught her, remembers: 'There was no surface brilliance about her: but a quiet assurance, almost an arrogance – a take-it-or-leave-it air about the way she wrote her essays.'

She married Clive Swift on leaving Cambridge in 1960; the marriage lasted 15 years. When (early on) he worked for the Royal Shakespeare Company at Stratford, she understudied Vanessa Redgrave as Imogen. But Vanessa 'was never ill'. And then her children arrived (two sons and a daughter). And so did her early novels.

They are stories of young women whose settings and experiences looked rather like their author's; and certain autobiographical similarities caused ripples.

A Summer Bird-Cage (1963), Margaret's first novel, had at its centre the antagonism relationship between two clever and competitive sisters. Four years later, Antonia Byatt's second novel, *The Game*, also contained (as the *Oxford Companion* records dispassionately) a relationship between two sisters: 'one an Oxford don, the other a popular novelist'. Margaret Drabble treats such matters with her usual aplomb. 'I continue to be surprised that people think that *A Summer Bird-Cage* was anything to do with my sister and me.'

Most people who recognise themselves in her fiction now declare themselves more amused than annoyed. But there have been arguments and anger in the past. Her elder son recalls his mother's unanswerable answer. 'She'd say: "Do you really not want me to write books? How do you think I paid for your supper?"'

Margaret Drabble's devotion and pleasure in bringing up her children are now crowned by the friendship she shares with them. (All are now in their twenties, living away from home.) They remember, with affectionate admiration, their mother's discipline and drive. Margaret Drabble has always been an early riser, and in Hampstead they would wake to the sound of the Hoover, followed by the clacking of the typewriter. 'It shook the whole house. We'd all still be in bed.'

They did not realise she was famous until they were grown up; they still find it hard to see her as ambitious. 'But she must be, mustn't she? – to do what she's done?'

She admits she does not like failure, which explains why she did not drive a car until she was 42. She failed her test at eighteen, then at 28, and was afraid of doing it again. The biographer, Michael Holroyd ('a saint,' in her view) recalls going to sleep in his car while she taught herself to drive it. They married soon afterwards, informing none of their friends except the two who witnessed the civil ceremony.

Now Margaret Drabble drives (as she writes) 'very fast, with great confidence,' observes a friend.

The couple's happiness is evident. They have kept their separate houses, but meet in evenings and at weekends; 'and of course,' says Holroyd, 'we see a lot of each other abroad'. In the past they have both given non-writing time to literary committees: they now devote more of it to British Council lecturing, at which Margaret has been both trouper and star since her first trip (to Czechoslovakia) in 1969.

'If you were to drop her in any country of the world with no clothes, no lecture notes, no books and no notice, she would still be a superb ambassador for Britain and British literature,' says the Council's Harriet Harvey Wood.

An American critic of Margaret Drabble's novels, recently noting the growth in their sociological scope and range, pronounced her 'the chronicler of contemporary Britain . . . the person who will have done for late twentiety-century London what Dickens did for Victorian London, what Balzac did for Paris'. Certainly she is now a queen of her city's literary world. She has had lunch with the real Queen, too, though she turns down invitations to Downing Street.

It is perhaps inevitable that friends can detect in her a touch of regality, a hint (in this judge's daughter) of something judgmental – 'though she fights against it' (one of them added hastily), 'and she's also very humane'. Another said: 'She is mostly right, but she can also be self-righteous; and she finds it quite hard to be wrong.'

Her parents and school endowed Margaret Drabble with a moral seriousness, a social conscience, a sense of duty and responsibility, which have meshed with the socialism she inherited from her father (who was twice an unsuccessful Labour candidate). She has herself twice joined and left the Labour Party, though she has not (yet) joined the SDP.

Her son Adam perceives in her – and her new book – uncertainty and division here. 'There are still large areas where she thinks she knows what's right and what's wrong. But there are also now tremendous doubts – about politics, about beliefs she held for a long time, and can no longer hold.'

Yet it is hard to imagine Margaret Drabble assailed by doubt for long. Certainty is her suit, and it suits her. She has a reassuring presence, and it may be that her inner security is now close to matching the outer confidence she has always presented.

She has no more money worries; her children are off her hands. In her house in Hampstead – a red brick Edwardian villa overlooking Keats's garden – she is an unflustered hostess, a splendid cook; her loyalty and kindness to friends – 'even to people she doesn't *like*' – is so unwavering as to be pronounced unwise. (She is also hoping to buy a house in Gloucestershire: she loves the countryside.)

She is doing what she likes, and thereby creating enjoyment both for herself and others. 'She is,' says her husband, 'a voluptuary in her work.' Yet still a voluptuary with a social conscience. She was glad, when editing the *Oxford Companion*, to find it was 'very hard work, but easier than writing a novel'; and in some way that labour has made her free. 'Maybe I've at last got the confidence to say I think writing novels is a very serious thing to do.'

MARK BOXER

24 June 1988

Mark Boxer, who died last week at the age of 57 and whose drawings regularly appeared on this page until last autumn, was quite simply the best caricaturist of his age. If Max Beerbohm had a lineal descendant, then he was it.

He had, of course, many other gifts – displayed as the first editor of the *Sunday Times* colour magazine, as the man who built and improved upon Tina Brown's achievement with the *Tatler* and who eventually became the editorial viceroy of the Condé Nast empire in London; but, above all, posterity will probably remember him for his drawings.

Oddly, Mark never seems to have been tempted to become a political cartoonist – indeed, the day-to-day flow of political news never really interested him: what fascinated him were the underlying social changes that the political battle often concealed. Thus a 'critical' Commons vote, which might have filled the newspapers for days, would leave him quite unmoved; the news, on the other hand, that a Thatcherite MP had had a visiting card printed with his own picture on it would divert and delight him.

This, no doubt, also explains why some of his most successful drawings were not of the famous or illustrious at all but of characters or social types he had invented. Sometimes these could be distinctly waspish – witness his strip on the NW1 trendies, 'The Stringalongs', which ran with great success (and considerable hurt for at least one family) in Karl Miller's *Listener* in the late 1960s.

More often, though, they were geniunely fictional creations. His brilliant series of drawings for the twelve paperbacks of Anthony Powell's *Dance to the Music of Time* was one of his greatest achievements: he had nothing to go on but what he felt each character ought to look like. He captured each one so perfectly that, to most Powell fans, his images – his Widmerpool, for example – are the ones they carry for life in their minds.

His pocket cartoons – which appeared by turn in *The Times*, the *Guardian* and the *Daily Telegraph* – were more mixed. His technique each morning was to phone up a collaborator – usually George Melly, when he wasn't on tour, sometimes the *Observer*'s Simon Hoggart, when he was – and chew over the day's news. His quest was normally for an idea – or, more precisely, a jokey caption. On good days this might take no more than minutes; on bleaker ones it could last easily half an hour (he always paid meticulously for any idea he used).

Again, he was never much excited by immediate political developments: what he wanted his pocket cartoons to reflect were shifts in the social fabric. Accordingly, some political stories were naturals. When the Duke of Devonshire joined the SDP, he promptly drew a cartoon showing two relieved members of the party, with one of them saying: 'At least it gets rid of our middle-class image.' Similarly, when it was revealed that African embassies were paying huge sums for residences in London, he had a woman twitching at her curtain, saying: 'At last the neighbourhood's moving up, the blacks are moving in.' (The slightly snobbish satire implicit in his pocket cartoons could be misleading: Mark remained a faithful Labour voter all his life.)

In the real world, he was at his best drawing people he knew well – and, since these tended to be raffish figures in café society, this could cause problems for the more earnest-minded of his editors (although some of his very best profile drawings did, in fact, appear in the *New Statesman* between 1970 and 1978 and, after that, in this column between 1982 and 1987).

He felt he had almost, as it were, to live in a face if he were to bring off an impression of it successfully: he would, therefore, go and see politicians in their offices (moving quickly and disturbingly around the room trying to get their expressions from every possible angle for his 'roughs') and sometimes even sit – lunchless – in a restaurant with his pad on his knee and a clear eyeline towards his subject. When all else failed – and there was no chance of a face-to-face encounter – he would conscientiously videotape his victims from the TV, though the results here were by no means uniformly successful.

Mark was always a perfectionist. He would normally send in some four or five drawings, all of the same subject – and to the lay eye with very little to choose between them: one, though, would generally be marked in pencil, 'This one?' (He would be hurt if it was not the one finally chosen – and even more aggrieved if something should go wrong with the reproduction. He was not above displays of temperament – especially if a drawing was lost or, worse, found its way into unauthorised hands.)

For most people an artistic career of this kind of distinction would have been enough – but for Mark it never quite was. From his earliest days as editor of *Granta* at Cambridge – from which he was rusticated for publishing a poem 'disrepectful to God' – half of him also always yearned for executive responsibility. He attained it early as art director (and, in effect, co-editor) of Jocelyn Stevens's *Queen*, the smartest magazine in London in the late 1950s. After that, he was lured to become the founding editor of the *Sunday Times* colour supplement in 1962 – after a wobbly commercial start making a great success of it and blazing the trial for all the other colour magazines (including the *Observer*'s in 1964) which followed.

At this stage there is little doubt that Mark had his sights firmly set on becoming a national newspaper editor. Indeed, even at the age of 23, he was taking the business of editorship very seriously, writing a letter of Polonius-type advice to the late Nicholas Tomalin, his successor as editor of *Granta* at Cambridge:

> You are sometimes too enthusiastic, you see through yourself ten minutes later but sometimes too late. You are not insensitive. An editor, however, must be ruthless. You just don't have impeccable manners – thank contributors formally, try and be polite at parties, try and be discreet.

In truth, 'discreet' was what Mark himself never was – but he was ambitious and, if things had gone according to plan, he might well have hoped to succeed Sir Denis Hamilton as editor of the *Sunday Times* in place of Harold Evans. That he was never even in with a chance of doing so in 1967 was the result of the one catastrophe of his career.

In 1965 he abandoned the safety of the colour magazine editor's chair at the *Sunday Times* to launch the then ailing *Tatler* (which had been bought by the Thomson Organisation) under the new title of *London Life*. It proved to be a disaster and, though the magazine itself limped on for a bit, Mark himself was relieved of his command of it after six weeks.

Accustomed to success, he took this reverse very hard, and thought seriously of leaving the Thomson Organisation. Probably he should have done – certainly the next thirteen years were years of humiliation for him at the *Sunday Times* (he even lost his seat on the paper's board, to which he had been appointed in 1962). Harold Evans, perhaps understandably, was wary of him and he was reduced to being little more than the serial-buyer for the paper. On the other hand, it was these fallow years that created him as a cartoonist: he started 'The Stringalongs' in the *Listener* in 1968, his pocket cartoons in *The Times* in 1969 and his profile portraits in the *New Statesman* in 1970.

Half of him still, however, felt unfulfilled – which was why, in 1983, after a brief and none-too-happy stint as a publisher at Weidenfeld's, he was delighted to accept the offer from Condé Nast of the editorship of the revived *Tatler*.

It was the ideal job for Mark, now securely settled into his second marriage with Anna Ford. The *Tatler* under his guiding hand (which he continued to exercise latterly as editor-in-chief) may have gone on carrying its usual pictures of bulging-eyed Horray-Henrys and their vacuous girl-friends; but it began also to publish penetrating analyses of the power structure of the new emerging post-Thatcher, neo-capitalist Britain. In one sense, Mark – who had come a long way from his seldom spoken of days at Berkhamsted School – was, of course, part of it; but that never stopped him from bringing his critical, quizzical eye to bear upon it.

Few things gave him a greater kick than being summoned to Sir James Goldsmith's triumphalist election party last summer. 'You know,' he said, dining out on the occasion afterwards, 'I'm virtually certain Anna and I were the only non-Tory voters there – we were the Quislings in the camp.' It was perhaps the role – from the base of a totally happy home in Brentford with his wife and two little girls – that Mark always relished most. It was that which made him what he was – a life-enhancer.

BRITISH POLITICIANS

British politicians probably form the highest number of profiles over the years. In today's editorial conferences, the politician making waves that week is likely to be first on the profile list. Inevitably someone will say 'Haven't we done him?' to which the answer is generally Yes. There will then be a debate over whether enough time has elapsed since his last profile (which hardly anyone present can remember anyway) to justify a 'fresh look' at so-and-so. The number of recent or contemporary politicians who have been profiled more than once is evidence of that. No domestic politician can match Harold Macmillan, who was profiled four times, nor can they equal his span: the first was in 1946, the last for his resurrection as a public figure in the shape of Lord Stockton in 1985. Roy Jenkins was the subject three times; many others figured twice. It would have been attractive to run contrasting profiles of the same person from different eras: the constraints of space dictated otherwise, alas.

Sir James Grigg is here because his was the very first *Observer* profile. Aneurin Bevan was profiled at the time of his resignation from the second Attlee government in 1951, over the extent of British rearmament. Churchill was featured at the end of the same year, two months into his second term as Prime Minister; Macmillan eighteen months into his first.

I have selected the 1961 profile of Enoch Powell because it seems to be a model of its kind, with a prophetic conclusion; and that of Jeremy Thorpe (which bore the byline of Ivan Yates) because it caught a man nearing his peak whose sudden and tragic downfall could not have been dreamt of at that time.

Of the three Roy Jenkins profiles available I have chosen the last, at the time of his triumph as SDP candidate at the Glasgow Hillhead by-election, when anything seemed possible for the new party whose inspiration he had been. The concluding paragraph of the profile of his Alliance co-leader David Steel was all too accurate. So was the summing up on Neil Kinnock, still a year away from becoming Labour Party leader (the analysis of his faults still held true too, eight years on). As for Michael Heseltine, neither his ambitions nor his frustration at not attaining the very top job had changed between 1982 and the time of writing.

The timing of the Norman Tebbit profile, on the eve of the Conservative Party conference in October 1984, was especially poignant: four days later he was badly injured and his wife paralysed by the IRA bombing of the Grand Hotel, Brighton. It was an event that the profile writer could not have foreseen.

The lasting effects of the bombing on Mr Tebbit and his wife were a big factor in the shaping of his political future.

At the time of her profile, in December 1988, Mrs Edwina Currie was still hanging on to office in the Department of Health after her gaffe on salmonella in eggs. But within days she had been forced to resign.

SIR JAMES GRIGG

1 March 1942

The initials 'P.J.' by which the new War Minister is known to his friends might well stand for Passion and Justice: add the G for Guts. Except for the second, these qualities are not now generally attributed to Whitehall, and P.J.'s success in the Civil Service is, nevertheless, so remarkable that one can only suppose that habitual tilting at bureaucratic windmills was counteracted by ability, and possible boredom with the machine counteracted by luck. The normal drudgery of a civil servant was escaped by a Wrangler who went from soldiering to nine years' secretaryship of successive Chancellors, and thence to India, where he had a taste of power such as India alone afforded, and a dose of the very violent criticism which the Indian Press and Assembly offer in abundance to harried Ministers.

Any attempt at a portrait of P.J. must be sketched with bold strokes, because his is essentially a bold and highly individualistic character. One must be careful: the British have a prejudice against strong individuality – until it proves itself in a crisis – and P.J. might certainly shock that section, however large it is, which, according to Mr Mathers, 'felt disgusted' by Joad's quotation of a Confucian aphorism. P.J.'s strongest likes are for Rabelaisian wit, claret, dogs, Dickens and fierce argument: his most violent hatreds, hypocrisy, whining people, inefficiency, Lord Haw-Haw and nearly all social functions. He is – or at least often is – devastatingly abrupt; he uses a ferocious candour like a surgeon's knife, ruthlessly cutting away from his environment all that savours of boredom, hypocisy or self-seeking. Those who survive the operation find in him an always wise counsellor, a supremely loyal, exhilarating and warm-hearted friend. The combination of extreme ruthlessness and extreme generosity gives to his character a sparkling and sometimes startling variety.

There are dangers as well as advantages in the sudden emergence of such a personality into the full glare of the limelight. Legends are apt to gather. P.J. is a man who, I suspect, will tend to shun or despise 'publicity'; he will be more concerned to get on with his job. It is immensely important that England should know him as he really is; he might too rapidly become the wrong sort of myth. There is a tendency to expect miracles – conversely, a tendency to identify him with bureaucracy; and too much chatter, *faute de mieux*, about his 'rudeness'. He cannot overhaul an army overnight: he has acquired a certain discipline from the bureaucratic machine but never succumbed to its apathies; his bluntness is, as I have tried to indicate, of a surgical and healing, but never unjust or unkind, quality. Towards youth particularly he has a great warmth of understanding and sympathy which will presently, I have no doubt, appear in his actions. He can inspire: but to do so he must be granted a measure of faith.

That faith is certainly held by those who know him. Grigg, like Cripps, possesses an acute, distinguished, disciplined mind, and, what is perhaps much more important now, a high and rare degree of passion and integrity. For all his bluntness he is a lovable and essentially modest man. If he and Cripps will go forward, not too modestly, together, sure of the faith of their fellow men, we shall find in them inspiration and leadership of a new and enduring quality.

ANEURIN BEVAN

29 April 1951

The weather was getting better; vague jokes about the Festival were beginning to appear; the basic sense of futility at living defenceless beside an unfriendly dictatorship was yielding slightly to a feeling that 'something was being done'; when a prosaic budget was introduced. Its only surprise interest was the scandal of Aneurin Bevan's preceding Bermondsey speech and subsequent embarrassing position.

Suddenly, there was a deafening report – MacArthur had been fired. The real meaning of this major world event was just sinking in, when there was a second noise, a sound of scuffle – Bevan had decided to resign.

It made Labour voters uncomfortable, Conservatives mildly pleased and gave the press exciting copy, but nobody quite understood it. When Mr Bevan explained himself in the House, the emotional content of his speech seemed to be mistrust or dislike of his former colleagues, some antipathy to rearmament, and an undertone of feeling that 'the Americans' were to blame.

The only people who seem to be actually pleased with him are the primarily anti-American wing of the Labour movement, mostly intellectuals, and trade unionists who, like the Communists, keeping pressing for more wages and less armaments, such as Mr Figgins. This may change, but at present it is the lack of many positive or negative emotional contact between him and any wide section of the public which is the most surprising feature of his situation. This emotional cut-off seems to be accidental, since he has hitherto consistently and successfully maintained himself as the most applauded and most booed-at of our politicians.

Aneurin Bevan was born in 1897 at the mining town of Tredegar, the son of David and Phoebe. His parents were unwilling immigrants to the coal valley from sheep farming, which was in decay; they clung to the old Welsh culture and christened their children such names as Blodwyn, Myfanwy, Arianwen, Iorwerth. The mother, a sensitive and temperamental woman, sought to alleviate the squalor of their home by religious observance, books and a fine print of Hereford Cathedral: there were thirteen children born of whom five died in this four-room house.

From this background, Aneurin set out into the world. His first experience came following in his father's footsteps. He went to work in the pit at thirteen, and remained working underground for seven years until he developed nystagmus, a mining disease, caused by inadequate lighting, affecting the nerves and eyesight.

This severe setback in his first dealings with the outside world seems to have had a fundamental effect: with a job at the pithead, he turned his attention to mental and verbal activity. He began to read a lot and to enter mining politics as an agitator.

It was at once clear that he was unusually gifted and energetic – but he was held back by a bad stammer. The way that he overcame this paralysing internal obstacle seems also to have been profoundly formative. He drove himself to speak in public – and discovered that, once involved in a fighting debate, his nervousness disappeared. His powers could be released only by this process; thus he was from the start self-driven to impassioned attack or exultant banter. This formula meant individual action against an adversary in public – it militated against committee discussion, peaceful solutions, and private life.

The social setting in which his adolescent character thus matured was the South Wales coalfield before and during the First World War. It was the grimmest part of the United Kingdom, the part that felt itself most disinherited, least connected with the war against the Kaiser. Aneurin came to manhood believing that the poor conditions of his fellows would not be affected by a war in France, but only by action against the coalowners.

In these circumstances, he first became a spokesman and leader at the age of nineteen; he was elected, in 1916, chairman of a lodge of 4,000 in the South Wales Miners' Federation. While the great North Welsh rebel, Lloyd George, was becoming the father of this country in its hour of need – taking confidence from the two thousand years of Celtic peasant history behind him – the young Aneurin, watching him with something of the ideology of an industrial 'dead-end kid', was rejecting the ways of his fathers. He felt he knew better what were the real needs of his like, and that patriotism was not a useful emotion; he did not answer his call-up papers. Although not a pacifist, he was only detained for a night, then left unmolested – such was the anxiety Whitehall felt about South Wales at that time.

The only part of his own father's outlook he adopted was that expressed by the

Tredegar Workingmen's Medical Aid Society (a miniature Health Service). His father was one of its founders, and Aneurin fought his first battle with a local outpost of the British Medical Association when they wished to boycott the miners' society. The only ideas he accepted from Lloyd George were those of his National Insurance Act. For the rest, he accepted no paternal ideas, indeed fought them, and sought his own traditions in the new Socialism.

After the war, Aneurin was sent by his union to their Central Labour College in London for two years. At this modest and short-lived establishment, he learned some politics and economics. When he returned to Tredegar, the coal-owners refused him any job. For three years he was partly unemployed, worked on the roads, was aggrieved. His union mates, determined that he should not be starved out of the valley, eventually forced him on the colliery company by electing him their checkweighman.

Soon afterwards he was elected to the Tredegar Urban District Council and here, for the first time, met the bourgeoisie in debate. He also ran up against the local press. Showing considerable courage, he accused the *Western Mail* of bribing unemployed men to attack the miners' cause. After a long struggle, he had the paper banned from the public library for the alleged unfairness of its reporting.

Throughout the depressed twenties, Bevan was active in mining politics and became a fighting champion in the valleys. In the General Strike of 1926, he was against any compromise or surrender. In 1928, he was elected to the Monmouthshire County Council. And in 1929 he arrived in Parliament with a consituency of fervant supporters at his back. He was the only *young* working man ever to reach Westminster at that time, and his arrival caused a considerable sensation.

It is 23 years since Bevan settled in London. In all that time he has, in part, never changed – this can be seen either as rare fidelity to his proletarian origins or as evidence of any incapacity to evolve. He has remained the vehement debater, the sly negotiator, the gifted 'outsider' who mistrusts authority, including that of his own party; and, above all, he has remained parochial.

In the 1930s, he did not visit the countries threatened or seized by Fascism, as Ellen Wilkinson did, but consolidated his position in Monmouthshire and spoke in the House on coal. He will not be remembered for his warning speeches against Hitler, but for his violent wartime onslaughts on Churchill. And, since the war, his intensity has remained concentrated on domestic issues – despite the evident crisis of the world. The great totalitarian issue of our time has always seemed to be outside his ambit.

On the other hand, it is equally true that London life has transformed Bevan – from a miners' leader into one of the most purely professional of politicians. It has become inconceivable to imagine him drinking any other draught than straight politics, hard for him to converse with ordinary people on ordinary things. He has become an exotic and an aristocrat (in the literal sense of that word).

This process was a natural extension of the sceptical individualism of his youth – he never really was one for a crowd, unless he was addressing it. And there was added to this the effects of his forensic success. It is not fair to compare him with John L. Lewis – the American miners' leader, who would never co-operate even with Roosevelt's New Deal, sticking obstinately to the rewarding trade of trouble-making. But it is perfectly fair to compare him with D. H. Lawrence – another miner's son, who developed his individuality to the point that towards the end he had less and less contact with ordinary people, more and more with his own feelings.

Naturally, few Labour MPs live in London as proletarians – their salaries would make that a pose. Most live, like the family men they are, in some quiet petit-bourgeois suburb or block of flats. But Aneurin Bevan has never chosen either of these courses. He has lived in London as an intellectual, joining the company of what might be termed the political bohemians.

At one time, he shared an apartment with Frank Owen, later editor of the *Evening Standard* and *Daily Mail* and now on the *Daily Express*. For a period, Bevan was a regular guest at Lord Beaverbrook country's seat, where he enjoyed high talk and badinage with the other regular guests, such as Randolph Churchill. Here his close ally, Michael Foot, was also to be found.

His marriage to a fellow politician, Miss Jennie Lee, stabilised the political nature of his social life, but confirmed its bohemian-intellectual character. He moved to Chelsea and transferred his weekending to the country houses of fellow-socialists, such as George Strauss and Tom Driberg; his home life did not become that of an ordinary family man.

These intellectual and aesthetic tendencies might have proved political assets, by broadening his nature; but their effect seems, rather, to have been an exaggeration of his individualism to the detriment of his judgment. There are only fairly exotic members of the Labour movement among those who have advised him to take his recent decision – it is the secession of a group that can be compared with the friends of the brilliant but ill-fated Lord Randolph Churchill (whom Bevan, in some respects, resembles).

Much the most solid and constructive effort of his political career is, of course, the establishment of the National Health Service. It is easy to see how his early training had equipped him to out-manoeuvre the doctors – he turned their flank and captured them by playing to the calloused appetite for power and money of some great consultant physicians. And his driving motive was plain – his own experiences had given him ample reason to believe sincerely in the need for a free medical service for the poor.

What is more surprising is his administrative success. He not only established the service promptly, despite all obstacles, but earned the regard of his own civil servants. This may be the one episode in his career which justifies comparisons in stature between him and Lloyd George. Had he gone forward and undertaken less enviable responsibilities – such as finding ways of economising on the NHS or remaining at the Ministry of Labour for long enough to tackle the basic problem of wage rates in a planned economy – he would have shown whether he has the emotional stamina required even in domestic statesmanship.

There is no reason to suppose that Bevan's unwillingness to remain in office, or his virtual silence on the great issue of our day, Communism, indicates pro-Communist sympathies. On the contrary, his editorship of *Tribune* during the war proves that he was anti-Soviet even at the height of the Anglo-Russian wartime honeymoon.

His failure to show interest in this most vital of all contemporary questions seems partly due to the facile transference of stale anti-Tory feelings into fresh anti-American ones (a common transferance among Left intellectuals). Moreover, to attack our local Communists would do him no good, and get him into trouble with some of his supporters. In any case, he is prone to underestimate grossly all other politicians, including Communist ones – a by-product, perhaps, of his too-easy local success in Ebbw Vale.

One of the most serious weaknesses of this able and lonely man is a lack of objectivity, of the ability to look and listen dispassionately. Where Lloyd George could sum up others precisely, Bevan can tell you little more than how *he* feels about them. Correspondingly, he lacks self-criticism.

It is not easy to change basic habits at 53, but there is little doubt that Aneurin Bevan will be able to command and give loyalty, on the scale required of a statesman, only if he can escape from the egocentricity that his life-story has induced. He will need to lose his feeling of being unloved, to learn love of this nation, to drop his patricidal passion for attacking authority and his disregard of ordinary dull men, such as Cabinet colleagues. And he will also need to become less of an old-fashioned orator and intriguer, and more of a patient explainer and team-worker, if he is to fit into the modern scene.

He has courage, resilience and a touch of gaiety. And he has learned much in the years. Perhaps he can yet right himself and become properly adult. If he cannot, he seems fated to end an elderly burlesque of an agitator, living in Chelsea.

WINSTON CHURCHILL

30 December 1951

He is probably the greatest man alive today – certainly the greatest living Englishman; yet many still doubt whether he will be a successful peacetime prime minister. He has been an outstanding landmark of our public life for more than 50 years; but he remains, at 77, something of an unknown quantity. In the course of a fantastic life, he has done enough to make half-a-dozen famous reputations; yet the final judgment of history on his career is hard to foresee.

He is universally admired and genuinely loved by his fellow countrymen, but he has rarely been accorded their complete confidence. Nor is it yet possible to judge whether their long refusal to entrust their destiny – except during one 'climacteric' period of supreme danger and stress – to this unique and revered man has been intuitive wisdom or base, ungrateful stupidity.

The refusal cannot be dismissed as the usual (and often justified) reaction of staid mediocrity to genius. For it would be inaccurate to call Mr Churchill a genius. He has a copious, original and powerful mind, and a wide range of remarkable gifts. But he has not 'genius' – if by that is meant the incalculable and erratic intuition which, for example, made Lloyd George pass through British history like an apparition. Compared with Lloyd George, Mr Churchill is very much one of us, sturdy, native, patriotic, loyal, dependable. Where he transcends ordinary humanity and inspires the awe due to greatness is not in genius, but in two other qualities: vitality and courage.

His vitality is of an heroic order and makes one think of pagan demi-gods. Counting his works and deeds – his books, his speeches, his parliamentary career, the offices he has held, his diplomatic conferences, his great political campaigns and his even greater war leadership – one fails to understand how all this could have been done in one life-time.

Nor has it been the result of ascetic discipline and strict self-organisation. All this enormous activity and productivity has gone side by side with gigantic hobbies – his painting alone would account for a respectable minor existence – and the indulgence of a taste for the civilised pleasures of the table and of nocturnal talk, which would spell the ruin of a mere mortal's constitution. But here the great man stands – approaching his eighties in the full splendour of his powers, keen-eyed and indomitable.

His courage is of an equally fabulous kind. It is neither that deliberate conquest of fear than can make a sensitive man fearless, nor, certainly, is it the fearlessness of insensitivity. Rather, it is a preternatural capacity for finding positive happiness in an endless struggle with danger and adversity. That Churchill has been a happy warrior throughout his life is obvious. To call him a 'war-monger' is a vulgar distortion of this instinctive enjoyment of struggle.

Moreover, its roots probably lie far from actual war experience. If we recall his stammer, his miserable school career and the fact that he was for long regarded as a stupid boy, we may suspect that he went through some inner crisis in his early days and triumphantly overcome his impediments, thus acquiring a taste for such exultant endeavours that has never left him. In any case, the exercise of courage, fortitude and endurance has always been to him a pleasurable activity, not a painful duty or penance.

Churchill's vitality and courage are superhuman, and inspire feelings of awestruck admiration. But it is his rich admixture of warmly human virtues and failings that change admiration into love. He has a brilliant and sympathetic sense of humour and boundless generosity; the most complete freedom from cruelty and malice; and a quickness to forgive and general readiness of the emotions that have made him the most devoted of husbands, the most long-suffering of parents, and the ideal of a friend and comrade.

With these virtues go his almost equally lovable, or equally amusing, frailties. He sometimes seems unable to lose gracefully, becoming involved in undignified arguments; he is capable of cynicism and of recklessness, and has a cosy tolerance of friends with these defects; he shows the broad contempt for discretion of a seventeenth century cavalier, a whiff of the capacity for misjudgment of an eighteenth century Jacobite, and a trace of the pushfulness of a nineteenth century American go-getter.

Withal he has a ready wit, an honesty of nature, a full-blooded good conscience and an indulgent self-enjoyment that bring to mind certain characters of Shakespeare – Mercutio, for instance, and even Sir John Falstaff. All this, added to the great and serious facts of Churchill's career, explains why he has, even in his lifetime, become a hero of popular legend, the central figure of a thousand anecdotes, and the inspiration of an adjective, Churchillian. Whatever his place in history, his place in folklore is secure. It is safe to say that in a thousand years from now his name will be popularly known; it will surely conjure up a warm glow, a proud smile, and signify what is most bold and generous in human nature.

But in the meantime, this great man is now entrusted, by the narrowest margin of votes, with the sober business of directing British policy at a highly difficult and delicate moment in our fortunes and, indeed, in the fortunes of humanity. He is today sailing for inevitably important talks with the American president. And we are confronted with the strange fact that it is hard to guess even the gist of what he will be asking in our name, that it is harder to sense even the general trend of his policy on key questions than it would be that of less illustrious figures, such as Mr Attlee or Mr Eden.

To think that Mr Churchill may seek war is, of course, sheer stupidity: no sane

British statesman could today do that. It is also a gross underestimate of Churchill's artistry in the shaping of his own life: he would not aim at a mere repetition of past glory for his final climax. He has himself said with considerable emphasis that he seeks nothing less than a settled peace as his 'last prize'. But there are several widely divergent ways of seeking that aim, and no indication which he may choose. It only seems 'safe to predict' that the course he will steer will be neither safe nor predictable.

Any consideration of Mr Churchill's career as a whole brings one up against the extraordinary fact that, for all its majestic scope, it remains to this day tragically unfulfilled and fragmentary. His political role has certainly not been meteoric and disastrous, like Napoleon's or Hitler's. But neither has it been linked to a definite achievement, like Richelieu's or Chatham's, Washington's or Lincoln's, Bismarck's or Lenin's. So far, he leaves no completed work, for even the war he won has not been ended. He leaves glory, tragedy and unfinished business.

In history, as opposed to legend, Mr Churchill's reputation will probably depend on his ability during his remaining lifetime to bring some kind of provisional order and stability out of the chaos and unsettlement left by the Second World War, and he is probably aware of this. That supreme moment in 1940, when he staked the existence of Britain on the undoing of Hitler's overwhelming conquest of Europe, made the Second World War in a peculiar sense his war. It is his tragedy that his influence on the political and military conduct of the war diminished with its progress, that from about the middle of 1943 onwards he lost practically every round in the Allied war councils and saw his every proposal turned down, until in the end the Allied victory, by bringing Russia half-way across Europe, concealed a heavy British defeat. Churchill can plead with justification that he, in contrast to Roosevelt, foresaw that such an outcome would in effect mean a defeat – which turned out to be also an American defeat; that this outcome would have been avoided had the policy and strategy which he passionately advocated been accepted in the Allied war councils; and that in this sense the responsibility for the present tragic situation is not his. But it is doubtful whether in his heart of hearts he would feel satisfied with such an exculpation. The question is whether he learned how to exert the maximum influence that his (and our) position could command. He himself has remarked that in the First World War, during the Gallipoli episode, he learned by bitter experience that one cannot shape grand strategy from a subordinate position. He had then been First Lord of the Admiralty. In the Second World War he was British prime minister, but as such he was again in a somewhat inferior position from the moment that the war became an Allied, and therefore primarily an American, war. Unfortunately, he lost his influence with President Roosevelt, who was bent on establishing an American–Russian entente and felt that Churchill was out to disturb this for narrowly-conceived British interests.

This feeling Mr Churchill never managed to dispel; indeed, as far as the published records show, he never tried to; and perhaps he did not do so because he secretly shared it. He could only have convinced Roosevelt of the dangers of his course, if he had argued his case from an entirely different premise – from an Anglo-American or, indeed a frankly American point of view. This he never did. He was content to appear as the upholder of a traditional British balance-of-power policy, which made no appeal to Roosevelt; and this although the idea of a political merging of Britain with America was not alien to his mind, as his Harvard speech of 1943 and again his Fulton speech of 1947 showed.

But Mr Churchill's mind has a peculiar capacity for holding contradictory ideas at the same time. In the years between 1943 and 1945 he entertained at the same time the following conflicting concepts as the aims of his policy: – the establishment of a continuing Anglo-American unity of policy, of a restored balance of power manipulated by Britain, and of a separate Anglo-Russian understanding; and, on a smaller scale, the concepts of a United Europe capable of checking Russia (and therefore presumably including Germany), and that of a totally disarmed and dismembered Germany. To consider all these possibilities, before discarding any, shows admirable flexibility of mind, but to follow them all up simultaneously, or waver between them undecidedly, was inevitably self-defeating.

Mr Churchill's early post-war speeches – especially those at Fulton and Zurich, which may come to be regarded as the most statesmanlike he ever made – show that he felt his responsibilty for the 1945 disaster keenly and was trying his hardest to help undo its consequences. He has, in general, shown a greater single-mindedness and clarity of political vision out of office than in it.

Indeed his speeches since he has been returned to power have shown the same tendencies that contributed to his frustration in the years 1943–5: the tendency to try to make a grand world strategy from a secondary and pseudo-independent power position (instead of aiming to gain the greater leverage of commitment to a permanent partnership with one great power or even with a group of secondary powers); and the tendency to hope that a grand solution would come out of a tangle of contradictory policies, like a rabbit out of a magician's hat. It is hard to see how this approach can be more successful in 1952 than it was in 1943–5.

Yet today most of the same, incompatible conceptions make their appearance again in various parts of a single Churchill speech: the need for American world-leadership based on Anglo-American unity; and the conflicting idea of British independence in world affairs; the idea of a peaceful division of the world with Russia; and the conflicting idea of a European unity that might include Eastern Europe; the primacy of the Commonwealth and Empire in British policy, and the contradictory assertion of an equal importance attaching to Britain's relations with both America and Europe.

Perhaps Mr Churchill's greatest handicap today is his deep understanding of British policy in the eighteenth and nineteenth centuries. Yet there are times when he seems to be explaining to us that any continuation of the traditional British policy of being a 'balancing' power has become fatally risky, that even an attempt to maintain one or more areas of exclusive British influence has become increasingly obsolescent. He has often appeared to realise more clearly than his contemporaries that this is an age of Super-Great-Powers, and that we are likely to see an embryonic system of world government formed around one or other of these giants – and has appeared about to recommend his countrymen and their neighbours wholeheartedly to think and act accordingly.

Whatever may be the comparative importance of tradition, historical knowledge and modern observation in Mr Churchill's great mind, it seems clear from his speeches that a dominant theme of his thought is a mistrust of the irrevocable political commitment. He has made bigger and bolder military decisions than any statesman of our age; but in the field of politics, he hesitates to close any door finally. Masterly indecision in ultimate policy aims may well be the peculiar blight which has kept Mr Churchill's statesmanship until now so curiously barren of great results.

Yet if anyone is in time of peace to lift this country's policy out of its historic course – so that we join in the revolutionary process of founding a new political unit capable first of defending Western civilisation and then of guaranteeing the peace of the whole world – he will need not only clarity of vision and political decisiveness. He will also need the special Churchillian qualities of vitality and courage. It is conceivable that those very qualities might yet transform the story of Winston Churchill's statecraft. It may yet be said that his final achievement was on as grand a scale as the epic endeavour by which he kept freedom alive in 1940. He might, in 1952, make the titanic wrench with the past needed to lay the foundation of a system of established world peace.

HAROLD MACMILLAN

8 June 1958

The inscrutable British Prime Minister who is this week practising one of his favourite skills – the art of maintaining Anglo-American relations – holds a very different position from when he last visited President Eisenhower, nine months ago.

It is true that his political party is in a nervous condition, and the President can have no great confidence that he will be dealing with the same man in a year's

time. But in the past year the British attitude to the Prime Minister, in Parliament if not among the public, has undergone a considerable transformation. From being an emergency pilot, he finds himself now well established in command, and even on the way to becoming the Tories' father-figure.

Mr Macmillan himself may not be surprised at this change, for he does not lack self-confidence; but the rest of his partly certainly is. Harold Macmillan has, indeed, often surprised people, and may yet again. There was even a time when some supercilious fellow-Tories used to refer to him as the Walter Mitty of the party, dreaming elder statesman dreams.

Part of his capacity to surprise is due, of course, to his appearance. The drooping face, the hooded eyes, the overhanging moustache, the Edwardian clothes and the tired cadences, have all, with the help of cartoonists, contributed to the popular picture of a haughty, old-fashioned fuddy-duddy.

The picture is misleading. He is, by general consent, one of the most intelligent British prime ministers of this century, combining academic ingenuity with quick practical skill. He is also, for a man of pre-1914 upbringing, startlingly up to date; he thrives on a changing world, is enthralled by science and talks cheerfully about the vanished age of Victorian stability, and the excitements of modern Britain, living 'on the verge of bankruptcy'.

Behind his proud appearance there is another surprise: he is acutely shy. Nervous and pompous in a large crowd, fidgety and sometimes rude in a small one, he is only really at home in the professional, forensic atmosphere of the House, or in a small company of friends, where his subtle disengaged humour quickly flowers.

Even his elaborate club life (he belongs to seven, including those exclusive rivals, The Club and The Other Club) is deceptive. He has never been 'one of the boys', and has always been inclined to prefer books to people. MPs remember with embarrassment how at one time, just after the war, he tried to overcome his diffidence by hearty approaches in the House of Commons smoking-room. He uses clubs not for relaxation, but for argument and stimulus, and for taking his party's pulse.

Even his patrician bearing, and his marriage to a Duke's daughter, are not quite what they seem. Though he shoots with the Duke of Devonshire, he has never become an integral part of the higher aristocracy. At Eton he was that peculiar bird, a King's Scholar or tug. In the Grenadiers, he was notorious for having read Aeschylus while wounded in a shell-hole. At Balliol, he worked hard and took a first in Mods.

In one important respect his appearance is not misleading: he is as detached as he looks. Not since Baldwin has Number Ten been bathed in such relaxing balm. 'Calm, cool deliberation solves all problems,' says a notice in the Prime Minister's hand, stuck up in one of the secretary's rooms. It has come as a welcome therapy afer the tenseness of Eden.

The unruffled comments about 'little local difficulties' had no doubt an element of pose, but they are very much part of his habit of looking at the world, as it were, through the window of a book-lined study. He is the most donnish man in the Cabinet: he reads, as he likes to tell people, an hour every night – Trollope, Homer, Virgil or history.

In the six weeks after he returned from Australia he read fourteen volumes of Froude's *History of England*. There are some who suspect that he views the week's crises as just one more page of Froude.

Much of the secret of his detachment lies in his firm family life: the picture of his crofter-grandfather's cottage, which he has taken with him from Ministry to Ministry, sums up his loyalty. He loves to talk about the 'old-fashioned virtues' of the family. His long weekends in his house at Chelwood Gate, surrounded by 2,000 rich Sussex acres, and with grandchildren all round him, have given him a calm escape from the anxieties of Westminster.

It is not easy to uncover, behind his Edwardian mask and his real detachment, the political motives of Macmillan. But clues can be picked up from the four most significant stages of his career.

The first was his time as a Tory rebel when, returning from serving bravely in the First World War, he was appalled by the squalor and misery of his first constituency, Stockton. His sixteen Conservative relations (through his wife) in the House did not noticeably influence him towards orthodoxy. He was one of the most outspoken of the young Tories, nicknamed the 'YMCA', who sharply attacked the 'second-class brewers and company promoters' (as he called them) in his party's hierarchy.

His record in those years, on both home and foreign affairs, was unusually impressive. On the issue of unemployment, he went so far as to have secret discussions with Labour leaders, and with Oswald Moseley, about the crisis, and wrote a provocative book, *The Middle Way*, about social reform.

He denounced the appeasement of Hitler and Mussolini from the start, crossing swords, among many others, with Mr R. A. Butler and Mr Quintin Hogg (now Lord Hailsham). Alone among the Tory rebels, he took the brave step of actually refusing the whip. His colleagues saw him as a clever young publisher, too idealistic to succeed in politics.

His second great turning point was Algiers, to which he was sent as Minister Resident by Churchill in 1942. His relationship with 'the Old Man' was one of mutual respect, though he was never in Churchill's closest circle. They were both courageous Tory rebels (both with American mothers), both with independent views and a strong sense of history.) Churchill was apt to see history as a challenge, a proof of the grandeur of the present. Macmillan, more of a pessimist and more of a scholar, saw history as a lesson in calm, a placid water into which the choppy present would soon pass.

Algiers marked the beginning of the transformation of a politician into a statesman. With Eisenhower and de Gaulle, it was a preliminary summit, and Macmillan realised with some excitement that he was 'in the big stuff'. His maturity and intellectual agility were just the qualities needed for his delicate diplomatic role; he handled the difficult problem of de Gaulle, who uneasily succeeded Giraud, with dexterity and modesty. Most important, he learnt the vital importance of Britain's friendship with America; he saw Britain's role in the war pass from senior partner, to equal partner, to junior partner.

'Never forget,' he told British officers in a pep-talk, after there had been signs of resentment against Americans, 'that we are the Greeks in their Roman Empire. It is our job to change their minds without them realising it.' He earned Eisenhower's gratitude for his unspikiness, his brains and his courage. Algiers moulded his post-war attitudes; just after the war, long before most Tories had faced the thought, he was boldly discussing Britain's role as a second-class power.

But it was not until Churchill gave him his second break, in 1951, that he showed his abilities as an administrator. Though at first he jibbed at being away from foreign affairs, he enjoyed being Minister of Housing more than any other job: 'Just like publishing: I had a job to do, and I did it,' he has said. His 300,000 houses were more than an administrative victory. His eloquence about the importance of houses was sincere: he had firm ideas about the moral importance of stable family life.

Two things emerged during his time in office; the first was his popularity in the ministries which he ran – Housing, Foreign Office (the least successful) and Treasury – where he presided with calm efficiency, and made witty Latin jokes in the margins of documents. (*Hock et praeterea nihil*, he cabled recently to the Foreign Office, when he decided to call on Lim Yew Hock at Singapore.)

The second was the disharmony between him and Eden, which became much more marked when Sir Anthony became Prime Minister. Partly, no doubt, it was a simple matter of ambition: nobody reaches No. 10 altogether by accident. But there was also a fundamental difference of character or personality between the two; the sturdier, more self-disciplined Macmillan became impatient of Eden's nervous involvement and of his moody outbursts.

How, then, can we explain the great enigma of Macmillan's career, his part in the Suez affair? And how would Macmillan, so mindful of history, expect it to be written? There can be no question of his responsibility: he was not actually Foreign Secretary at the time, it is true. But he was fully with Eden, even at one point in front of him, in urging the use of force against Nasser. Eden would not have pressed on with his policy had he not had the support of Macmillan, who by how had the right-wing following which Eden lacked.

How in particular could Macmillan, so aware of being a Greek in a Roman Empire, countenance an action which was deliberately kept secret from the Americans, and must surely endanger the Western alliance?

Those close to Macmillan say that, although the Suez plans were kept from the Americans, he (with Eden and Lloyd) believed that Dulles would accept a *fait accompli*: but this could hardly explain the other major misjudgments of Britain's role (which Macmillan now in private seems to acknowledge). Perhaps Macmillan, like Eden, mistook the expedition against Nasser for defiance of a Hitler.

The most likely explanation may be that Macmillan, in the fascination of the diplomatic chess-game, lost sight of the implications, both practical and moral. Upright and religious though he is, it must not be forgotten that his favourite prime minister is Disraeli.

Whatever his role at the time of Suez, his performance since has been astonishing. It seemed only by chance that he, and not Butler, succeeded Eden; but in the last eighteen months he has behaved as if built for the part. The fact that he took over when his party was on the rocks (he himself made no secret of his pessimism) added to his prestige when he succeeded in salvaging it.

His proud Tory look has made it easier for him to perform the tricky navigational task of pointing to the Right, and steering to the Left. As his fellow officers realised which way the ship was going, some of them, like Salisbury and Thorneycroft, stumped off the bridge. But by choosing his crew with ingenuity (Edward Boyle on the Left, Julian Amery on the Right) he avoided mutiny, even though the ship has had a shockingly rough passage.

Now sixty-eight, with a very broad experience behind him, he has developed curiously late; and his Commonwealth tour early this year showed that he is still growing. He was observed to have gained a new confidence as the tour went on; it was as though the blighting presence of Churchill and Eden, who had both outshone him in the public eye, was being forgotten in this new pioneering adventure.

Since that tour, he has not only appeared more aware of the 'floating voters' of the Commonwealth, who were so ruthlessly ignored at the time of Suez. He has also begun to emerge at last as a public personality at home – through television, an instrument of political education of which he is unexpectedly fond.

He is by no means the perfect Prime Minister; with his odd aloofness, and his intellectual arrogance, he is more respected than loved; and in his fascination with manoeuvres, and his strict ideas of loyalty, he is apt to land himself with unsatisfactory appointments (e.g. Hailsham, Lloyd).

But he has great strengths. He has courage, toughness, sensitivity and a first-class original mind. He inspires confidences and has none of the vindictiveness and bias that marks some more emotional leaders. In the present condition of his party, lying uneasily between uninspiring administrators and unrealistic adventurers, he has succeeded in providing a dignified compromise: who could have done better?

This week, at a time when the Western alliance is once more in danger, he will no doubt appear again in the role of the good Anglo-American, the man with no illusions about the limits of Britain's greatness and with no chips on his shoulder – a welcome contrast to de Gaulle.

It may be that since Suez he has taught not only himself, but his party, the importance of realism and restraint in world affairs: certainly in his Commonwealth tour he avoided, to an impressive degree, any impression of British tub-thumping.

If so, he may well go down in the history books as the man who, after a spasm of wildness, succeeded in reassuring the Tory Party, and bringing it to terms with the post-war world of Nehru, Nasser and Cousins.

ENOCH POWELL

5 February 1961

Since Powell was appointed Health Minister last July, no one has been in much doubt that this potential iron man of the Tories would be prepared to take strong measures if he honestly thought they were necessary. That he *does* think, now, that they are necessary is accepted even by the cynics.

Last week's measures mean a shift away from direct and towards indirect taxation – an idea which is widely supported by the right wing of the Tory Party. But to assume that Powell is their mouthpiece would be wrong, just as it would be wrong to see him as the doctrinaire butcher of the Health Services – it is only a week or so since he announced increased spending on hospitals. Powell is an honest man, who will act in any situation as he thinks best.

For a long time Powell's critics have been saying how extraordinary it is that a man who could have risen to somewhere near the top as proconsul, staff officer, civil servant or academic should have chosen politics, the one career which seemed certain to defeat him. For the outstanding thing about Powell has been that he is not a politician, which means, quite honourably, a compromiser.

A teetotaller except for an occasional glass of sherry, a non-smoker, with an intense white face and very pale blue eyes, Powell's intellectual austerity has been such that he has come to represent a kind of metaphorical hair-shirt for Conservatives, the sort of man to whom they felt they could turn if things went disastrously wrong for the rootless expediences of Macmillan's neo-liberalism.

Three times Powell has either refused office or resigned from it on a point of principle. In becoming MP for South-West Wolverhampton with a tenuous majority in 1950 – the twentieth candidature he tried for – one of his first acts was to have a row with the bigwigs of his local Conservative Association. Within a few months of entering Parliament, he had defied a three-line whip on the Schuman Plan.

He went on record against higher pay for MPs, against housing subsidies, against life peerages as offending against the hereditary principle, against abandonment of the Canal Zone base, against the Queen's compromise title as Head of the Commonwealth – she was, in Powell's eyes, Queen, and that was that.

As Parliamentary Secretary at the Ministry of Housing he was credited with responsibility for the more unpopular austerities of the Rent Act. In July 1959 his passionate protest over the Hola outrages won him increased respect – but for a man who had fairly recently resigned from the Government, was this, asked MPs, really the way to work his passage back into office? 'Ah, Enoch,' those in the know said. 'A brilliant brain, of course. What a pity he's not a politician.'

It would still be a wrong assessment of Powell to assume that he was brought back because he is prepared to be a good boy and forget those inconvenient principles of his. But there are at least three Powells, of whom the politician is certainly one. He himself says, with characteristic lucidity and honesty, that he took to politics partly because he is ambitious for rank and office but mainly because he rejoices in the despatch of business. 'I think that's quite a good phrase for describing it – I love to see business done.' He seems to smack his lips at the idea.

Another side, though increasingly overlaid by the politician, is the boy who wanted to be a musician, but found that he couldn't become a full-time one, sold his clarinet and has never played a note again; the romantic poet who has published three books of verse, the last in 1951, shortly after he became an MP, and whose manner – gentle, courteous, almost shy – comes as a shock to those who know only his fire-eating political reputation.

Finally, there is the ferocious pedant, the ferret-like hunter of facts, a terror to his civil servants and, in one of his previous careers, a noted textual critic and translator of Herodotus.

It is the ferret-like Powell that some Conservative MPs would like to see let loose one day on the Ministry of Defence, that rabbit-warren of technical jargon and security mumbo-jumbo likely to baffle anyone with less than Powell's determination. Others have hailed him as the only MP (including the Chancellor of the Exchequer) who understood the technicalities of the 1960 Finance Bill; if it had been left to a free vote of the Parliamentary Party, he would probably have succeeded Heathcoat Amory last July.

Powell seems to have been born a Tory. Taken round Caernarvon Castle at the age of six, he removed his cap on entering one of the rooms. His father, a Lloyd George Radical, asked him why, and the young Enoch answered quite unselfconsciously that it was the room in which the first Prince of Wales was born.

He has never known the deeper kind of social discontent which makes a reformer, and is happiest among the ordered forms of any established institution – university, army, Conservative Party, House of Commons. The veneration he has for them doesn't blind him to their inefficiencies, but, rather, adds a righteous indignation to his determination to keep them up to the mark.

Powell was born at Stechford, in Birmingham, educated through scholarships at Birmingham schools, and still has a Midlands grittiness which fits incongruously into Macmillan's Government of dukes, earls and Old Etonians. But his ancestry on both sides is Welsh. His mother came from a line of border yeomen, his father was the fourth-generation descendant of Welsh emigrants to Staffordshire.

It was his mother, the daughter of a Liverpool policeman, who influenced him more – his father, says Powell, was a gentleman, an unenquiring, easy-going man, who could never understand why people wanted to make trouble for themselves by pushing things too far. His mother was not like that, and neither is he. 'We fight, we are not gentlemen.' It was his mother, largely self-educated, who taught Enoch Greek when, at King Edward's School in Birmingham, he transferred late from science to the classics.

Both parents were teachers, and met and married while teaching in Birmingham elementary schools. Powell himself, after a scholarship to Trinity College, Cambridge, and two years there as a Fellow, became Professor of Greek at Sydney University – said to be the youngest in the Commonwealth – and was, according to old pupils, a gifted teacher.

Both in private conversation and while addressing the Commons, he still tends to lecture, as if explaining complicated matters to an undergraduate audience – he has been accused, in fact, of being lucid to the point of incomprehensibility. Partly this is intellectual arrogance, to which he admits, but it is also caused by his intense desire to explain, to educate, which makes him an excellent pamphleteer and a favourite speaker among the more intelligent young Conservatives.

Heretics have occasionally questioned whether he is quite such an intellectual as he, and Conservative MPs in general, believe, and it is probable that among the over-fertile intellectual ranks of the Labour Party, he wouldn't stand out with quite such sharp distinction. He has something of the self-made intellectual's compulsive need to impress with his cleverness which Aneurin Bevan also had in marked degree. Powell, like Bevan, is inclined to drop into his talk asides which are calculated to shock: 'When I was learning a language a year for the fun of it' – he claims to be able to read, though not to speak, twelve languages.

There is no doubt that if he had not gone into politics, he would have been in the running for the Regius Professorship of Greek at Cambridge; and his work on Herodotus – most of it done before he was 30 – is respected by scholars. The same can't be said of his verse, which jogs along some way after Housman, Masefield and Edward Thomas.

Powell's entry into politics was characteristically unconventional. Early in 1940 he was due to take up the professorship of Greek at Durham University. When war broke out he abandoned both that and the Australian chair, and came home to join up as a private in the Royal Warwickshire Regiment. He quickly became a brilliant if somewhat unusual staff officer, and eventually found himself in India at the age of 32 as a brigadier, general staff.

India – the wonder of the British imposition of order on that untidy subcontinent – had a lasting effect on him. He says that if he had gone a century earlier, he would have left his bones there; and he would probably have made an admirable provincial governor. As it was he took note of Burke's words on the trial of Warren Hastings – 'The keys of India are not in Calcutta, they are not in Delhi, they are in this House' – and set out for home and Parliament.'

Arriving in England, the obvious step seemed to be to ring up the Conservative Central Office, where he knew no one, and demand to speak to the chairman. He failed to get him, but made enough impact to be taken on the staff of the parliamentary secretariat and later the Conservative Research Department. There, his intensity is said to have reduced successive secretaries to nervous breakdowns; he married the one who survived.

He also had a hand in the great Conservative post-war re-furbish, did a lot of work with that equally devout Tory Angus Maude on the pamphlet *One Nation*, and eventually arrived in the Commons in 1950 among the batch of bright young men – Macleod, Maudling, Heath – which still seems certain to produce a prime minister.

This is unlikely to be Powell, who is too much outside the refashioned Conservative image to reach Number 10, though he may well, if he doesn't resign once too often, get to Number 11. Of the famous resignation, that from the Treasury in 1958 over economic policy, it has been said that Powell was the man who put backbone into the more pliant Thorneycroft. What in fact happened was that each of the Treasury trio – Thorneycroft, the Chancellor, Nigel Birch, the Economic Secretary, and Powell, the Financial Secretary – had made his own independent assessment of the situation, and come to roughly the same conclusions.

On the decisive morning Powell took his paper to Thorneycroft, to be greeted with the words: 'I'm going, but that doesn't mean you have to.' Powell had no hesitation in backing Thorneycroft, but it is probable that, while Birch would have resigned anyway, Powell would have stayed with Thorneycroft if the latter had decided to remain Chancellor.

Resignations at moments embarrassing for a government are not lightly forgiven. On the other hand, it is the principles, as much as the intellectual brilliance, which have won him Conservative respect. He may well be rememberd as one of those politicians whose merits rather than defects come between them and the top.

JEREMY THORPE

27 September 1970

Last July, in Westminster Abbey, Jeremy Thorpe walked down the aisle with the Prime Minister on one side of him and Harold Wilson on the other. They were at a ceremony to unveil a memorial to David Lloyd George. Thorpe delivered the panegyric. He was the Liberal Leader, after all, and, unlike Heath and Wilson, he had known Lloyd George. Visits to Criccieth are among his childhood memories.

The historical thread depends on a purely personal link; Lloyd George's gifted daughter, Megan, was his mother's best friend and bridesmaid. But it has given him a deep devotion to his Liberal heroes. He must be the only Liberal of his generation – he is still only 41 – with direct experience of the great figures of the Liberal decline. Samuel, Layton, Sinclair, Isaac Foot. His comfortable mansion flat in Westminster is filled with Beerbohm cartoons of Campbell-Bannerman's front bench colleagues. And you can sometimes surprise him in his room at the House of Commons admiring some presentation silver salver for which he has triumphantly secured the signature, say, of the only surviving Liberal MP from the 1923 Parliament.

This vein of nostalgic ancestor-worship cuts no ice whatever with the new waves of young Liberals, for whom the past is nothing and social action means immeasurably more than parliamentary or party politics. Jeremy Thorpe is a dedicated parliamentarian and a tough, highly professional politician in a way that his predecessor, Jo Grimmond, was not and could never have been. (But then nor has he Grimond's gift for original, if occasionally woolly, ideas.) He is a politician's politician. He deals in facts and arguments and precedents, and revels in the cut and thrust of debate. This is what made his position at Eastbourne last week so poignantly paradoxical.

There he was leading a once-great party now reduced, as in the 1950s, to a rump of half a dozen MPs. Single-handed, before the election, he had rescued its finances from the brink of banruptcy. He gets 15,000 letters a year, employs three secretaries and has two personal assistants. And all his professionalism is at the service of a raggle-taggle army of amateurs with increasingly little idea of where it wants to go and how it means to get there.

He could be forgiven if he sometimes wondered how much longer the game was going to be worth the candle. In his time, he has said, he has been offered opportunities by both the major parties, and he would not deny that the sight of some of their front-benchers, whose gifts are manifestly inferior to his own, occasionally gives him cause to think. Yet he has never been tempted to cross the floor. None of his colleagues has invested so much emotional capital in the Liberal Party.

The personal tragedy that overcame him after the election, when his wife, Caroline, whose dignity and charm had made her widely loved in their two short years of marriage, was killed in a road accident, must have temporarily heightened the strain, the element of unreality in his position as the Liberal leader. For a time, very naturally, the savour has gone out of politics. He will need more than ordinary courage and patience to rebuild his personal and political life.

Both his father and his grandfather were Tory MPs, but his devotion to the Liberal Party, though it was always had a strongly anti-Tory bias, is not a reaction to their influence. He never knew his grandfather. And he never discussed politics with his father whom he adored and who, anyway, in his later years, after Jeremy was born, devoted himself exclusively to the parliamentary bar.

In the war, like others of his class and age-group, he was shipped to America where he certainly reacted against the strong Republicanism of his American cousins. (He was a Roosevelt Democrat before he was a Liberal.) Back home again, at Eton, he gave most of his spare time to music, playing the violin and nursing his taste for Bach and Beethoven. Politics had to wait for Oxford, where he flung himself into the whirl of sociable clubs, dinners and elections, becoming in turn President of the Liberal Club, the Law Society and the Union.

Already he was a natural orator with a grand dramatic manner and a brilliant gift for mimickry, a little showy for the prudish – with his brown bowler and his buttonholes – a little tiring for the conventional with his taste for horseplay and his panache. But what immense fun and fizz! And, what was less noticed, perhaps at the time, what effort and energy he devoted to achieving the successes he sought!

This was the nadir of the Liberal Party's fortunes. In the 1951 election, it had fought only 100 seats and won fewer than a million votes. Candidatures were going begging. Before Jeremy took his law finals at Oxford in 1952 he had been offered North Devon, his present seat, on a plate. But he wanted to wait until he had made his way at the Bar. He promised that if he were tempted by other approaches he would give them the first refusal. Soon afterwards in the same week, two other constituencies in the west country later to become Liberal seats, North Cornwall and Torrington, asked him to be their candidate. So he went to North Devon, fought it and lost in 1955, fought it again and won in 1959. The day after that victory 10,000 people packed the covered market in Barnstaple for a rally and torchlight procession.

He is idolised there. His unusual histrionic gifts – old-fashioned in an increasingly conversational age – are ideally suited to the large open-air meetings that are still common in an area without too many other entertainments to distract people. His exotic, joker-ish persona persists, but it conceals fibre and character unsuspected by the casual observer.

Throughout the 1950s he combined law with television. His practice at the Bar, though never extensive, helped him to discipline his speaking, cutting down the flamboyance but improving the argument. His effectiveness on television is one of the Liberals' more important assets.

Words are important to a politician, but not all-important. The Liberal Party offers many opportunities for their use. Indeed, it offers little else. Jeremy Thorpe, who was the obvious choice for the leadership when Jo Grimond retired in 1967, is certainly a big fish in a pond that is now growing smaller and more turbulent. He has the capacity to be more than that. Whether he will ever have the chance depends partly on him, partly on his party and partly, perhaps, on the developments in British politics as the country moves towards the Common Market with all the strains and upheaval that that may cause.

DAVID OWEN

14 February 1982

Kensington Town Hall offers a fairly sedate setting for political drama. Nor is there anything especially exciting about the vision of some 300 people dutifully dealing with resolutions on, and amendments to, a party constitution that already exists in draft.

But, of course, everyone knows that what will dominate the SDP's first constitutional convention this weekend is not any minor matter of what does, or does not, ultimately appear in 'line 1, clause 2' but rather the power struggle that lies behind the whole constitutional debate. At the centre of the power struggle is the youngest member of 'the Gang of Four' – Dr David Owen, already at 43 almost as controversial a figure among the Social Democrats as he was once within the Labour Party.

True, he himself is getting a bit tired of that 'controversial' label – and especially of the way it has affixed itself to him (even within the SDP) as a result of his declared intention to run against Roy Jenkins for the leadership. David Owen is particularly resentful of the charge that his decision is to be explained in terms of personal ambition: 'Hell,' he says, 'if I was really ambitious, given how young I am, I wouldn't even be contemplating challenging Roy.'

Why, then, should he not merely be ready but apparently eager to take on the challenge? In the first place there can be no doubt that Owen really does believe –

it was, after all, the issue that finally led him to leave the Labour Party – in the 'one member, one vote' formula that the SDP Convention will be asked to adopt this morning in preference to the more oligarchic recommendation of the party's steering committee. And, like Tony Benn, he maintains that there is no point in having a new piece of machinery if you then shrink from testing it. (Revealingly, he freely confesses that he will not be contesting the leadership at all if the official recommendation favouring the parliamentary party goes through.)

More significantly, however, Owen does increasingly seem to see himself as the custodian of the SDP's radical conscience, even to the point of being the person who keeps Shirley Williams up to the mark. Admittedly, he went along with the majority decision to back Norman Tebbit's trade union Bill last Monday, but he remains unrepentantly convinced that the SDP will be doomed if it ends up by merely bringing about 'some rearrangement of the Right' in British politics. He still retains all the reforming zeal of a socialist (even the title of his book published last year, *Face the Future*, was derived from Labour's 1945 election slogan); and his disenchantment with the Foot Labour Party came about, he claims, as much through his irritation with its inherent conservatism as anything else.

It is symbolic perhaps that the most famous phrase he has given to the vocabulary of British politics should be the one about 'nudge and fudge, slush and mush' – for even in his Labour Party days he tended to display an impatience and impetuousity more frequently associated with the Left rather than the Right.

On the other hand, ideologically he has always travelled pretty light. Too young to play any part in the Gaitskellite wars of the 1950s and early 1960s he was never marked by the scars of CDS, CND or even Clause IV. If he embodied anything in his fifteen years as a Labour MP, it was perhaps a rather old-fashioned strain of idealistic middle-class socialism founded in Christianity.

Certainly that was the nature of his background. When he was appointed Foreign Secretary at the age of 38 in February 1977 ('the Young Lochinvar' as James Callaghan then called him), there were complaints, not least from trade unionists, that he had 'no roots in the movement'. In the narrow sense at least, his critics had a case. The son of a doctor and the grandson of a Church of Wales clergyman, there was only one hint of a political influence in his family's history – his dentist mother's membership (as an Independent) in the 1950s of the Devon County Council.

Owen had the classic middle-class upbringing – private preparatory school, where he did well, followed by Bradfield College in Berkshire, where he was relatively undistinguished. Even when he went up to Cambridge to read medicine he played no part at all in politics ('I joined the Union on my first day there, went to one debate and found it so awful and mannered that I never went again'). He did, however, come under the influence of Mervyn Stockwood, then Vicar of Great St Mary's (it was Stockwood who, on hearing that he proposed to stand for Parliament in 1964, unkindly enquired 'Which party?').

It was not, in fact, until he went as a medical student to St Thomas's that he actually joined the Labour Party – as a result, he recalls, of hearing Hugh Gaitskell talk disparagingly about 'armchair socialists' and suddenly realising that he was one of them. After that, however, preferment came miraculously quickly. At the age of 26 he was a parliamentary candidate, at 27 an MP, at 30 a junior minister, at 38 a senior member of the Cabinet.

Promotion like that necessarily arouses jealousies – and it is not perhaps surprising that the adjective most often applied to Owen is 'arrogant'. Even the arrogance, however, has its attractive side. As a government backbencher he joined in 1967 with Professor David Marquand (also now of the SDP) and the late John Mackintosh in producing a pamphlet criticising the Wilson Government's economic policy – a pamphlet that sufficiently infuriated Harold Wilson for him to let it be known that none of its three authors need look forward to ever holding office in any government of which he was in charge.

Shortly afterwards Owen happened to find himself in a Commons lift with the then Prime Minister. 'If you have any criticisms of me in future,' the 29-year-old Owen took it upon himself to remark, 'I'll thank you to make them to my face rather than behind my back.' Whether Harold Wilson simply admired his courage – or, cynically, recognised the need to neutralise a potential enemy – we may never know: the fact remains that within twelve months Owen was the youngest member of the Wilson government.

From then on it was a career of copy-book political success. Indeed, by 1970, when the first Wilson Government fell, Denis Healey, under whom Owen had served at the Ministry of Defence, was openly speaking of him as a future leader of the Labour Party.

Owen, however, did not initially take to life in Opposition – and, for a short period, even appears to have contemplated returning to his first love, medicine. Instead, however, he took a job with an American computer company (he had married his American wife, Debbie Owen, the literary agent, in 1968) and the next two and a half years, as he ran the European side of the business, saw his first incarnation as 'the Flying Doctor'. He resigned, reluctantly, with Roy Jenkins from the Opposition front bench in April 1972 over Labour's support for a referendum on the Common Market and devoted his energies thereafter to getting his Private Member's Children's Bill of 1973 (the Owens have three children of their own) through the House of Commons.

Never one to underestimate his own worth, Owen was openly offended when all he found himself offered in March 1974, on Labour's return to office, was a Parliamentary Secretaryship at the DHSS. He took it, though – according to his boss, Barbara Castle – with a slightly bad grace. Incongruously , however, the two of them eventually formed a political alliance, even a personal friendship, and Owen did not seek to hide his regret when Jim Callaghan celebrated his accession to Number 10 in April 1976 by sacking Mrs Castle from his Cabinet.

At first Owen was certainly not a beneficiary of the Callaghan succession: he was forced, in fact, to soldier on for six months at the DHSS under a Secretary of State (David Ennels) for whom he felt nothing but an ill-concealed disdain. Even when that autumn other 'young lions' like Roy Hattersley and Bill Rogers were promoted to the Cabinet, Owen, by now a Minister of State at the DHSS, had to be content with a sideways move to being a Minister of State at the Foreign Office.

The consolation of the new job was, however, that it meant working under the late Tony Crosland – who remains even to this day Owen's political hero (in the Labour Right's War of the Roses he always belonged, both by temperament and instinct, to the defeated Crosland side rather than to the victorious Jenkins one). There is no reason to doubt, therefore, that Owen genuinely meant it when he told one of those who wrote to him when he succeeded to the Foreign Secretaryship after Crossland's death, 'I know I can never fill *his* shoes'.

His detractors would, no doubt, say, that the next two-and-a-quarter years merely proved his point for him. As Foreign Secretary, the dimension of his achievement never quite lived up to the energy of his performance. Even if Labour had won the 1979 election, Jim Callaghan was going to move him – to an economic role that might, or might not, have placed him in a subsidiary position to a new Labour Chancellor.

Certainly the Foreign Office – 'those bloody Europeans,' as Owen still refers to them – were mightly relieved to see the back of him. Sir Michael Palliser, the present Permanent Under-Secretary, may look a cool enough customer but even he has been heard to remark, 'No one has ever spoken to me as David Owen did'.

Whitehall of course, has its own ways of redress – and it was not perhaps surprising that the damaging anecdotes soon began to surface. Owen was reputed to have drawn more lavishly on the government stock of official photographs of himself than any other Foreign Secretary in history; he had been through half-a-dozen government drivers before he had even been two years in office; he was a man who thought nothing of sending a private secretary twenty miles to buy a particular favourite sandwich.

Inevitably, some of the mud tended to stick – and in many ways, despite his 'Dr Kildare' good looks, Owen cannot help seeming an uncharacteristic figure to find among the essentially well-mannered Social Democrats (in fact he was not only the first of the original 'Gang of Three' to decide to leave the Labour Party but easily the firmest in his resolve to go). Unlike Bill Rodgers and Shirley Williams he has, however, no long-term bonds tying him to Roy Jenkins, to whom from the beginning he has deliberately gone out of his way to pay no form of obeisance.

'Sometimes I am,' he himself acknowledges, 'perhaps a bit too tough' – and it can hardly have been a coincidence that Denis Healey should have chosen a week ago to dub him as the Social Democrats' 'JR'. But JR does, after all, run the Ewing oil-firm.

It is by no means inconceivable, after the Kiddington Hall Liberal Social Democrat 'summit' last weekend, that even with Roy Jenkins as titular leader of the alliance, David Owen could end up by running the SDP. If he were to do so, at least the electorate would not be in any doubt that what was on offer was a realignment on the Left rather than the Right of British politics. And that, given the continuing tendency towards 'nudge and fudge, slush and mush' within the SDP itself, might even be no bad thing.

ROY JENKINS

28 March 1982

There comes a point in most by-elections when the tide suddenly turns with the candidate who is going to win. The electorate has made up its collective mind, and nothing short of a scandal involving boy scouts and rubberwear will change it.

This moment came for Roy Jenkins in Hillhead about ten days ago. An old campaigner, he sensed it almost immediately. People seemed friendlier, more relaxed; as he outlined his policies in that orotund and wordy manner of his, they nodded in agreement rather than quibbling. Voters who a fortnight ago had muttered mild insults as they passed by were indulging in what Jenkins chose to term 'responsive waving'.

A canvasser from one of the other parties detected this shift a week or so ago when he spoke to a woman who had made up her mind to vote for Jenkins. He asked her why. 'Because I've always been against the Common Market,' she said. But, the astonished party worker said, Jenkins was the ultimate pro-European. He had even been president of the European Commission, 'Aye' the voter replied, 'but he packed it in!'

Jenkins's triumph is very much his own. Lots of people, including David Steel and Shirley Williams, advised him not to stand in Hillhead. Scotland, they said, was not interested in the SDP. The middle-class vote in Scotland would stay doggedly loyal to the Tories. The protest vote, such as it was, would go to the Nationalists. Even if he won, he would face the draining chore of flying 400 miles every week to a demanding constituency, while being, quite probably, leader of his own party. For a long time it looked as if the pessimists had been right and

Jenkins might end up like a beached whale, stuck outside Parliament and too proud or too tired to fight again.

Because it was a personal decision to stand, his success adds the more to his personal political lustre. He is, for instance, a first-rate campaigner. The jokes about his claret drinking (he does drink a lot of fine wine, with a slight preference for burgundy) and his pompous manner are almost always made by his sworn opponents; they don't seem to offend the ordinary floating voter one whit.

Indeed, his very ponderousness can be an advantage; whereas other candidates tend to leap about, with a swift handshake here, a sharp 'glad to meet you' there and then a rapid escape, Jenkins gives every casual enquiry the weight that he would on TV, being interviewed by Sir Robin Day. 'Would he support such and such a measure?' 'I would not be disposed to go against it,' he replied, choosing his words rather as he would if a Hansard writer were at his elbow. He doesn't suggest anything, but 'postulates'. He doesn't agree with someone, but 'holds the proposition to be true'. There's no reason to think that the voters find this ludicrous or patronising, as the Labour Party seems to think they ought.

Talking about Hillhead itself, he declared – often – that 'if its qualities, its social mix, its architecture, its achievements in medicine and science, did not *seize* my imagination, I would not want to be its Member of Parliament'. He always left out its most striking quality, that until Thursday last it had a dead MP, but even this description of west Glasgow as a modern day Athens did not make the electors burst into cynical guffaws. Nor did his absurd suggestion that he couldn't actually remember how much money he was paid in Brussels, since the Belgian franc kept changing its value. Rightly or wrongly, Jenkins inspires great trust.

Which will be exceedingly useful to his fellow members of the SDP. Roy's return home will solve quite a few nagging little problems for them. Puzzlingly, because his views are often different from theirs, he is the most popular members of the Gang of Four with Liberal activists. He is certainly the best respected among Liberal MPs. As Jo Grimond remarked last year, the Alliance is bound to be a success since David Steel is really an SDP man and Roy Jenkins is really a Liberal.

He is too – though more of an old-fashioned Asquithian Liberal than a soul-mate of most keen Liberal workers these days who are, if such is possible, extremist moderates, ideologues of the Centre. Most of them are well to the left of Jenkins, though they respect him for his honesty and his political courage. He is rightish on economic policy while distinctly left on social issues. One close colleague says that though he calls himself a radical, 'he hasn't a real radical idea in his head. He believes in letting people get on with it, whether it's making money or screwing. But he certainly doesn't want to change society. He wouldn't know where to start.'

Jenkins likes and enjoys money, and has absolutely no sense of shame about it. Had his political career come to a juddering end on Thursday he would have quite happily become a full-time banker. He says that steering the British economy (he was a successful Chancellor of the Exchequer, though is still blamed by many Labour MPs for losing the 1970 election through refusing to buy votes) is like riding a bike along a cliff edge; get it wrong in one way and you bruise your elbow; get it wrong in the other and you fall 1,000 feet.

He is also one of those fortunate people which British society continually produces who will always, somehow, find themselves in an excellent and lucrative job. Richard Marsh and William Rees-Mogg are others; they can resign or be sacked, and there will always be something waiting. Jenkins didn't even specially want to be European President. The job was first marked in for Denis Healey by Helmut Schmidt, but before Harold Wilson could mention it to him, Healey was vetoed by Giscard.

Jenkins was chosen as a compromise, and when in January 1976 Wilson asked if he would like it, his first reaction was to refuse firmly. Then as he walked out of the room, he said he would think about it. Wilson had not told him that he planned to retire, but when in March Jenkins was humiliatingly beaten in the first Labour leadership ballot, this splendid and remunerative job was waiting for him.

What he lacks is the ability to make himself loved by his fellow MPs. This is far more important than it ought to be. Jenkins has never whiled away the hours chatting in the tea-room, and has always preferred an elegant supper in his Kensington Park Gardens flat with a few friends of similar persuasion and habits. There is a famous story of him being persuaded to buy a drink for a Welsh Labour MP. The MP, pleased and surprised, asked for a pint of bitter, which Jenkins bought. Then he added, 'I'm terribly sorry that I can't join you, but I have an urgent meeting . . .' and left. This inability to suffer boring people gladly has destroyed the careers of many party leaders – Jeremy Thorpe and Ted Heath had few friends at the end – and Jenkins will need to be careful.

He is, however, the only SDP leader for whom David Steel would be prepared to step down. Jenkins arrived at the SDP by a different route from Owen, Williams and Rodgers; they were wrenched painfully away from the Labour Party they had once adored, while he had reached a more bloodless intellectual commitment to realignment. His Dimbleby Lecture, the new party's Book of Mormon, was seen by Steel before it was delivered. Steel helped convince him that a new party, rather than a re-vamped Liberal party, was the only way for either of them to get near to power.

Yet even though Steel accepts that at the next election it will have to be Jenkins who stands as putative Prime Minister of the Alliance, he will insist that it is made quite clear that while Jenkins may be first through the Palace gates to kiss hands, there will in effect be a joint premiership. One thing Jenkins cannot assume: that he will be another British president, ruling almost unchecked like a Thatcher or a Wilson. The apter comparison is much more likely to be with the post-1915 Asquith – though whether Steel has it in him to be another Lloyd George is quite another question.

David Steel

19 September 1982

Politicians who try to change the direction of their parties have usually been reviled. Yet, after six years during which David Steel has forced the Liberals to abandon their irrational horror of alliance and then deprived many of them of the chance to fight long cherished seats, he remains, on the eve of this week's party conference, respected – even by the minority who still distrust his strategy. He is a living refutation of Churchill's dictum that the venom of a man's enemies is a measure of his strength.

He has certainly not achieved this by gentlemanly diffidence. The idea of Steel as the Mr Nice Guy of British Politics – the young man you would have liked your daughter to marry but wouldn't dream of putting in charge of the family business – is a sentimental fiction. He is capable of ruthless action.

In 1964, when as a television interviewer in Scotland he was offered the winnable seat of Roxburgh, he unceremoniously abandoned the hopeless constituency of Pentlands which had selected him as candidate.

In 1967, during the 24-hour leadership struggle in the parliamentary party after Jo Grimond's sudden resignation, he swiftly outflanked a grassroots 'Stop Jeremy' movement, ensuring Thorpe's victory with the almost intuitive grasp of political management that has barely deserted him.

Last year, believing success in the Croydon by-election to be essential to the momentum of the Alliance, he worked hard (needlessly, as it turned out) to displace Bill Pitt, the long-established local choice, first by Shirley Williams, then by John Pardoe.

Behind the conciliatory manner, the private smile hovering so deceptively between mockery and self-deprecation, is one of the most forceful tactical minds in the game. Perhaps the missionary zeal owes something to his upbringing as a son of the manse.

The party he inherited in 1976 was deeply divided over strategy long before it became demoralised by the Thorpe affair. Lacking a solid class base, Liberals believed that any alliance to the right or left would lose them votes from the opposite end of the spectrum. In the absence of electoral reform, the party seemed condemned to an irresolute centrist programme.

This had opened up a rift between the hierarchy and the increasingly confident constituency activists, who were arguing for a radical redefinition (or rediscovery) of Liberalism as the enemy of the great state and corporate bureaucracies, even if this meant alienating floating voters.

Both of Steel's immediate predecessors had been prevented from breaking out of this trap. In 1965, Grimond proposed a deal with Harold Wilson, arguing (with Steel's support) that the Liberals now had 'their teeth in the real meat of politics'. The members, however, proved to be fastidious herbivores. In March 1974, when Ted Heath offered the Liberals posts in a coalition government, Steel opposed keeping the defeated Tories in office. But he watched in dismay that summer as Thorpe, a brilliant showman but a weak tactician, failed to carry the party on the principle of realignment.

He recognised that the only way to pull it off was to take the initiative, not beseech approval. He has been staggeringly successful: first leading his mutinous troops into the Lib–Lab pact; then acting as accoucheur at the long, slow birth of the SDP, darting out of the delivery-room from time to time to reassure nervous Liberals pacing the corridors that all that screaming was really quite natural; and now officiating at the shotgun wedding.

In 1976, he knew that he possessed three advantages lacked by Grimond and Thorpe.

First, the party was in such a demoralised state after the Thorpe affair that it was disposed to welcome any clear assertion of purpose. Second, as the only leader to have been elected by the rank-and-file, he was virtually impregnable against any radical campaign to unseat him. In a crisis, he appeals to the membership over the heads of the activists.

Above all, he was the combat-hardened veteran of a campaign that made the internal feuding of the Liberal Party look like a nursery game. At the age of 28, after only eighteen months in Parliament, he had carried through reform of the abortion law by the arduous Private Member's Bill procedure, often under savage personal attack. That experience left him with a confidence, courage and sureness of touch that no other Liberal can match.

His tactics have been astute and subtle. In the summer of 1977, he was shaken to find himself at odds with the party's heavyweight machine politicians about whether the pact should continue into the next session. He prevailed only by threatening resignation.

This time around, in the debate over the Alliance, he has taken care to secure their support. He has used the Liberal slice of the official patronage pie not to reward favourites but to strengthen allies.

His general line of advance is known, but every new position is captured under a smokescreen of speculative debate.

'David eases the party forward in an extraordinarily calculating way,' says a colleague. 'He has a very fine sense of how far *not* to involve people without actually alienating them. They just find that some new stage has been reached and they have to accommodate themselves to it. Each step is clothed in an air of mild confusion: did he mean exactly what he seemed to be saying in that TV interview? Is the interpretation placed on it by the commentators the right one? Then, the party having arrived at that position, there's no going back. He does it all with a frank charm that defuses opposition.'

He can currently be seen playing this game of grandmother's footsteps (most entertainingly) over the next moves to strengthen the Alliance: the nomination of a 'Prime Minister-designate,' the unified manifesto and the joint Shadow Cabinet.

If opposition crystallises, however, he meets it head on by reasoned argument, conciliating rather than confronting. 'In personal relations, he's absolutely straight,' says a fundamental critic, Michael Meadowcroft. 'Jeremy never forgave anyone he believed to be against him. I don't think David ever stops to think whether you're against him personally. Criticism doesn't affect him in that way at all.'

At two crucial points, he has helped to shape the SDP. At a private dinner with Roy Jenkins in Brussels in July 1979, he argued that individual defections from Labour to the Liberals would not be enough to break the pattern of British politics, and that a fourth party was essential to attract hitherto uncommitted voters. And at a luncheon during the Königswinter Conference in April last year, he argued with Bill Rodgers and Shirley Williams that it was essential to have a positive alliance between the two parties with a joint programme, and not merely a non-aggression pact.

Steel is criticised for under-estimating his own strength in dealing with Jim Callaghan (over the key issue of proportional representation for elections to the European Parliament) and with the Social Democrats (over sharing out constituencies). 'He's so anxious to promote the Alliance,' says Gordon Lishman, editor of the Liberal journal *New Outlook*, 'that he sometimes appears to be more an ambassador of the SDP to the Liberals than of the Liberals to the SDP.'

At 44, he can be amusing company but is a curiously undemonstrative man whose deeper thoughts and feelings are a mystery to his closest friends – quite unlike his outgoing wife Judy. Their relationship reminds one of Goethe's observation that a marriage between a high-spirited woman and a sober man can succeed, whereas the reverse is often a disaster.

He has a flat in Pimlico, but spends as much time as he can at his Scottish home at Ettrick Bridge, where he keeps a horse and is an elder of the Kirk. He has two sons (one adopted) and two daughters.

He is a mediocre platform orator, but a superb exponent of the conversational style in television interviews, the context in which most people form their judgments about politicians. While Mrs Thatcher lectures, Michael Foot mumbles furtively, and Tony Benn signals wildly to 'the people sitting at home', Steel gives the convincing impression of conducting a rational argument.

Despite his qualities, however, he will ultimately be judged by a cruelly simple test. Unless he succeeds in breaking the two-party system at the General Election, David Steel will have been just another in the long succession of Liberal hopefuls.

NEIL KINNOCK

26 September 1982

Neil Kinnock's greatest political failing is probably naïvety. He has yet to come to terms with the fact that politics is a rough and unpleasant business, and that many of the people who engage in it are as trustworthy as black mambas.

For instance, shortly after James Callaghan had appointed him to the Shadow Cabinet, he came under a fierce and well-orchestrated attack at the PLP, the weekly meeting of Labour MPs. It was a wounding experience, made much worse by the discovery that the person behind the assault was an MP whose claims to promotion Kinnock had strongly and successfully pressed.

The incident was really a professional foul, though he was deeply hurt at the time. 'The problem is,' says a friend, 'that it hasn't really dawned on Neil that other people aren't as nice as he is.'

It is possible that this week Neil Kinnock will get another shock, quite as unpleasant though rather less unexpected, if the Labour Party constituencies vote him off the National Executive Committee. Kinnock has been a member since 1978, and while nobody in his right mind would actually feel deprived at not having to attend the monthly deliberations of this committee, it is still a traumatic experience for many to be voted off.

If he is despatched, one of the principal reasons will be his loyalty to Michael Foot. Despite having defeated (even humiliated) him over the Welsh devolution proposal in 1979, Kinnock was one of the people who spent most time persuading the unwilling and indecisive Foot to stand for the party leadership in 1980 – not an achievement for which all his colleagues would now wish to thank him. In the leadership contest of two years ago, Kinnock, though, certainly provided the gumption and flair which Foot's own campaigning style so conspicuously lacked. His relationship today with the leader is one of affection tempered by occasional exasperation; he reveres Foot while often wanting to save him from himself, like a newly grown up son caring for a father who suddenly faces the problems of old age.

Kinnock's intense dislike of Benn and the Bennites is his own, but it is intensified by the loyalty to Foot. His argument against Benn is that he dangerously misleads the party faithful by claiming that the new dawn of socialism can be ushered in as easily and as painlessly as a white fisheries amendment Bill, and that the only reason it has not come about yet is the timorous cowardice of past Labour governments. Kinnock himself refused Callaghan's several pleas to join his Labour Government, at a time when Callaghan was desperate to get some

credibility with the party's left wing. It is, therefore, particularly galling for him to watch Benn, who served happily as a Cabinet Minister all the way from 1974, abusing the Government from which he failed to resign.

The net effect was that last year Kinnock, together with a small group of other left-wing MPs, decided he could not bring himself to vote for Benn in the bitter deputy leadership election. Kinnock was the most public of these conscientious objectors, and defended his position in *Tribune* and on television. Since he and his colleagues were just as unwilling to vote for Denis Healey, – indeed it was unimaginable that they could support the man they had fought in 1980 – once John Silkin had been eliminated they abstained.

People who do not follow the passionate intricacies of internal Labour politics would be surprised by the hatred this decision inspired. Many activists, and quite a few Bennite MPs, saw the issue purely as a Left/Right battle in which, for the first time in living memory, the Left had a real chance of winning. To opt out of the struggle at the moment it was about to be won struck them as grotesque, even despicable, disloyalty. Their anger was heightened by the fact that, if the left-wing MPs had swallowed their scruples and voted for Benn, he would just have scraped to victory.

For years now, Kinnock has been making the traditional annual fund-raising appeal at the *Tribune* rally, ostensibly a celebratory jamboree for the Left, but more usually a poisonous snake-pit of personal hatred. Kinnock on form is one of the half-dozen funniest politicians in Britain today, and in the past his spot was always eagerly awaited. Last year it was interrupted by jeers and boos, and cries of 'Judas', 'thirty pieces of silver' and the like.

In fact, his reception was much milder than he had feared and expected. Then Mrs Margaret Beckett, the former MP for Lincoln, stood up and made a speech dripping with venom, a lengthy attack on Kinnock which avoided mentioning his name. The gist of it was that there are times when everyone must jump into line for the common cause, and that in the first serious test of his loyalty to the Left, Kinnock had failed. The subject of this tirade sat white and numbed, as if watching his torturer plunge the poker into the coals.

Kinnock comes from, and represents, a mining community, although he never worked in a pit himself. He was a WEA lecturer in South Wales after leaving Cardiff University College. Aberfan at the time of the pit disaster was one of the towns where he taught. In this part of Britain the gap between socialist idealism and what ordinary working people feel and believe is less wide than it is elsewhere; Kinnock's unswerving belief in unilateral disarmament, his passionate dislike of the public schools, and his wish to pull Britain out of the EEC, are almost populist issues in South Wales, drawing their force from the beliefs and conversation of everyday working people. This sense of being directly connected with the aspirations of real voters increases his suspicion of Benn's more cerebral, theoretical socialism.

He has an extraordinary ability to get on with virtually everyone who knows him, and even some of the more ardent supporters of Mr Benn will tell you plaintively that they actually *like* Kinnock very much. The corollary is that his success at the House and in the media (he is a good journalist but a better broadcaster) has aroused the usual jealousy. There has always been a powerful element in the Labour Party which resents and mistrusts success.

He is, to put it bluntly, too fond of the sound of his own voice. He often has to be told to shut up by his wife Glenys, who is also his closest friend and severest political adviser. He takes on too much work, from radio panel games to addressing small Labour Party meetings in distant parts of the country. He says that in his days as secretary of the Socialist Society at Cardiff there was always a moment of misery when he opened a refusal, and he doesn't want to inflict that on more people than he has to. Critics say he is trying to ingratiate himself with as many constituency parties as possible.

Because he takes on too much work, he occasionally fails through lack of preparation or complacency. A few of his speeches in Parliament have flopped because he hasn't done the spade-work, and one or two TV appearances have been embarrassing, simply because he has taken easy success for granted. When he knows the subject and is speaking with feeling, however, there is probably no one in the Labour Party who can touch him.

The Kinnocks live with their two children in Ealing, where they moved because it had a real comprehensive education scheme, unlike Kingston where they lived before. He has a furious temper which he does not often display, and even then it is as likely to be over a bad football refereeing decision as about politics.

Although he has more outside interests than many politicians, he remains every inch a political animal. It is partly, no doubt, for that reason that the smart money is already going on him as the party's next leader. He remains, of course, absurdly young – at just 40 he is ten years younger than Roy Hattersley and nearly twenty younger than Peter Shore. But if the present leadership team – Michael Foot at 69 and Denis Healey 65 – fails to take the party to victory in the next election, the cry will almost certainly go up for jumping the generation gap. The beneficiaries of any such feeling seem bound to be Hattersley and Kinnock – though, given the tradition that the party is best led from left-of-centre, by no means necessarily in that order.

MICHAEL HESELTINE

3 October 1982

For almost a decade now Michael Heseltine has been 'the darling of the Tory Party conference.' It is not a title which is necessarily worth all that much (as Lord Hailsham, that Brighton bell-ringer of a quarter of a century ago, has survived to discover), for the holder of it always runs the risk of gravely offending his ministerial colleagues.

Last year, for instance, at Blackpool one Cabinet Minister was to be observed leaving the hall just as Michael Heseltine rose to speak. Why was he off? 'I'm afraid,' he said, 'Michael's special brand of demagogic ranting is more than I can take – especially just before lunch.'

In fact, as things turned out, he was being less than fair. Last year's conference performance marked the emergence of a new, more serious Heseltine – capable of jolting the party's conscience on, of all unpromising issues, the plight of the inner cities and the need, even for a non-interventionist government, to prevent there being simply a cycle of racial deprivation.

It was a brave speech – if also perhaps from the man who had been Secretary of

State for the Environment for the past two years (and who still has to redeem his promises to Toxteth) a belated one. Yet infuriatingly for his tougher-minded colleagues, it did absolutely nothing to diminish the matinée idol hero-worship in which Heseltine is held by the mass of constituency representatives.

Insofar as he has one, the party conference remains Heseltine's power base in Tory politics. Like Lord Randolph Churchill and Iain Macleod before him, Heseltine has always been an 'outside rails' politician, not an 'inside track' one. At 49 he owes remarkably little to anyone – unless it be to the man who originally encouraged him when he first came into the House sixteen years ago, Peter Walker. Yet even there, since Heseltine did not stand with Walker at Heath's Alamo in 1975, the relationship is not nowadays particularly close. Nor, interestingly, is it with the two members of the present Cabinet – Norman Tebbit and Cecil Parkinson – who served, in turn, during the years of the Heath Government as PPS to him.

In the Commons Heseltine has always been very much a 'loner' – neither 'wet' nor 'dry', only briefly a Heathite and never a Thatcherite. Rumour, indeed, has always had it that when Mrs Thatcher first came to the Tory leadership in February 1975, Heseltine was among those she had marked down for the chop – and that he was saved only by the coincidence that on the morrow of her victory both of them were due to address together the quarterly meeting of the party's Central Council (making the abrupt termination of his Shadow Cabinet responsibilities a little too messy even for the Iron Lady to contemplate).

Since then, without at all bending him to her will, the Prime Minister is said to have developed a wary respect for him – though friends on each side still insist that 'the chemistry between them simply is not right'. If it had been, it would, no doubt, have been Michael Heseltine (and not his own former protégé, Cecil Parkinson) who became chairman of the party this time last year. It was the natural, almost inevitable, appointment and the fact that it was not made serves to suggest that whatever measure of respect Heseltine has garnered for himself by the way in which he has, for example, cut down on the vast bureaucracy within the D of E is more than balanced by a feeling of wariness inside No. 10 as to his ultimate political designs and intentions.

About those there need be no doubt. Heseltine means to be Prime Minister – and, unlike many equally ambitious politicians, is honest enough to say so. It may, of course, never come to pass, though it is probably worth noticing that nearly all the things he has wanted in life he has up till now attained.

Certainly, he started out with few advantages, at least in terms of the traditional Conservative Party. Born in 1933 in South Wales, the son of a structural engineer, and the grandson of a coal merchant, he was recognisably, even when he arrived at Pembroke College, Oxford, from Shrewsbury in 1951, a first-generation public schoolboy. Finding no welcome for the boy from the valleys in the then somewhat snobbish university Conservative Association, he promptly set to work and formed a rival body to it – the Oxford Blue Ribbon Club (a precursor of the branches of the Tory Reform Group that can now be found in most universities).

What, above all, he was determined to become was President of the Union – and he finally made it, if only by persuading his college to let him stay up an extra term simply to occupy the office. In those days he was not much of a speaker and he owed his election more to his neo-Keynesian attentiveness to the Union's dining-room accounts than to any classic flights of oratory on the debating hall floor.

The writer of a profile of him in *Isis* at that time spotted that he was already 'dreaming of pavements of gold' and predicted that 'one day he would walk along them'. Sure enough, he very soon did. A legacy of £1,000 was promptly invested in a Notting Hill boarding-house, which within a year or two was translated into a Bayswater hotel; the 'Monopoly'-style property boom of the late 1950s did the rest.

By 1961, Michael Heseltine was not only one of the few articled clerks in chartered accountancy to own half the side of a street in South Kensington: he also had his own chauffeur complete with uniform and peaked cap.

He never passed the chartered accountancy exams but that has not stopped him from being a millionaire today, with a smart town house in Belgravia and a lavish country estate (acquired from the widow of an old-line Tory backbencher) near his own constituency on the borders of Oxfordshire. He possesses, in fact, all the trappings of conventional Tory success – including an outstandingly attractive wife, a son at Harrow and two very pretty daughters, to say nothing of horse, dogs and even a private aviary which, in his middle years, has become his heart's delight.

Why, then, do the doubts, at least among his colleagues, still linger around him? Is it perhaps that it all seems too good to be true, that somehow other Tories want there to be a blot or two on the career of copybook success?

There have, of course, been blots – the protest waving of the Mace in the Commons in the mid-1970s (which caused even Mrs Thatcher to purse her lips), the lack of frankness about the Hovertrain before a Commons Select Committee while he was still Aerospace Minister (still muttered about by older backbenchers within the 1922 Committee), even the collapse, before his days of publishing success with the Haymarket Press and *Management Today*, of both a glossy and a news magazine that he owned in the early 1960s (about which the *Daily Telegraph*, never a particular friend of his, was delivering him a tart reminder only last month). Yet none of these incidents, nor even a more recent indirect personal threat to his career, appears to have done anything to relax his relentless grip on the Tory grassroots.

Maybe that is what his colleagues cannot forgive – and why Mrs Thatcher is wise to remain wary of him. Heroes of political romances, who effortlessly overcome all sorts of vicissitudes, are still perhaps safest left to the storybooks.

SHIRLEY WILLIAMS

10 October 1982

A lady once asked Adlai Stevenson, the liberal Democrat who ran twice against Eisenhower for the US Presidency in the 1950s, whether the public adulation was doing him any harm. 'It's all right,' Stevenson replied, 'so long as you don't inhale.'

Mrs Shirley Williams is too self-aware an individual to inhale, but the billowing affection that surrounds her sometimes distorts the popular perception of her political influence. The cheers for her, as she presides this week over the second annual roadshow of the Social Democratic Party, will be warm and genuine. Yet within the inner circle of the party her standing is lower now than seemed possible way back in the heady days of the SDP's launch.

She was, of course, the defector Labour most regretted, the one they loved the best. She is a crowd-puller without whose emotional appeal the professional calculation that lay behind the birth of the SDP would now look far more naked. Of the four founders, she seemed much the most likely, eighteen months ago, to emerge as leader.

Instead, she was overtaken by a sequence of misadvantures. In June last year she dodged the draft at Warrington, leaving Roy Jenkins, lately the forgotten man of British politics, to establish the party's credibility with the voters and become its eldest standard-bearer – extinguishing doubts about whether four years in exile at Brussels had put him out of touch.

A few weeks later, she became entangled in the misbegotten attempt (by an alliance ostensibly opposed to machine politics) to dump the locally selected Liberal candidate at Croydon. Then, at Bradford in October, she horrified her advisers, angered David Steel and embarrassed constituency Social Democrats by impulsively announcing a pre-emptive bid for the Crosby nomination while the deceased Tory MP was not yet in his grave.

If it were merely a question of relative placings on the ephemeral squash-ladder of Westminster reputations (Mrs Williams did, after all, not only win at Crosby but score a convincing victory over William Rodgers last month in a contest for the rather shadowy role of party president), it would scarcely matter. But this is the critical formative period of the SDP. Once its still-fluid principles solidify, they will gather an accretion of loyalty and passion that will be hard to crack. A Roy party will be a markedly different organism from a Shirley party.

There has always been the question as to whether Mrs Williams, with all her energy and idealism, had the steel required for political leadership. 'They want to make me Joan of Arc,' she protested to friends in 1976 when, after initial reluctance to fight, she came astonishingly close to beating Michael Foot in the election for Labour's deputy leader. 'But I don't *want* to be Joan of Arc.'

While still a young girl, she had been given an incomparable insight into the world of political thought and action. Her father, George Catlin, stood twice as Labour candidate in the 1930s, and covered the Spanish civil war as a correspondent. Her mother, Vera Brittain, was an untiring campaigner for socialism, feminism and the League of Nations. Leading left-wing figures of the period drifted through their house in Cheyne Walk.

At her eight schools in England and North America, where her father lectured in political science, and later at Somerville College, Oxford, Shirley Williams discovered that people responded to her natural charm and authority.

Her appeal lies in the directness and sincerity that spring from this self-confidence. She has never developed the carapace of assumed superiority or defensive irony behind which most politicians conceal their self-doubts. What you see is what you get, as they say in Washington.

At the same time, she has failed to acquire – during a long apprenticeship which began as general secretary of the Fabian Society and continued with junior posts in the Wilson governments of the 1960s – several of the most elementary political skills.

At 52, she still diffuses her formidable energy. She finds it hard to concentrate on two or three priorities. She becomes immersed in detail, enjoying intellectual debate for its own sake. In office, she was conscientious to a fault in considering every conceivable option before making a decision.

The attempt to stop overloading her life, so that she is perpetually late for everything, has defeated two generations of private secretaries. After Jenkins offered his celebrated explanation of her absence from a press conference last year that she had 'got on the wrong train' (he made the mistake of grinning as he spoke) – railway stations were staked out by reporters who watched in amazement as Mrs Williams would come panting along the platform with twenty seconds to spare.

She doesn't have a total commitment to politics. She wants other things as well: a night off at the opera or to cook a meal for her daughter Becky. (Her marriage to the Cambridge philosopher Bernard Williams was dissolved in 1974.) She loves parties and usually stays to the end. Callaghan once had to forbid her from rushing off to yet another private engagement in America after several previous visits.

Nevertheless, the effect of this frazzled life style has been ridiculously exaggerated. Few of the top civil servants who worked with her would assent to *The Times*'s majestic put-down last year: 'A somewhat indecisive woman, of middling intellectual attainments.'

As Education Secretary from 1976 to 1979, she admittedly had a tough task.

Her record was not distinguished, but it was certainly not a bad one – no worse than the average.

It is probably her lack of time to think through problems, rather than any serious defect in her political reflexes, that allows her to make so many miscalculations.

She had to be pressed to stand against Foot in 1976, though not to have done so would have critically damaged her base on the Centre-Right of the Labour Party. In May 1980, only three months before the Gang of Three mooted the idea of the SDP in their famous letter to the *Guardian*, she was still telling the Manifesto Group that the idea was all nonsense: 'I am not interested in a third party. I do not believe it has any future.'

Worst of all, against advice at a time when she could have waited for the pick of the by-elections, she saddled herself with a constituency that would have been hard to hold at a general election even if the Boundary Commissioners had not decided to transfer the ward with the strongest SDP support to the neighbouring Labour seat of Bootle. Her reputation for muddle may be inflated, but it is hardly surprising.

Whether she could, in any event, have become leader of either party is questionable. Many MPs believe that the apotheosis of Mrs Thatcher ruled it out – presumably on the grounds that to have one woman party leader may be regarded as a misfortune, but to elect two looks like carelessness.

So far, the debate within the SDP about principles and policy has been a decorous one, remarkably free from rancour. It is too soon to judge the outcome with certainty. But the first indications suggest that the dominant strain in the party will be the anti-statist/libertarian one, and that the democratic socialist tradition with which Mrs Williams is identified – egalitarian and redistributive – will be subordinate.

The two are not incompatible. Indeed, many Social Democrats (including Mrs Williams herself) argue that they are interdependent. In practice, however, at any particular time there have been key issues on which democratic socialists have been willing to sacrifice a degree of individual freedom to attain greater equality.

The most important of these issues at present is the future of fee-paying education. Mrs Williams has retreated from her opposition to private schooling. On other issues, like private health care and mortgage relief for the better-off owner-occupiers, the party as a whole seems likely to take a soft line.

Mrs Williams could hardly, in any case, have determined the policy of the party, but she could have affected its socialist emphasis. The danger now is that, in seeking cautious institutional reforms that will not offend the former Tory voters whose continuing support is essential, the SDP will be producing an essentially conservative programme that, in Ralf Dahrendorf's sardonic aphorism, 'promises them a better yesterday'.

Norman Tebbit

7 October 1984

The received wisdom about Norman Tebbit is that he is much nicer than he seems. He could hardly be worse. Like many people with a powerful public image, he has come to resemble increasingly his caricatures.

When he loses his temper – which is fairly often – his eyes go cold and black, the bags underneath them stand out against the pallor of his face, and his whole lanky body quivers with tension. These occasional spasms are, for the most part, tactical: like a cat arching his back, they are designed to intimidate the nearest opponent, and they often succeed. They rarely last very long. Civil servants who have been rubbished by Tebbit in departmental meetings find to their surprise that he has recommended them for promotion. Like the Piranha Brothers, Tebbit is cruel but fair.

This week he will be speaking at the Tory Conference on the subject of privatisation and political liberty – a favourite topic. The pundits will be looking to see whether he wins for the second year his annual undeclared war against Michael Heseltine. Last year Tebbit had marginally the longer standing ovation and a similar success will be seen as marginally improving his chances of the ultimate succession.

Yet the coming political year may well prove a critical one for Tebbit's career. Nearly twelve months ago he took over the Department of Trade and Industry from his old friend and rival Cecil Parkinson; and since then he has deliberately kept much quieter than before, with the exception of a few remarks, culminating in his waspish attack last week on Neil Kinnock, about the miners' strike. As it hapens, he has a lot of sympathy with the miners, but he detests Scargill and would pay virtually any political or economic price to see him defeated.

Nevertheless his abrasive image has remained with him, and would give serious pause to those who might ponder choosing him as Mrs Thatcher's successor. One minister says that 'it may well be that we will need to signal a much softer line when Margaret goes, and that would rule Norman out'. You meet plenty of people who say he will be the next leader, but a lot fewer who say they will vote for him.

The question remains whether he even wants the job all that desperately: friends say he would have a go, but that his life (unlike Heseltine's) would not be blighted by defeat.

Tebbit's other problem is that he seems to have lost the love of the Prime Minister. He is less often invited for cosy chats at Number 10, and, according to one eye-witness, 'she is absolutely bloody to him in meetings. She humiliates him in front of other people. It is quite extraordinary.' For example, she roundly defeated him on the sale of Jaguar shares. Tebbit supported BL's wish to keep back some of the company but Thatcher wanted the lot sold. He came out of the meeting furious with rage, demanding to know why people didn't keep their noses out of subjects they didn't understand. The defeat on an important departmental subject still rankles. His public praise for the Prime Minister, an old Tory convention, is perhaps a shade less glowing than it was.

Nobody knows exactly what brought about her change of mood, though it seemed to coincide with the departure of Parkinson and the general acknowledgment that Tebbit was her most likely successor. The King never feels easy with the Dauphin, the reminder of his own mortality. Tebbit's own relationship with Parkinson was tricky. Parkinson railed against him ('my worst enemy') after his resignation last year, and Tebbit drove from the Tory Conference to Parkinson's house to clear the matter up.

He was born in 1931 in North London. His father, a jobbing builder, became posthumously famous when Norman described his reaction to losing his job during the 1930s. 'He didn't riot. He got on his bike and he looked for work.' 'On your bike,' which he never said, has stuck with him nevertheless, a fact about which he is rueful but philosophical. He was educated at Edmonton Grammar School, at a time when university was rarely contemplated for the sons of builders (though his younger brother became secretary of Aston University, a post from which he resigned last month).

Tebbit says he became a Tory at school, roughly from the age of fourteen: 'I liked the concept of social mobility in a free market economy, and the opposite struck me as rigid and restrained. I felt you should be able to make your own fortune; you should be the master of your fate.'

If that sounds a shade abstract for a fourteen-year-old boy, the beliefs have certainly remained and hardened. The idea of social mobility, both upward and downward, is at the core of Tebbit's thinking. A world in which people are prepared to take, perhaps temporarily, a job they don't like is a world where equally they have the chance of great success later. (He himself, after all, started off in the lower reaches of journalism before progressing upwards to become an airline pilot.)

'The point about Norman,' says an MP well to the left of the Tory Party, 'is that he is very, very clever.' 'He has an untrained mind,' says another colleague, 'yet he can read a brief prepared by some mandarin with a double-first and tear it to shreds.' Another Tebbit-watcher records: 'It is unnerving to see someone with that collection of prejudices be so brilliant as well.' Tebbit's own account is more modest: 'I'm not a great intellectual or a scholar, so to understand something myself I have to reduce it to its bare essentials. I try to keep in touch with the average bloke.'

The average bloke he refers to is himself. 'Norman will sound off about something, such as he can't get a phone installed, or there's no one to mend his garden gate, then he'll suddenly step to one side and become the politician, and note what he has said for future use. He actually examines himself as a typical example of what the British people are thinking,' says another colleague.

There are mixed views about his skills in the field of industry and commerce – some think he has scant understanding, others that he has done well to pick up the nuances so fast. His greatest art, though, is as a politician and specifically as a short-term tactical thinker. 'He sees everything in terms of who wins and who loses. Who'll be at the meeting? Whose support is he going to need? He goes all out to win, and he doesn't lose with grace. The American adage, "don't get mad, get even," doesn't apply to Norman. He gets mad *and* even.'

He tends to see all issues in terms of black-and-white. Wealth creation and profit, good. Public spending, bad. Getting rid of government red tape, good. Yet there are subtleties in his positions, too. He was, for example, much less hard on the unions than both he and their leaders chose to believe. There are Tebbit admirers who are certain that the great GCHQ fiasco would not have taken place if he had still been one of the Prime Minister's intimate advisers. As it was, the first the Cabinet heard was on the morning of the original statement. Not that he would have approved of a leak; he loathes and detests people who give away confidential documents and has hardly less contempt for the journalists who receive them.

His ferocity is given free rein in the Commons. He is especially savage with MPs who interrupt from their seats, and a Tebbit speech is generally listened to in a hush born of fear. It was his skill as a political knife-man (Michael Foot called him a 'semi-house-trained polecat') which attracted him to Mrs Thatcher, and he was one of the members of the first British 'Gang of Four' which met on Tuesdays and Thursdays to plot her response to Prime Minister's Questions.

Tebbit's private life is peaceful and quiet. He married a warm and humorous nurse called Margaret Daines in 1956 ('She is quite the nicest Cabinet wife I know,' says one MP), and they have three children. Their daughter has recently presented them with their first grandchild, a girl. Having sold their bungalow in Hertfordshire, the Tebbits now have a flat in the Barbican, and a small cottage in Devon where Tebbit loves gardening. He gave his hobby in one directory as 'peace and quiet'. The contrast with the rich, showy and glamorous Heseltines is often remarked upon.

How much further Norman Tebbit goes towards the top depends on many factors – much the most important being the circumstances of Mrs Thatcher's going. However, being admired by his civil servants and the darling of the Tory Conference are unlikely to be enough. Tebbit not only requires being liked: he needs to look as if he's liked. That will take some hard work in the coming years.

JOHN SMITH

2 November 1986

Labour's industry spokesman, John Smith, has become the rising star of his party over the past year, earning his reward in last week's Shadow Cabinet elections by moving up from seventh to second place.

This weekend he is in Frankfurt deputising for Neil Kinnock at a conference held by West Germany's trade union bank. His diary has suddenly become crowded with political events (removing the reproach that he was prepared to give up to his family what was meant for the party). Next weekend he will speak at a fringe meeting at the Confederation of British Industry's annual conference.

'I have been in the House of Commons for sixteen years, but it's only this year that I've been noticed outside it,' he admits. Both the Westland affair and the Government's attempt to sell off Austin Rover to the American-owned General Motors transformed his political position.

His scintillating performances at the despatch box – deadly combinations of wit and attention to detail – eclipsed the hapless Government front-bench. Conservative MPs were impressed into sullen silence while Labour left-wingers (not his obvious allies) cheered him on. 'He is the right man at the right time,' admits one of Smith's many admirers at Westminster.

Until this year Smith's high reputation was mainly limited to the *cognoscenti* of the political world. In his television performances, especially on the BBC's *Question Time*, the tubby Scot seemed to exude plenty of plain commonsense but not much charisma. Unlike others in the People's Party, Smith is no flashy exponent of self-promotion. 'He is essentially a politician's politician,' says one friend. In a party prone to sloganising and vendettas, Smith stands apart, though he is hardly fastidious – not least in his language.

'I am a party man,' he admits, but he is no hack or apparatchik. His democratic socialism is moral-based on a keen sense of social injustice. Yet he speaks up strongly for the creation of wealth as much as for its redistribution.

Essentially, Smith is a man who wants to get things done. He remains a well-organised and tough combatant who dislikes the waste of being in Opposition. But he can wheel and deal with the best operators in the Labour movement. As a stalwart of the centre-right Solidarity group, he acted as Roy Hattersley's campaign manager in the 1983 party leadership election. As a sponsored member of the Boilermakers, later the General and Municipal Workers' Union, he keeps in touch with the world of the shopfloor.

'John is not just a pragmatist who goes with the trend,' says one friend. 'He hates sloppy thought wherever it comes from and he will face unpleasant facts head-on.' The very ordinariness of his reassuring appearance – conservative blue suits, white shirts, spectacles and portly stomach – is very deceptive. 'He may not light up a room when he enters it but when he starts to speak you know he has an alpha mind,' says one admirer on the Left.

Smith was born on 13 September 1938, in the village of Ardrishaig in mid-Argyll, the son of a primary school headmaster. He was brought up in a radical Presbyterian household where copies of Kingsley Martin's *New Statesman* were read. But, unlike other Scottish socialists, he was not reared in the class struggle of inner city slums. At the age of fourteen, young Smith left home and went into lodgings in the nearby town of Dunoon to attend the local grammar school.

He excelled there and went on to read history and then jurisprudence at Glasgow University, where he stayed for seven years. Smith shone alongside contemporaries like Donald Dewar, a life-long friend and Labour's Scottish spokesman; Teddy Taylor, the Tory MP for Southend; and the television presenter Donald MacCormick. A chairman of the University Labour Club, he became a powerful debater and won the *Observer* mace in 1962. While still a student, Smith stood in the East Fife by-election that year and again in 1964.

With no money of his own, nor personal connections, Smith built up a swift reputation as a lawyer, becoming an advocate in 1967. Keen to ensure his sole means of making a living was not politics, he was also anxious to get into Parliament as soon as he could. At the 1970 general election he was elected for the mining seat of North Lanarkshire.

In his early years in the Commons Smith concentrated on Scottish affairs and impressed Labour's chief Scottish spokesman, Willie Ross. For his part, Smith liked Ross's attacking style of politics. But he was ready to break ranks with the party leadership if he felt deeply enough about an issue. Smith defied a three-line Labour Whip to vote for Britain's entry into the Common Market in 1972. Most of his fellow Labour rebels joined the Social Democrats. He suffered some trouble in his constituency for what he had done, but has never regretted it.

When Labour came back into office in February 1974, Harold Wilson offered Smith the post of Solicitor-General for Scotland, but he refused, wanting to avoid being over-identified with things Scottish. For a few months he was Ross's parliamentary private secretary, but in October 1974, after that year's second general election, he was offered and accepted the junior post at the Energy Department under Eric Varley.

His main task was to pilot the Petroleum and Sub-Pipelines Bill through the Commons, which he did very skilfully. That regulatory measure was hated by the American oil companies, but they found Smith to be an awkward customer, far more so than his supposedly more left-wing colleague, Tony Benn, when he later became Energy Secretary in July 1975.

Although having little in common, Benn and Smith worked well together, and it was on Benn's insistence that Smith was promoted to Minister of State at the department. He helped to create the British National Oil Corporation and his efforts ensured that its head office was based in Glasgow. Smith is still knowledgeable about North Sea oil and a map of Britain's reserves remains pinned to his office wall. In April 1976, his diligence at Energy was rewarded with promotion.

The incoming Jim Callaghan had taken a keen interest in Smith's career from the start, seeing in him a potential Labour leader. Smith likes Callaghan and readily agreed to work at the Privy Council office under Michael Foot on the thankless job of pushing through devolution for Scotland and Wales. Foot came to admire Smith's skills and ensured his promotion to the Cabinet as Trade Secretary in November 1978.

Smith became the youngest member of Callaghan's Cabinet at the age of 40. He took little active part in the dying months of the Labour Government through the 'winter of discontent', spending much time abroad on trade missions.

Out of office in May 1979, Smith recoiled from the tactics of Opposition. He looked with horror at the bloody civil war inside the party that threatened to tear it to pieces. His power base has always been the Parliamentary Labour Party and in the autumn of 1979 he scraped into the Shadow Cabinet for the first time. With spells shadowing trade, energy, employment and now industry, Smith has made himself indispensable. He never ever thought of breaking with the party to join the Social Democrats and speaks with contempt of those who did.

'Smith is no trimmer for the safe option. He pins his colours to the mast,' says one friend. Now he has become the crucial figure in Labour's plans to revive manufacturing industry. He speaks eloquently about the need to change our antique industrial training system, to invest in research and development, and to stimulate the mixed economy. Always he is concerned with practicalities. The party's new commitment to social ownership reflects this. He and Sheffield's David Blunkett combined to press for a more flexible attitude to nationalisation.

Smith is no nationalist but he loves Scotland and his family still lives in a solid Victorian house in the Morningside district of Edinburgh. His wife Elizabeth – herself an attractive and strong-minded socialist in the Glenys Kinnock mould – works for the Great Britain-USSR Association, and their three daughters have all been educated north of the border. Early in his career he decided not to move the family south to what he sees as the rootless cosmopolitanism of London life.

But Smith is not a dour man. He likes to unwind over a dram of whisky with friends. He loves opera and has been known to sing Gaelic folk songs with relish. His idea of relaxation is sailing, tennis and hill-walking. Ever conscious of his weight, he is a devoted member of the Commons Club for the Well Proportioned.

Smith is hardly self-effacing but does not go out of his way to frequent the Commons bars or the company of journalists. He works very long hours at the Commons and has a *pied-à-terre* in the Barbican. Both Kinnock and Hattersley rate him very highly and some even predict he could be leader himself one day.

Certainly, Smith would be a formidable force for stability and order in a Labour government in crisis. He is perhaps the one Labour man whom the Conservatives genuinely respect and fear.

DENIS HEALEY

5 April 1987

It was a black week for anyone who feels a sympathetic interest in the fate of the Labour Party. On *Panorama*: Brent council's insufferably patronising race-and-gender *apparat*, every shot a vote-loser. On *This Week Next Week*: a painful inquest into the leadership's bafflingly ill-judged call on the President.

Characteristically, Denis Healey had privately tried to dissuade Neil Kinnock from making the trip, then loyally defended it on TV. Little good it did him. In the public mind, he is ineradicably identified with the central dilemma of Labour foreign policy: how could an anti-nuclear government remain in an alliance predicated on the possession of nuclear weapons?

Watching him gamely landing a punch or two on Donald MacCormick, one wondered again why the old bruiser hasn't hung up his gloves. He could have had his pick of top jobs outside Westminster: Nato in 1970, the IMF in 1979, GEC in 1984.

Why on earth doesn't he cart Edna off to some agreeable posting in Paris or Rome or Washington, with plenty of time left over for playing Chopin, translating Theocritus, perhaps writing that book on German aesthetics he never got round to?

It's partly sheer fascination with politics,' says a fellow-member of the Shadow Cabinet, 'partly that Denis hasn't given up hope of becoming Foreign Secretary in some kind of Labour government.' In a sense, Healey's entire career has been an apprenticeship for the Foreign Office. He and his brother grew up in an internationalist family. His father, Principal of Keighley technical college, was a Congregationalist and Asquithian Liberal. At Bradford Grammar School, Denis resigned from the OTC on grounds of pacifism.

At Balliol, where he got twelve alphas in Mods, and did rather less well in Greats (but managed a comfortable first), he was briefly a Communist. In Combined Operations during the war, he took part in the American invasion of North Africa and the British invasions of Sicily and Anzio.

In 1945, he turned down a fellowship at Merton and a job as war historian to become secretary of the Labour Party's international department, helping to re-establish several European socialist parties. For 40 years, he has been a leading participant in international seminars on foreign relations, for twenty a respected strategic theoretician on both sides of the Atlantic.

Ronald Reagan's Mister Magoo-like greeting last week, 'Good to see you again, Mr Ambassador' (confusing Healey with the last British ambassador, Sir Oliver Wright – same eyebrows) was sublime comedy.

Healey, now 69, has represented Leeds East (previously Leeds SE) in Parliament for 25 years. As Defence Secretary (1964–70), he began the process of restructuring the armed services after the retreat from empire. As Chancellor (1974–9), he inherited a dual OPEC and balance-of-payments crisis. In the end, Labour's pay pact with the trade unions fell apart, and the entire policy is now derided as a disaster.

But he took the British economy through a uniquely critical period with a minimum of pain for ordinary citizens, and ended with both unemployment and inflation falling. The economic historians may hand down a more charitable judgment.

Healey was deeply disappointed when, after Anthony Crosland's death in February 1977, Jim Callaghan made David Owen and not himself Foreign Secretary. But, so soon after he had fought the £1 billion IMF cuts through the Cabinet, he was needed at the Treasury to sustain confidence.

Defence and the Treasury are, at best, paths to respect, not admiration, in Labour circles. 'In my student days we used to ask one another, "Who does the dirty work under socialism"' he says. 'I found out in later life. It was Denis Healey. I don't think either job helped my political position.'

Nor did his rudeness. He is a warm, generous-spirited man who nevertheless appears to have little notion of how much punishment the average individual's *amour-propre* can take in the course of political argument. 'Get out! You're wasting my time,' he once told a group of top brass at the climax of a discussion of defence cuts.

His civil servants, many of whom greatly admired him, resented his aggressiveness less than his party colleagues. 'You could get bruised,' says Sir Leo Pliatzky, recalling the intense arguments at the Treasury during the autumn 1976 negotiations with the IMF, 'but you could answer back. However rough he was, Denis was always willing to be stood up to.'

His bullying is not informed by personal animus. It's simply Denis's natural way of settling an argument. He is a bit like a character in a John Ford movie. He will cheerfully deliver a couple of jabs and a roundhouse right, and then slope off with Beethoven's Ninth on his Walkman.

A week before the 1976 leadership election, he spectacularly lost his temper on the floor of the House with a bunch of left-wing MPs voting against the

Government. 'You bastard!' roared the Left. 'You fuckers!' bellowed Healey. ('They questioned my paternity, so I praised their virility,' is how Healey now recalls this altercation.) He got only 30 votes in the first ballot, below Michael Foot, Callaghan, Roy Jenkins and Tony Benn. Even the centre-right had been alienated.

Next time, in 1980, Healey came top in the first ballot, beating Foot by 29 votes, but was defeated by 10 votes in the second. 'Denis lost at least 10 votes because he had antagonised people,' says one of his allies. 'More – *far* more,' says another.

He fought his hardest battle in 1981, when Benn challenged him for the deputy leadership. It was crucial. If Benn had won, the party would certainly have split or been irrecoverably ruined at the general election.

It was a bitter and, although he had friends and organisers, a somewhat lonely experience. He had never cultivated a clique of supporters, having been disgusted by party cabals during the Attlee governments in the late 1940s. The deputy leadership campaign forced him to seek friends. He spent a lot of time on the 1979 intake. But the hard Left were intimidating, and some of his natural allies kept at arm's length. Today, he is a much more popular figure throughout the parliamentary party.

He had a final shadow of a chance in February 1983 when sections of the parliamentary party discussed the possibility of dumping Foot. The Australian Labour Party had just won an election triumph after a similar tactic.

Healey prudently held aloof. (He was always utterly loyal to Foot, as he is now to Kinnock and Roy Hattersley.) It came to nothing because of the difficulty of ensuring a clean substitution.

'The PLP wanted the trade union bosses to tell Michael to go,' says a former colleague, 'and the unions said it was the MPs' responsibility. Everyone knew Denis was *papabile*, but the college of cardinals couldn't get their act together.'

After that, it was too late for him. During the 1983 general election, Hattersley assiduously promoted his own leadership potential, arguing that Labour might well not win the next two elections, and should therefore 'skip a generation'. A member of the campaign committee recalls this exchange:

Healey: I enjoyed your election address yesterday, Roy.

Hattersley: I didn't know you were in Sparkbrook, Denis.

Healey (brandishing Hattersley article in *The Times*): I meant your *other* election address – the one for the leadership.

It would be wrong to portray Healey as a Rab figure. He has never lacked determination. He is a showman – but, unlike the greatest of that breed (Dizzy, Lloyd George, Churchill, Macmillan), his political feel is surprisingly uncertain.

He adores an audience, hence the private banter, the comic accents, the whole bag of repertory tricks deployed in TV interviews – like his favourite response to unanswerable points: a slow, derisive smile exploding into an abrupt chortle of disbelief, followed by a brisk shift of ground. In the 1970s, the comedian Mike Yarwood tapped an unexpected vein of popular affection for him.

Yet he often misunderstands the audience. In recent months he has been arguing forcefully (as in current number of *Foreign Affairs*) that the change in Soviet policy under Gorbachov offers an unprecedented opportunity to rethink Nato strategy, which has remained the same since the adoption of flexible response (under Healey's own influence) twenty years ago.

It is an honest and necessary argument. His difficulty is that most of his audience are not listening to it. They simply see a politician attempting to rationalise a position he has been compelled to accept for reasons of expediency.

He is still vigorous, absorbed by political debate, possibly a smidgeon less intellectually intolerant than he used to be. In the dark night of the soul, he sees that final prize slipping away from him. But cheerfulness keeps breaking through.

EDWINA CURRIE

11 December 1988

One glance around Edwina Currie's office at the Department of Health reveals her abiding passion. Herself.

A noticeboard in one corner is filled with the latest Edwina press clippings. A whole wall is covered with framed originals of Edwina cartoons. At the centre of this self-created shrine sits Her Majesty's Parliamentary Under-Secretary for Health: a woman who appears to have taken the old adage that 'all publicity is good publicity' and turned it into a philosophy of life. 'Edwina,' said one disgruntled Tory MP last week, 'makes Jeffrey Archer look like a recluse.'

Even by her own exacting standards, 1988 has been an exceptional year. In January she suggested we should all 'postpone that second holiday and use the money for a non-urgent operation . . . put off decorating the living-room and get our teeth done instead.' Result: uproar.

In March she pointed out that 'something like half our pensioners have their own homes': why couldn't they sell them, she wondered, and use the money to pay for their private health care? Result: uproar again.

In September, she gave an audience of bemused old folk in Reading the benefit of her advice on avoiding hypothermia: 'Buy long-johns, find your woolly socks, check your hot water bottles, knit some gloves and scarves and get your grandchildren to give you a woolly nightcap.'

A fortnight ago she suggested scrapping child benefit. Last week she turned

her attention to eggs. It takes a special kind of genius to make eggs the main domestic front page story for three successive days, but Mrs Currie managed it when, on ITN last Saturday, she stated that 'most of the country's egg production' is affected by salmonella.

Egg sales dropped overnight by fifteen per cent. The British Egg Industry Council threatened to issue writs for damages against Mrs Currie and ITN. A Tory MP asked the Prime Minister to repudiate 'this reckless and uninformed statement by a junior Minister with an uncontrollable tongue'.

Mrs Thatcher (who had already demanded that Mrs Currie's evidence be sent over to No 10) replied that she had had 'scrambled egg on toast for lunch and enjoyed it' – a pointed rebuke for the woman the tabloids have dubbed 'Eggwina'.

And yet, despite it all, the lady herself appeared last week quite unruffled. She has received sacksful of mail, the majority favourable. She refuses to apologise and insists that her only mistake was to say that 'most' rather than 'many' eggs were infected. Indeed, evidence does suggest that up to one in 200 eggs may now contain traces of salmonella. In terms of public awareness of a serious health hazard, the junior minister has probably done us all a favour.

The truth is that Edwina Currie is a most effective politician. She is disliked by Labour for her hard-line, right-wing views. She is disliked by her own side because she is so obviously on the make.

It was noticeable last week that the Tories who harbour the greatest hostility towards her are the Knights of the Shires. She epitomises everything they find most obnoxious about the social revolution Mrs Thatcher has wrought in the party since 1975. She is a woman. She is pushy. Her background is working-class. She speaks in an accent compounded of Birmingham and Liverpool. She wears heavy make-up and flashy clothes in bright, man-made fabrics. Conservative Party Conferences these days are full of Edwina Curries. Hers is the rise of a Tory Everywoman.

She was born in Liverpool on 13 October 1946 (she never tires of pointing out that she shares the same birthday as Margaret Thatcher: 'I expect she altered her birth certificate,' says one parliamentary colleague). Her father, Simon Cohen, ran a gentlemen's outfitters.

The Cohens were orthodox Jews – one of Edwina's uncles lost his family in Auschwitz – yet today she is a member of the Church of England, and her parents do not even figure in her *Who's Who* entry. Friends believe this conscious break with her upbringing is the key to her relentless ambition.

First, in order to get away from home, she applied to St Anne's College, Oxford to read chemistry (she had to apply to an Oxbridge college, she says: her father would never have let her leave to attend a mere Redbrick university). Then, after taking a degree in PPE, she entered a firm of chartered accountants and married a non-Jew, Ray Currie. Her parents refused to attend the wedding. Her father never spoke to her again, and died a few years later.

Cut free from her roots, Edwina soared upwards. In the 1970s, the Curries moved to Birmingham and she stood for the city council. In 1977, four months pregnant with her second child, she became chairman of the social services department with a budget of £15 million. Subsequently she became chairman of housing and of the vast Central Birmingham Health Authority.

She made national headlines at the 1981 Tory Party conference when she brandished a pair of handcuffs at the Home Secretary during the law and order debate. This was the famous occasion on which the then Arts Minister, Lord Gowrie, is said to have watched the manacle-flourishing Edwina and experienced 'a bat's squeak of desire'.

In 1983, after applying to more than 40 constituencies, she was selected to fight the then marginal seat of Derbyshire South. Her Labour opponent, she recalled, was 'a nice little lad called Peter Kent – and I eat people like Peter Kent for breakfast'. She increased the Tory majority from 900 to 9,000.

Edwina proceeded to hit Westminster like a typhoon in a twin-set. Startled journalists found themselves being rung up with demands to be taken out to lunch. She and her husband were the subject of a TV documentary. She wrote to the producers of BBC's *Question Time* insisting on an invitation ('I have been on just about every other serious TV programme, on all four channels, but I still pine for *Question Time* . . .').

Small wonder, then, that some of her colleagues regarded her with undisguised loathing. One MP pretended to smoke 40 cigarettes a day in order to get out of sharing a room with her. The Government Whips are said to have decided to recommend her for promotion in the vain hope that it would quieten her down.

In 1985 she was the unlikely choice to be Sir Keith Joseph's Parliamentary Private Secretary (she once shocked the donnish Education Secretary by producing a copy of Spike Milligan's *Adolf Hitler – My Part In His Downfall* to read on a train journey). Two years later she was made a junior Minister at the DHSS.

Her chief characteristics as a minister are boundless enthusiasm and a certain flirtatiousness. 'At ministerial meetings she's relentlessly positive,' says one official. 'Everyone else is worried about some issue or another, then when it's her turn to speak she says: 'Well, *I've* got six *marvellous* pieces of news to announce.'

'She's very quick. She grabs hold of a brief in the way a bright schoolgirl would – she grasps the point but doesn't necessarily deal with it in a mature way.'

She is quite open about her willingness to use her femininity as a political tool. 'I like being with men,' she told *Marxism Today* in 1987. 'I like pulling out all the stops and trying to figure out how to get my own way . . . And if that means being slightly underhand and teasing them, or flattering them or whatever, I don't give a damn.' One fastidious civil servant was recently alarmed to find his Minister running her finger down his spine in an attempt to cajole him into doing something.

Her husband and her two daughters – Debbie, fourteen and Susie, eleven – are the rocks in her life. 'My home and family matter a great deal to me,' she told Anthony Clare in a characteristically frank interview on *In the Psychiatrist's Chair*. 'Having abandoned one family, I needed the security of another.'

Ray Currie – rather like Denis Thatcher – is the ideal foil for his ambitious, famous wife. The director of training at the accountancy firm of Arthur Anderson, he has little interest in politics. His passions are rugby and snooker.

He can, however, be fiercely protective. Travelling down from their Derbyshire home last Monday morning, with the Great Egg Row in full swing, his wife had to restrain him from laying into some Fleet Street photographers besieging their compartment.

That would indeed have been unwise. In the strange way of British politics,

Mrs Currie and the tabloid press have forged a mutually beneficial relationship. She makes outrageous remarks and gives them colourful stories. They have made her, according to a recent *Economist* poll, the most recognised member of the Government.

Sometimes, like last week, the relationship turns sour. But Edwina Currie is shrewd enough and tough enough to know that those who live by the press release, must occasionally expect to perish by it.

SPORTS STARS

The *Observer* was a pioneer of good sports writing: that is, good writers treating sport as a subject as worthy of their attention as politics or the arts. These sporting profiles are confirmation of that fact. Don Bradman was profiled at 38 in 1946. He had been written off by many in 1938 when England regained the Ashes and Len Hutton (later, incidentally, to be a regular commentator on cricket for the *Observer*) had taken away his world record individual score. Then the war intervened and suspended sporting careers for five years. Now sporting life had resumed and MCC were touring Australia, to find Bradman rejuvenated. The writer got his ending right: the story was concluded in 1948 when Bradman led Australia to a devastating 4–0 Ashes win in England. He retired and was knighted the following year. His duels with Hedley Verity would never be resumed (penultimate paragraph) because Verity had been killed in the war. The profile of his adversary Denis Compton captures that free spirit perfectly. The opening paragraph of the Stanley Matthews profile refers to hopes of a knighthood for him: it eventually came in 1965, the first to be awarded to a professional footballer.

David Astor instanced Lester Piggott in his memo on profile writing: people were more interested in how he rode a race, he wrote, than in 'too many stories about Mrs Piggott and the kids'. This 1957 profile fulfilled all his demands. It was remarkably accurate: it could have been reprinted at any time of Piggott's career as Britain's top jockey over the next 30 years but naturally could not have forecast that, far from being 'completely honest' as the conclusion had it, Piggott would eventually go to prison for tax evasion.

Virginia Wade's profile bore the by-line of Christopher Brasher, the paper's distinguished athletics correspondent, who for a couple of weeks every summer during Wimbledon would turn his attention to tennis (there was a family connection: his wife Shirley had been a top player and was the *Oberver*'s tennis correspondent for many years). As a former Olympic gold medallist, he was just the man to explain the factors that had turned a perennial English loser into Wimbledon champion in the tournament's centenary year. The George Best profile was written by Arthur Hopcraft, one of the paper's many fine football writers, who was also a distinguished television dramatist and author of one of the most original books on soccer *The Football Man*. Diego Maradona was portrayed on the day of his finest hour, when he led Argentina to victory in the 1986 World Cup Final. Ian Botham overhauled Trueman to become England's leading wicket-taker, without having to resort to off-breaks as his profile had predicted. But he never came near to beating Boycott's aggregate of Test runs and though he carried on playing cricket past his promised retirement age of 30 his career went into an unforeseen decline marred by injury and off-field controversy.

DON BRADMAN

1 December 1946

Just over eight years ago Don Bradman was carried from the field at the Oval, in a vast silence, with a vast score by England on the board.

He had injured his leg when bowling; a function which, as matters then stood, might more successfully, if less legally, have been delegated to any willing spectator of either sex; under-arm, over-arm, or round-arm; roll, bowl, or pitch.

Then, at the sepulchral hour of seven last Friday morning, a Voice, striving heroically for tact, stated that Bradman had made a century at Brisbane, his sixteenth, single, double, or treble against England. Later and ample, such very ample, reports sought to ease disappointment's bread with the margarine of comfort; Bradman had started shakily; he had offered what would have been chances if they had happened to go to hand; he had even been caught at slip; but it had proved not to be a catch. And it all boiled down to this, that Bradman had done it again. The most devastating return since Sherlock Holmes surprised the iniquitous Colonel Sebastian Moran.

In a purely cricketing, and Pickwickian, sense the obituary of Bradman has several times been written of recent years. At the start of this Australian cricket season, rays of rumour flickered through clouds of mystery. Bradman was an old man, with no interest except for commerce. He had batted in the nets at Adelaide, where some found him as wonderful as ever, while to others he was just a memory of splendour, a husk of genius, or even a different man altogether, batting under the same name. He proved his identity by playing against the MCC. But his performance was, for him, only moderate. He was grey and tired and wizened. He might conceivably appear in the first Test, but not as captain. So much for rumour.

Donald George Bradman, lord in the nonpareilage of New South Wales and South Australia, was born on 27 August 1908 at Cootamundra, a small up-country town in New South Wales. When he was still not much higher than a short-handled bat he moved, with his parents, to Bowral, fifty miles or so from Sydney. Here, in the back-yard, against a wall, with himself as batsman, bowler, and ten fielders, and the sky as sole spectator, he taught himself cricket. From this one-man show he graduated to pick-up matches with the Bowral High School. In 1926, at the request of the New South Wales State selectors, he appeared in the practice nets on the Sydney cricket ground. His style of batting was described as uncouth, even eccentric. But the less hilarious judges noticed that hardly a single ball reached the back-netting. Arthur Mailey, one of the subtlest dealers in the leg-break that cricket has known, was called in to tax this turbulent novice and was treated as just another practice-bowler.

When the Australian team came here in 1930, there was a quiet confidence that the 'Ashes' would not sail away with the challengers. Bradman was the exploder-in-chief of that comfortable view. He began, reasonably enough, wih only 131 in the first Test, at Nottingham. He followed with 254, at Lords, 334 (a new record), at Leeds, and 232 in the deciding match at the Oval. The pundits might argue about his right place in the galaxy of the great, or even deny him greatness. But they had to admit that he had set a new standard of arithmetic. Once, batsmen, even in Test matches, had tended to depart, decently or with a flourish, somewhere between the first and second century. But Bradman batted on.

Few, if any, had so disciplined themselves to physical excellence, or fielded and thrown with such agility and accuracy. The critics were not educated to such perfection, and it was fashionable to decry the supreme artist as an automaton. But Bradman, the breaker of records, was not reflecting the spirit, even the demands, of a record-hunting age. He was only 21, but he knew the market. He was something new and strange, an Australian Test cricketer who could capitalise his skill and even dare, successfully, to defy authority and contractual clauses.

Bradman was now the greatest figure in world sport. Envious fate sent to Australia Larwood and Jardine, a very fast and accurate bowler directed by a very able and realistic captain. Under the Leg Theory attack Bradman's art wilted but never wholly collapsed. It may be allowed that he was reduced, numerically, to the ordinary, but ordinary is no epithet for square cuts played past point from mobile headquarters on and outside the leg stump.

In 1934, Australia again arrived as challengers. At the start of the season a different Bradman was seen on English grounds. He was in a perpetual hurry. Was it nerves? or weariness of being Bradman? or just an agreeable expression of *joie de vivre*? There was a wonderful 160 against Middlesex; then a failure in the first Test; then, on a sticky pitch in the second Test at Lord's – Verity's match – a catastrophe, which profoundly shocked the wise and paternal Woodfull. Bradman's answer was to play innings of 304 and 244 in the last two Tests, he and the scarcely less magnificent Ponsford aggregating over 800 in two partnerships. As soon as the tour ended, Bradman was operated on for appendicitis.

In the last two series of Tests before the Hitler war Bradman was captain of Australia. Against Allen's visiting team he led Australia to victory after losing the first two Tests. Then, eight or eighty years ago, according to taste, he had to content himself with three single Test centuries and a drawn Rubber, saw Leonard Hutton beat the Bradman record of 334 and sustained the heaviest defeat in any single Test match. As to his place among captains, the argument still awaits full evidence. But, whatever verdict the immediate future begets, none who saw that Oval Test of 1938 will forget the difference between Australia fielding under Bradman and Australia on the field without him.

To the connoisseur, the most exquisite duel in cricket was between Bradman and the left-handed Verity; the back-chatting urchin versus the Professor of Logic, Don against don. The last time that it was fought, or, alas, can be fought, was in the 1938 match between the Australians and Yorkshire at Smoky Bramall Lane. The pitch varied from the sportive to the cantankerous. Verity used every trick of spin and flight; stuff that might have won two matches in a day, and Bradman played him, for over after over, in the middle of the bat. 'Don't ever tell me,' Verity used to say, 'that Don is just ordinary on the sticky ones.'

So, the story is 'to be concluded', perhaps in England, 1948; of the slight, high-shouldered batsman, walking out from the pavilion, slowly, pensively, to slice the enemy into ribbons.

DENIS COMPTON

6 June 1948

Everybody knows who is the Boys' Own Hero of Australia: and the Men's, Women's and Wallabies' Hero, too. Bradman, about whom everything possible has been said, has a powerful English rival for the championship of the young heart.

He is Denis Compton, ten years younger, still on the record-makers' up-and-up, but outreaching even 'the Don' in width of favour because of his excellence at football, too.

The possession of 'all eyes' will be shared by these two at Nottingham on Thursday when the First Test is held on a wicket long known as sweet, serene and fruitful for the batsman and a source of affliction to the bowler. Facing Denis as well as Donald, if the sun shines, is a task for the pertinacious, the imperturbable, the optimist.

Compton, the most entertaining of great batsmen today, cannot help his abundance. The song of his bat is as natural as summer's warmth. But he is like those natural wits whose sayings are waited for by professional joke-gatherers. The statisticians prowl and prowl around.

Arithmetical digits are provocative things. They beget comparisons; and the last thing to do with Denis Compton is to compare him; as if he were an adjective, or a length of linoleum. He is, in the strictest sense, incomparable, though

Captain C. B. Fry has been heard to compare him, without final judgment, to Victor Trumper.

No athlete of modern times has been so popular with the young. The shout that greets Denis Compton when he walks out to bat at Lord's is mainly of treble and alto pitch. He is, of course, what each shouter would himself like to be; and these hero-worshippers, while their eyes watch him moving in white flannels, call up also the image of Compton (D.) dribbling the ball down the left touchline at Highbury and cracking it across into the top corner of the net. These are the more obvious attractions. But the deeper alliance is in the kinship of temperament. Compton is just 30 years old, as years are officially measured. But his youth does not mean to listen to that old nagger, Time, and keeps easy company with the skill and strength of the man.

In the grimmest Test, Compton cannot quite shake off the half-holiday idea. A match lost is still in the nature of 'a swizz', and an immortal century is 'a bit of a fluke'. Thus, at a time when others would be awaiting their innings, padded and silent, Compton is engaged, far from the dressing-room, in a delirious finish at shove-ha'penny.

What of the style, the technique? Above all, easy; nature, concealing but strengthened by hours of study and practice. In all great batsmen there is the distinguishing trait; in Ranjitsinhji, the glide to leg; in Frank Woolley, the length ball driven over the despairing bowler's head; in Macartney, the half-volley chopped, late, crack to the rails behind third-man; in Bradman, the prolific diversion of worthy balls to the space wide of mid-on. Compton, above all batsmen, is a teaser of cover-point. No one has quite his gift of so delaying or advancing the impact of the off-drive that the fielder needs to run both ways at once.

Denis Charles Scott Compton is a Londoner. His home and school and first cricket were at Hendon. His father, a competent club-cricketer, took the boy to matches, as scorer and occasional filler-up of a gap. 'We can't play against such a small lad,' said an opposing captain. 'Don't worry,' said the father, 'just bowl normally.'

On 13 September 1932, at the age of fourteen, Compton played his first match at Lord's, captaining the Elementary Schools against Mr C. F. Tufnell's Public School eleven. He scored 114. His partner, A. Macintyre, now the Surrey wicket-keeper, scored 44. The Elementary Schools won by 148. Compton, slow left-hand, took two wickets.

Luck went paired with skill. Sir Pelham Warner was watching, and soon Compton joined the ground staff at Lord's. He sold scorecards; with Young, Robertson and Brown, today his companions in the Middlesex team, he helped to pull the heavy roller over the pitch on which Hedley Verity overthrew Australia, and, at the end of that match, found that, by foregoing lunch, he had netted a profit of £14 6*s* 1½*d* from the sale of cards. The money was banked. He also bowled in the nets; and once, at request, batted in them to the bowling of Mr P. G. H. Fender. Good practice, for a boy.

Compton, began, like the great Hendren before him, as Number Eleven for Middlesex, and helped G. O. Allen to head the Sussex total in the Whitsun match at Lord's. Ten years afterwards, with Godfrey Evans, in the breathless heat of Adelaide, he was to control *the* last-wicket stand of latter years. In his third County match, he made 87 against Northamptonshire. By the end of this season, 1936, he had arrived. A year later he had settled in as an England batsman, scoring 65 against New Zealand at the Oval Test.

In 1938 came 'the Tiger', W. J. O'Reilly, and that erratic genius, L. O'B. Fleetwood-Smith, whose experiments with the left-handed googly Compton is still following up, as yet some way behind. At Nottingham, in his first Test against Australia, Compton scored 102. Arithmetically, this innings was swamped by the concurrent triumphs of Paynter, Barnett, and Hutton. Temperamentally, it was significant. For here was a batsman with care but no cares. And, at Lord's, in the second Test, came the sealing answer; a 76 not out in the second innings, on a difficult pitch, against bowlers who scented victory near.

Then the war; with army service; cricket in India; football in 'War' internationals 1946 summer; and the one 'bad patch' with which fortune chastises her favourites. And so to the Test matches in Australia, heavy, argumentative matches, in which even Compton for some time lost his bearings and, almost, his spirit; till the Test at Adelaide, where, after struggling each painful inch to 50, he reached that famous 100, then added another.

Last summer, light returned. With W. J. Edrich, he perplexed and caned the bowlers of South Africa and the English Counties. Crash went the records of those old masters, Hayward and Hobbs. The Championship came south. A perfect physique surmounted the strain; a perfect balance met the fame. Above all, whether for Middlesex or England, he remains a team man. There's nothing of the showman about him, and, in his highest triumphs, he has kept that happiness without which no game is worth playing or watching.

STANLEY MATTHEWS

6 January 1957

After a quarter of a century in professional football, Stanley Matthews stands out as the most remarkable, if no longer the best, player in the world. The award of CBE in the New Years Honours List has been received by his admirers with qualified delight. They will not be fully satisfied until he is given a knighthood.

Current literary fashions have inured us to the hero with feet of clay. Matthews, however, has never disappointed his idolaters with outbursts of petty temper on the football field. In his most recent match for England at Wembley, he did not even show emotion when the Yugoslav left-back, quite desperate, stopped him by clinging to his knees.

Two qualities distinguish Matthews as a footballer: his elusiveness and his longevity. He will shortly celebrate his forty-second birthday, but the years show no decline in his transcendent ball control, nor has there been any appreciable falling off in his great speed off the mark. It is bad enough for a left-back to be beaten by Matthews; worse still is the knowledge that he will seldom have the chance to recover. Even now, few outside-rights are so fast, over the first, vital twenty yards.

Matthews has a superb body balance and technical equipment, and his self-confidence is immense. He can bring the most difficult pass under control in a moment, and then he is away, slowly at first, the rather slight figure hunched over the ball, tantalisingly kept between his two feet. He invites opponents to the tackle, a spider beckoning a fly, and when they are lured he is past them with a wriggle of the hips and a flick of the inside or outside of the foot.

His body swerve is his most bewildering weapon. Even today, with the prestige of twenty-five years' sorcery behind it, it seems remarkable that defenders should fall to it so often. Where they waver and hesitate, Matthews is utterly sure of his ability to pass them, and once he has done so, he seldom wastes the ball. His centres are cunning and precise, gently floated to elude the hands of the goalkeeper.

Matthews was born in the Potteries, the son of Jack Matthews, a prominent boxer known as 'The Fighting Barber at Hanley', who was a favourite at the National Sporting Club. His son has paid tribute to his father's insistence on physical conditioning; he would make his children stand by the open window to carry out deep breathing exercises, regardless of the weather. Today, Matthews is as fit as a man ten years his junior. He has always made training a fetish, and he has been amply repaid.

His promise was very soon evident, even in the Potteries, where good footballers grew like dragon's teeth in every street and alley. Once, in a schoolboys' match, he scored ten goals from centre-half, and as soon as he left school he signed for Stoke City. At the age of seventeen, he was a regular member of their League side; at nineteen, he was an English international.

It is strange, in view of his later flair for the great occasion, that he should begin poorly in England's colours. After an early, disappointing game against Italy, in 1934, a journalist wrote, 'I saw Matthews play just as moderately in the inter-League match, exhibiting the slowness and hesitation. Perhaps he lacks the big match temperament.'

That was his second international, and it was not for three seasons that he really established himself in England's team. His reputation was assured by a brilliant exhibition against Czechoslovakia, at Tottenham, in 1937. England were forced to reorganise their team through an injury to Crayston, now manager of Arsenal, and Matthews moved to inside-right. He scored three fine goals, every one of them taken with his left foot, and England won the game 5—4. The match is sufficient answer to those who have maintained that Matthews cannot score goals, though it is true that, as time went on, he became increasingly interested in making them for others – surely a sign of maturity.

The following year, he bewitched the Irish defence at Manchester, enabling his partner, Hall, to score five goals. Meanwhile, his popularity in Stoke was such that when he asked for a transfer from the club, the town hall was hired – and packed – for a meeting of protest.

In 1947, however, Matthews did leave Stoke, going to Blackpool, for whom he had played regularly, as a 'guest', during the war. He has been there ever since, representing the club in three Cup Finals, the third of which is remembered for perhaps the finest display which even he has ever given. That was in 1953, when Blackpool, with twenty minutes to play, were losing to Bolton Wanderers. Matthews sensed that possibly his last chance of a Cup-winning medal was slipping away from him. He proceeded to transform the game, dribbling the Bolton defence off its feet, and Blackpool won by four goals to three.

It is an irony of his career that, despite his celebrity, he is not a rich man; far less wealthy than many, more obscure, footballers playing in Italy and Spain. He has always been shrewd to exploit his name, with articles in the press, two autobiographical books, and sponsorship of many different products, ranging from breakfast cereals to parlour games. During the close season he goes abroad to counrtries in the Commonwealth, to play series of exhibition matches, for which he is liberally rewarded. Yet although these supplementary earnings make his income far larger than the average British professional's, it is still negligible by comparison with a boxer, professional baseball or tennis player of equal status.

He trains throughout the year, living most abstemiously. He and his wife, the daughter of a Stoke City trainer, once ran a boarding house in Blackpool, though they eventually gave it up. His daughter, Jean, is a promising tennis player – a game at which Matthews himself is proficient – and his small son was taught to kick a football at the earliest possible age.

If Matthews has a 'secret', he has never analysed it himself. Once, when a journalist who had been a footballer asked him to demonstrate his swerve, he replied, 'Honestly, I couldn't do it in cold blood. It just comes out of me under pressure.' He is not one of football's thinkers; he is an intepretative artist rather than a teacher. Trends and tactics appear to interest him very little, and he is too shy a man to command a team.

Reserve, in fact, is the principal impression which Matthews leaves, off the field. He is quiet and withdrawn, unwilling to talk to the press, though he showed at a recent dinner at the National Sporting Club that he is quite a proficient speaker. These qualities have only increased his reputation in a country where admiration for modesty is carried to excess.

One rare occasion when he unburdened was after the match between England and Brazil at Wembley, last May. The choice of Matthews had been criticised by certain newspapers on the grounds of his age, yet he played magnificently, turning a game that might have been lost by England without his presence. 'Too old,' he remarked, with sober disgust. 'Do you know, there have been times when I've read that, and I've wanted to tear the paper across!'

LESTER PIGGOTT

18 August 1957

Apart from Prince Charles, who is exceptionally well handicapped, and Tommy Steele, the Bermondsey songbird, who may not stay, the most famous Englishman under the age of twenty-five is surely Lester Piggott, the jockey – now approaching his hundredth win of the season.

No other young man's daily activities are followed so closely by so many people: no one else's whereabouts and plans can be discovered practically every afternoon of the year merely by looking in a newspaper.

Over £300 million are wagered, legally and illegally, on horses every year in Britain; what Piggott does every week may well cause £1 million to change hands. Those who feel inclined to deplore his economic influence may find some

comfort in the thought that jockeyship, as parliamentary government, is one of the arts in which Britain has always held her own.

Piggott is undoubtedly the outstanding new figure on the Turf since the war. His successes this season include the Derby (Gordon Richards had to wait till the end of his career to win this race; Piggott has already won it twice), the Two Thousand Guineas, the Oaks, the Eclipse Stakes and the German Derby.

He is tall for the job – a well-constructed five feet six inches – and he rides at eight stone five pounds, which puts him at a disadvantage with light men such as D. Smith and Breasley, but in spite of his weight Piggott last season was third on the winners' list to these two, and this year he is again near the top. Good judges think he is probably the best jockey riding.

The odd thing is that he lacks some of the qualities which might be thought essential for success. His mental reactions are not outstandingly fast. No apprentice would ever be advised to copy his style. It is true that he has an easy, nonchalant seat on a horse which shows good nerves and self-confidence, and he rides with a nice length of rein, but he is inclined to round his back, lift his seat in the air and stick his elbows out – as some of the pictures of him winning this year's Derby show. Most striking of all, he has no noticeable sympathy with horses. A racehorse, for him, is primarily the vehicle for riding a winner.

One most important reason for his excellence is undoubtedly that he was virtually born with a bit in his mouth. The Piggott name is famous in racing: his grandfather won the Grand National three times; his father, now a trainer, was a first class National Hunt rider (he used to ride, as his son does, with pretty short stirrup-leathers, even over fences); his uncle was a well-known trainer. On his mother's side, he is a Rickaby: his uncle won the Oaks, and One Thousand Guineas four times; another uncle trains in South Africa; a cousin, W. Rickaby, is among the most successful jockeys riding today. Piggott is the product of the Trevelyans and Macaulays of the Turf. He is bred to ride.

His second blessing is his single-mindedness: he is absorbed in the task of riding winners to the exclusion of everything else. His spare time at home is spent almost entirely in resting for his next ride, looking up form, going through the racing calendar, reading every authoritative book on racing he can find.

Like models, jockeys are obsessed by their figures. Piggott is heavy. He could, theoretically, ride lighter, but excessive wasting saps a man's strength and constitution – the great Fred Archer, depressed by too much of it, shot himself – and wisely Piggott does not try. But he has to watch his weight all the time. His theory is that expenditure of energy makes him hungry, a very undesirable condition, so the only activity he allows himself outside riding is an occasional swim. He keeps to a spare diet, alleviated by a good meal about once a week, followed by a spell in the sweat box later in the day to counteract the effects.

Holidays do not appeal to him. He has been abroad for short spells during the off season, but he prefers travel when there is a good ride at the end of it: given this condition, he is always prepared to fly to the Continent on a Sunday. In the winter, when other jockeys migrate or take it easy, Piggott instead stays in England and rides over hurdles.

This practice causes consternation among those owners who retain his services on the flat – racing people not associated with the jumping part of the business tend to regard riding over fences or hurdles as if it were going into battle – but Piggott, unlike most other flat-racing jockeys, is not afraid of riding over obstacles and, besides, he likes money and cannot see the point of turning down a chance to earn it. This full programme probably gives Piggott an income tax return of around £15,000 or £20,000 a year.

He was born on Guy Fawkes Day, 1935, started his apprenticeship with his father when he was twelve and rode his first winner at the same age. Before he started to ride regularly, he went as a boarder to King Alfred's School at Wantage – near his father's training establishment at Lambourn – and later to a small private school, making up the hours he lost on the racecourse with a tutor at home.

By 1950, Piggott was leading apprentice with 52 winners. The next year, he again was at the top; he rode 51 winners against the next best of nineteen. In 1952, he was fifth on the list of winning jockeys.

This rapid rise was not entirely smooth; he had been steadily gaining a name for rough and dangerous riding, and he had been in trouble with the stewards. There was nothing more to it than youthful impetuosity and the desire to ride winners, but the rules of racing cannot be continually flouted without causing the offender to be penalised sooner or later. Piggott's fellow jockeys, in the circumstances, were extraordinarily tolerant: had he been a little older, those who suffered from his indiscretions might have given him one or two rough rides in return.

In 1954, his career reached its crisis. That year on Never Say Die he won the Derby, the race every jockey would give his right arm to win; immediately before him he had the prospect of his second classic success, on the same horse in the St Leger. Then, in the King Edward VII Stakes at Ascot, Never Say Die got involved in a mêlée which the stewards considered Piggott had caused by trying to drive his way through too narrow a gap between two horses, and he was stood down for the rest of the season.

To his bitter disappointment, Piggott thus missed the ride in the St Leger, which Smirke won on Never Say Die. To make the experience more traumatic, many reliable observers of the incident held that, in this instance, he was not to blame – an opinion given some support by the newsreel of the race. Still, if the stewards' justice was rough it was also poetic, and Piggott accepted it with a phlegm remarkable in a boy of nineteen. His father was advised that it might be good for him to be transferred to another stable for a time, and for the rest of the season he worked for Jack Jarvis at Newmarket.

There, he at once came up against a discipline which possibly he had not experienced at home: on his first morning he was told that it was not the custom for the stable's apprentices to arrive at work in a car, and told to remove it from the yard forthwith. Like any other apprentice he thereafter 'did' his two horses, rode out two lots a day and received no privileges. He also had a fight with a board wageman. The change of environment seems to have been Piggott's turning-point. His licence to ride was renewed the following season and he has never been in trouble since.

As his character settled down under Jack Jarvis, so the quality of his jockeyship has improved since he became first jockey to Noel Murless, trainer of Crepello. Murless has taught Piggott that most horses run as well without being hit as they do under the whip and that a couple of slaps are as effective as several hard cuts.

His riding instructions more than once have been to the effect that 'if you touch this one it's the last you'll ride for me'. Piggot has also learned the art of riding a horse smoothly throughout a race, letting him settle down early on, making up ground gradually, and not coming to the front too soon. In this he is reminiscent of Harry Wragg; his riding of Rue de Romance in the Newbury Cup this year was a superb example of judgment and confidence in bringing a horse from behind to win with the least possible effort.

But though Piggott rides with quite unusual confidence, he is never over-confident. When the occasion requires it he is a powerful and effective finisher. In spite of his spectacular rise, there isn't a shred of conceit about him. His outlook in many ways is surprisingly mature: he is neither hilarious in victory nor despondent in defeat.

He is a polite and agreeable fellow, but no one would call him forthcoming. He is in any case rather deaf – for that reason he was unfit for National Service (other top-class sporting figures to have been unfit for National Service are Terry Spinks, the boxer, and Colin Cowdrey, the cricketer). Even when he hears what is being said to him, he has a rather indistinct, nasal way of replying and is not an easy man to talk to.

'Well, Lester,' said a bright television interviewer to him the other day, 'and which is your favourite course?' 'Newbury,' said Piggott, after a pause. 'Aha, I suppose that's because you've ridden so many winners there?' 'Nearest home,' said Piggott.

Hard going for interviewers, Piggott is very popular with the racing public: they know he will always give them a fair run for their money. In this respect, no jockey could have a better reputation: he is completely honest. Apart from accidents or a sudden increase in weight, Piggott's future looks assured. He is just about at the top of his tree and he is young and brave.

GEORGE BEST

10 December 1972

It is a matter of common regret among photographers who specialise in sport that George Best seldom makes good action pictures for them. The reason is that, unlike Bobby Charlton or Denis Law or Brazil's Pelé or Italy's Riva, there is nothing exaggerated in any of Best's movements on the football field. There is none of the strut and swagger of Law, although Best is as combative and can head goals as improbably; none of the majesty of Charlton, although Best can kick goals as powerfully.

No other player in Europe, and only Pelé in the world, has excited crowds as much as Best has; and he is equally thrilling on the television screen, because the film camera can encompass his intricacy and the scope of his play as the human eye can. But when the moment of action is frozen, the man hardly ever appears stretched or to be straining, or even urging. This is instructive about Best. There is nothing in his personality, in total contrast to the image of flamboyant irresponsibility that has grown in the public mind, that makes him naturally conceal himself. Just as he hides intention on the field he is secretive off it. He is an intensely private person.

Here is the paradox. The media hunt him. Best is seen so often, in newspaper and magazine pictures, looking haggard after some all-night debauch or stretched out in the Mediterranean sun, because the press go looking for him, not because he goes to more parties, nightclubs and expensive holiday resorts than every other footballer or most young pop-music stars. But he is the antithesis of a self-publicist. He *wants* anonymity, but cannot possibly be permitted it: he is physically too arresting, too gifted, too retaliatory, too interesting. It is his own problem, and football's deep disappointment, that he is not equipped to absorb equably the attention he does not ask for, yet attracts so insistently.

It is tempting to set up Best as the defining representative of the modern British footballer – of the generation that has never known the construction of a mandatory maximum wage and the modest lifestyle that went with it. But being the most glamorous, most talented and most brazenly rebellious of this generation does not make him characteristic of it. The point about Best that is of overriding importance is that he is unique. When he is is considered as a footballer, ignoring his behaviour away from the pitch, one cannot find another player of any era to compare him with satisfactorily.

When he was introduced in Manchester United's First Division team, at seventeen, in September 1963, the immediate response of the writers and

watchers of football was to welcome 'a second Stanley Matthews'. British football then was in love with, or at any rate gripped by, the new concept of the ever-running, passing and never-holding-the-ball player; the game was simultaneously busy and dull, and much more so than it is now, in spite of the current alarm at low scoring and declining attendances. So the slight figure of Best, as he dribbled the ball with endless invention around defenders, was a startling sight. There were charm and courage in this boy. (The degree of gratitude and affection that reporters and spectators felt for the shy, audacious young George has much to do, one feels, with the notable vindictiveness in the headlines and the spoken comment he is getting now.)

But it was not long before the parallel with Matthews, the shuffling dazzler of the thirties and forties, had to be abandoned. Best was seen to relish the thick of the in-fighting of a match in a way Matthews never did. Best liked to win the ball, possessing, as he still does, one of the most effective sliding tackles in the Football League. We saw Best to be aggressive as well as supremely subtle. He showed the kind of brave, almost reckless, improvisation that Matthews never attempted, taking the ball so close to a tackler that he could use the tackle itself against the defender. He would deliberately seek contact to claim the ball back off the opponent and thus dismiss him irrevocably.

In his most telling seasons with Manchester United, from 1964 to 1970, Best declared himself as a player almost without flaw: dribbling, passing, shooting, heading – all the skills were present in exceptional quality. Also there was a range in his game, the factor that is largely a matter of intuitive understanding of what ought to happen next – Danny Blanchflower had it, Pelé possessed it incomparably – and this was the extra dimension that made so massive an aggregate of the specific talents.

When Best was eighteen he was already a 'great player' in the judgment of United's manager, Matt Busby, already a Northern Irish international. At 21 he was Footballer of the Year in England, the youngest ever. It is interesting to recall now that on the Saturday afternoon when he was told of this award he surprised us all with a little, acid impudence that momentarily opened up the sardonic interior behind the shy, bland front. He was sitting, neat and gleaming from the bath, in Busby's huge office armchair, and he was dwarfed in it like a child. Someone asked him which player *he* would have voted for, and he said, with a twist of the lips: 'Bobby Charlton's mother.' (The story of Mrs Cissy Charlton's devoted 'coaching' of Bobby as a schoolboy player has long ago taken its place in the folklore of English football.) There was a gasp at the irreverence of the youth, before the room chuckled. Busby, who heard Best's reply as he was half-way out of the door, whipped round in embarrassment, only half smiling. 'That's not for publication,' he said. Best then bore the same wicked, mirthless grin that has come to be familiar as an accompaniment to his numerous, contemptuous dissensions with referees.

That incident has sprung to my mind frequently in the past five years. There was something in Best's manner, not arrogance or malice but a kind of disregard, a dismissiveness, an alone-ness, that affected the atmosphere. Here was a very young man, who didn't even look his age, who possessed enormous ability, who from the age of fifteen had known only the insular, protected, self-nurturing world of the leading professional football club, who was so set apart as an individual that he could confuse its father-figure, normally so assured, and disconcert a score of men, most of them twice his age, by simply releasing a reflex action of the personality.

We, of course, established the atmosphere – the convention of a middle-aged, rather sentimental, very approving prize-giving. Best was neither intimidated nor much flattered, but his verbal flick of irritation was like the pound-for-pound kick on the ankle or jab of the elbow he was already beginning to deal out to tacklers in matches.

It is important to remember that Best reacts to the given situation. He is a singular man, a singular talent, in a team game, a collective approach, a group environment. If one can imagine his degree of individual ability projected into a man-for-man sport, like motor-racing or tennis it's possible to see him in a very different light from the one we now are stuck with. Vivid, troublesome personality stands out much more sharply when it occurs in a component of a team. And it is Best's sad destiny that he appeared on the scene in English football when his club was already on the slide and its manager, that admirable and far-seeing man, was growing old and tired.

Manchester United have retained glamour by reputation and the astonishing longevity of Busby's reliance on forward play. But hindsight now tells us what some of the players always knew: that the management and coaching and recruiting fell behind years ago in terms of firm grasp and energy and flair. Fortune helped to obscure the facts: United, with Busby as manager and Charlton as captain, won the European Cup in circumstances of unbearable emotion in 1968, with a weaker team and against weaker opposition than had contested the competition in the three earlier years when Busby's team reached the semi-finals.

What kind of mature player might Best have become had he grown up with an improving team instead of a shakily established one? The question is imponderable. The man is father to the player; Best's skills come out of his personality, and the personality is informed by the rewards of its skills. Best is a conundrum; brilliance, uncertainty, wilfulness, vulnerability, callousness. He drinks too much; he regrets his drinking. He wants to find repose; he flits from girl to girl. He is capable of turning a game; he vaporises from it while you watch. He can be as charming as a child; he brushes his way through a crowd of children without a moment's pause.

If Best were a poet, or a ballet dancer, or an actor his behaviour would both be less resented and less reported. But the British view of football is still very old-fashioned. Managers who were star players 20 or 30 years ago still insist, against the evidence of match after match, that the teams they played with were just as violent, just as committed. The hard core of the game's following, which is of the managers' generation, likes to believe this.

Best was taken to its heart as long as he was a youth with youth's resilience – that blithe acceptance of outrageous ill-treatment from defenders. The grown man, who sees that his loyalty is to a poor side, who remembers the years when he was unprotected by inadequate referees stubbornly supported by the ostrich-head of an executive, who knows he can only be slower in the future, and who shows his scars and turns in frustration and fear – I believe he is afraid of the future – to booze (sometimes), and fawning sycophants (regularly), offends this following because it cannot bear the accusation from the player that is implied.

Football expresses itself – as much by the sound of its crowd as by the methods of its coaches. A separate man like Best is adored only as long as he rides the violence of the rest of the game. If he complains about it he is crying out of turn; if he joins it is he is prostituting his God-given talent. Why wouldn't Best show some bewilderment?

He was born in Belfast, into a Protestant, working-class family, and that fact alone must be significant in considering his nature. In that environment, at its least an uneasy influence and commonly unbalancing, it is hardly surprising that a boy should acquire a *particular* attitude to authority, to the means of survival, to the pride of person. There was early enough evidence of his restlessness, his sensitivity to instruction.

United's scouting organisation picked him up when he was fifteen, and with another fifteen-year-old, the (now) Middlesbrough and Irish inside-forward, Eric McMordie, he was delivered to the pebble-dash council house in Chorlton-cum-Hardy where one of the club 'mums', Mrs Mary Fullaway, had twins beds ready for them. Within 24 hours both were on a boat, going home. To this day Best insists that it was McMordie who was homesick; Mrs Fullaway smiles about that.

Best returned to Manchester, under Busby's persuasion, a fortnight later. But he had been an obstinate truant at school, and now he left the job the club found him as an office boy near the ground because he was not at ease with his employer. Did it matter? Of course not. Busby and his assistant, Jimmy Murphy, knew they had a player of rare gift. Best stood five feet three inches, and weighed four pounds under eight stone.

By the time he was 18 Best was famous. He was being paid between £70 and £100 a week (in 1964). At that stage he was still visibly and touchingly immature: tight suits, a sheen on his face, baby's brown eyes, a bag of sweets in his pocket, shyly playing snooker in a Temperance Hall. He was talking about the glamorous possibility of owning a sports shop when he was 21. There was a scrapbook on a table under the window of Mrs Fullaway's living-room, and it had 'George Best' written in painstaking, round characters on the cover. 'A lovely lad,' Mrs Fullaway said of him; and she has never said anything less.

When he *was* 21 how different it was: the gilded bachelor with a white Jaguar, photogenic girl friends; the freedom of Manchester's night life, such as that awkward mimicry of Jermyn Street is; an agent, a secretary, boutiques with his name in gold paint: a blasé indifference to the needs and ambitions of the Ulster football team. Football had made him wealthy, given him a hard surface, begun to punish him physically.

The winter and spring of 1970 established Best the Problem Boy. In January he was fined £100 and suspended for a month, after knocking the ball out of the referee's hands in anger. In April he behaved so badly, when playing for Northern Ireland against Scotland in Belfast, that he soured the match irredeemably. After complaining to the referee, the Englishman, Eric Jennings, that a defender had dragged him away from the ball by his shirt, he picked up a handful of mud and threw it, with a mocking, girlish, under-arm gesture, at the official, and then spat at his feet. The crowd, overwhelmingly Irish, booed him as he was sent off.

Since then the list of misdemeanours, almost all of them more regrettable for their petulance and silliness than for any violence, has grown relentlessly. The more one thinks about his conduct the more saddened, rather than angered, one becomes. It's the money that gives so much pain. How recent were those marvellous, lilting soliloquies of his in the late sixties, yet how distant from his play now.

Alan Hardaker, the secretary of the Football League, told a national newspaper last week that he was tired of hearing Best's name. What a deep slough of dismal mean-mindedness is shown by our foremost football official with that wretched comment. Ten thousand Alan Hardakers don't make a minute of football. One hour of Best, at his most glorious, justifies the game: reminds us that it is capable of supreme theatre. If only we have a single George Best, as one remembers him resisting brutal tackles and whipping in a goal with that liftless, electric action, we can even carry Alan Hardaker.

At the moment we do not have Best. It may be that English football will lose him to Spain, or Holland. Even if he stays in England it is difficult to rid one's mind of the sense of obituary. Best is now 26. It is improbable that he can expect to rediscover the instant acceleration that made him so exciting – the loss is critical.

He has shown this season that, if he really wants to do it, he can play in midfield to great effect. His club has yet to find another player, to replace Charlton, who can strike the ball with the accuracy and cunning that Best can achieve. He is as good a tackler, except for the young Scot, Buchan, as is available to the manager. There would be nothing demeaning, and much of value, in such a job for Best.

It seems, after last week's squalid sulking, that the rift is too wide for him ever to do it for Manchester United now. The question is whether Best can bring himself to work that way for anybody else. His nature resists anything so tedious as industry. Yet he would bring to it a beautiful intuition.

BEST'S WORST

1966. Two speeding convictions.
1967. August: Fined £10 for careless driving.
1968. July: Banned from driving for six months after a collision.
1970. January: Suspended 28 days, fined £100, for knocking the ball out of the referee's hands after a League Cup semi-final in which he had been booked.

March: Former fiancée, Eva Haraldsted, says she will sue for breach of promise. April: Sent off during Northern Ireland v. Scotland match.

1971. January: Six months suspended suspension and £250 fine from FA for having received three bookings in twelve months. Dropped for missing training. Suspended fourteen days by Manchester United, after disappearing to London. August: Sent off against Chelsea.

1972. January: Dropped by United for missing training. Fined two weeks' wages, made to leave his home and move back into lodgings. May: Missed Northern Ireland match in Scotland, disappeared to Spain and announced in a *Sunday Mirror* article he had quit football. July: Suspended two weeks by United for 'breach of club discipline' and told to move into the home of youth coach Pat Crerand. October: Sent off in Northern Ireland's World Cup match against Bulgaria. December: Charge of assaulting a young woman during an incident in a Manchester night club: charge deferred for a month. Banned by United from night clubs. Missed training and turned up in London. Placed on transfer list.

Arthur Hopcraft

VIRGINIA WADE

3 July 1977

At nine o'clock on Friday morning the doorbell rang in Virginia Wade's London flat, just off Eaton Square, and there on the steps were some press photographers. Her first reaction was what one would expect from someone about to play the centenary Wimbledon final in front of the Queen: 'Oh, just leave me in peace.' And then she changed her mind: 'I thought: "This is your big moment . . . so why not just enjoy it?"' That thought would never have crossed her mind during any of the other fifteen Wimbledon championships she has played in. Truly we have witnessed the transformation of a lady: a prickly, complex cocoon has opened and revealed what we least expected – a highly excited, completely professional British champion.

She has confounded us all and made life exciting not only for herself but for millions of people who could hardly believe that she, the woman named Virginia Wade who has disappointed us so often, was actually going to win the premier championship of the world in the one year when it meant so much.

Five years ago she said: 'I'm not equipped mentally to play week after week. I should never play more than three weeks on the trot because I get stale so quickly.' That is a classic English amateur attitude to sport.

This year she has played almost continuously – indeed for four weeks before she came back to Britain, at the end of the first week of June, she was 'on the road' with the New York Apples. They are just one of the teams in the American inter-city tennis league, which sprang up four years ago, and which has survived, contrary to many expectations. The Apples played on average, four matches a week, travelling vast distances, practising every day, moving on from city to city.

As one player says: 'You would think it was the worst possible schedule just before Wimbledon.' And certainly when Virginia came to Eastbourne three weeks ago to play for Britain in the Federation Cup, she looked awful and played awfully. But she soon readapted her game to grass, and within a fortnight was playing some of the best tennis of her life against Chris Evert in the semi-final on Wednesday.

There is no doubt that her team-mates on the Apples have had a profound effect on her. First, she has seen the ultimate professional, Billie Jean King, at work – seen her train 'like a mad thing', as another English player puts it. And she has had to live with that and with the intensity of the men – Ray Ruffels, Sandy Mayer and Fred Stolle. They practise three hours a day on non-match days and two hours before every match – sometimes with two playing against one, sometimes with four players at the net banging balls at one another to speed their reactions.

When they are 'at home' in New York – they have attracted a crowd of 13,000 to Madison Square Garden this year – they train on two courts covered with an air balloon, on top of a garage. Virginia generally bicycles there from her flat on the East Side. She has in a sense lived with professionals and become a professional. They have laughed at her bad technique until she has laughed with them and gradually changed until there are now few weaknesses.

Five years ago she said: 'I hate people who work too hard. I think laziness is the absolute end, but it is overwork that I really despise.' That, too, is a typically amateur English attitude. It has all gone now – replaced by a hard working professional.

And like a good pro she has been brave. Last year her service – generally regarded as the best in women's tennis – had got into such a mess that she couldn't even toss the ball up properly. So just before Christmas she started working in New York with Ham Richardson, the American player who reached the Wimbledon semi-finals in 1956. He said that it nearly killed him to see her wasting all that energy to so little effect. They made changes, but Virginia was not entirely happy. Her confidence was in shreds, and she had what she must have considered to be two very bad losses to Sue Barker. So she went to Jerry Teeguarden, a well-known American coach, and between them they have worked on a compromise which just happens to suit her. As she herself says: 'You have to have a lot of courage to give up what you've got to get something better, and you have to try not to worry too much if you don't do quite so well in the meantime.'

It was, in fact, a very close run thing. Her new serve still wasn't working at Eastbourne. So on that rainy Sunday two weeks ago she went on to what she calls the Bambi court at her family home in Kent and served 60 or 70 balls, 'and then I felt the rhythm and I knew that I had it'.

Five years ago I wrote: 'If only someone could control her sociability, make her singleminded for a few months and tune that fine mind of hers to the one single purpose of winning.' And five years ago she said: 'It is very difficult to find someone who tells you the right thing, so that your mind can interpret it into your own style. That is what we lack in so many sports in Britain.'

She never found that one person, but maturity and a combination of circumstances in her American way of life have achieved a similar result: the sheer professionalism of Billie Jean dripping on her like a tap; the philosophy of her friend Mary-Lou Mellace (with whom she shares her New York flat) that ambition can be achieved by guts and determination. And finally there has been the presence of Jerry Teeguarden during this past fortnight, taking the worry from her practice sessions and giving self-confidence.

Five years ago she said: 'I may seem at my ease with people, but underneath there is still a terrible lack of self-confidence.' On Friday, when I repeated that to her, she said: 'I am so much more secure as a person now. When I'm at close quarter with the other players, this is very obvious. When you are thrown together in dressing rooms you can see who is feeling at rest with themselves and who isn't. I just felt this week that I was far the strongest person in the dressing room. I just felt that I had more guts and felt more secure than anybody else this week.'

Part of that security stems from the New York Apples, Billie Jean, and Fred Stolle, their coach. The attitude of these Americans and Australians is that you prepare yourself as well as you can, and then, knowing that you have done everything, you go out and play your heart out – and you do not get tight if things start to go wrong. Instead you relax, confident in the knowledge that they will come right.

That is not as easy as it sounds. It requires confidence and the intelligence to read yourself. For instance when Virginia was playing Chris Evert there were signs that she was beginning to tense up. As one player puts it: 'The old Ginny would have gone on until the blood vessels were sticking out on her forehead, and she would have blown four games in the meantime. The new Virginia went and sat on the grass by the umpire's chair and relaxed her neck and back muscles. She sees the signs now. It's the same car, but it's being driven by a different person.'

That different person has also acted very differently during this past week. Instead of attempting to reject the pressure of people's expectation – something which she has accomplished easily in the past by losing to unknowns – she has put the pressure on herself by declaring that she could win. But that is just part of her perverse nature. Ten days ago, spotting my wife, who has been doing some commentating for BBC Television, she came across and said: 'Why are those BBC people writing me off? The more they do it, the more I'll prove them wrong.'

And she has handled herself so well. Five years ago she said: 'Wimbledon is so difficult. The phone rings all morning with people saying "Good Luck" . . . "Are you going to do well?" . . . all this sort of thing, and you can't just turn off the phone. I don't know what one does about it. Maybe one should just be mean and horrible and selfish.'

On Friday I asked her how she had avoided all those people who wanted a part of her, and she said: 'I've been much stricter. If you once look into the eyes of all those children who want autographs you've had it. You've just got to brace yourself and say I'm sorry, I can't. And I've had the pillow over the phone. This morning I had Rachmaninov's second symphony on so loud that I couldn't have heard it if it did ring!'

But all this ignores her athleticism and the talent that she has displayed over many years – she was, after all, the American champion at the age of 23. She comes from an athletic family. Her eldest brother Anthony was brilliant academically (he won a Rhodes Scholarship) and was a good tennis and squash player – a squash Blue at Oxford. He died of cancer last autumn.

Her younger brother Chris is a good athlete – a distance runner who was never able to break into the British international scene (where our best distance men are in the world class), but good enough to become Swedish marathon champion. He is now based permanently in Sweden. And her elder sister plays squash for her county.

Virginia herself is a natural athlete, a most beautiful mover. She is often described as tigerish, but there is a more urgent intensity about her. She is feline, but it is the movement of a feline who has her prey in sight. And she has stamina. One of the clichés trotted out this week was that Virginia, at the age of 31, would suffer most from the long baseline rallies against 22-year-old Chris Evert in the semi-final. But, of course, it is the other way round – a 31-year-old, particularly one as lean and fit as Virginia, has far more stamina than a 22-year-old who is slightly above her best fighting weight.

The Wades are the children of a South African mother (with Scottish blood) and an English father, a Church of England clergyman. When Virginia was very small the whole family moved to South Africa, where her father became Archdeacon of Durban.

'I was a very energetic child, and I suppose a bit of an exhibitionist,' she says, 'always doing things that were adventurous and exciting. I had endless energy, and at school I couldn't bear ever not doing well at something I thought I could do well. I was always determined never to let myself down. Somehow we were all expected to do well, but without any pressure being put on us. Of course, there was a lot of excitement when anybody did well, but absolutely no pressure.'

When Virginia was fifteen, the family came back to England, to Kent, and it was automatically assumed that after a couple of more years at school she would go to university. And so she did – to Sussex to study maths and physics (nuclear and atomic physics). But she did not really like her subjects: 'I much preferred the imagination of the artist rather than the disciplined intellectualism of the scientist. Really the English education system is ridiculous: you are forced to decide your subjects so early, committed to a course before you really know your own mind. It was only a very strong will that kept me at university.'

She had already decided that when she left she would go on to the tennis circuit for two years to see how she fared, because there is a chasm between the world class player who can earn a fortune every year and, say, the seventh ranked British player who struggles to avoid bankruptcy. And there is an equally large chasm between those who can earn fortunes and those who can become great champions as well.

Virginia's motivation has never been money. She earns over £100,000 a year, but she doesn't need it – like all her family she can live very frugally. Instead her motivation has been to prove to all of us, the unbelievers, that 'I deserve to be out there amongst the champions. I have felt that I have been the best player who has not won Wimbledon, and that if only I had a high opinion of myself I would feel I belonged out there.'

It was, of course, merely a question of believing in her place in the world. She has believed. And she has taken her rightful place.

Chris Brasher

IAN BOTHAM

18 July 1982

With his Henry VIII appearance of porcine eyes, massive bulk and animal good looks, Ian Botham, the cricketer, has in the past year become a symbol of the resurgent energy that this country evidently yearns to feel.

Unlike Henry VIII, however, Botham has not allowed his early promise to turn sour. Instead, a year ago, he recognised his limits by taking the unprecedented step of resigning the England captaincy. He had been a failure against Australia especially as a batsman and was wondering whether he would be picked for the next Test.

This Tuesday will be the anniversary of a born-again cricketer. At Headingley last year, hitting as he had never hit before in a Test, Botham made 149 not out, and his fame and reputation have been growing ever since. Last week, after he had made 208 against India, his celebrity reached some sort of peak of popular esteem when the *Sun* newspaper announced that he was the best player of the century, and 'as good as W. G. Grace'.

He was a success from the beginning. He was born on 24 November 1955 in Heswall, Cheshire, where his father, a chief petty officer in the Fleet Air Arm, and mother, who trained as a nurse, lived while the father was stationed in Northern Ireland.

Both parents played cricket. When the family moved to Yeovil in Somerset, after Botham senior retired and took a job with Westland Helicopters, Ian was sent first to Milford Junior School. By the age of nine he was already prodigious, both at cricket and football. Aged ten, he hit a six out of the ground and out of sight. He went next to Butler's Mead Secondary School nearby, where his feats continued. His father used to tell him that it was the next success, not the last one, that mattered. His hero was Gary Sobers.

By the time he was fifteen, he could have chosen a career in either football or cricket. Crystal Palace offered him a contract. Instead, he joined the Lord's ground staff, where he was reckoned to be a promising batsman but no sort of bowler. He is remembered for flinging down bad bouncers at elderly members of MCC.

He played his first full season for Somerset in 1974, was selected for England in 1977, aged 21, and two years later achieved the Test double of 1,000 runs and 100 wickets in what was then record time. He was married in 1976, to Kathryn Waller, a Yorkshire girl, and they have a son, Liam, five next month, and a daughter, Sarah, who is three.

His physique has certainly helped his success, even though first-class cricketers come in all shapes and sizes. When Botham was seventeen, Brian Close, the former England captain who was then captaining Somerset, pointed him out to a friend and said: 'Take a good look at that bloke. He's going to be a great player, and he's built like a shithouse door.'

He is six foot two inches, and weighs nearly fifteen stone. One winter, after an accident, he went up to seventeen stone. His shoulders, despite all the sixes, are not particularly broad, but he has a colossal torso and thighs.

He likes to appear indestructible. After he had smashed up two sports cars on a motor-racing circuit near Andover earlier this season, although badly shaken in private, he surfaced like Superman for the public and the photographers. In Sydney in 1979, when it was so hot that Willis, the England fast bowler, left the field dehydrated, Botham bowled eighteen overs as England's only surviving pace bowler and that night, while everyone else flopped early to bed, went to see *Midnight Express* for the second time to watch the gruesome bits. Yet he is prone to occasional migraines, and is partially colour blind.

Because of his raw energy, his blatant desire to be a winner, and his occasional spectacular rudeness, some people in the outside world regard him, not to put too fine a point on it, as a lout, though a lout, to be sure, of exceptional sporting talents. This is not how he is viewed by his team-mates. They see him as basically a shy character who would much prefer to be one of the lads, and who likes to submerge himself in the camaraderie and protection of whatever cricketing company he happens to be in.

He is loyal. If he hears a stranger criticising one of his colleagues, he is liable to barge over and ask for the evidence. If a member of the Somerset team is in financial trouble, it is usually Botham who helps him out.

Botham is not a thinker, though he has common sense. However, he was forced into a period of self-doubt when, after being made at the age of 24 the youngest England captain of the century, his world slowly began to crack last year. He stopped making runs – a matter of luck, according to him, not the burden of captaincy. His bowling lost effectiveness, owing to trouble with a vertebra in his back. He was up on a charge of 'occasioning actual bodily harm'. He felt the press was out to get him.

But he was found not guilty of the charge, and he fought back as a cricketer. He had averaged thirteen as captain, since giving the job up, he has averaged 64.26.

No doubt he was made captain too young. One of his best friends in the Somerset side says he is 'really a simple country lad at heart'. He likes shooting and fishing, and goes salmon-fishing in Scotland every autumn, though he has yet to catch a salmon. He stays in the best hotels, but drinks lager in the pubs round the corner. In the West Indies, when he was captain of England, he showed himself to lack the capacity to make small talk to the local officials, but was superb at fostering good relations between the two teams. At the end of two Test matches, he arrived back at his hotel at dawn after a night's carousing with his West Indian cricketing mates. In his drinking he is in a long West Country cricketing tradition: Sammy Woods of Somerset used to drink champagne (and eat lobsters) for breakfast.

Botham could afford the same breakfasts, if he liked. These days he is said to earn, with sponsorships and endorsements, £60,000 to £70,000 a year. South Africa offered him over £50,000 last winter for four 'rebel' Tests, which he declined. He owns two racehorses. But not long ago he was nearly broke, and as recently as the spring of last year did not find it easy to raise the money for his court case.

His current cash flow means that he can afford to take flying lessons regularly, and he has done so for a year. He sees it as another challenge. In his Saab turbo car he has reached his limits of speed on earth (while he was England captain he was fined for speeding) so he has now conceived the ambition of flying to Australia and, eventually, round the world. (W. G. Grace went ballooning over the Avon Gorge.)

As his father long ago advised, Botham is always looking to the next milestone. At Kanpur at the beginning of February, he accepted a bet of 20-1 with an English reporter that he would make 1,000 Test runs during this calendar year: not a unique feat, but at the time of the bet he had made only 2,000-odd Test runs since 1977. Already this year he has made 699, with three Tests against Pakistan still to come and four in Australia. Challenges keep Botham going.

He has set himself another statistical goal, connected with Boycott. The relationship between the two might be described as one of mutual disrespect. It was Botham who ran out Boycott in New Zealand, when Boycott, who was captain, appeared to be absorbed in remaining not out and to have forgotten the good of the side. Botham is now determined to overtake Boycott's record aggregate of Test runs. If it were Hutton or Compton or Hammond who held the record, he might be much less interested. Boycott made over 8,000, but if Botham, whose total is now 2,833, keeps going at his current rate, he should dethrone Boycott before he hangs up his boots.

He has one more ambition. One of the few cricket skills he still has to master is that of bowling off-breaks. Again there is a spur. The two current players he regards as his equals, Viv Richards and Mike Proctor, can also bowl them. Botham reckons he can bowl off-breaks better than either of the two specialists on the Somerset side, and on the last day's play at the Oval last week all four of his overs were off-breaks. He knows that his pace bowling will get fewer wickets as he gets older and stiffens up – already, as his batting improves, his average haul of wickets per Test match has gone done from five to three – so he will need his off-break if he is going to break Fred Trueman's England record of 307 Test dismissals. So far, in 51 Tests, he has taken 231.

But is he really, as the *Sun* thinks, 'as good as W. G. Grace'? Comparisons with Grace are futile, except in the matter of vitality. Botham has had no part in shaping the game's evolution or techniques. Richie Benaud, the former Australian captain, ranks him with Sir Garfield Sobers and Keith Miller, two of the outstanding all-rounders in cricket history. T. E. Bailey says he is the best cricketer England has produced this century.

These judgments sound extravagant, but they are particularly endorsed by Sir Leonard Hutton, an exacting judge. 'Botham is not as good a bowler as Miller, who could bowl slow as well as fast: at least, he has some way to go before he is as good an off-spinner as Miller. He is very close to being as good as Sobers, but not quite, either with bat or ball. The variety that Sobers had with his bowling was unique.' It may safely be concluded, in sum, that Botham is as exceptional in his era as any cricketer has been in any former era, apart from Grace himself and Bradman.

He says he will retire at 30. So long as he does not seriously injure himself flying or driving, what will Sir Ian do then? Governor of the Falklands?

Diego Maradona

29 June 1986

At noon today local time, the eyes of half the world will be focused on a patch of turf in Mexico City – and on one man in particular. The Azteca Stadium will be the setting for the World Cup final between Argentina and West Germany, and much of the watching world will be hoping it is the stage for the apotheosis of the most extravagantly gifted footballer the world has ever seen: Diego Armando Maradona.

At an altitude of 7,400 feet the Azteca Stadium is the nearest stadium to heaven this world possesses and an appropriate setting for Maradona's miraculous talents to flower in. The skills of the little Argentine have added a different dimension to a competition that many feared would be a drab succession of stalemates between over-trained teams lacking individual stars.

The Maradona miracle has been a long time coming, though it was obvious from the moment he burst on to the international scene as a teenage candidate for the Argentine World Cup Squad of 1978 that he was something out of the ordinary. The comparisons with another superlatively gifted South American, Pelé, were swiftly being drawn – and still are.

The Brazilians took a chance with the seventeen-year-old Pelé in the 1978 World Cup finals and it paid off. He starred, they won and he was launched on a career that was to bring another two World Cup winning medals.

Maradona did not get that early chance. He was left out of his country's 1978 squad and Argentina still won the title. Maradona agreed with the decision. 'I was too immature,' he said, and four years later in Spain he still was. The team wasn't as good, and he was a marked man in every sense. Eventually he boiled over and was sent off for retaliating, he and his country departing the tournament almost simultaneously.

It has been a similar story at club level. His periods at his two Argentine clubs, Argentine Juniors and Boca Juniors, were marked more by financial scandals and murky deals than by success in league or cup competitions. He has fared little better since transferring to Europe after the 1982 débâcle. He failed to ignite the ever-promising Barcelona (who won the Spanish League under Terry Venables the season after he left) and he has attracted full houses to Naples but brought them no nearer the Italian League title.

At 25, he arrived in Mexico having achieved fame and riches but absolutely nothing for club or country where it really matters – on the playing field. What Maradona needed was the stage Mexico offered, and the world has seen him emerge onto it as the complete player he has always threatened to become.

He has taken the opportunity with both feet (and one hand). With every game Argentina have played he has grown in stature and confidence. At first he created a wealth of scoring opportunities for his team-mates but in the last two knock-out games, against England and Belgium, he took over the game himself, scoring all four of Argentina's goals (three with breathtaking individual efforts) and displaying the whole awesome repertoire of his skills.

Maradona does not look much like an athlete. He stands five feet five inches tall, weighs ten stone eight pounds and wears an earstud, sometimes a diamond one. His dark, attractive face bears just the suspicion of another layer beneath the chin; it is the sort of face that you might see behind a Buenos Aires bar.

Part of the reason for the adoration he receives from the Argentine people is that he comes from the lowest sector of society: his is a real rags-to-riches story. He was born into a family of Italian descent in a poor suburb of the Argentine capital, behind the stadium of Argentinos Juniors, a club with strong working-class support. He has eight brothers and sisters – two of his younger brothers are also promising footballers.

In a country where football is king, the hunt for young talent is intense. The young Diego was spotted by an Argentinos Junior scout playing in the street and signed up at the age of twelve. He made his league début at fifteen and his first appearance for his country only a year later, coming on as a substitute against Hungary. He went to a bigger Buenos Aires club, Boca Juniors, the move financed by a consortium of local businessmen. The deal nearly collapsed in a financial tangle and the Argentine Football Association had to step in to guarantee the money to keep their little star in the country until after the 1982 World Cup.

After that he moved to Barcelona, who paid £6.5 million for him, of which he himself received £1.5 million. But it was to be a two-year disaster for him. He never settled, surrounding himself with a huge retinue of family and camp followers whose arrogant behaviour swiftly attracted the dislike of the Catalans. He found the city too gossipy and the press only too willing to attack him. Probably too much was expected of him. He missed half of one season through hepatitis, and half of another through an appalling leg injury inflicted by Andoni Goicoechea, known as the 'Butcher of Bilbao.'

All too often he was to be the target for Spain's hatchet men and the referees did little to protect him. Finally he was suspended for three months for his part in a cup-tie brawl. He had yet to conquer his temperament.

Spain had also been a financial nightmare for him. Since he was a teenager his affairs had been managed by a Rasputin-like figure called Jorge Cysterzpiller, a cripple who had been a childhood friend. He set up a company, Maradona Productions, to handle the commercial side. It made and lost them a fortune. It is estimated Maradona lost £1.5 million in Spain, much of the money being frittered away on his entourage. There were plenty of hangers-on and Maradona was a sucker for a tear-jerking story. He has parted company with Cysterzpiller; his affairs are now managed by an older and more experienced man, Guillermo Coppola.

He is much happier in Naples where he moved for a fee of £5.5 million. There he was instantly deified, the people of Naples identifying with the working-class kid who had come back to his ancestors' country. Within a day of his signing, 100 Naples babies had been christened Diego Armando. He is paid at least £500,000 a year by the club.

He lives in a large villa in Naples with his long-time girlfriend Claudia (though the scandal sheets regularly link him with a variety of other lovelies), and, usually, several other members of his family. He also has a villa in the middle-class Buenos Aires suburb of Villafane, where he has installed his parents and his five unmarried sisters.

He has clearly grown up a lot in the last couple of years and can handle the public adulation and constant media attention. In Mexico he has been notable for his patience with the press, though he now habitually refers to himself in the third person: 'Maradona doesn't like . . .'

The new Maradona is unlikely to find himself detained by the police, as he was for 'public aggression' after a match in Buenos Aires in 1980 following an incident with a spectator. More typical now is the good humour he showed against England, when he smilingly replaced the corner flag at the linesman's insistence before he could take a corner.

How does that image square with the natural English accusation that he cheated us out of the World Cup by pushing in the first goal with his hand? To Argentines, there is no contradiction. It is applauded as a display of *viveza* – craftiness – which won the game. The gauchos always cheated at cards or over women – it is a quality to be admired, not condemned.

What is the secret of Maradona's footballing success? For the experts, it is his amazing control and touch, especially with the left foot he favours (though he is no slouch with the right). His astonishingly stocky thighs give him a balance which enables him to ride over many of the roughest tackles. Above all, there is his imagination, the (justified) belief that he can do the most outrageous things with the ball in the most confined spaces. He has explosive acceleration which gives him that extra yard over his pursuer within a split second and he has now added the self-discipline that means his preliminary magic is more likely to end up in goals.

Today, at the peak of his career, he carries a heavy burden: nothing less than a country's pride rides on his shoulders. His fortunes have somehow strangely coincided with those of Argentina: in 1982, the Falklands defeat came at the same time as Argentina's ignominious exit from the World Cup. Maradona was blamed for it and vied on the front pages with the unfortunate General Menéndez as the villain of the hour.

He has long since been forgiven, although if Argentina lose today his countrymen may turn on him again. It is no exaggeration to say that he is being regarded as the potential saviour of the nation by a country with a long history of venerating such figures, come to rescue them in their hour of need. For the rest of us, the little man from Buenos Aires has already done enough in this World Cup for it to be forever remembered as Maradona's monument.

MISCELLANEOUS

A collection of half-a-dozen who do not fit neatly into the other categories. As mentioned in the Introduction, the profile of Evan Edwards, a Welsh shepherd, was written by Paul Ferris, himself a Welshman and the future author of biographies of Dylan Thomas and Huw Wheldon, among many other books. It was published on Christmas Day, 1960. Sir Timothy Cargill was the work of Philip Toynbee, for long the *Observer*'s chief book reviewer. The date is worth noting. Robin Day continued to be television's leading political interviewer for nearly twenty more years. The profile's parting thought came true with the BBC TV programme *Question Time*, which Day (later Sir Robin) chaired for a decade. Its huge popularity was in large part due to his highly individual and irreverent style. Sir William (later Lord) Rees-Mogg had his way with the appointment of Luke Rittner as Secretary-General of the Arts Council, and later made a perhaps unexpected return to journalism in the shape of a weekly column in the *Independent*, in addition to all his public offices. I have included Elizabeth David as an example of a profile which casts some light on an influential figure in her own field about whom the public would probably know very little – an important task for the profile genre. The rollicking portrait of Denis Thatcher was the work of staff feature writer John Sweeney and formed part of a special section which examined various aspects of Mrs Thatcher and Thatcherism to mark her tenth anniversary as Prime Minister.

EVAN EDWARDS

25 December 1960

Christmas in the countryside is supposed to be more traditional than Christmas anywhere else. Innocence, in Christmas cards and many hearts, still means snow-covered slopes, small birds in trees, holly, lonely cottages, village greens, skaters, inns, innkeepers and shepherds. Evan Edwards is a Welsh shepherd. His life is hardly romantic; his Christmas will be commonplace; but because we are all susceptible to the season, this is the kind of man who comes to mind.

Shepherds keep dogs, blow whistles, carry crooks, wear oilskins in storms and know one sheep from another. On the Scottish border and in the north of England they may have a couple of thousand acres to look after: in South Wales one farm has 15,000 acres and nine shepherds, and a sheep-stealer with a van can make a dozen disappear in a night.

Mr Edwards has a 500-acre sheep-walk on a mountain, with 400 sheep, employers who never bother him, and no thieves. He comes from the mountains, and, like most people, does what he does for the simple reason that anything else would be worse.

He has a hard, quiet face, with dark hair: he is in his mid-forties. Welsh is his first language. The small stone house where he lives with his wife and two children is 1,000 feet up, in central Wales, facing east into the Cambrian Mountains, which are among the oldest rocks in the world.

Above the thin, perpetual wind a jet can almost always be heard, very high. A lot of rain falls, and at times of bomb-testing has given this part of Britain more radio-activity than most: the village of Cwmystwyth, five miles away, was renamed Cwmstrontium by the wags.

Shepherds usually turn out to have had shepherds for fathers. The father of Mr Edwards lived deeper and higher in the mountains, but the army took over the land for an artillery range in the Second World War, and the family moved down to the present house. Now the son has it, rent-free from the three brothers who employ him.

All he has to do for long stretches of the year is to get up at 7.30, hear the weather forecast on the new red battery radio with antennae, have breakfast – with his wife's salty butter, and cocoa, which he drinks instead of tea – then go out to see the sheep are all right at the top of the mountain, 1,500 feet up, where they will have spent the night.

After that he can get on with mending a fence or chopping wood or digging a

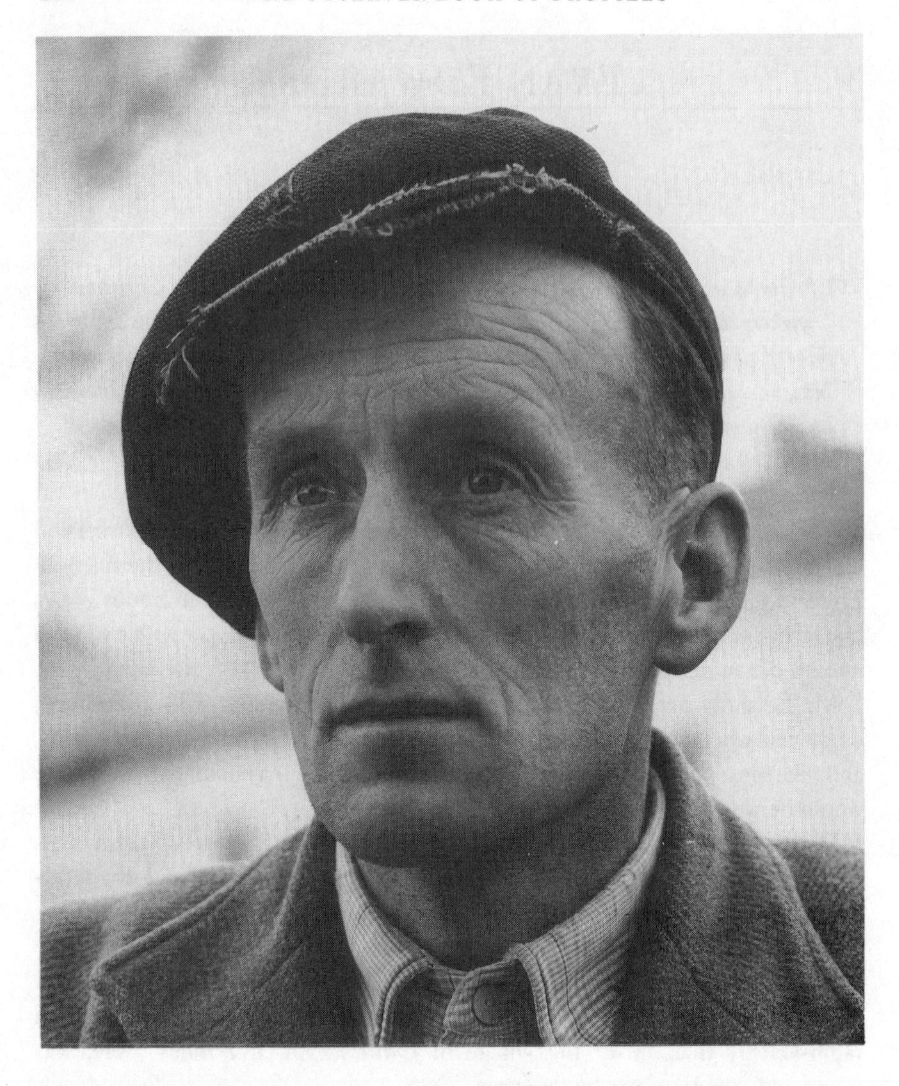

ditch; he goes home for midday dinner, and may doze by the fire for half an hour with one of his weekly newspapers; the *Cymro* or the *Cambrian News*, while the draught sings through the patched-up hole where the wind has blown a pane out.

But the fixed points of his year turn Mr Edwards into a furious man of action. His voice is harsh when he calls to his dogs. At lambing time he will kneel with the sheep – 'Sometimes you've got to take hold of the lambs and bring them out.' A month or two later comes the ear-marking – 'We always keep the day, the last Thursday in May.' With a sharp knife the ears are nicked in a pattern distinctive to this flock, a slit in the left ear and a piece off the top of the right.

Above the dresser, in the kitchen with mats and linoleum on the floor, is a tattered notebook containing 355 earmarks from the surrounding hills. Mr Edwards lifts it down carefully and turns the pages slowly with thick fingers. He knows the marks as far as Rhayader, fifteen miles away. Some of them go back for centuries.

Shearing is in July, when twenty men and boys, with wives and other interested parties outnumbering them, come up the track from below and over the top from the next valley. Mrs Edwards cooks a sheep and eighteen pounds of beef, and the noise is tremendous.

Among the hill-farmers and shepherds, there is still quite a lot of getting together in one another's houses. The other evening Mr Edwards went over the mountain to help roll a side of a pig: 'Pull it with a rope and a ire-on bar. Roll it tight and it's keeping better like that.' Mrs Edwards said: 'He wasn't home till three.'

While he is out on the hill, keeping the sheep together, whenever he catches an animal turning it upside down to trim its horny foot, he watches for kites, which breed round about in secret places, and reports to the Nature Conservancy. He sees a few grouse, and wild geese flying from the bog up to the mountain lakes.

In the summer Mr Edwards rides a pony. There are campers in the valley, and for twenty years now they have had a regular summer visitor, a retired soldier from the Midlands who comes for the fishing, or, as Mrs Edwards says approvingly, just to go off for the day with sandwiches and lie on the grass. There are hikers. Extra sheep have come up for the summer pasture, at ten bob a head from May to October.

There is the marking and dipping, and sheep to be driven down to the lorries for market. The hills are busy. Then, in mid-autumn, the rams are let out among the ewes. Then winter settles down, black and wet.

The school taxi squelches through the field to the bottom of the track, a quarter of a mile away. It's too cold to ride a pony. Mr Edwards squelches over the hills in wellingtons, stuffing pills of carbon tetrachloride down unwilling throats to prevent the fluke. In the evenings the parents play whist with Lewis, aged fourteen, and Sara Eleanor, aged ten, while the paraffin lamp hisses and Luxembourg comes through powerfully on the radio.

Lewis is mad about sheep and football, but it's not clear, whether he'll be a footballer or even a shepherd. His father says: 'If it goes on like now there'll be no need for shepherds here. The other side from us, it's all bought for forests. No one wants to come and live up the mountain now. When a sheep farm is going for sale the Forestry Commission give good money. They say they've got trees to grow anywhere, right up the mountain.'

This doesn't depress Mr Edwards unduly. It's fact of life, like snow in February. He is reasonably content: goes to chapel occasionally, visits Aberystwyth for the pictures, has never been to London, of course, has a bank account at Tregaron, thinks 'the electric is very handy' but doesn't pine for it, never tires of eating mutton; has five good dogs, a few cows, a hazel crook made by his cousin with 'E.E.' cut into the curly part, and a pair of geese for Christmas.

On Boxing Night there will be a whist drive in Bont, the nearest village, while the children stay with grandparents there. Soon it will be next year, and Mr Edwards will be busy again.

SIR TIMOTHY CARGILL

1 April 1962

As Sir Charles Snow has reason to regret, the scientific expert in this country has rarely exercised much power-behind-the-throne. In his heyday Lord Cherwell may have aspired to Rasputin status, but his evident delight in the role detracted from the necessary air of mystery. Perhaps Tim Cargill (whose 57th birthday falls today) has come nearer than any other Englishman to being a man of science who is also a major Grey Eminence.

His name seldom appears in newspapers, and a list of the posts Sir Timothy has held gives little away – in wartime, Co-ordinator of Information and Supplies; under the Attlee Government, Chairman of the Parliamentary Commission; more recently, Secretary to the Duchy of Lancaster. Yet each post has involved its holder in positions of effective political power. For although Cargill is a distinguished physicist, who studied under Niels Bohr in Copenhagen, it is as a patient negotiator and brilliant administrator that he is equally well known in Whitehall and Washington, and now, of course, also in Brussels.

The Cargills have been Somerset squires since the sixteenth century, and Sir Timothy's father, 'Panther' Cargill, was one of the most famous of Edwardian eccentrics. Readers of Sir Osbert Sitwell's autobiography will remember the many delightful encounters between 'Panther' and old Sir George. Yet until the present generation the family had produced little of intellectual achievement.

It was a shock to his father when Timothy won a scholarship to Eton and joined the highbrow inhabitants of College. But he was no mere bookworm. A considerable athlete, his exceptional height (he is six feet eight inches) was matched by speed and stamina: he is still remembered in College as the last scholar to score a goal in the Wall Game. He went up to King's in the early 1920s and there, apart from setting up a new record in the quarter-mile and rowing in the defeated Cambridge crew of 1923 – itself a distinction in those years of monotonous

Cambridge victories – he first began to retire into that brilliant obscurity that suits him so well.

He took a first in physics, and a distinguished academic career seemed almost inevitable: many of his fellow-scientists still regret his loss to the world of pure science. But Tim Cargill himself believes that the comparatively minor contributions which he made to nuclear physics in his three years in Copenhagen and five at the Cavendish Laboratory are all that it was in him to make.

His real career began when Ramsay Macdonald offered him a private-secretaryship. Much has been said against Macdonald, but every subsequent prime minister has had reason to be thankful for his acumen on this occasion. Cargill made himself indispensable to Macdonald and indispensable is what he has remained ever since. He is immensely proud of being a public *servant* – although some of his 'masters' must have smiled a little wryly at the term. What he means is certainly not that he is a simple follower of instructions from on high – that he has never been – but rather that he will stay at his post in all circumstances, performing his functions as he himself sees fit.

The Suez adventure was an example of Cargill at his most active. His role in planning the operation – successfully concealed under the pageantry of the Duchy – was as positive as his part in the subsequent feat of extrication. It was largely due to the brilliant tactics suggested by Cargill (based on a personal knowledge of Nasser – an old squash opponent from his student days) that the Government was able to withdraw with such a lack of ostensible damage. It is not generally known that Harold Macmillan's discreet call to retreat, itself decisive with the then Prime Minister, was made only after the then Chancellor had been closeted with Cargill for more than two hours.

One day, the publication of official papers will no doubt reveal the full extent of Sir Timothy's great influence in nearly every national crisis of the last 30 years. What already clearly emerges is that he was wholly responsible during the war for the organisation of the hideously dangerous 'X' convoys. This is sufficiently hinted at in Churchill's memoirs. Cargill was as well aware as any admiral that the losses would be heavy; it was his special contribution to final victory that he endured the news of the repeated losses without flinching and absolutely refused to vary a plan which was the product of profound mathematical calculations, based on an inspired insight into the enemy's intentions. 'It was all really a frightful shambles,' he says disarmingly.

Charm, of a peculiarly English kind, is a key to Cargill's achievements. It is the charm of absolute naturalness. Still remarkably youthful-looking despite his thinning hair, he and his handsome Lithuanian wife are famous in Somerset for the undemonstrative splendour of their entertaining. Tim is a renowned connoisseur of Burgundy, and so enthusiastic a cook that for a short time he contributed a column on the subject to a well-known magazine, under a (female) pseudonym. He is prouder that his daughter, Mairi, is art editor of a Cuban monthly review, *Prog*, than that his son, Hugo, was recently appointed Assistant Keeper of the Queen's Statisticks at Windsor Castle.

The contrast between his family home, Samberley Hall, now and as it was in his father's day, marks a change of epoch. 'Panther' was frankly in the Squire Western tradition, and it is no secret that he and his male guests often ended a dinner party under the table. The present Sir Timothy is no prude, but he has a natural fastidiousness which is hostile to all forms of excess. What would certainly not be approved by his 'hunting fathers' is his unique collection of handbells and the Légers and Dufys, with one superb ferro-concrete Hunk Spurrier, which now adorn the Long Gallery, itself recently redecorated in a style which Lady Cargill describes as 'a mild version of the "new brutalism" of a red-brick university corridor.'

It would be a mistake to assume that Cargill is no more than a peculiarly complete example of the Establishment Man. It was while James Joyce's *Ulysses* was still generally regarded as a bad joke, that he published, pseudonymously, his now famous interpretation of the book as a prophecy. The outbreak of war in 1939 was to vindicate his perception. The fallacy of thinking in Establishment terms is shown by the fact that Dylan Thomas was asked to stay at Samberley – and then asked again!

Perhaps his greatest gift is his knack of foreseeing who or what will next be in the news. He was the first Whitehall man to call Dr Hastings Banda by his Christian name. And anyone in the Treasury will admit that Cargill was for joining the Common Market before the first suggestion of this plan was ever made.

In the company of his closest friends – Connolly, Ehrenburg, John Glenn, Colin MacInnes – the conversation seldom touches on politics. But among his wider circle – which includes Ian Mikardo, Charles Clore, Arthur Schlesinger, Tony Snowdon, Huckleberry Hound and John Osborne – he will often make a bitingly realistic analysis of some contemporary political phenomenon.

But he has one failing which some find inexcusable – he indulges a taste for feeble practical jokes. This he attributes to having been born on April Fools' Day. 'It has made nonsense of my life,' he says, with devastating perception.

ROBIN DAY

30 January 1972

When Robin Day left *Panorama* last week after twelve controversial years, it meant not just the end of an era for the BBC's most eminent political programme. It was also an unexpected turning point in the career of one of the ablest and most frightening interviewers television has yet produced.

'It all depends on whether you are more frightened of him,' says Richard Crossman, 'than he is of you.' The idea of Robin Day being frightened of anyone is surprising, yet newcomers to the *Panorama* studios have been struck by his nervousness before transmission, as well as his kindness. He can be a pompous, contentious man, yet his private persona sometimes contrasts sharply with his more abrasive public image. On such occasions, he can seem a less assured, even a vulnerable, figure, particularly sensitive to criticism and surprisingly angered by it.

He has made enemies – partly among television people who resent his independence and his high salary, reputedly more than £20,000 a year. There is also opposition to him among some of the new, young BBC producers who are trying to revamp *Panorama*, only to be blocked, it is said, by the patriarchal presence of Day. 'I've known almost as many programme editors,' he says, 'as Queen Victoria knew prime ministers.' While it is true that he left for something fresh, he has been featured less and less prominently on *Panorama* of late.

Even his severest critics acknowledge, however, that Day is still one of the most provocative and fearless among those who interview leading politicians on TV. He can look more formidable than some of the people he interviews, but he asks the questions the public wants to know the answer to. Unlike his blander colleagues, he refuses to let politicians off the hook. He has also kept his dignity, consistently refusing to exploit or trivialise his public persona in the lucrative entertainment field. 'He's tough, fair, courteous, does his homework, and knows his facts,' says Jeremy Thorpe. It is difficult to imagine *Panorama* without him.

In the early 1950s, Day had been an impecunious barrister for a year and was a temporary, and unknown, radio producer when ITN took him on, with Christopher Chataway, as one of their first newscasters. (BBC-TV had turned him down.) Then the traditional role of television announcers was neutral and impersonal. Under the guidance of Aidan Crawley, former editor of ITN, Day and Chataway were encouraged to develop their own personalities. They became something that was to be crucial to the development of television – the first tele-journalists.

Hunched intently before the cameras, wearing what Frankie Howerd later described as 'those cruel glasses', Day gave the public something it had literally never experienced before. People were astonished that he was permitted to sign off one programme with the remark, 'Goodnight to you all – including the lady who wishes to put a bomb under me and describes me as a swollen-headed pip-squeak.'

His major innovation, the source of his celebrity, was his incisive and, in the early days, sacrilegious treatment of public figures. 'Is it right,' he asked Nasser after the Suez crisis 'that you now accept the permanent existence of Israel as an independent state?' 'Well,' Nasser replied. 'You are jumping to conclusions.' 'No,' replied Day. 'I am asking a question.' In the 1950s such an approach required nerve, as it still does.

'I'm tired of being governed by babies, women and children,' Randolph Churchill once boomed at him, referring to the previous Labour Government. 'Now, Harold Macmillan is a grown-up man.' 'At 63,' said Day, 'he ought to be.'

Politicians have since learned to cope with his vigorous cross-examinations: it is difficult for Day to appear to be tough and uncompromising when prime ministers call him 'Robin'. When he began in television, he took on the Establishment – with no quarter given. Now, at 48, though his interviews may be as relentless as ever, he has himself become an institution. He speaks with genuine authority about the difficulties and dangers of television as a journalistic medium. Yet, for a former Liberal candidate, he sometimes seems to have drifted Rightwards over the years. His world, too, is very much that of the banter and cigar smoke of the Garrick Club.

But if one catches him relaxing at home without his familiar bow-tie, he can look a large, unkempt man with a bit of a belly, not quite so much master of the situation as one might expect. Television has also given him three physical distortions: it's made him look older, darker, and shorter than he is. His fine and rather stately Victorian house in the fashionable area of Holland Park has such an imposing front door that it looks as if a foreign embassy might lie behind it. There are framed cartoons of Day in the hall, and a portrait of his young wife, Katherine, a former Oxford don. 'She's frighteningly clever,' says Day. 'Much cleverer than me.'

In the basement he has a small functional office filled with files, reference books and encyclopedias. A leopard-skin rug, which Day bought from a game warden in Tanganyika, covers the floor. On the wall hangs a picture of him, as President of the Oxford Union, in round Billy Bunter spectacles: Day was then seventeen stone. 'I speak for the little man,' he was fond of saying in debates. In the picture he is flanked by his two guest speakers for the occasion – Randolph Churchill and Dr C. E. M. Joad, the celebrated Brains Truster.

He is good company, though a better talker than a listener. An old barrister chum once said of him, 'He has developed provocation as a social style.' For the past seventeen years he has also developed it as a television style, and the question now facing this ambitious, self-made man is whether or not there is sufficient interest in it any longer.

He may have sensed the danger: for some time he has wanted to switch to an executive role. He applied for the Director-Generalship of the ITA and would dearly have liked to get the job. He may now turn to commercial radio – his *It's Your Line* programme on Radio 4 has been very successful. But what he wants, perhaps more than anything, is his own prestigious television programme – something which the BBC has mysteriously never given him.

SIR WILLIAM REES-MOGG

19 December 1982

Those who have ventured out of the editorial chairs of our great newspapers to run other institutions – Sir Gordon Newton at Vavasour, Lord Crowther at Trusthouse Forte, Sir William Haley at Encyclopedia Britannica, Alastair Hetherington at BBC Scotland – have usually found them less than responsive to what has been called 'the instinctive autocracy of the newspaper editor'. The phrase was used last week of the latest in this line, Sir William Rees-Mogg, now at the centre of the biggest row ever to rage in public at the Arts Council.

The row is over the key appointment of its next Secretary-General. As the Council's chairman, Sir William chaired the selection committee that recommended 35-year-old Luke Rittner, director of the Association for Business Sponsorship of the Arts. Instead of rubber-stamping this choice, however, the Council threw it out. Since the case against Rittner was presented in letters from the Council's own staff – solemnly read out by the present Secretary-General, Sir Roy Shaw – the row has been seen as 'democracy breaking out at the Arts Council'.

Sir William refutes the suggestion calmly. 'I would say it is conservatism defending entrenched positions at the Council. Before Luke Rittner was named, Lord Birkett of the GLC was considered the favourite, and almost as much of a head of steam built up against him. A lot of it is fear of change, hostility from some people to the idea of somebody coming from outside.'

After fourteen years at the top of *The Times*, William Rees-Mogg is a watchful, guarded, elusive man, elegant in phrase and dress. There is something Victorian

about his presence (though his interests lie in the century before that), and his courtesy conveys the impression of a man who does not like rows.

It is misleading – 'I quite enjoy controversy.' He expresses distress about the pain all this has caused Luke Rittner – 'a young man of excellent reputation' – but insists (convincingly) that 'as far as I'm concerned, it hasn't chipped the paintwork at all. If one's been through as many rows as an editor of a daily paper is bound to go through in fourteen years, you end up not taking them personally.'

The editorial crown in Sir William's wardrobe of hats has in fact been seen as the root of the trouble. This row follows a series of rumours and press leaks about the unpopularity of his chairmanship (he joined the Council in April). There are stories of Sir William 'going his own way', seeing clients without consulting or informing his officers or panellists; taking unilateral decisions; pushing through personal preferences. There are also a few grumbles about his Garrick Club lunches and his chauffeur-driven Arts Council Jaguar.

Sir William was a surprise appointment to the post, which came as quite a surprise to him, too. He was not known as a defender of the arts before he got it, but he claims he is a lover of the arts, and once wrote that 'Shakespeare matters to most civilised people and Alexander Pope matters to some of us'. He is certainly a lover of books, and can be expected to shift the emphasis of the Council's work gently towards literature from music and drama. Perhaps more important, he points out that he has been involved with public affairs for 25 years, and he feels 'able to handle what are really public problems' and 'comfortable with politicians, civil servants, and the press'.

'Comfortable' is a word that recurs in his deliberations. He has lived in comfort most of his life – 'I can't pretend I'm not well-off,' he once told an interviewer. He was born in 1928 into a family of Somerset gentry (he was High Sheriff of Somerset in 1978) and when he was editor of *The Times* he bought Ston Easton, a stately Palladian house in the county. He sold it five years ago, and it is now Egon Ronay's Hotel of the Year: William and Gillian Rees-Mogg and their five children now occupy a pleasant rectory not far away at weekends. In London they live in Lord Butler's former house in Smith Square; there is also a flat over the bookshop at 17 Pall Mall.

He has also turned the less comfortable areas of his life to advantage. At Charterhouse, where his Catholicism and lack of physical prowess could have caused him problems, he commanded respect through well-timed revelations of his learning and his investments, and his affectation of middle age. A contemporary recalls that he founded 'all the right societies', and he became Head of School; at Balliol he became president of the Oxford University Conservative Association (after serving as a junior committee member under Margaret Thatcher's presidency), and ('to everyone's surprise') President of the Union.

Rees-Mogg does not deny his ambition. As a young journalist on the *Financial Times*, a colleague asked what would satisfy him as a career. Editorship of the *FT*? He shook his head. A Cabinet post? Yes. ('It would have had to be a *senior* Cabinet post,' qualified a friend.) Editorship of *The Times?* Yes, that would do.

It came in 1967, when he was 38, and was announced on the same day as the appointment of Harold Evans as editor of the *Sunday Times* at the same age. Evans's reputation came from campaigning journalism in the north. Rees-Mogg had twice unsuccessfully contested Chester-le-Street as a Conservative candidate (at a by-election in 1956 he lost by 21,287 votes); he had also progressed from the

FT to the *Sunday Times* in 1960, and there from the city to the political-economic to the deputy editorship.

At *The Times* his editorship was generally popular, though some of his staff grumbled that it erred on the Olympian side, and some of his readers could be startled when its passionate conservatism of morality and politics could go beyond thundering into a sort of dottiness.

A memorable leader on the Cambridge traitors in November 1979 contemplated the 'broader moral relativism' of their homosexuality and suggested that even in Maynard Keynes, a notably loyal product of the same culture, there might have been a link between his rejection of conventional sexual morality and 'his emotional resentment of the monetary rules which prevented inflation, particularly the gold standard'. Keynes, brooded *The Times*, 'did not like rules'. (And Rees-Mogg has always liked the gold standard.) As editor, he stubbornly defended Richard Nixon against all the evidence.

In March 1981 he left *The Times* to the mercies of Rupert Murdoch, declaring that he felt like the prisoners at the end of *Fidelio*, 'bursting out of their jailhouse with a song of joy on their lips'. He had been 'too sensible for too long'.

He was knighted three months later (unlike Evans), and took on a directorship at GEC, the vice-chairmanship of the BBC and his own antiquarian bookselling business, Pickering & Chatto. One suspects that it is in the latter that he is most at ease.

On the invisible list of the great and good who are appointed to the controlling bodies of British institutions, William Rees-Mogg's name must come near the top. Comfortably ensconced in his mellow bookshop, under a portrait of Alexander Pope, Sir William had the grace to look uncomfortable at this compliment. 'I think I was given these jobs much more accidentally than that.' Yet presented with a fact that might discomfort another ex-journalist – that he has clearly become a pillar of the Establishment – Sir William looked, simply, extremely pleased. 'Well, yes, I think I am: and that seems to me – provided one doesn't allow oneself to become pompous and opinionated – a useful and helpful thing to be. I think its a good thing, the Establishment.'

He credits himself with expertise in what he calls 'the seamanship of public life'; and he understands (and perhaps shares) what he discerns as the 'negative confidence' of the people who ask him to take on such jobs. (Lord Weinstock of GEC and Paul Channon, the Arts Minister, are old friends.) 'They don't expect you to do them brilliantly, though they hope you'll do them well: but they do hope you'll do them in such a way as not to bring the institutions into disrepute.'

He does not consider the present dispute damaging to the Arts Council. 'This level of dispute reveals pressures, but it doesn't create them. These rows occur at focal points in the history of institutions, when an institution is facing fundamental questions about its future.'

Some of these questions will be raised in acute form shortly when the Arts

Council grant is revealed. Sir William certainly does not see the present impasse as a resigning matter. 'Heavens, no!' In fact, he thinks the rows (of which there will be more) will probably do some good. 'If there can be sleeping beauties – well, there were a lot of sleeping uglies about.' Which he has awoken with a kiss? 'They've been woken up, anyway.'

ELIZABETH DAVID

5 January 1986

'Of course,' said one English gourmet last week, on hearing of Elizabeth David's award of a CBE in the New Year's Honours, 'if Britain were a truly civilised nation she would have been made a Dame.' But even if 'Dame Elizabeth' will have to wait, there is in this latest low-key, almost grudging award – she was given the OBE in 1976 – a recognition of Elizabeth David's extraordinary and considerable contribution to the quality of British life.

It is hard to credit today how exciting and inspiring the writing of Mrs David seemed to a war generation starved of good food ingredients for over ten years. Her first book, *Mediterranean Food*, was published in 1950, a full four years before food rationing ended. As one close friend put it: 'We all read it as escapist literature.' And, as she remembers, 'I don't think I used the word "margarine" once'.

But it wasn't just the abscence of dried egg, snoek, Namco or Woolton pie in the recipes which was important. Many of the ingredients were, in any case, still unobtainable at that time. What was important was the effect of the book – and subsequent books – on the morale of the middle class, who were as starved of sunshine and foreign travel as they were of oranges and olive oil.

Elizabeth David reminded a war-weary Britain that the whole world was not as grey as austerity demanded and that only 21 miles away across the Channel was a land where the lemon trees flowered, where there was also cream and butter, meat and cheese, real bread and wine – *and* that, one day soon, it would be possible to go there again.

Since that important start in 1950 there has been a steady trickle of David books on food – not to mention a prodigious output of journalism – which has set the standard for the boom in the appreciation of good food in this country. Precise, no-nonsense prose and an admirable detachment from the food industry, always eager to bend a writer to its will through payola, has given her the most daunting authority.

As one food writer put it: 'it is the sheer confidence with which she makes a judgment which is so awe-inspiring. Doubt does not enter any of her pronouncements – and she is almost always right. And that lack of compromise gives her work the bite which sets her apart from the rest.'

Born in 1913, Mrs David was brought up in Sussex, the second of four daughters of Rupert Sackville Gwynne, the Conservative MP for Eastbourne, and the Hon. Stella Ridley. (It is a pedigree which puts the Transport Secretary, Nicholas Ridley, and the artist, Jessica Gwynne, among her many cousins.) Her parents had no special interest in, or knowledge of, food; but in one of her essays she writes, with tantalising brevity, about a childhood food experience which must have been a key to her later passion.

'The real field mushrooms which, as children, we had so often brought home for breakfast after a dawn search in the fields round our home in the Sussex Downs. . . . We had had a nannie who always used to cook our breakfast mushrooms over the nursery fire in cream.'

After this conventional upper-class childhood, the sixteen-year-old Elizabeth Gwynne left school and went to France for eighteen months, where she studied at the Sorbonne and lived – and ate – with a Norman family who had a farmhouse near Caen as well as a Paris household. She returned to England, having learnt how to eat well, determined to learn how to cook well.

Her lack of income was a spur. 'I was living very frugally,' she said. 'Maybe that is why I did what I did. I didn't get out to restaurants much. I had to learn to cook in order to eat good food.'

In her youth she was a very great beauty. She was an actress for a time, and today she says that although 'I had no talent in that sphere whatever, the brief experience was very, very interesting and I do not regret it.' At one time she was employed as a *vendeuse* at Worth in London.

In the late 1930s she met the writer Norman Douglas. He was 72 to her 24 and he came to have a great influence upon her. She has written of 'an entanglement' that he advised her to break off: 'Had I listened to Norman's advice I should have been saved a deal of trouble. Also, I should not, perhaps, have seen Greece and the islands, or spent the war years working in Alexandria and Cairo' – where she worked for the Ministry of Information as librarian at Cairo – 'nor have got married' – to Lt-Col. Ivor Anthony David in 1944 and divorced in 1960 – 'and gone to India, nor returned to England, nor become involved in the painful business of learning to write about food and cookery.'

It was John Lehmann, her first publisher, who encouraged her to write in a novel way about the pleasures of the table. Despite the fact that other publishers had rejected *Mediterranean Food*, Lehmann took it, it sold well and it continues to do so.

She was taken on as a food journalist by Leonard Russell at the *Sunday Times* in 1955, where she much disliked working for the then woman's editor, the late

Ernestine Carter, who was 'always appropriately ready with her cutting-out shears when it came to my cookery pieces'. She was much happier at *Vogue* and the *Spectator*, during the golden years of Ian Gilmour and Brian Inglis.

Her journalism was quite different from the cookery writing that had gone before. Elizabeth David's journalism treated food seriously and as a subject which should concern everybody. Her writing was, and is, elegant, written first in longhand, typed then revised up to six times before the final copy is ready. She was as at home telling of Madame Barattero at the Hotel du Midi and her excellent fare as she was at laying into Walls for producing poor sausages. Her shyness and reserve, which many misinterpret as aloofness, allowed her to keep a respectable distance from those she wrote about.

In the mid-1950s Mrs David suffered a mild stroke and for a time she feared that it might damage her sense of taste. She recovered fully, but not from the car crash she endured in the late 1970s which, according to a close friend 'had a much delayed and long-lasting effect'.

By 1965 Elizabeth David had become such a byword for good food and good cooking that she opened a shop for kitchen utensils bearing her name near Sloane Square, close to her Halsey Street home in Chelsea. She took shopkeeping very seriously, often serving in the shop herself, yet in 1973 she fell out with her partners in the venture and she withdrew. The shop, still called Elizabeth David, persists.

But her lasting contribution to British life is the collection of definitive books on food and cooking. *Mediterranean Food* was followed by *French Country Cooking*, *Italian Food*, *Summer Cooking* and *French Provincial Cooking*, all edited in the influential Penguin edition by her close friend, Jill Norman. More recently she has become increasingly specialised and scholarly, even donnish, venturing into *Spices, Salt and Aromatics in the English Kitchen* and *English Bread and Yeast Cookery*. Such work has been rewarded by the Fellowship of the Royal Society of Literature in 1982 and an honorary doctorate from Essex University in 1979.

From this lofty perspective Mrs David now sits in judgment on the new generation of food writers and chefs who have introduced a self-consciousness and a deliberate, often distracting fashionability to the presentation of food. Take this from the Introduction to *An Omelette and a Glass of Wine*, the latest in the David canon: 'Today's young restaurant chefs, amateurs usually, tend to imagine that they can with impunity take some recently evolved *style moderne* recipe, omit one of only two key components and with a flourish present a customer with nothing more than one and a half mushrooms and one small *croûton* in the centre of a vast expanse of otherwise empty plate.' And in her current *Tatler* columns she has heaped abuse on the proponents of the Foodie culture.

Her own taste is increasingly for simple, well-prepared food, chiefly vegetables and fish, or for 'ethnic food', especially Indian and Middle-Eastern. Her appetite is not large, she drinks wine almost exclusively, and shops for herself at her local

Italian delicatessen. She is less reclusive than in recent years, although she declines to be photographed and has avoided interviews, preferring the company of close friends.

When she entertains, it is almost always at the kitchen table in the basement of the house she shares with her sister Felicity. Rarely are more than two others invited. She is the best of dinner companions – and still the best of cooks.

DENIS THATCHER

30 April 1989

Pour yourself a tincture and cuddle up, if you will, with *Accounting and Costing in the Paint Industry*. Not, it has to be said, the catchiest of titles, but the book has a certain curiosity value because of the identity of its co-author: Denis Thatcher, company director, nineteenth hole habitué and life-long consort to The Boss.

It's a tribute to the wildly successful subversion of *Private Eye's* 'Dear Bill' column that our picture of Denis is that of a juniper-soused half-wit, forever downing snifters behind The Boss's back. The letters are finely crafted forgeries, ostensibly from Denis, ensconced in his den in Number 10, assisted by his shadowy Russian valet, Boris, to Denis's real-life golfing crony, Bill Deedes, former editor of the *Daily Telegraph*.

From the first 'Dear Bill', dated 18 May 1979, writers Richard Ingrams and John Wells have each fortnight created and re-worked 'Denis' into one of these totemic characters which so enrich the national sitcom; the fictional Denis Thatcher can be properly mentioned in the same breath as P. G. Wodehouse's Bertie Wooster and the *Beano*'s very own Dennis The Menace.

What is so fascinating about the 'Dear Bill' letters is how close they are to the real man. Insiders like Rodney Tyler, the journalist who is trusted by Number 10 to polish his adulatory adjectives until they sparkle, has written: 'He is in many ways the curiously-dated author of "Dear Bill".' Daughter Carol agrees: 'There is a lot of Dad in *Private Eye*.'

Palpable hit though the caricature may be, it is not enough. *Accounting and Costing in the Paint Industry* may be ditchwater-dull, but Denis Thatcher, author, gives the lie to Denis Thatcher, half-wit.

He was born in Kent in the second year of the First World War, the child of

prosperous farming stock, made wealthy by a sheep-dip cocktail. His grandfather had discovered that sodium arsenite was an effective killer of sheep parasites and also weeds. To market the cocktail he founded a company, Atlas Preservatives. The firm, which was eventually passed on to his grandson, later diversified into wallpaper and paint – hence the book title.

Young Denis was sent to Mill Hill, a minor public school in north London overshadowed by nearby Harrow – where son Mark was subsequently to hone his intellect. Like son, father did not dazzle academically, but shone on the sports field. Denis's sporting prowess stood him in good stead when he joined up. He served in the Royal Artillery in France, Sicily and Italy, rose to the rank of Major, won the MBE (Military) and was mentioned in despatches.

Tall, athletic and broadshouldered, Denis has real, unfussed physical courage and an upper lip so stiff it could be starched. His only comment on the Brighton bomb – which almost did for him and the Prime Minister – could have been lifted from a Noël Coward war movie: 'It was quite a thump. You should have seen our bathroom. It looks as if it's been through a wringer.'

His fine war record – not to mention the Thatcher sheep-dip fortune – must have been a strong pull when the young, rather glamorous Margaret Roberts first met Denis at her successful adoption meeting for the Dartford constituency in Kent in 1949, then a safe Labour seat. Denis, a Tory supporter who actually lived in Chelsea, had gone to the meeting because the family firm was based in the constituency. He offered to give the successful candidate, prettily flushed by her triumph, a lift to London in his Jaguar: the love affair blossomed from there.

Bizarre – preposterous even – as it may sound to today's generation, there are a number of Conservative bigwigs around who will admit over their whiskies-and-water that young Margaret was in those days what the tabloids now term a 'stunna'. Denis certainly was smitten: 'Who could meet Margaret without being completely slain by her personality and intellectual brilliance?' he once volunteered. There was a problem for Margaret, given her Methodist upbringing: Denis was divorced. He had married Margaret Kempson shortly before the war. Like many war marriages it finished when, come victory, the couple realised they were strangers. By the time Denis met his second Margaret, the first Mrs Thatcher had been married to Sir Howard (now Lord) Hickman for nearly a year.

The Thatchers Mark Two ploughed on, marrying in Wesley's Chapel in the City Road, the Methodist equivalent of the Sistine Chapel, in 1951. Two years later the twins were born on the day England won the Ashes. In spite of the babies, Margaret put her name down for the Bar Finals in December, but it was Denis's money that made it possible to hire the nanny. Margaret has never forgotten her debt to Denis; even though she may have under-played the enabling power of his wealth in her personal success when she has frequently urged others to better themselves.

While Margaret slowly climbed up Westminster's greasy pole after she finally took Finchley in 1959, Denis's business career quietly flourished. As well as writing the book, he served one term as chairman of the London Association of Paint and Varnish Manufacturers and became of liveryman of the Worshipful Company of Painters and Stainers. These positions may not have been the commanding heights of British commerce, but he clearly had some acumen.

He sold the family firm to Castrol Ltd in 1965 for more than half a million pounds – with the Thatchers' financial security assured – after which Castrol was absorbed by Burmah Oil Company. It would have been easy for the oil firms to have junked a small-time local businessman, but each time Denis moved on to the bigger board. One former Cabinet Minister said of him last week: 'He really does have a smart eye for the balance sheet.'

He currently sits on a handful of boards, where his position as consort to the West's longest-serving leader must have a value. He continues to wheel and deal, partly to keep his mind from vegetating, partly to finance the Thatchers' energetic and expensive party-giving at Number 10.

Denis misses few tricks, and on one prime ministerial factory visit during the last election campaign he was overheard fixing up a bit of business by an eavesdropping reporter.

Considering how exposed Denis is, he has remained remarkably unscathed. Mud has been flung, but it has never properly stuck. The nearest thing to improper influence from Denis was when during the first term he wrote to Nicholas Edwards, the then Secretary of State for Wales, about the slow progress of a planning application made by a firm with which he was connected. In a note to his civil servants, Edwards scrawled on Denis's letter – written on Downing Street notepaper – that he wanted a reply and 'it had better be quick'. The letter was leaked to the press, to everyone's huge embarrassment. But the incident proved to be the exception.

Denis keeps himself very well hidden beneath the parapet. He recently refused to take part in a book of celebrity confessions but offered this characteristically courteous explanation: 'So long as I keep the lowest possible profile and neither write nor say anything, I avoid getting into trouble.' Occasionally, he takes this self-imposed *omertà* to farcical lengths. There is television footage of Denis refusing to answer an off-the-cuff question, shaking his head and putting his hand to his lips in the fashion of The Monkey That Speaks No Evil.

Very, very rarely he is caught out. In May 1985, during the Prime Minister's visit of condolence to Bradford after the football disaster, he was offered an ashtray and said: 'Oh good, we don't want another fire, do we?' It was one of those awful howlers professional politicians spend a lifetime avoiding: there is no guile to Denis.

He keeps his political views – a touch to the right of Vlad the Impaler on one of his more crotchety days – to himself too. One close friend calls him 'an honest-to-God right-winger'. He hates the media's fascination with him and regards the BBC as 'a nest of vipers'. He has been a frequent visitor to South Africa in his business life; his son Mark started his more controversial business career in the land of apartheid, presumably with his father's sanction. Denis's consistent championing of rugby tours to South Africa reveal his views – views which are probably more in keeping with his wife's personal feelings than her public detestation of apartheid would suggest.

Ferocious reactionary he may be, but in person he is – they say – not a bad bloke: funny, brave, loyal, however unthinkingly. In her choice of partner for life, as in many things, Mrs Thatcher has been rather lucky.

SHOWBUSINESS

I believe this section contains some of the best writing in the book. This is, on the face of it, odd: the *Observer* has never been a 'showbiz' paper; quite the opposite. Yet the showbusiness profiles are generally racy and readable, full of good stories and sharp insights. For although the paper has always had a reputation for being rather 'worthy', it has also been home to a long series of journalists to whom that adjective could never be applied, the likes of Maurice Richardson, Kenneth Tynan, John Gale, John Heilpern and so on. The profile was a good outlet for their talents, their ability to spot what made a star tick. It is their spirit which infuses this section. The verve of the Mae West profile, for instance, is in sharp contrast to the general tone of the paper in 1947. The Chaplin of 1952 is, by contrast, treated more reverentially. The young Brando bears the stamp of Tynan. The 1959 profile of Tommy Steele reads like an early example of what became known as the New Journalism of the 1960s: it could come from an early edition of *Rolling Stone* magazine. Tony Hancock's melancholia is hinted at; it had taken a deeper grip when he died in Australia only eight years later. Peter Sellers was profiled at the same age, 35, in the same year, 1960. There were similarities: their private lives were of a similar turmoil but Sellers went on to some of the 'important acting' the profile thought he had in him, before he too died prematurely, of heart disease, in 1980. Albert Finney was not the first, nor would be the last, British actor to have 'Olivier's mantle' cast around his shoulders but he more than fulfilled the profile's high expectations. There is a pleasing symmetry about Nicholas Garland's portrait of Barry Humphries, which accompanied his 1987 profile. As the profile mentions, Garland and Humphries produced the Barry McKenzie cartoon strip for *Private Eye* for nine years before both went on to greater things elsewhere. The section is brought up to date with two cult heroes of the 1990s, Lenny Henry and Madonna, profiled by John Sweeney and Andrew Stephen, the paper's American correspondent, respectively.

MAE WEST

26 October 1947

In electing to open her 'Diamond Lil' tour in Manchester Mae West has not merely followed theatrical routine; she has also shown a nice regard for history and humour. The North West is justly famed for its ancient loyalty to *laisser-faire* and the basically liberal approach to life. Never have the ideals of the Manchester School had a more sardonic exponent than this flaunter of hips, eye-lashes, plumed hats and resurrected boas.

In other aspects, however, Manchester and Mae West are antithetical. The one is bedrock reality. The other is the century's most efficient hallucination. Mae West as seen by 46,000,000 cinemagoers has no common denominator whatever – except, perhaps, the curiously arched upper lip – with the Mae West of humdrum dailiness. Never was the gap between art and nature more bewildering.

The screen has accustomed us to an opulent hussy with eye-lashes like trout hooks, a creature ruched, brocaded, sheathed, corsaged, and bejewelled, with Bowery talk slurring sensually from a mouth shaped exclusively for salty innuendo. Somewhere behind the unspeakable goings-on, somewhere above and beyond the hints and the leers, there was, of course, a saving decency, a heroic kindliness. In the end one always glimpsed an outsize heart of gold. But the interim accent was on shock and shamelessness.

So much for the grand hallucination. The real Mae West is small and almost trim. Where, one wonders on meeting her, are the 'elephantine proportions' of legend? The arched upper lip gives her almost an ingénue air as she sits in the stalls watching a rehearsal. When pondering she has a way of biting her thumb like an abstracted schoolgirl. The eyelashes, artificial admittedly, have lost their corruption and seem rooted in grace.

The reference books say brutally that she was born in 1892. That is only another aspect of the hallucination. In a well-lit lounge she looks under 35; in daylight hardly more. Mindful of stories which publicity men have been mailing from Hollywood for half a generation, one expects her talk to be stuck all over with raffish puns and synthetic apophthegms like fake jewellery. But no. One is spared such things as, 'I climbed fame's ladder wrong by wrong', and 'Love can't live on fur coats'. Her casual conversation is earnest, unbrilliant, and cosy, seasoned merely with kindas, sortas, and sump'ns. She is at pains to let you know that the vaudeville theatres in which she spent her early professional years were nice and the audiences 'polite'. One has the impression that if Miss West were on the English stage she would give her leisure to embroidery and good works, ending as a Dame Commander of the British Empire.

Mae West's mother was of Franco-German parentage; her father a prize-fighter. They put her in stock drama at the Gotham Theatre, Brooklyn, at the age of five, as though certain already of her destiny. There she stayed until too old for child parts and not big enough for grown-up ones. She was Jessie in *The Fatal Wedding*, the Angel Child in *Ten Nights in a Bar Room*, and the princeling in *Richard III* – probably her only contact with Shakespeare. Weeks when there was no call for a child player she did a song and dance in the intervals. Every day the leading man of the company called for her at the Wests' home in Brooklyn and took her to the theatre in his horse carriage. With her she took three dolls, one of them a favourite which watched her nightly from the wings. All three wore copies of her stage dresses.

Too young to read theatre scripts herself, she had her parts read over to her and learned them by ear, a habit she retains to this day. Even roles such as Diamond Lil which she writes herself have to be recited before she can get them into her head. Private teachers drilled her in spelling, sums, and the rest. At ten she had six months of school. That was more than enough for pupil and school authorities alike. Any routine outside the theatre revolted her.

At fourteen, she blossomed into a Baby Vamp. Wearing a black velvet train gown cut low, her hair up, she gyrated in a blue spot against a red velvet curtain, with a long-handled mirror in one hand and a rope of imitation pearls in the other. The grand hallucination had begun. In Miss West's own idiom, 'That's how I really started. There was something about me. It was just natural. I had a flair to know what to do. I took on a personality, and I developed it.'

A vaudeville tour took her to Chicago, where she happened to see coloured couples on a café dance floor performing a prolonged wriggle which was already obscurely known as the shimmy. Here again Mae West found something that was sorta natural. Back in her theatrical lodging she aped the dance, burlesquing it lightly. 'You'd never dare do that on the stage!' said her sisters in vaudeville. In daring Miss West has never been deficient. Not long afterwards she shimmied her way to celebrity in a Shubert revue. Again one has recourse to Miss West's idiom: 'I perfected the shimmy round to a point where I could use it on the stage. I made the shimmy possible for the theatre. And it went over big.'

When the Shubert management resolved to lift her into 'straight' stardom, Miss West, who has always had ideas of her own, wrinkled her nose at the play-tailors and, taking up pad and pencil, began writing something after her own heart. 'Sex' was the result, a piece no less provocative than its title, which packed Daly's Theatre, New York, and brought its author, in addition to a fortune, ten days of detention on Welfare Island, the outcome of an indecency prosecution.

Miss West has often written plaintively of this episode. The evidence was thin. The police raids on her play – and others – had an occult political motive. And, anyway, what constitutes indecency? On this subject eight persons could hold eight views. The trouble was that she couldn't speak a line without people peering at it for a double meaning . . . One gathered that Miss West had suffered a grievous wrong.

Defiantly she continued on the same path with *The Wicked Age*, *Pleasure Man*, and *The Drag*. She extended her forays to radio as well as to the films. An Adam and Eve burlesque, which the National Broadcasting Company unluckily allowed on the air in 1937, made America ring with resentment. Miss West, having spoken the part of Eve, was the target of telegrams from the embattled church guilds and women's clubs of a nation.

Bans and raids had little effect upon her raging popularity. In the mid 1930s one of the high-income scrutinies permitted by US law showed Miss West as having earned from films and other sources in one year 480,000 dollars, only 20,000 dollars less than the plutocrat of them all, W. R. Hearst, who, by a stroke of irony, was then assailing her films and excluding Mae West advertising from all his prints.

It is true that in 1938 there were signs of a falling off in the clamour and acclaim. The independent theatre owners of Manhattan classed Miss West among a baker's dozen of film eminences who had become 'box office poison'. Her retort is the brightest sally on the record. 'Why pick on me?' she asked. 'Box office business in the entire industry is down by 30 per cent. The only picture to make money recently was *Snow White and the Seven Dwarfs*, and that would have made twice as much if they had let me play Snow White.'

However questionable the uses to which she has sometimes put it, the talent of Mae West is in its own class supreme. It takes something like genius to conjure up and sustain a hallucination which captures a world.

Coco The Clown

2 January 1949

At the day's end Coco the Clown leaves the Olympia ring with the roar of delighted thousands in his ears. His changing room, with its trestle table and oval mirrors, is along a circular alleyway behind the scenes, facing horse and pony boxes. Here he sheds the baggy trousers, the oversize jacket of red-yellow check, the vast, bulb-toed boots.

From his middle he unhitches the concealed pressure tank with brass and rubber tubes leading to the trick wig. This is the device which enables him to produce jets of water from his ears and the crown of his head. He peels off his simpleton's nose of paste and drops it into a waste pail. Then, blowing and spluttering over a washbasin, he rids himself of the make-up which has been familiar on English hoardings since 1929: the horseshoe mouth painted across his own, the black blobs beneath the eyes, the immense eyebrow arches which express unending surprise at a world full of pitfalls, water douches and booby traps generally.

Coco disintegrates. Bits of him hang on wardrobe pegs. The rest goes down the washbowl drain. In his stead appears Mr Poliakoff, aged 48, father of six, grandfather of five. He wears a striped brown suit, a cable-stitch pullover and a black City hat with circus dust on its brim. His aquiline nose is a direct denial of Coco's ingenuous knob. His entire personality, indeed, is a denial of Coco: the mask and the reality behind it are antithetical. The scar on the upper lip is a sort of trademark. It was made by a bucket of water which, instead of landing in the top of Coco's baggy pants as a fellow droll intended, knocked out two teeth.

Nicolai Poliakoff was born in Dvinsk, a subject of the Tsar. His early years are like a chapter from Gorky. He remembers vaguely the 1905 Revolution; red flags over street crowds, Cossacks cracking their whips, an uncle who talked revolt from a soap box and fled to Canada. Father was a 'props' man in small theatres, more often out of work than in. When, driven by hunger, he moved to Riga in search of a job, his three young sons travelled with him on platform tickets. During the journey they hid under carriage seats among dirt, baggage, and heating pipes.

This became Nicolai's preferred travel method when he broke away from his family to earn his own bread as a nomad entertainer. He was not yet ten. From street buskers and fairground acts he had picked up a few acrobatic tricks, and could sing a comic song or two. Sometimes he would sleep under sacking in a disused shed with the stars shining through roofgaps, sometimes in sinister doss houses, protected from taint by some quality of shrewd innocence. Often he was beaten brutally by underlings in circuses with which he toured. But all the time he was mastering ring technique and getting the feel of ringside crowds.

Apprenticeship with the Rudolpho Truzi circus, a famous touring outfit in its day, completed his probation. At thirteen he was modestly prospering as an all-rounder: rider, acrobat, juggler, trapeze artist, and funny man. He knew St Petersburg and the old Moscow during their last pre-Revolution days. The glittering crust of society dazzled him. And he saw the misery beneath it.

At fourteen, an outrider with the 11th Siberian Infantry, which he joined on the outbreak of the Kaiser's war, he swaggered before old circus friends in a long cavalry coat, won a medal, cowered in trenches under shellfire, was wounded in both legs, and, with discharge papers in his pocket, hobbled into a starving Petrograd where Cossacks had taken to sabreing their officers. The civil war years that followed were a fantastic see-saw. As the front line shifted back and forth, Nicolai was pressed (usually as an entertainer) into the Red and White Armies alternately. He escaped execution as a renegade by a fluke. The uneasy peace of 1919 found him in Riga, out of Bolshevik reach and thankful for it. The Reds had shot his elder brother Alexander, and left him bleeding to death in the snow of his garden. That he would never forget. Valentina was his solace. On a June day of famine he married Valentina in the Orthodox Church at Riga. Their marriage feast was a pound of bread and one salt herring.

There were many setbacks in the decade that followed. Whenever Nicolai was on the point of founding a little circus of his own, something adverse happened. He would wrench his side or scald himself from chest to knees with boiling water in a trick-samovar act. There were penniless months in hospital, on crutches, or in a wheeled chair. In Berlin during the late twenties, the sun at last began to shine on Coco. The Circus Busch gloried in him. But England was the truer haven. As soon as possible after his first season for Bertram Mills, he settled his family here. Life can be lived freely in England, says Nicolai, and there is no cause to be afraid. And that makes English people kind.

Nicolai writes English as he speaks it, fluently though not without fault. When he set down his life story, another hand turned the sentences back to front and made the verbs agree in number with the nouns. Otherwise there was no re-touching. The result is a masterpiece of simple narration. Nicolai cannot bear to re-read it. He is too soft-hearted, he explains. Mrs Poliakoff sits in the dressing room stitching spangles on costumes for the younger Poliakoffs, Michael, Sasha, and Tamara, who are clowns by hereditary right. Nicolai nods in Valentina's direction and says: 'After all that Mother and I have been through I wouldn't want to live my life over again.'

Past hardship is not allowed to corrode present fun, however, under the green and scarlet tenting of Olympia, Coco is a happy man. They call him Coco the Clown. Strictly considered, the label is inaccurate. Your Clown is white-faced and spangled; droll and nimble beneath his conical hat; always, or nearly always, the master of the situation. Coco, on the other hand, is as grotesque as a gargoyle and immersed in misadventure. His true category is that of the Continent 'auguste', the type who takes Life's buffets with a grin, perhaps because he doesn't quite understand what it's all about, more probably because he's so much riper a philosopher than the rest of us.

CHARLIE CHAPLIN

28 September 1952

He is so legendary a figure that it is sometimes hard to believe that he really exists: and it is extremely hard to relate the universally appealing Charlie of the screen with someone who is of apparently serious interest to the US Attorney-General.

Perhaps the truth stares one in the face – the real Chaplin and the screen one are very much alike, and the Attorney is, by analogy, one of those angry figures of respectability that Charlie always finds himself up against by accident.

The Charlie Chaplin of the screen is, after all, an idealistic, sensitive, over-romantic, impulsive creature: it is these characteristics that bring the complications into his life – yet they are characteristics that arise from an almost naïve simplicity.

Charles Spencer Chaplin was born in Kennington on 16 April 1889. He spent most of his Dickensian childhood south of the river – in Kennington, Brixton and Lambeth.

His father, also Charles, was a comedian; his mother was a singer, with the stage name of Lily Harley. It has been said that Chaplin is a Franco-Jewish name and that Chaplin's mother was of Irish, or, alternatively, of Spanish descent. Chaplin has never bothered publicly to deny or to confirm these stories. But he has told friends that he believes his father's family came originally from Suffolk, and that his mother had Gipsy blood.

He has spoken of this Gipsy ancestry with pride, claiming that it explains the basic element in his comedy, which is his instinct to bypass trouble, rather than face it. It might also explain his musical ability, his dignity and jauntiness, his resilience in face of appalling odds and his general skilfulness at getting by.

At the time of Chaplin's birth his parents were touring with their own act. As soon as it was possible, they set off again, taking with them the new baby and his two-year-old half-brother, Sidney. It was a life lived in the dreariness of theatrical lodgings.

The early death of his father was to have a great influence on Charlie's life: it brought the family to the depths of poverty. The boy's mother had no regular income. Charlie shared her worries, and there grew the closest bond between them, which was to last until her death in Hollywood in 1930. The brothers made money as best they could, running errands, selling newspapers, dancing in the streets. Occasionally one of the family would get some minor engagement on the halls which brought momentary relief.

Mrs Chaplin's health and nerves at last gave way, and she was taken to a public hospital. When the boys were questioned as to what they would do, Charlie spontaneously ducked the clutch of authority by saying that they had arranged to stay with an aunt. Chaplin has told how, after sleeping in parks and living on fruit snatched from the stalls of street traders, they made friends with a carpenter, who allowed them to sleep on the wood shavings in his workshop. For a time the boys made money by carving toys from spare pieces of wood and selling them to other children. It was not long, however, before the authorities discovered the life they were leading: they were sent to Hanwell Institution and the workhouse school. Although the boys were not long at Hanwell, the institution's Cuckoo School provided Chaplin with his longest period of regular education; thereafter he attended various schools, but none for long.

The family reunion when Mrs Chaplin was released from hospital produced a scene that her son still remembers with emotion. They had no money, no home; they sat on a seat in a public square, the two small boys and their mother, and she discussed what they should do. Even in this extremity, 'Lily Harley' behaved with a gentleness and dignity that made their loneliness beautiful and tragic.

The imprint of those early days has never left him; his desperate childhood is responsible for his sad side and the particular character of his success. There is always the recurring theme of loneliness and there is the triumphant survival by skill and cunning.

The date of Chaplin's first stage appearance is uncertain. Certainly by the time he was eight he was a veteran of a troupe of child clog dancers, the 'Eight Lancashire Lads'. At eleven he played the part of 'Billy' in *Sherlock Holmes*; it is said that when he was handed the script of this part he dared not confess that he could neither read nor write, but rushed home to his mother, who stayed up all night with him, teaching him the part word by word.

It was with Fred Karno, the great impresario, that Chaplin learnt his trade as a comedian and a clown. Even in some of his most recent films one can find traces of Karno's influence; in the juggling and tumbling, and sudden disappearances through windows.

Karno had also an American company whose artists were in great demand in the incipient film sheds of Hollywood. Chaplin resisted the lure on his first American tour. But on his second trip to the States he accepted, after some hesitation, a contract with a firm called Keystone productions.

Some time before he went to America Chaplin fell in love. She was a young actress, who possibly never realised his feelings for her; certainly the love affair never prospered. Yet the girl, Hetty Kelly, who died in the influenza epidemic after the first world war, and whose brother is now one of Chaplin's executives, was to have a great effect on his later life. She remained for him an ideal. It is likely that in his first two marriages Chaplin sought that ideal. Neither girl had anything in common with him: only in looks did they appeal to his wounded romanticism.

Chaplin was some time adapting himself to the technique of films. But from the time he put on the costume of the tramp, with the turned-out boots, bowler hat, walking-stick and baggy trousers, he began to feel at ease. The costume personified shabby gentility. Chaplin has said that the cane is a symbol of dignity – no mishap can part him from it – and that the moustache stands for vanity.

In 1914, his first year in California, Chaplin made 35 films – some of them in a matter of days, even of hours. These early productions – indeed all his films – show a character that is not simply the pathetic underdog. The Charlie character is a respecter of overwhelming odds, of policemen, if they are large: but if the chances seem good he will cheat, elope with other people's wives, return home drunk and exploit old men. The slapstick is toned down in his later work, and the underlying vein of pathos is developed; yet Chaplin, although an unworldly character, a misfit, is always maintaining a strange dignity by the most immoral of tactics.

In *The Champion*, made in 1915, he enters a boxer's training camp with the idea of earning money as a sparring partner. A succession of unconscious men are carried past as he awaits his turn to enter the ring. This appals him: eventually, with a sad shrug, indicating that there seems no other course left to him, Chaplin slips a horseshoe into his glove.

Despite the pathos of Chaplin's films, he is rarely worsted by a powerful opponent. It is his relationship with women or children, who often laugh at him, that induces the sadness. Yet the small tramp of the early days invariably retains an air of hope. Apparently broken by misfortune, he will remove the finger of a tattered glove, in order more freely to snap that finger at fate; in *City Lights*, as he passes through the prison gates between two policemen, he chucks his cigarette butt over his shoulder and, as it falls, flips it sideways with the heel of his boot, in a neat and typically Cockney gesture of defiance. In *The Idle Class* (an early farce of golf and fancy dress balls) he plays both a tramp and an immaculate Verdoux-like husband who is spurned because of his drunkenness: he receives a final note from his wife, turns, his shoulders shaking with broken sobs – which continue till he turns again and is found to be shaking a cocktail with slightly pursed lips.

In real life, even success brought loneliness. Working in Hollywood, he was not at first aware of the extent of his fame. When he visited New York and saw his name in lights and the children in the streets imitating his walk, he was filled with dread. Later, he grew accustomed to success and enjoyed acclaim; yet adulation never affected his work.

In 1920 he joined with Douglas Fairbanks and Mary Pickford to form the United Artists' Corporation. From then on he was able to work as he chose. He did not welcome the introduction of sound films, feeling that his art was already whole. He realised, too, that once he had spoken, his universal appeal would be gone. So he held out. But in *City Lights*, released in 1931, he added a musical sound track. He had set about learning the art of composing and had written the music himself.

Even *Modern Times*, released in 1936, was not a 'talkie'. Some felt that it was marred by the compromise between speech and mime. But there was no doubting the skill of Chaplin's peformance. The most unsuccessful of his major films was *The Great Dictator*, a sound film, made at the beginning of the last war. In it he stepped beyond the bounds of his art: Hitler was too vulgar a character to deserve his attention. And the dictator of the film lacked sympathy, without which a Chaplin character must fail.

The almost obsessional dislike of Chaplin in some quarters in America is not easily explained. He has been reviled for his erratic private life, for his 'red' sympathies, his refusal to become an American citizen and for his mockery of the industrial aspect of the American tradition. Yet, when the lists of complaints is drawn up, it is not wholly convincing; the antagonism must remain something of a mystery. Bitter controversy seems out of keeping with the man, for he is a warm and sympathetic figure. Indeed, his sympathies have dominated his life.

Modern Times is said to have gained him powerful enemies – although its satire of twentieth-century industrialism is essentially good-humoured. He has spoken, too, of the political persecution that he endured as the result of 'liberal views' expressed in *The Great Dictator*. It is scarcely credible that feelings were so easily aroused. Yet certainly he became a favourite target of sections of the American press. He was once a friend of the late William Randolph Hearst, the newspaper magnate; but they had little in common and the friendship foundered. It is believed that Hearst never forgave him.

Earlier even than this, following his matrimonial failures, Chaplin was denounced for his private life – although this differed little from that of many other Hollywood stars. His indictment under the Mann Act and the Barry Paternity suit formed the climax of the campaign against him, and revealed the influence of his opponents.

But all this was nothing to the vilification he endured as a result of his Left-wing sympathies. 'They came on like wolves,' Chaplin has said.

Due to temperament and background, he has always had a social conscience. He is simple enough to say that he seeks nothing less than a happier world. Many years ago he was interested in panaceas, including the Social Credit system of Major Douglas. But he is not a Communist; indeed before the war he refused more than one invitation to go to Russia.

Yet in the last six or seven years Chaplin has said and done a number of things, not a few of them ill-timed, that must certainly have brought him to the notice of the Department of Justice. In 1949 the House of Representatives Un-American Activities Committee denounced him as a pro-Communist, referring to the support he had recently lent to the World Peace Congress in Paris.

Senator Cain on the floor of the Senate demanded his deportation, mentioning that in 1946 Chaplin had attended a champagne party on a Russian tanker in the Bay of California, and that although he had said several good things about

Marshal Stalin and his form of government, he 'had never said a kind word for the United States'.

Chaplin replied: 'I am an internationalist. Yes, I am a guest of America. But a paying guest. Up to ten million dollars. I feel as American as any American.'

Another local cause of unpopularity may have been his contempt for the film world. He has written, 'Hollywood has no identity. It is the tremble of a young girl's lip, the torture of a writer's mind, the counting of dollars and the scramble for recognition. To understand these things is to understand Hollywood. There is nothing else to know.'

In the last few years, however, Chaplin has probably been happier than ever before. He has lived quietly at home with his fourth wife, the daughter of Eugene O'Neill, and with their family of a boy and three girls: he has his swimming pool and tennis court and, above all, old friends for the talk that he loves.

Many people believed that sound films would mean the end of him. They were wrong; and yet, the improvement of screen technique has added nothing to his genius. It is a genius in harmony with the rain of the flickering screen and the tired piano jangling in the darkness, rather than with the pneumatic carpets of the modern cinema and the treacly message of the electric organ. Perhaps *Shoulder Arms, The Circus, The Gold Rush* and *The Kid* will remain his masterpieces.

In *Limelight*, the story of a fading clown and a young ballet dancer, Chaplin not only plays the lead, but he has written, produced and directed the film; he has also composed the music and arranged the choreography. He spent years considering the plot and working on the script. When at last the time came for shooting, he exhausted men half his age, supervising personally every detail of production. Often he was in despair, sometimes near to tears. Although 63, he repeated his clowning scenes countless times to gain perfection; to obtain satisfaction in small details, he was willing to shoot hundreds of yards of film, which were later discarded.

There are always rumours that Chaplin will retire, but he has said: 'I shall go on making films until I die, and I shall always have to think the last one the greatest of them all.'

He has been white-haired many years now, but he retains his grace and elegance. His sensitive face, wrinkled near the eyes by laughter, is a face that has felt much. We wish him a happy stay in England. He is a great man.

Marlon Brando

3 October 1954

'For voice, eye, action and expression,' wrote Hazlitt of Edmund Kean's debut at Drury Lane in 1814, 'no actor has come out for many years at all equal to him.'

A pivotal performance in the history of acting had been given and observed: for it was Kean who began the movement towards what is now called naturalism, the reproduction in the theater of the audible and visible surfaces of life.

That movement, gathering pace, became a revolution, which has reached its fulfilment, according to many good judges, in the performance of Marlon Brando in Elia Kazan's film, *On the Waterfront* (which, having ended a successful showing in one West End cinema, moves on Thursday to another – the Ritz – and will be 'Coming Shortly' to your local).

The theorists have lately decried naturalism, pronouncing it a dead heresy and swearing that the theatre should return to the 'larger-than-life' techniques of rhetoric. Brando has outfaced them by presenting, perhaps for the first time in a leading role, naturalism in its pure state; his pauses, his shrugs, his eloquently unfinished sentences have the smell of unrehearsed reality, the ragged poetry of truth.

His springy walk and dodging head proclaim Terry Molloy the prize-fighter, whose spiritual dimension is implied by Brando's searching eyes and soft, bruised smile. He joins a gang of dockyard bullies because his brother is one of them, and the film explores his slow awakening to the sense of shame. He is subpoena'd to testify before a federal investigating commission; his gangster brother advises silence, even makes threats, whereupon Terry, baffled and reproachful, shakes his hangdog head. This fraternal encounter, in the back seat of a taxi, has already taken its place among the lasting documents of the actor's craft.

Most actors unconsciously assert the moral stature of the people they play: this man is a hero, that one a villain: but Brando takes no sides. If Molloy is a hero, he knows nothing of it; because he is Molloy. His performance befits one who has been described by the critic-director Harold Clurman as 'all in all the most talented actor in America today'.

Brando's career has been cometary in the dictionary sense of the word: 'revolving round the sun in a very eccentric orbit.' His character has the anarchic streak which marks many fine actors and a multitude of bad ones. He was born in Omaha, Nebraska, on 3 April 1924, the son of an art-loving businessman and a diligent amateur actress. The family (of French descent and originally spelled Brandeau) was well-to-do and a trifle bizarre, preferring artists to Babbitts at its parties; one of Brando's sisters has since become an actress, and another a painter. Leaving school before graduation, he went off for two months digging ditches for a drainage construction company. His father, instead of lecturing him, offered to finance him in any career he chose.

Marlon went off to the Dramatic Workshop in New York where for a year he studied the improvisational Stanislavsky technique known to its *alumni* as 'The Method'. Applied in the 1930s to the plays of Clifford Odets, it had become the mainspring of American acting, and had shaped the style of John Garfield, Brando's precursor as the representative 'New Deal' hero, the moody, rebellious innocent to be found brooding in the pages of Hemingway and Steinbeck, the boy for whom speech is the last resort of the human animal.

At the age of twenty, Brando made his first Broadway appearance in John van Druten's *I Remember Mama*, which ran through two theatre seasons. He then played a small but eye-catching part in Maxwell Anderson's *Truckline Cafe*. Already the anarch was visible: in a programme note he announced that he had been born in Bangkok during a zoological expedition. Now professionally established, he played Marchbanks to Katherine Cornell's Candida and appeared, for an explosive spell, opposite Tallulah Bankhead in *The Eagle Has Two Heads*. These experiments over, he went into *A Flag is Born*, Ben Hecht's short-lived eulogy of the State of Israel – a crucial engagement, for it inspired Elia Kazan to cast him as Stanley Kowalski in Tennessee Williams's *A Streetcar Named Desire*.

He hitchhiked to Cape Cod to meet the author, arriving penniless and travel-stained at 6 a.m. His opening performance (the first of 855) in December 1947 was an announcement of triumph. He measures less than six feet and is not heavily built, but on stage he expands gigantically: one writer called him a fusion of poet and gladiator. He was now definably a 'star', as strong in the whiplash comedy scenes (such as the derisive evisceration of his sister-in-law's suitcase) as in the strident displays of animalism which mobbed the headlines. Yet he continued, and still continues, to take lessons at Kazan's Actors' Studio.

In 1950 he went to Hollywood, as he put it, 'for the loot', which he has invested in a profitable cattle ranch. A good script (*The Men*) and a good director (Fred Zinnemann) seduced him; and before shooting began he spent a month of reconnaissance in a hospital for paraplegic war veterans. Asked what he thought of his performance as the film's crippled hero, he murmured thickly into his coat-collar, 'I think I show promise'.

Back with Kazan, he made the film version of *Streetcar* and afterwards *Viva Zapata*. 'In his presence,' wrote one critic, 'the screen mutters with the sort of sultry menace that precedes an earthquake.' The earthquake broke with the revelation that he was to play Antony in Joseph Mankiewicz's adaptation of *Julius Caesar*. The resulting performance was a coherently anti-romantic portrait of an adroit politician; and many purists bewailed the loss of the conventional Antony. In fact, it was Brando's execution rather than his conception that was at fault: the thick conformation of his speech was unable to take the full strain of the verse. Yet he had declared his range, the extent of which may be judged by imagining the performance Sir John Gielgud might give as a lustful Polack hooligan.

Since *Caesar* he has made *The Wild One* and *On the Waterfront*: the former, which concerns the impact on a small town of a group of destructive adolescents, has been banned outright in this country because of its brutality. He has just played Napoleon in an 'epic'; and will shortly play a gambler in a musical, *Guys and Dolls*.

For Brando, in life as in art, there are no class distinctions. The anarch obstreperously guides him. He abhors formal clothes ('You might as well wear armour'); he keeps a pet raccoon; he breakfasts off raw eggs, and has been known to slip one into his palm before shaking hands. He is unmarried: content with a casual tenancy of his friends' divans, he has seldom sought a home of his own, though he once put a plaintive advertisement into a New York paper: 'Apartment wanted – Any Old Thing.'

His imitators, who throng the bars of Broadway, slouching and monosyllabic, bear witness to his persuasiveness as a symbolic figure: the undeceivable ego which can see through 'phoneyness' at a glance, the distinctively post-war type, deriving ultimately from Huckleberry Finn, which can be traced in such novels as J. D. Salinger's *The Catcher in the Rye* and Kingsley Amis's *Lucky Jim*.

One hopes he will soon return to the stage. And if he takes the bait, let it not be held against him that he is not a classical actor. The American theatre, maturing, has evolved its own style: would one berate Lorca for not writing like Pope, or Picasso for not painting like Rembrandt? Brando has a responsibility already tremendous enough – as the first actor to achieve poetry in a theatre dedicated, by strict historical conviction, to prose.

MARILYN MONROE

15 July 1956

All film stars owe much of their success to their personal legend, to the charm or the enigma of their 'real-life' personality. For all that, they generally owe something to their films. In this respect, as in others, Marilyn Monroe is out of the ordinary. She, the brightest star of this decade, has won her renown in spite of the films she has made; the scripts have mostly been undistinguished. And the parts she has played have usually failed to provide the kind of vehicle worthy of a highly glamorous star; above all, perhaps, they have been too diverse to allow her to develop a continuous, unified screen personality. There has been no centre to her career, which seems up till now to have been all experiment and improvisation, ranging between the extremes of the glittering inanity of Lorelei in *Gentlemen Prefer Blondes* and the pathetic solemnity of Nell in *Don't Bother To Knock* – a career whose only unifying element has had to come from within herself.

Not only can it be claimed that Miss Monroe has achieved and maintained her position in the firmament without help from consistent casting; it is also true that she had acquired the status of a star before she was ever given star-billing in a picture. The personal myth came first, actual stardom second.

It is, of course, not unusual for an actress, especially if born in Hungary, to achieve the notoriety of a star through involvement in interesting marriages or personal relationships without ever actually starring in an important film. But this kind of reputation has none of the stamina of an authentic star's. Authentic stars cannot help keeping the public constantly alerted: their most negative actions become somehow invested with meaning and mystery. The spurious celebrity, by contrast, can sustain interest only by living a peculiarly rich and varied life. Now, Marilyn Monroe has had such a life, all the ingredients are there: the remarkable marriages, the improbable friendships, the quarrels with production chiefs, the endearing background of an unhappy childhood. So it is necessary to ask whether her life alone accounts for the public's enduring interest in her.

She was born in Los Angeles on 1 June 1926. Her childhood was spent partly in an orphanage, partly in the care of a wide variety of uniformly unsuitable foster-parents. She has spoken of more than one traumatic episode during these early years. At the age of sixteen she was married off to a man she did not love: the marriage lasted a year, and in 1943 she went to work as a paint-sprayer in a factory. Here she was discovered by a photographer, and by 1947 she was a highly sought-after model and cover girl. This led to her first contract in films, at $125 a week. This and another contract were short-lived, and, after being out of work for some time, she consented to pose in the nude for a photographer, who sold two of his pictures to publishers of calendars.

Shortly after this, she played a small part in John Huston's *The Asphalt Jungle*, and achieved a spectacular success. She was at once put under a contract, at $750 a week. At last she seemed on the point of breaking through. Suddenly a columnist revealed the identity of the girl on the calendars. And it was her reaction to the resultant scandal that did more than anything to create the Monroe myth – her reaction to the scandal rather than the scandal itself. Which seems to answer the question about the secret of her success.

Alarmed by the fuss, she was perfectly frank: 'I needed the money,' she said. And then, when asked by a lady journalist, 'You mean you didn't have anything on?' she replied: 'Oh yes, I had the radio on.'

An innocent, almost involuntary wit, and an engaging acceptance of all the facts of life – these, as much as the appalling biography, the 'vital statistics' and the radiant beauty, are the sources of the Monroe myth. 'The Johnston Office,' she said recently, 'spends a lot of time wondering whether a girl has cleavage or not. They ought to worry if she doesn't have any. That really would make people emotionally disturbed.'

This blonde is not a dumb one. Indeed, leaving aside the sayings attributed to her (and which do seem to have been her own), the sound of her speaking voice contributes as much as her looks to her peculiar magic. It is a little girl's voice, small and earnest and imperfectly articulate, a voice which can render any film script ambiguous and unexpected, simply because we are never quite clear what she is thinking about what it is saying. And with the voice, in all its disarming sense of vulnerability, goes the wide-eyed, soft-featured baby-face and a sort of innocent paganism.

The total effect is a personality that is curiously lovable because whether in life or on the screen, it is so remote from any form of viciousness or meanness. There can be few stars who are so universally liked by people who have come in contact with her. As Dame Edith Sitwell puts it: 'She's a very nice girl, quiet and well-behaved.'

Her encounter with dame Edith – in point of fact a single half-hour meeting – has been transformed by the press into an intimate friendship. Yet not altogether without rhyme or reason. For this meeting was a symbol of a new development in Miss Monroe's life. In 1953, the year in which she won the Photoplay Award for the year's most popular actress, she began to show signs of higher aspirations. She took to reading serious literature and listening to serious music, expressed a desire to play Grushenka in *The Brothers Karamazov*, asked her studio for parts which would give her a chance to act, and declined one in a musical called *Pink Tights*.

Early in 1954 she married Joe DiMaggio, the baseball star. Within a year this marriage, too, had failed: it seems they had nothing to say to each other. Meanwhile, she made *The Seven-Year Itch*, a coyly bowdlerised version (which seemed designed to prove that men will be boys) of the Axelrod stage-play which nevertheless presented her at last with a fairly worthwhile part.

But not worthwhile enough. She walked out on her contract and installed herself in New York, there to knuckle down in earnest to improving her mind. She made friends in the intense world of the enlightened theatre, joined Lee Strasberg's Actors Studio, painted in watercolours, read poetry aloud, formed Marilyn Monroe Productions, Inc., and played her meatiest part to date, in *Bus Stop*. Her plans for the immediate future include *The Sleeping Prince*, co-starring Olivier, and (in America) a television production of the *Lysistrata*.

The release in this country of *Bus Stop* will be awaited with interest. For it may allow us to see how far we can agree with the opinion of her acting held by Arthur Miller, the author of *Death of a Salesman*, who has just become her third husband: 'She has a terrific instinct for the basic reality of a character or a situation. She gets to the core.'

THE GOONS

23 December 1956

The suburb of Shepherd's Bush, an amorphous area of dull houses entirely surrounded by trolleybuses and hidden sidings, is the unlikely home of many strange fantasies intimately affecting the life of Britain in the mid-1950s.

Not only does it contain the high concrete barns of Lime Grove, where television developed from a tiny, private sideline of the BBC to its present ubiquity; over a fruit shop in Shepherd's Bush, up three flights of narrow brown stairs, there is an office containing teapots, typewriters, electronic devices, encyclopaedias, and books ranging from *The Dialogues of Plato* (translated by Jowett, in four volumes) and *The Tragedy of the Caesars*, to *Birds of Our Country*, and it is here that the extraordinary hallucinations of *The Goon Show* are hammered into script form every week by Spike Milligan and Larry Stephens. The result is the purest form of surrealist humour yet reached on steam radio (in Goon parlance, 'talking type wireless') – or anywhere else, for that matter.

Milligan is the key figure, both as scriptwriter and as one of the three protean performers who dodge, giggling, from one microphone to another, in some sad hall or ex-theatre where the show is recorded on Sunday nights. They populate the air with a dozen or so weirdly compulsive characters who are now familiar to most people under 40 (and many over). Milligan is The Famous Eccles, a lovable, toothless dimwit who owes something, but not all, to Disney's cartoon figure Goofy. He is a character called Spriggs, who is always making nasal objections from the back of the hall at meetings. He is Abdul the twittering bearer or dragoman; he is the vague, hen-like Minnie Bannister; he is Count Jim Moriarty, that impoverished cosmopolitan of the 1920s.

The last-named acts as a sort of seedy Leporello for the larger, smoother villainies of Grytpype Thynne, played by Peter Sellers in his George Sanders voice. Other Sellers roles are the shameless, ex-Indian Army Major Bloodnok, Henry

Crun (also vague and poultry-like, living in a dubious Victorian relationship with Minnie Bannister), Willium, a croaking, despairing Cockney ('I bin 'ere all night, mate'), Bluebottle, a ludicrous personification of schoolboy dreams of glory – and, in the Goons' not infrequent representation of the House of Commons, Sir Winston Churchill!

These, and other remarkable figures, revolve around the central figure in the plot, Neddy Seagoon, played by Harry Secombe, who looks but does not sound like an owl that has taken Benzedrine. There are certain basic, unchanging elements. Seagoon is usually involved in a quest – an empire-building mission, laying a telephone line to '17a, Africa,' a drum race from John o'Groat's to Land's End, or he is after some prize or treasure of which the villains easily defraud him.

The essential thing, however, is the combination of a quite special, ultra-modern humorous idiom with a nostalgia for our Victorian, imperial past. It is as though Britannia were having not a nightmare but a sort of comic dream; it is as though Dali, Kipling and Dickens had co-operated. The character called Henry Crun, for instance (in full, Henry Albert Sebastopol Queen Victoria Crun), was originally conceived as one of a firm of lawyers called Wacklow, Furrell and Crun, who might well have been in *Bleak House*.

The dialogue contains lines not unworthy of Groucho Marx. 'Minnie, I'm taking you away from the squalor that you live in – to the squalor that *I* live in'; or, in a brisk Service voice on the intercom of a criminal airship which has stolen a bank by lifting it with hooks, 'What course are you on?' – 'Prunes and Custard'. These shade off into a post-Marxist surrealism. Thus, Seagoon (King Morte d'Arthur Seagoon) is trying to get into a Cornish castle ('Excuse the mess, but we've got the sea in') and demands the key. He is told 'There are no keys to this ladder, it's always open'.

This, with an equally surrealist use of sound effects (an important figure in the control room at *The Goon Show* is a small, bearded man who speeds up records of bugles, trotting feet, railway trains, etc., by whizzing them round with his finger), is part of what Mr Milligan calls, with undoubted seriousness, 'Dimensionalism'. The radio listener, he maintains, is in a dream world, where the rigid dimensions of time-space unity need not confine him. ('Open this door and let's get this room in.')

Milligan is a much more aggressive and uninhibited man than the other Goons. The big, mobile mouth in the long face, the sudden relapses from laughter into genuine, bitter sadness ('The human race has failed. We ought to be *fighting* for *Hungary*') remind one of his Irish ancestry. But he is also a born eccentric, almost a professional misfit ('the people who like the Goons are Outsiders'), and a sworn enemy of bureaucracy and greyness.

A lot of the 'imperial' background to the show is a reflection of Milligan's personal life. He was born in India, where his father was a regimental sergeant-major. He came to England to train as a pilot, failed the examination disastrously, and ended up in the Royal Artillery. In Italy he met Lance-Bombadier Harry Secombe, when both were working in the Central Pool of Artists.

After the war, while Secombe was making his name as a comic, at the Windmill and elsewhere, and Sellers establishing himself as a wonderful mimic, Milligan was playing the guitar in 'The Bill Hall Trio'; he also plays the trumpet, and one of the best things in *the Goon Show* is never broadcast – it is the riotous jam session during the audience warm-up. He found efforts to break into the conventional music-hall dispiriting, and later he simply signed on at Deptford Labour Exhange.

But the old friendship with Secombe, and a newer one with Sellers, was kept alive, and *The Goon Show* was born in 1952 when the BBC had finally showed interest in a privately made recording. Although Milligan admits a debt to no one, the organisation which had known ITMA was adventurous enough to take a chance, which has been amply repaid. The listening figures in this country are six million, and *The Goon Show* is increasingly popular on American, Canadian and Australian networks.

Milligan is the centripetal element. In him goonery is actual. In Secombe and Sellers it is potential, sparked into brilliant reality when they are together. These two naturally contribute ideas; there is a strong sympathy of temperament with Milligan. But they have other pursuits.

Secombe, who comes from Swansea, is a kind of Ideal South Walian. Like Michael Bentine, a founder member of the Goons who left them to tour Australia, he is fundamentally a visual comic, and he creates his own material almost spontaneously. The act with which he convulsed Windmill audiences, a glum lot who do not really go to be *amused*, depicted shaving as practised by a boy for the first time, by a man using ice-cold water, and by a nervous case. But he also possesses a heroic tenor voice of real promise. He studies singing seriously, and has made records of *Vesti la giubba* and other arias which have been respectfully received by the critics. Off-stage he is exuberant, kindly – and a well-informed, voracious reader. He lives in Sutton, and like all the Goons is a husband and father.

He has no theatrical antecedents. But Peter Sellers, the youngest of the trio (he is 31), appeared in films at the age of five. His uncle was manager of the Victoria Pavilion at Ilfracombe, and here he learnt the repertory business from the bottom, beginning as assistant stage-manager. Gradually his impressions of the famous superseded his other work, and formed the basis of the act in which he, too, appeared at the Windmill. His private manner is quiet. He looks like a scholarly, well-dressed young house agent. He is in demand as a character actor, supplies UPA with cartoon film voices – and, like Secombe, can sustain a top billing in variety.

So much talent makes for a centrifugal tendency and a strong need for discipline and forceful direction, if the Goons are ever to do something less ephemeral than their weekly broadcast: a film, for instance. And that means a very strong director indeed. Milligan himself is not very hopeful. A certain British director of comedies was once pointed out to him on a small rock off a fashionable *plage*. Milligan put on his mask and flippers, swam under water and popped up to greet the great man with 'Do you come here often?' The raised eyebrow he got was typical of the reaction so far of the British film industry to the scenario for a Goon film which he has up his sleeve.

Doubtless there would be great clashes of personality, just as there were over the promising venture of the Goons into television, *A Show Called Fred*. But those who love pure, quicksilver, and above all *new* comedy must continue to hope that films will one day be made. In the meantime they are grateful that *The Goon Show*, as is obvious to anyone physically present at the broadcast, is performed by these brilliant and talented young men at least as much for love and high enjoyment as for money.

TOMMY STEELE

21 December 1958

Rodgers and Hammerstein's *Cinderella* at the Coliseum has a young and famous 'Buttons' with fluffy fair hair and a rather fetching costume by Loudon Sainthill: it's Tommy Steele, 22 this month, one of the highest-paid British entertainers ever and one who has quite transformed show business in this country.

Most people have heard of the Prince of Rock and many, not always the young, are worshippers. There are those who find the whole thing a little absurd. And there are those who, linking him with the drape, juvenile delinquency and hysteria (for instance, that time he got laid out cold by teenage girls in Dundee), disapprove more or less automatically. A small, gloomy school of thought is also inclined to discover in the circumstances of his entry into show business ominous resemblances to *A Face in the Crowd* or similar American sagas of the mass-media.

This entry was made in an interesting way. One day, two years ago, Steele, or Tommy Hicks as he then was known, was just another Bermondsey boy singing rock in the smaller clubs and coffee bars of Soho. While singing a song composed by himself and two friends, 'Rock with the Caveman', he was approached by a young

man in the publicity game, John Kennedy. 'I could do something for you,' said Kennedy. Tommy thought that this was 'the same old schmooze' he had heard before, but it wasn't.

Rock with the caveman
Roll with the caveman
Stalactite, stalagmite
Hold your baby very tight
Piltdown poppa sings this song
Archaeologist done me wrong
The British Museum's got my head
Most unfortunate 'cause I ain't dead.

What Kennedy could do and did for the young singer was provide him with publicity. In his book, *Tommy Steele*, Kennedy makes this statement of faith:

'Once you get a person talked about – no matter how you do it – he becomes news in himself and creates his own publicity. But the difficulty lies in getting the initial impetus. After that it's like a snowball.'

In Steele's case Kennedy conceived the idea that rock must become respectable. Steel must be seen playing for the 'debs'. Difficult to arrange? Not if you hire models who pretend to be debs and then pull the wool over some newspapers' eyes. This was the initial impetus. Photograph the Duke of Kent as he comes from a theatre, pretend he is emerging from the club Tommy is playing at, ascribe to him the remark that 'Tommy is great' and the snowball begins to grow. Why not two debs fighting over Tommy? Hire a couple of girls and let them pretend to fight. Out of this jungle, as it were, rolled a huge snowball.

Kennedy soon had Steele fixed up with a three-weeks' time-filler at the Stork Club. Next it was a six-week tour at £150 a week with a four-piece band. Then it was twelve weeks at £350 a week. Within a year it was £1,000 a week. Fan mail started piling up, and so did requests for a lock of the Steele hair, his old ties, even buttons. 'Fabulous' and 'Magic', Mr Mendl of Decca had said of Tommy's first record. Steele discs were high on the hit parade.

The snowball rolled on from the Café de Paris, where Steele followed Noël Coward, Marlene Dietrich and Eartha Kitt, to the Royal Command Performance, to tours of Scandinavia and South Africa, where he came near being killed by admirers, to films (*The Tommy Steele Story* and *The Duke Wore Jeans*), in size and speed unprecedented for a British performer.

But the truth is, Steele is a surprise. Off duty, he is likely to be late and in a hurry, and wearing (carelessly) a well-cut pale blue suit and narrow unpolished tan shoes; he doesn't care much what he looks like. He has a husky cockney voice and a round, dreamy face, floury-complexioned, a little toothy, with wide-apart blue eyes.

At first meeting he will be very enthusiastic about whatever crops up in conversation, probably to avoid awkward silences. It happened to be firework night and he burst out: 'I love fireworks. We let off a Roman candle on Camber Sands. You know Camber Sands? It was the most beautiful thing you ever saw in your life, Boom! Then it fell over.' He's frail, highly strung, and there's something about him: he's alive.

The Prince of Rock was born Thomas Hicks on 17 December 1936 in Mason Street, just off the Old Kent Road, the second son of a professional backer (his elder brother died, as did a younger brother and sister, none reaching the age of two). There are three other children: Colin, seventeen; Roy, fourteen and Sandra, nine.

During the war, Tommy was evacuated for a time, but saw a good deal of the Blitz. Just after the war, he went to his first pantomime at the Elephant and

Castle. Next day he ran away to find the leading lady, but was brought back by a policeman. At school, he seems to have been, on his own admission, a bit fly and pie-faced, and on the side of authority (which he still is). He was fond of writing short plays, and the master let the class act them.

On leaving school, he was four feet eleven inches and destined to be a bell-boy at the Savoy. But he had romantic ideas about writing, and felt that travel would be the thing. And so he found himself at the age of fifteen at sea in the Scythia. After eighteen months on the Quebec run, he was laid up for four months with spinal meningitis. In Guy's Hospital a busker taught him a few chords on the guitar.

Back at sea, as a bell-boy and waiter, he played his guitar. In New York, he heard jazz. He sang calypsos on the beaches of Bermuda.

Aboard the Mauretania he was encouraged to sing by another waiter, Kurt ('Brushes') Littner, a pleasant and sardonic former Austrian who'd served in the Foreign Legion and who thought Tommy's 'Guitar Boogie' pretty good. Together they composed short revues for the first-class passengers. It was while at home on compassionate leave that Tommy Hicks took his guitar to Soho and met Kennedy and became Tommy Steele, and when he next went to sea was waited upon.

His success doesn't seem to have gone to his head. 'I come from an area where you're taught to be pleased with what you've got regardless of what your income is. If I changed my ways I could never face my people.' He's done little more extravagant that buy one or two cars for himself and a house for his mother in Catford.

He's essentially serious (recently he signed an appeal against colour prejudice), but says of his career: 'I treat the whole thing as a joke. I'm forever laughing at it. When it's over I don't want people to be sorry for me. I want to say 'thanks a lot everybody, I've had a ball.' He pauses, and then adds: 'Unquote.'

'I know I must go down. I can't go up any further. I hope the people of Bermondsey will stand by with the mat' (this feeling for Bermondsey and his own people is very real).

He likes the cinema and reading: to write is still his real ambition. 'Did you ever read George Orwell?' he may ask. '*Down and Out in Paris and London*? There's a book. And did you read *No Mean City*? About the Gorbals. Fabulous. I sit down and knock out ideas. But I have no discipline. I'm still in the process of writing some music: a symphony. What's it called? Crikey! Oh, yes, "Ode to a Trend".'

Before he goes on for one of his routine shows, Steele is pretty nervous and edgy. He wears a white shirt, old yellow shoes and dark blue jeans-ish trousers, rather thin and soggy, with silver notes painted down the seams. 'I go on unrehearsed, but with the skeleton, to which I add the flesh. I get the feel of the audience. Sometimes I may be a tramp, sometimes a gentleman. It depends. There may be a strike in the area.'

'My object is to entertain and I've got to give them their money's worth. I have

45 minutes on and I come off exhausted. But it's good fun if it's a happy audience. I haven't had an acting lesson, I'm not tall, dark and handsome, I haven't even got a voice. All I can say is I don't know what I've got. I can only just ask people to tell themselves.'

When he comes on stage there is piercing teenage mewing and squealing. From this moment he never lets up. He gives them 'Caveman'; 'Butter Fingers' ('Bu-hhhater Fingers'); 'A Handful of Songs'; 'Mabeline'; 'Hound Dog'; 'Rebel Rock'; 'Doomsday Rock'; 'Elevator Rock'; and 'Teenage Party'. Most of the time he is bending his knees in time, or dancing about the stage, sometimes swinging a leg. He knows how to be still for a sad song. It certainly isn't much of a voice: it's flat and tenorish, with a rather pleasant catch to it. He has a fine sense of rhythm. Kennedy did not create his snowball out of nothing.

There's plenty of patter: 'I'd like to say on behalf of the boys and myself that it's very nice to be here in mush land.' 'Our first recital' (laughs) . . . 'Look, I do wish you'd shut your gate. Our first recital was composed way back in 1863 by a feller called Pushini, and it's called Rigor Mortis.'

Sometimes he puts on a very posh voice. His timing is good; he's intuitive, with a great feeling for the mood of the audience. Sometimes, in flashes, he looks almost like the young Chaplin. Yet it's hardly artistry that he relies on.

The biggest squeals come when he performs remarkable electric shakings, or revolves his head like a fair gollywog's, the hair flying; or does strange contortions, leaning far back with his shoulders brushing the stage. The squeals are a convention. The whole thing's happy and healthy. The audience feel he's one of them, and that maybe they could do it, too.

And there is a kind of magic. You realise it at the end, when he sings 'Princess': the words of the last line go, 'And I'm your Prince'. Perhaps that is it.

BRIGITTE BARDOT

27 September 1959

The French film star Miss Brigitte Bardot, who is 25 tomorrow, shares with Mr Khrushchev the distinction of being recognised throughout the world by initials alone.

In Europe, the Americas and the Far East, the letters 'BB' produce a marked response even from people who have seen none of Miss Bardot's 24 films. The spread and speed of her rise to fame are a tribute to the power and efficiency of modern means of communication. For her establishment as a 'sex symbol' owes at least as much to the international publicity machine as to her cinema appearances.

The advertising campaign which made her as well known as the master of the Soviet Union did not merely make clever use of long blonde hair, a rare shape and lips set in a childish pout. Nor did it promise brilliant new talent. In Miss Bardot's case, the publicity men persuaded the world that she was 'authentic' – the same person both on the screen and off. They sold a personality, not an actress.

Modestly crediting the Devil with her creation, they maintained: 'She doesn't act – she simply exists.' But few people were interested in this existence until in 1956 she appeared in *And Woman Was Created*, which assembled all the elements of the Bardot personality.

She played Juliette, a lazy beauty who worked at St Tropez only at being happy, who thought 'the future was invented to spoil the present', acted on impulse and followed her instincts with the aggressive frankness of a young animal. She undressed frequently, flirted with a middle-aged man, married a timid admirer and seduced her brother-in-law. But while she broke all the rules, she retained a look of innocence and showed affection for animals.

The combination of childish face and mature body, innocence and sexuality is the basis of the Bardot myth.

A succession of similar film parts and a skilfully organised public relations campaign established BB as an unsophisticated schoolgirl vamp, contemptuous of bourgeois conventions and the opposite of what a well-bred young woman should be.

Miss Bardot was, in fact, well brought up and the grooming of BB was the reverse of Eliza Doolittle's.

She was born in Paris on 28 September 1934 into a wealthy middle-class family. Her father was proprietor of Bardot and Company, manufacturers of liquid oxygen and acetylene. Brigitte and her sister, Marie-Jeanne, led a quiet, sheltered existence, growing up in the family's large flat in one of the best residential districts in Paris and in the country house at Louveciennes near Versailles.

At a private girls' school in Paris, Brigitte showed average intelligence and was good at French and Latin. At the age of six she began taking private ballet lessons, and Madame Bardot hoped her pretty long-legged daughter might one day be a dancer.

When Brigitte was in her early teens, her mother allowed her to model junior-miss dresses for friends in the fashion world. In May 1950 she appeared on the cover of the women's popular weekly *Elle*. It caught the eye of Marc Allégret, the film director. She reminded him of Simone Simon, the kittenish *enfant terrible* he had made a star in the 1930s, and he invited her to make a screen test for a part in his new picture. The film was never made, but the test brought her at the age of fifteen into contact with her future husband and mentor. M. Vadim Plemianikov, a tall, handsome journalist of 22 intent on a film career, then acting as assistant to Marc Allégret.

M. Roger Vadim, as he is professionally known, encouraged Brigitte to persevere with the career that had begun disappointingly. He is a persuasive and charming talker, full of ideas about the future of the cinema, and with a theory about the immorality of the post-war generation.

Under his tuition, Brigitte Bardot obtained a number of small, scantily clad parts in insignificant films. The lessons were intensified after their marriage in December 1952 when Brigitte was eighteen. Vadim taught her the tricks of strip-tease, persuaded her to act as an empty-headed child given to infantile questions, and fed copy to his journalist friends about the beguiling mixture. But progress was slow until 1955, when Brigitte Bardot made a brief appearance in René Clair's *Les Grandes Manoeuvres* and obtained the lead in a slight farce, *Cette Sacrée Gamine.*

The following year an astute young producer, M. Raoul Levy, gave the couple their chance and Vadim directed his wife for the first time in *And Woman Was Created.* The story, written by Vadim and Levy, was unconvincing; but it served to link a series of numbers for Brigitte Bardot with a provocative mambo as the finale. During the shooting the press was informed that the love scenes were the most realistic ever filmed – so much so that they continued after the cameras had stopped. Miss Bardot's flirtation with her leading man, Jean-Louis Trintignant, and her estrangement from Vadim (they were finally divorced in 1957) were exploited to give substance to the publicity. A running commentary on Vadim's difficulties with censors kept the film talked about.

The results in France were disappointing, but in the United States the same softening-up process, helped by attempts to have the film banned, ensured its success. It obtained a general release and is said to have earned over four million dollars (about ten times its cost).

But a beautiful body, strip-tease and insistent press ballyhoo do not explain Miss Bardot's continued success. Her nationality no doubt helps outside France, but she is not the first French actress to appear unclothed.

A number of solemn attempts have been made to isolate her sociological significance. One American critic described her as 'the symbol of the loneliness and insecurity of modern youth'. In a recent analysis of the Bardot myth, Simone de Beauvoir, the novelist, compares her with James Dean and detects the same dominant traits: 'the fever of living, the passion for the absolute, the sense of the imminence of death.'

In some respects she does represent the *blouson-noir* teddy-boy type of problem child, who gratuitously flouts conventional standards without replacing them with any coherent new philosophy. Family, politics, religion and thought are excluded from the myth. Instinct and self-satisfaction are the driving force.

Yet BB, on the screen, is not simply a selfish delinquent. She has freshness, charm and a touch of mischievousness. She is irresponsible and immoral, but not deliberately cruel. She does not fit into any of the previously accepted categories of film personality – the sweet, pure, clinging type (Phyllis Calvert, Grace Kelly), the *femme fatale* (Marlene Dietrich, Greta Garbo), the full-blown pin-up (Jayne Mansfield, Jane Russell), or the bright-eyed adolescent (Audrey Hepburn, Leslie Caron).

In *En Cas de Malheur* (*Love is my Profession*) the contrast between BB and the sophisticated woman of the world played by Edwige Feuillère is revealing. The clash is between the fundamental honesty of the child from the gutter and the hypocritical discretion of the grown-up bourgeois world. The Bardot child-woman is never sentimental or mysterious. She has no time for the tantalising wiles of a Cleopatra. She is a frank man-hunter and her methods of seduction are forthright – she lifts her skirt or bites her partner's shoulder to indicate what she has in mind. Colette's Gigi has to be taught about sex. BB, though as young, knows about it and enjoys it for its own sake.

But perhaps the child-woman is already on the way out, having reached its ultimate expression in Nabokov's *Lolita* and Raymond Queneau's best-selling novel *Zazie dans le Metro*, whose heroine is an immensely knowing, foul-mouthed little girl impatient of adult pretence and stupidity.

M. Vadim does not think so. His latest film is a modern dress version of Laclos's near-pornographic eighteenth-century classic *Les Liaisons Dangereuses*, which also has a teenage heroine.

Miss Bardot, however, after at least pretending to believe her own propaganda, has already turned away from it. She occasionally refers to her public personality in the third person and is hurt by unkind press comment. Her second husband, M. Jacques Charrier, the actor, has a solid reliable look about him. He is the son of a retired army colonel and the kind of young man Brigitte Bardot might have married had she never embarked on a film career. Then in her latest film, *Babette s'en va-t-en Guerre*, which recently charmed Russian critics in Moscow, she plays a Resistance heroine and remains fully clothed throughout.

Miss Bardot is spoiled by everyone around her, but to meet she is likeable and unpretentious. She speaks slowly and simply. She is not profound and does not try to be. Her reading, she admits, is limited to film scripts and scenarios. She likes Mozart and Handel, but only as background music when she is tired. She shows little interest in politics, though she admires General de Gaulle for his courage in assuming control of the country last year. She is keenly interested in money and has a reputation as a clever business woman. Her reaction to being imitated by young girls of many countries is typically hard-headed: 'It's a sign of popularity and that's what a film career is based on.'

She is evidently aware of the need for a change, and is no longer content with parts that are 'just pretty pictures', but she is too good a business woman to destroy her profitable myth out of hand. Her problem is to establish a new meaning to her initials without losing the international credit that at present goes with them. But to the countless devotees of 'bardolatry', a mature, adult BB may appear a contradiction in terms.

TONY HANCOCK

30 March 1960

In his dressing-room after the show, Hancock needs a vodka, cigarettes and conversation. In vest and trousers he is a solid, fleshy figure, and the flesh gives an occasional tremble for some minutes after the camera lights have cooled and the studio audience, flushed with enormous pleasure, has stumbled out into the river-smelling Hammersmith backstreets.

Another *Hancock's Half Hour* has gone on tape for television, and the gentle Hancock face is left lightly creased, like the lining of a hat. A muscle twitches high in his cheek, and he talks about the show; about holidays in France; and about the the prospects of a Third World War.

Even in television, where they go out of their way to encourage new categories of talent, the funny man remains king. With one simple old-fashioned asset he can earn a fortune: and at the same time find himself exposed to the shrivelling light where nothing survives but an outline. His comic personality may be safe, but what about his own?

Many of those who saw Hancock interviewed recently in *Face to Face*, that curious prelude to the *Half Hour* series now running, wrote to sympathise with him for having endured such surgical questions from John Freeman. Hancock refused to hear a word against Freeman – it had been 'a great experience,' he said.

Yet sympathy was natural enough. Hancock the comic is a highly competent contemporary buffoon. Hancock the man, caught in the great beam of light, was seen to be an anxious, fragmentary, endearing individual: and the buffoonery, which includes some of the funniest things of the day, was seen to be no more than a brilliant suit of armour.

Anthony John Hancock, aged 35, has none of the flamboyant characteristics of showbiz; he doesn't speak the jargon, haunt the parties or generally live in the mainstream of organised entertainment.

He is serious, humble, sometimes lonely. He would like to be better: to be a funnier comic, a cleverer man. Till he was 30 he read scarcely anything; now hungrily he wades into history, philosophy and biology, reading Wells and Bertrand Russell and Joad and, incredibly, Herodotus. He has been psycho-analysed. He worries about forgetting his lines and about his weight, and periodically goes into a nursing home to reduce.

In private life he is excellent company – funny without hogging the conversation, and ready to talk about anything. When the Bomb comes up he doesn't have a comic routine for changing the subject. He likes student-type arguments about politics and religion, and argued till 3 a.m. recently with Harry Secombe's brother, who's a parson.

Where he came from is immaterial, except in the sense that he doesn't want to go back to it. He was born in Birmingham – the flat accent is still there sometimes – but his parents moved to Bournemouth when he was three; he grew up restlessly. His father did various things: ran a shipping office and a laundry, and owned a small hotel. He was a semi-professional entertainer, in demand at Masonic concerts, and though he died when Tony was eleven, the business was in the blood.

By the outbreak of war he was in a concert party called the Black Dominoes. Things didn't come naturally. At seventeen he couldn't make himself go on stage in a hat. But the war, which was forcing the growth of a whole generation of comedians, nourished Hancock with the rest. He joined the RAF and ended up in the RAF Gang Show.

Big-boots-and-slapstick acts saw him through for the duration. There was a Tommy Trinder period and a Cyril Fletcher period. He was funny, but so were a lot of other people. After 1945 came long gaps without work; and when the work arrived it was likely to be bit parts in pantomime or even repertory.

Then came a Windmill engagement, the turning-point in many comedians' careers. He learned, as they say, to 'die with a smile'. Then radio, in 1949. The narrative, single-theme comedy show was still embryonic. *ITMA* had shown the way, but comedians remained essentially men who ran on, made a row of jokes, and ran off.

Hancock made rows of jokes. Among those who fed him with material were two men just into their twenties, Alan Simpson and Ray Galton, who had met in a TB sanatorium and gone into business as gag-writers. They peddled jokes to the BBC at 10s each. Hancock and the jokes seemed to match, and later they wrote sketches for him in *Calling All Forces*.

In 1954, by which time he had appeared successfully at the Adelphi Theatre with Jimmy Edwards, the BBC tried him in a show of his own; and with *Hancock's Half Hour* the rocket started climbing.

The music-hall background is sometimes recalled in his present shows with a cod-nostalgia, a corny vaudeville presentation, a joke preceded by 'I say, I say, I say!' Early Hancock can also be found in the 'warm-up', the often embarrasing session before a television programme when producer and performers soften up the studio audience.

Hancock, uneasy at warm-ups, includes material from a show he gave to a navy audience years ago. There is an imitation of an upper-class naval officer. He shouts: 'Up periscope!' and staggers back as it slaps him in the face.

It's good clean fun, but it would hardly have put Hancock where he is. 'You change because you throw away,' he says 'because you become more economical.' After six years of slaving at narrative shows, Hancock the performer has moved much closer to Hancock the man, the plump worrier who told Freeman in passing that he doesn't expect happiness because he doesn't think it's possible.

The same writers, Simpson and Galton, and the same producer, Duncan Wood, have been with him all along as the character of 'Ancock has swollen into a national image of indestructible middle-class clown.

He is not especially pathetic; he comes somewhere between two of his heroes, early Chaplin and Jacques Tati. He isn't a man you feel sorry for, but a man you want to cheer because he uses his wits and a kind of elasticity of spirit to fight his way through the natural disasters of life in trains, cafés, flats and hospitals.

His standards in all this are exacting. When the unions can be squared he wants to film the show piece by piece, if necessary taking days to produce a single 30 minutes; as it is, the whole thing goes on tape and a sequence can be reshot. He was one of the first to insist on pre-recording a TV comedy show.

His writers don't give him too long to read a script for fear he'll turn against it; at the start of a series, he usually rejects one or two. Gimmicks worry him, and he is even afraid of overworking 'East Cheam', his fictitious locale.

Catch-phrases and stock characters are avoided. What his writers call a 'no-plot', a simple situation in which Hancock can be left to burn away for half an hour, has remained the favourite formula since the first radio series lit upon the idea of Hancock and Sid James (who is really Hancock's extrovert brother-figure) lost in the deserts of a suburban Sunday afternoon.

Television has made it both more necessary and more possible for him to perfect a dead-pan realism within which to perform; and unlike many radio comics, he is funnier and gets a higher appreciation-figure on television.

The past doesn't mean much to Hancock. He has no friends from childhood. He likes the countryside, enjoys the feeling of being enclosed with his wife, a very good-looking ex-model, in their comfortable house in a Surrey village – but he has no roots in one place, only an accidental passion for France (his wife used to work in Paris).

He's an honest, unphoney man. He loves driving but gave it up when it became a dangerous pastime – 'I am,' he says, 'a proper Mr Toad behind the wheel.' To be recognised by taxi drivers pleases him and he *says* it pleases him.

The important thing is that every facet of his character becomes ammunition.

The clown reflects the age; all Hancock has to do is turn the mirror on himself, and translate the image into audience material. To do this and be an artist involves the mechanical skills of speech and expression and timing; it embraces human absurdity and dogged human dignity; it takes a nice chap like Hancock.

PETER SELLERS

6 November 1960

Sellers was never a natural comic, despite his early reputation as a Goon in radio's *Goon Show*. But he is a natural actor.

Fifty years ago, perhaps, no one would have had a chance to consider him as an important comedian. *The Goon Show* was an original kind of surrealist drama, its scripts and thinking-power supplied by Spike Milligan, its point of contact with the ordinary world supplied by Harry Secombe, and its maddest cleverest voices supplied by Sellers – he was Grytpype Thynne, Bloodnok, Henry Crun, Bluebottle, and, till the BBC forbade such lese-majesty, Churchill.

Of the three Goons, only Secombe is a true, pure, rollicking comedian. Milligan is a satirist with a bitter laugh. Sellers shared the Goons' anti-pomposity, but his real contribution lay in mimicry.

As an actor, he was funny because it was a funny programme; now that it's gone – struck down in its prime by the growing success of the Goons, who could all make more money elsewhere, as well as by the hard fact that Goonery proved untranslatable into television, where it might have escaped from the backwater atmosphere of radio – Sellers, still only 35, is busily expanding as a high-powered character-actor, aiming to make three films a year.

None of his recent characters is in the category of quaintly obvious targets, eccentrics who are amusing without having much relevance to everyday life. Lionel Meadows, the vicious businessman-crook in *Never Let Go*, and Kite, the plaintive shop steward in *I'm All Right, Jack*, can be found in the newspapers – particularly Kite, whose portrait brought a roar of protest when the film came out last year. Trade unions complained, and there was a widespread feeling among people of the Left that while the film merely caricatured the bosses, and was thus harmless tomfoolery as far as the board-rooms were concerned, Sellers's pompous, pathetic Kite ('I tell you, brothers, everybody's coming out') was really a bit too accurate.

Sellers has no politics. Kite was a type he studied in television newsreels provided for him by the Boulting Brothers, and at meetings arranged with several shop stewards, whose conversation was tape-recorded and played back at length; when Kite said a matter was 'relevant', or asked 'Do you imbibe?', Sellers knew what he was talking about.

The part seizes Sellers, to the point where he declares that, believing as he does in spiritualism, 'One acts as an open wavelength and maybe something comes through.' Of Lionel Meadows he says, seriously and with his full face quite placid behind the glittering, heavy spectacles: 'Maybe you trap evil spirits somehow.'

As a person there is nothing dogmatic or high-powered about him, and like Tony Hancock, whom he resembles in some ways, he doesn't have the flamboyant show-business personality. His mother is Jewish; his education was at a Catholic school. He has a wry, rueful way of talking about matters of personal belief; he thinks of himself as a Jew, without any orthodox pretensions; a medium has told him that Dan Leno is his spirit guide, and he half accepts this; he will say that 'I pray to myself and not in church', and then his rich, springy voice tails away, leaving him with a slightly puzzled expression.

His view of people, including himself, tends to be wry, hard-headed, sometimes biting: an asset to his kind of highly observant acting. Milligan recalls all three Goons at society parties, standing in a corner and laughing at the debs. Sellers recalls the local vicar in the country, where he, his wife and two children went to live in a large house outside a village earlier this year, pressing him to open a fête: 'Nonsense, Mr Sellers, you're sure to be funny.' 'You're so wrong, boy,' answered Sellers. 'I will louse this up for you good and proper.'

Eventually he was persuaded. It was shortly after the release of *Never Let Go*, where the scene in which he stamps on an old man's pet terrapin was called 'nasty' by some reviewers. Sellers's account of his speech at the fête, with full mimicry, is as merciless as any of his LP records.

'I said: "You mustn't think I'm like that Lionel Meadows – I don't want you to think it was a *real* terrapin" (murmur of disgust). "It was a *plastic* terrapin" (chorus of "Ah-h-h's") . . . "Anyway, God bless this fête and all who sail in her" – and they all rushed in and bought wicker baskets.'

Sellers, whose great-great-grand-father was Daniel Mendoza, the prizefighter, was born into a family of theatricals. He played drums, piano and ukelele, took the familiar Second-War entertainer's route via Ensa and gang show, worked in radio, met Spike Milligan, and was in at the start of the Goons in 1951.

A few years later he started making films, appeared with Alec Guinness – with whom he bears comparison for his chameleon qualities – in *The Ladykillers*, and built his reputation through the 1950s in such films as *Carlton-Browne of the F.O.* (where he was a Levantine politician), *The Mouse that Roared* (a duchess, a grand-marshal and a prime minister) and *Battle of the Sexes* (an accountant). His movements, as well as his voice, can be splendidly funny. For his stiff-walking Kite in *I'm All Right, Jack* he won a British Oscar as the actor of the year; as with one or two other of his films, the joke went down well in the United States (where *Life* has written him up at length).

His voice has been used in many cartoons and television commercials, earning what are reported to be fabulous amounts for a few hours' work. On television proper, things have been different. Goon-style ITV programmes such as *The Idiot Weekly, Price* 2d and *Yes, It's the Cathode Ray Tube Show* amused the critics but got poor audience-ratings, and there was talk of scripts being 'too outrageous'.

With the BBC, so easily flummoxed by unorthodoxy, Sellers was involved in a strange row in 1958, when he filled in a few moments at the end of a television programme by tearing up the roller caption and crying: 'It's all lies! It's all Tom Sloan's fault, him and his liniment!' (Tom Sloan was the Assistant Head of TV Light Entertainment). Since then, angry at being reprimanded for what he saw as a harmless piece of fooling, and in any case busy with the central job of film-making, he hasn't appeared on BBC television, apart from news programmes.

His standards are high, his dissatisfaction considerable. He would like to be things he isn't, such as an after-dinner speaker. He buys a succession of expensive cars and surrounds himself with gadgets, including a mechanical elephant with a Ford engine which will travel at ten m.p.h. Asked why, he says that 'At the time I bought this elephant I was terribly aware I was trying to get into the international class. I was thinking of things I could fall back on – it was a security if I ever failed.' The explanation is weird, a little touching and typical.

In his acting, Sellers has taken on increasingly difficult parts, and learned to play them absolutely straight. The bland saintliness of the little Muslim doctor in *The Millionairess* had to be conveyed without a breath of caricature, of an implied snigger at the expense of the part, and Sellers carries it off magnificently.

This month he starts on a new film, where he will both direct and play a schoolmaster; before the end of the year he also has a small part in the Kubrick-directed version of *Lolita*.

Between times he may produce phenomena like the *Running, Jumping and Standing Still Film*, a piece of magnificent nonsense, eleven minutes long, filmed with Milligan anda few others in a field off the Great North Road. There is even a chance of a small series of half a dozen new *Goon Shows* on radio.

But Sellers has already gone a long way since he was a row of funny voices. If he can continue to impersonate without ever taking the short, fatal step into caricature, he has some important acting ahead of him.

ALBERT FINNEY

6 August 1961

Versatility is not necessarily a hallmark of a great actor. On the level of greatness, Guinness must yield to Gielgud. But few actors have equalled Albert Finney's feat of achieving international success in such contrasting roles

as Arthur Seaton (*Saturday Night and Sunday Morning*) and Martin Luther in so short a time. To have done so is something like genius.

Most actors have to isolate a marketable commodity in themselves and accept the limitation as the price of a steady living. For the highly talented and determined one, the occasional Finney, this sort of goldfish bowl restriction has to be denied. His range of experience, at 24, with his career only in the fledgling stage, has been wider than most theatregoers realise. And there is something in his looks that suggests not only simple, stocky capability – the young village carpenter, perhaps – but also interesting contradictions, a feeling for complexity. An urban Wordsworth, some might say, with common sense and poetry nicely amalgamated. A mobile, sensitive face – but one that would not look entirely out of place in a coming welterweight.

Every director who has worked with him has been impressed by his unusual gift for concentration. It is when he is on stage, totally absorbed in a part – 'working', as he likes to call it, flatly – that you get the sense of repose, the power that comes from a closeness to the centre of things. He clearly owes something to the modern American school of acting; like other young actors of his generation, he was struck by the early Brando films. But his ability is also something personal to him – a combination of hard work on a part, to the exclusion of pretty well everything else in his life at the time, and a high degree of natural stage intelligence.

He is not an actor who can depend largely on technique. He likes to edge his way carefully into a part, and begins to feel comfortable only when he has found, say, the molecular make-up of an Arthur Seaton, not just of any young worker in a bicycle factory; of the veritable Billy Liar, with background, habits and private thoughts, not just any confused Yorkshire youth.

He takes pains to get this; he has had a professional streak in him from the start. Playing a Negro in a school production once, he spent hours at Salford docks doing some private study on West Indian movements and mannerisms. On the set of *Saturday Night* he had long discussions with his director, Karel Reisz, about how exactly the hero would walk, dress, smoke a cigarette, or hold a fishing-rod. Rehearsing *Luther* – in which he throws an epileptic fit, convincingly – he had a long and earnest discussion with a neurologist friend about the symptoms of epilepsy.

Finney has perhaps been lucky in having been noticed and encouraged by intelligent people at the right time. He has kept his freshness, spared from any long spell of mechanical hackwork in unsympathetic company. Though his talent looks so strong now, it might well have been overlooked or left too late.

The son of a Salford bookmaker, he was born near Manchester racecourse and a few streets away from Shelagh Delaney; his parents are still slightly amazed about him. He was noted at Salford Grammar School, where such things are noted, for his high intelligence, his powers of exact mimicry and off-the-cuff comedy, and his slender interest in academic work. He did poorly in examinations.

But by that time he had shown enough promise in a long line of school productions from the age of twelve onwards – Mrs Gargary, a padded Falstaff, Emperor Jones – to make an acting career look a sensible proposition.

He took a scholarship to RADA under John Fernald in 1956, and came quickly to notice. It was a vintage period for promising young actors – Alan Bates, Peter O'Toole and Brian Bedford were all there at this time – but he stood out as an original character actor who felt happiest, as he still does, when allowed plenty of freedom for personal invention. Other strengths were beginning to show and he made most impact in a modern-dress *Troilus*. Tynan noted him as 'a smouldering young Spencer Tracy'.

From there, turning down more lucrative offers, he went for two years to Birmingham Repertory Theatre, first playing small parts, then coming to the front in Shakespeare's plays, particularly as a memorable Henry V. Charles Laughton and the impresario Oscar Lewenstein saw him do a moderate Macbeth; but Laughton was much impressed with his potentiality, and Finney was signed on for the West End production of *The Party*. Working with Laughton, who retained his flat Yorkshire vowels, was something of a formative experience for the young Finney, still trying to find himself both as an actor and as a person.

After the short run of *The Party*, Finney again turned his back on the better-paid world of the West End and television for two more apprenticeship seasons at Stratford. He made an impression there when, understudying Olivier in *Coriolanus*, he took over the part for a six weeks' spell and, showing nerve, found an interpretation that was not at all the master's.

But generally Stratford was a bleak time for him. His marriage to an actress, Jane Wenham, broke up and illness caused him to lose, to Peter O'Toole, the leading part in *The Long and the Short and the Tall*. Then in 1958 his second chance at the Royal Court came with *The Lily White Boys*; and here, with a company that suited his temperament and feeling for realism, and the sympathetic direction of Lindsay Anderson, who understood and encouraged Finney's liking for creative freedom as well as discipline, he began to find the threads again.

Anderson has been an influence. His similarly square-jawed approach to the art of theatre, his determination to cut away the usual *chi-chi* trappings, were exactly what Finney had been looking for. They were soon to work together again on *Billy Liar*, but meanwhile came the enormously successful *Saturday Night and Sunday Morning*. It was during the run of *Billy Liar* that Finney turned down a small fortune for a five-year Hollywood contract, and the chance to play Lawrence of Arabia. He didn't want to become someone's investment, he said; he wanted freedom to develop on his own lines.

To meet, he is quite without side of any sort, and people find themselves calling him '*Albie*'. Unlike many young actors, he doesn't click away like a computer, wondering what use acquaintances might be to him. There is a slow, shy grin, and an amiable acceptance. In conversation he is liable to drop without warning into another voice, usually one of his two favourites, Peter Woodthorpe or Wilfred Lawson.

His private life is, he admits, nebulous. There is usually some uncertainty about his fixed address. He enjoys living out of a suitcase. He has a habit of dropping in on friends for talk and coffee at odd hours of the night. He expresses distaste for his celebrity appeal and, on the whole, it doesn't look like affectation. His off-duty clothes – windcheater, old trousers, beige golf cap (indoors and out) – are unconventional but not aggressively intended.

His single-mindedness about the theatre and his dedication to his own possibilities in it stand out even in a profession where self-absorption is a kind of fraternity badge. He feels himself, he has said, still 'unformed'; and the search for himself is pursued not only privately but also on stage in every part he plays. In some, like Billy Liar, he has felt personally released, as though some sector of himself had suddenly come into view under the spotlights and a flag of occupation planted there.

There is no doubt that Finney has a big idea of his own potentiality – so big, perhaps, that as yet he can hardly articulate it. Certainly, when anyone in pre-Luther days hinted that he was accepting working-class type-casting, he rustled with impatience.

Several good judges think he will eventually take over Olivier's mantle. Characteristically, the man himself insists that he would prefer to be the first Finney, and suggests that this need not be of any noticeably smaller size.

SIR JOHN GIELGUD

14 April 1974

Sir John Gielgud is 70 today. He is someone for whom the tributes and birthday junketings will be genuine. In a profession in which loyalty and affection are thin on the ground, Sir John is outstandingly popular.

At an early age he learnt the full value of teamwork in the theatre and has never forgotten it. He astonishes strangers by the outgoing wit and relish concealed behind his patrician face with its hooked nose, pale skin and sensitive eyes. He is, in fact, a modest man and finds it difficult to believe that anyone might be shy in his presence.

He doesn't look his age and doesn't feel it. Blessed with plenty of energy and a

good memory (he writes out all his lines in longhand first), he says he has always been lucky in that the right parts have kept rolling up. But those who know him say that 'luck' has played a very small part in his superb career. They know that this supreme professional rarely shelters behind his formidable technique, but is as ardent, vulnerable and dedicated as any young apprentice.

Arthur John Gielgud (Jack until it became inappropriate) was born in London, the son of a well-to-do stockbroker. The family were typical comfortable Edwardians living in Campden Hill, but with one small difference – the blood link, through his mother, with that romantic acting clan, the Terrys. Gielgud caught the infection early, and was allowed to try the stage instead of going to university, like his brothers Val (who later became the head of radio drama at the BBC) and Lewis. The Terry connections helped, but the Terry talent helped more. In his first acting year, when he was eighteen, his second cousin, Phyllis Neilson Terry, then at her zenith, announced to his parents that she saw 'all the family gestures coming out again'.

His birthright included charm, panache, presence and 'weak lachrymal glands' (like all the Terrys he can cry at the drop of an adjective). Like them he finds it almost impossible to allow himself to be disliked on stage, which explains some of his failures, notably Shylock. It was a family saying: 'You must never say it is a bad audience. It is your business to make it a good one.'

He also inherited a fastidiously keen ear – 'Some actors can't tell one inflection from another, you know. Such a pity,' he remarks – and a strong visual sense like his second cousin, the revolutionary stage designer Gordon Craig. Along with the gifts came 'a certain facility' which he recognised as dangerous. He remembers his early setbacks with gratitude.

As a student he was told by a near-hysterical Lady Benson, when he was at her drama school, that he walked like a cat with rickets. 'It dealt a severe blow to my conceit – which was a good thing.' Since then he has become disarmingly self-critical, especially of the tendencies (such as using his beautiful tenor voice to make 'empty music') that he used to be mocked for.

A turning point in his already promising career came when he joined the Old Vic in 1929 under the iron regime of Lilian Baylis. He opened the season as Romeo, the youngest actor for several years to tackle the part (at that time romantic leads were thought to be the preserve of middle-aged stalwarts). He has never been happy with any of his Romeo interpretations. 'I don't take myself too seriously. And a sense of humour is important when you're playing tragedy; I can find the humour in Hamlet and Lear, but not in Romeo or Othello or Macbeth,' he explains.

He made his mark that same season when he played Richard II. 'Richard was a shallow, spoilt young man, vain of his looks and with lovely things to say. I fancied myself no end in the part.' He went on to play Hamlet to great acclaim and, incredibly for a 25-year-old, Prospero, Lear and Macbeth.

By 1931 Gielgud was the acknowledged first player of the town. He has stayed at the top of the profession, though his supremacy has been matched, and in some areas superseded, by his great contemporary, Laurence Olivier. Gielgud's range is narrower, less strongly masculine. He lacks Olivier's animal force, his gift for mimicry and the capacity for creating a sense of danger on stage. But his comic talent is much less self-conscious and his projection of lyric language unchallenged. Both as actors and as men, our two greatest actors are polar opposites; they admire but do not understand each other.

Gielgud remains primarily a stage actor and, coming a fair second, a stage director. He has done very little television and only a smattering of films, maintaining a detachment from the mass media which few young actors today would either seek or be able to afford. In retrospect, he wishes he had conquered his early suspicions of the camera and taken up an offer – which Olivier seized – from Alexander Korda, the film tycoon, to film *Hamlet*. 'Korda never asked me again'; then wistfully: 'All those actors who worked for him managed to afford such lovely big houses.'

For much of his career he worked under the comfortable umbrella of H. M. Tennent, whose chief, Hugh ('Binkie') Beaumont, ruled Shaftesbury Avenue like a latter-day Catherine the Great. Perhaps as a result, although Gielgud always had an eye for new acting talent, or designing and directing ability, he did little to pioneer new work. The possible exception is Chekhov – who had been dead for twenty years when Gielgud first played in *The Cherry Orchard* in 1925, to outraged London audiences.

On the whole, he stuck to the classics – taking a memorable second wind as a Shakespearean virtuoso at Stratford in 1950 with Peter Brook. Most of the West End plays he appeared in were pet projects of Beaumont's: one remembers, and wishes one didn't, *Nude with Violin*, a mediocre play by Noel Coward; Enid Bagnold's ill-conceived *The Last Joke*, and Peter Shaffer's dispiriting *The Battle of Shrivings*.

In 1961 Gielgud said: 'The theatre has given me all I ever asked for, but too soon.' He was nervous of Beckett and of all the Osborne-and-after school. Again this was in contrast to Olivier, who plunged in with Osborne's *The Entertainer*. It was a fallow patch for Gielgud, of whom Agate had written: 'He is much too fine and romantic an actor to be happy away from rhetoric and robes.'

It seemed at that time that he was on the shelf, doomed only to flick the dust off occasionally with a tour of his solo Shakespearean anthology, *The Ages of Man*. Then the energy flared up again: friends were encouraging; he stopped worrying about his incompatibility with modern dress.

In the past ten years he has amazed and delighted a new generation of actors and audiences and has experienced the combination of box office success and critical kudos that often eluded him in the Tennent empire: as the headmaster in Alan Bennett's *Forty Years On*, in Peter Brook's *Oedipus*, in *Home* and in *Veterans*, in which, despite disapproving clucks from his old fans, he caricatured himself playing Lord Raglan in the film of *The Charge of the Light Brigade*. 'I do use charm to get my own way. I know I do. That's why the part was so well written. I couldn't resist it.'

After his stint in *The Tempest* at the Old Vic, he is to tackle the work of another dramatist in the Royal Court stable. He will play the lead in Edward Bond's *Bingo*, a play about Shakespeare's last days. He sees natural parallels between Prospero abandoning his magic powers on the island and Shakespeare retiring from the charmed life of London to late middle age in Stratford. He's already worrying about getting tight with Ben Jonson. 'I'm no good at drunk scenes. . . .'

Gielgud is not, as some people imagine, an intellectual actor. He is a very intelligent, emotional actor, who can sustain a line of poetic thought as no other. He has never been interested in politics or world affairs and intensely dislikes propaganda in the theatre. In his search for dramatic truth, he places his trust in his observation of people, in his emotional feelings and in instinct; these are the essential tools of his craft, behind his professional discipline and quest for perfection.

MAX WALL

9 March 1975

Mr Max Wall, who is related to the Great Wall of China, a brick, is a man who came back from oblivion to be hailed a comic genius.

His run, which ended last night at the Garrick Theatre, proved so triumphant that it reopens immediately at the Greenwich Theatre tomorrow night. No greater justice, none could be as sweet.

Now 66, he appears in his outrageous tights alone for two hours on the stage like an apparition: a ghost of the music halls. 'You've heard of the music hall,' he says, 'it used to be in the newspapers.' Perhaps comparisons with Osborne's Archie Rice are inevitable, particularly as he played Rice in a recent revival of *The Entertainer*. Many claimed he was the equal of Olivier's famous performance. But there's a difference. Unlike Archie Rice, Mr Wall isn't dead behind the eyes. Whatever the despair of his wrecked private life, whatever the put-on hopelessness of his legendary act, to watch him perform is to witness one of the greatest clowns the British theatre has known. His decline and triumph aren't without irony.

'Frankly, ladies and gentlemen,' he announces at the start of a performance. 'I don't see any reason, while you're sitting there, I don't see *any reason* why you shouldn't be entertained.' The logic of this can be lethal. 'Mark you!' he adds, for he's fond of unexpected exclamations: 'By the Lord Harry!' or for no apparent reason, 'Get *in* there, Arthur.' '*Mark you*, I wish I was out there where you're sitting – enjoying a marvellous show.' There's a sense of danger about him. He plays with the audience, improvising. He's neither the lovable red-nosed clown nor the straight comedian. He's something unique: his own invention.

Always he ends each performance with the insane Professor Wallofsky, that timeless, hysterical creation, who discovers one arm growing longer than the other as he attempts to play the pianoforte with the aid of an AA map and a spirit level. A new generation of admirers is convulsed with laughter. Yet there's a harsh, cutting edge about Max Wall which takes the audience by surprise. No one is ever quite at ease, never knowing which way he's going to play it. It's part of his almost perverse appeal.

He can be sentimental and warm, yet he presents a spectacle of human disaster and misery that can be harrowing. At times it's as if he despises both himself and the audience that acclaims him. He's a true eccentric, yet the ridicule he invites, feeds off, leaves you more than thoughtful after the lights go down. 'Don't laugh,' he's been known to say to his audience in a hollow voice, stopping them in their tracks, 'it's unkind.' Each night, he receives an ovation. 'I *know*,' says Mr Wall.

Born in Brixton in 1908, he was christened Maxwell Lorimer, the son of a famous Scottish comedian. His mother, aunt and uncle, grandfather and grandmother, were also stars of the music hall. The lineage stretches back to the 1860s. He first appeared on the stage at two years of age, when his father carried him on in a kilt. One of his earliest memories in life is of seeing Marie Lloyd from the wings. Dan Leno, with whom he's sometimes compared, was a hero. Another was Grock, the great Swiss clown. His eyes light up whenever Grock's name is mentioned. He worked with him in Paris.

Max Wall's own act was what was known as 'acrobatic dancing'. It's how he learned to contort his body. For some fifteen years he performed without speaking at all. If you spoke in those days, the management had to increase the salary. By the time he was 30, there was little anyone could teach him about stagecraft. More than anything, he had learned never, never to give in.

His face is sad and open, honest: without guile. When he smiles, he grins from ear to ear, a clown's smile. Like so many naturally funny men, he was born into unhappiness, and was never to overcome it. His father was an alcoholic, who drank himself to death. During the First World War, his home was bombed by a Zeppelin, killing a baby brother. Max was buried in the rubble, but survived.

Since then, his three marriages have all failed. Last year, he was declared a bankrupt. 'Marriage,' he says now, 'there's no percentage in it. *The lion's den*. I've never understood women, really. No one ever has.' He describes himself as a fool in his private life. But there's no obvious trace of self-pity or bitterness in him. He just states it as a melancholy fact.

Twenty years ago, when he was still at his height, one of the most popular comedians in the country, the break-up of his first marriage occurred and almost finished him. By then, he had appeared in two Royal Command Performances; he ran a Rolls. But he fell in love with a former Miss Britain, 26 years his junior. They married eventually. The five children from Max's first marriage, though adult now, still don't speak to him.

Partly because of the bad publicity, some of it vindictive, partly because of the stricter moral climate of the 1950s, his career began to slide. He could never have been an easy man. He had a reputation for independence, moodiness, awkwardness on occasions. But he felt victimised by what happened. He says the impresarios closed the leading theatres to him. Certainly, at a time when music hall was dying, he was forced off the TV screens, only to appear from time to time as a shadow, victim of a few imitators. He received poison-pen letters, which hurt him deeply. Bouts of severe depression followed; guilt, drink, a suicide attempt. He was just about to do it, when what he described as A Voice On High was heard to say: 'Don't be a silly sod.'

He survived: in rough and crude conditions, he worked the Northern workingmen's clubs, notorious graveyards. Changing his costume in the Gents, competing against the more immediate appeal of booze and scampi – that's where Max Wall has been all these lost years. The act for which he's currently hailed as a genius is exactly the same as the one he performed in the wilderness. He's married to his craft, and an audience. 'Show business is like sex,' he announces cheerfully during his act. 'When it's wonderful, it's wonderful. But when it isn't very good, it's still all right.'

He lives alone now, in a bedsitter outside the centre of London. His only possessions are his props, hundreds of letters and a 35-year-old typewriter. He thinks, schemes and writes all his own material. He's still a hopeful man: very gentle. Away from the theatre he's almost a recluse. He drinks Guinness at his local pub, sometimes gambles at roulette: always alone.

He's pleased by his present success, though scarcely overwhelmed by it. Over the past few years he must have been discovered more times than North Sea oil. He's a fatalist. 'There's a time to be a success and a time to be a failure. Fate decrees it. What was it Aristotle said? The will of the masses will prevail. Well, I think he might have had something there. People say I could fill the Albert Hall. I don't think so. But if you put a medium-sized hut in the middle of nowhere and said, "Max Wall Appearing Tonight", you might find quite a few people trickling along. Yes, I think that might be true. It's *written*. If the Lord says it, it will be. *Something* will happen. Because the Lord is saying, "This is the day of Max Wall".'

He laughed.

Inside his profession, and outside, he is well loved.

His signature tune is called 'Say it while dancing'.

ANDREW LLOYD WEBBER

18 March 1984

The musical *Starlight Express*, which opens for preview tomorrow, has a lot going against it. It concerns a race to find the fastest engine on the old American railroad. Much of the action is taken up by the cast, many of whom have no previous theatrical experience, whizzing around the Apollo Victoria theatre on roller skates. It sounds like a recipe for disaster.

It will probably be a smash hit and for one reason above all: the music is by

Andrew Lloyd Webber. It is costing more than £2 million to put on and will take 40 weeks to start showing a profit for its backers. There are no safe bets in the theatre but the odds shorten when Lloyd Webber is involved.

He will be 36 on Thursday yet already he has five hit musicals under his belt – and only one flop. He has a genius for turning the unlikeliest subjects into musicals: the life of Jesus, Evita Perón, the poems of T. S. Eliot. Songs like 'Don't cry for me Argentina' and 'Memory' are whistled all over the world. *Jesus Christ Superstar* ran for eight years in London. Lloyd Webber is the first person to have three musicals in performance at the same time in both London and New York. He could turn the Reykjavik telephone directory into a box office hit.

He is as dominant a figure in the modern musical as Richard Rodgers was in his heyday. Rodgers was, and remains, his idol and the parallels between their careers are remarkable. Both were musically precocious, writing shows from boyhood. Both went to university but left well before graduation, both were commercially successful by their early twenties. Both were innovators who maintained the ability to write strong, haunting melodies that stick in the memory of the most unmusical listener. Where Rodgers's name is inextricably twinned with the lyricists Lorenz Hart and Oscar Hammerstein, Lloyd Webber's goes with that of Tim Rice.

Lloyd Webber's background shaped him perfectly for his subsequent career. He comes from a totally musical family. His father, Dr William Lloyd Webber, was an outstanding organist and principal of the London College of Music. His mother was an inspirational piano teacher, numbering John Lill among her pupils, and his brother Julian is now Britain's most noted cellist.

He grew up in a house over South Kensington tube station in an atmosphere he describes as 'extremely Bohemian'. When, much later, he wanted to buy his parents a thank-you present he racked his brains before hitting on a refrigerator to replace the one in the kitchen that had not worked in living memory.

But the greatest influence on his musical development was his Aunt Vi, who knew many of the leading lights of the British musical in the 1950s. From early on he was going to more West End shows than would normally be accessible to one so young. This theatrical experience was tempered with rock and roll gleaned from radio and television.

From the age of eight he was producing his own musicals in a model theatre he built himself, which included such embellishments as a revolving stage made from an old gramophone turntable. With the acumen that was to become apparent in his later commercial dealings, he eventually turned it into a model television studio.

The constant theatregoing was to stimulate his other great passion, Victorian art and architecture. While at Westminster School, where he was a scholar, he would tramp the streets of London on games afternoons to track down churches. He can still, he says proudly, name every important Victorian church or building in the City of London. He remembers pleading with his grandmother, unsuccessfully, to lend him £18 to buy a sketch of Rossetti for 'Desdemona' which he spotted in an antique shop. He has since built up a private collection which for obvious reasons he prefers to keep quiet about.

At Westminster he wrote two more musicals. One or two of the tunes have, he says, survived and surfaced in other works. Although he did badly in his 'A' levels he won an Open award in History to Magdalen College, Oxford, largely on the strength of a paper on Victorian buildings. He had insisted against school advice on trying for Oxford because he thought it harboured the country's most promising young lyricists.

He was wrong. After the first term he asked for the rest of the year off and never went back. He was still only seventeen but he had already met Tim Rice, through a publisher. Rice was older by three years, but they got on together, writing a musical based on Dr Barnardo. It was never performed but the authors were not deterred. On his father's advice Lloyd Webber went to the Royal College of Music for a year to pick up the rudiments of orchestration and conducting.

That year he and Rice wrote a 40-minute pop oratorio, *Joseph and the Amazing Technicolour Dreamcoat*, whose mixture of Biblical theme and catchy music was to reappear later in *Jesus Christ Superstar*. It was put on by a school and made into an album. It attracted the attention of Sefton Myers, a young property man interested in developing show business talent. He signed up the pair on a ten-year contract at £3,000 a year each, good money for a teenager in the late 1960s.

Their next effort was a musical about Richard the Lionheart, entitled *Come Back Richard, Your Country Needs You*. Nobody needed the show (though part of it was to re-emerge as Rice's *Blondel* last year) but *Jesus Christ Superstar* soon followed in the fashion Lloyd Webber and Rice pioneered. It was launched as a double album and only later turned into a stage show, a reversal of the usual practice.

Superstar did nothing for two months, then suddenly took off in the United States, where its mixture of schmaltzy religion and punchy music was in perfect tune with the naïve enthusiasm of young Americans. The album broke all records, becoming the biggest seller of all time. Its authors, however, made nothing from the numerous stage productions and inevitable film – control of their work having passed to the Robert Stigwood Organisation. It was not until 1979 that Lloyd Webber gained total control of his affairs, which he now runs through his firm, The Really Useful Company.

After *Superstar* came his one flop, the musical *Jeeves*. It taught him that the director is as important as composer and lyricist and must understand the special demands of the musical. For *Evita* it was Hal Prince, for *Cats* and now *Starlight Express*, Trevor Nunn, an at first unlikely but, as it turned out, inspired choice.

Although their names are still coupled almost automatically, Lloyd Webber and Rice have not worked together for eight years now, since completing the *Evita* album. The split has a lot to do with Lloyd Webber's need to free himself from Rice's bluff embrace and go his own way. He is basically still shy but the photographs, which always portray him as a schoolboy with a slightly daft smile, are misleading. Close up, he is harder and more intense, a self-confident man who knows where he is going.

He laughs at the notion that he is a multi-millionaire in the McCartney class. His shows pull in enormous revenue but the outgoings are immense too. His one big personal moneyspinner has been *Cats*, now playing in six cities and scheduled to be on at nine by the summer of 1985. The latest venues are Budapest and Tokyo. An associate says: 'He understands money. He knows how to spend it to create more.' The most tangible example of that came with last year's purchase of the Palace Theatre for £1.3 million. It is an apt choice, combining his passions for musicals and Victoriana. It housed *Superstar* for eight years, and is currently the venue for his latest hit *Song and Dance*. It is also where he first met Richard Rodgers (during *The Sound of Music*) and the next production is to be the 1936 Rodgers and Hart classic *On Your Toes*. He wants to make the theatre the natural home of the musical in London.

Financial affairs are complicated by the present expensive divorce settlement being negotiated by his first wife Sarah, whom he left for a 23-year-old dancer, singer and operatic hopeful Sarah Brightman. They plan to marry later this year.

The one drawback to his seemingly limitless success is that it tends to obscure the musical talent which makes it possible. His brother Julian, for whom he wrote *Variations*, based on a Paganini theme, thinks he is underrated.

'*Variations* is the best piece of cello music since Benjamin Britten's cello work,' he said. 'When I first sat down and played it right through, I was astonished at his ability to come up with a succession of winning phrases.'

The next project is probably a musical setting of David Garnett's *Aspects of Love*. What he needs most, he says, is a lyricist. On *Starlight* it is Richard Stilgoe, and Trevor Nunn is working with him on the Garnett adaptation. But one senses that Britain's Rodgers, having found his Hart in Tim Rice, is still looking for his Hammerstein.

IAN MCKELLEN

16 December 1984

When Ian McKellen murmured to Sir Peter Hall last year that he might like to join the National Theatre as 'something more than a visitor', Sir Peter clearly bore no grudge from past times when McKellen had turned down his

offers and criticised his building. McKellen was welcomed into the company as an associate director to play four roles – only three of them on the stage.

Two have already won acclaim: Platonov in Michael Frayn's version of Chekhov's *Wild Honey* (for which he won a Laurence Olivier award last week), and Pierre in Otway's *Venice Preserv'd.* McKellen is now playing the third as Coriolanus in Hall's new production, which opened last night. The fourth job is the focus of different but equal speculation and hope. Under Hall's recent restructuring of his company, McKellen and his chosen colleague, Edward Petherbridge, will be running one of the five groups of actors that will compose the new National Theatre.

The first and last time Hall and McKellen worked together was in 1980, when McKellen replaced Paul Scofield as Salieri in Hall's production of Peter Shaffer's *Amadeus* on Broadway, for which he won a Tony award. Hall, like many observers of McKellen's performing life over the past twenty years, does not hesitate to call him a star – 'which, for me, is an actor who can be downstage with his back to the audience in the dark, and still be the centre of attention'.

McKellen demurs. His cell-like dressing-room at the National (a building he still likens to a prison) is neatly pasted with a collection of postcards: Brando, David Bowie, Raquel Welch, Guy the Gorilla, Sir Henry Irving. 'No one ever paid a penny for a postcard of me.' A colleague agrees. 'A star is someone who can fill a theatre, *no matter what*. Ian can't do that.' The key to that sort of stardom is popular success on film, and 'that's the one area he still hasn't cracked,' said a friend. 'I think it may irk him a bit. He'd really love to be Robert Redford.' McKellen contains such feelings in wry amusement over his last meeting with Sir John Gielgud on a film set with Meryl Streep, both men savouring their one-scene cameo roles.

He is 45. He was born in Burnley and brought up in Wigan and Bolton, where his father was borough engineer. Though acting might seem a breakaway from his Nonconformist, north-country, lower-middle-class beginnings, he points out that both his grandfathers performed in public every week (one was a Baptist lay preacher, the other the Congregationalist minister in the village of Romiley near Stockport); and his father was a big man in Bolton, whose name appeared on Corporation lorries ('I've never had my name on a car').

His family was pacifist, socialist, and temperate: both his parents went to church 'every Sunday of their lives'. He still supports Labour and CND, but his churchgoing stopped 'the minute I left home'. The death of his mother when he was thirteen affected him deeply. But he became head boy of Bolton School, and found early fame in the Hopefield Miniature Theatre, run by its Latin master, George Sawtell, who also took boys on a week's camp in bell tents in Stratford every summer. Sawtell recalls the day that young McKellen queued to stand through a matinée of Olivier's Coriolanus, tore back to camp for tea, then charged off to stand through the evening show – *Coriolanus* again (directed by the 28-year-old Peter Hall).

McKellen's career emerged from an anonymous performance as Justice Shallow in his first year at Cambridge in 1959. 'One would like to know the name of this Shallow,' said Alan Dent in the *New Chronicle*, 'because it might become a name to remember.' McKellen has not let it be forgotten ever since. 'What's special about me among actors,' he says, 'is that I've usually been in work.'

At Cambridge he became president of the Marlowe Society and played 21 parts. He sneaked into the seminars F. R. Leavis gave in his rooms, and with the rest of his generation (Trevor Nunn, Corin Redgrave, Derek Jacobi, Margaret Drabble) was moved by the imperative of moral seriousness. His acting has always been characterised by intense thought, textual scrutiny, and total commitment to whatever he undertakes.

'He's given up *everything* for Coriolanus,' said a friend: beginning his days with a workout at his gym much as a religious plunges into his early devotions. And he spares colleagues no less than himself. 'He's a perfectionist, and it irritates him if other people don't work as hard as he does,' said a director. 'Everything I've done in my career has been about becoming *the best*,' says McKellen: 'and *best* is being better than you were last time, and stretched as far as you can make it.'

There is an avidity about McKellen, both on and off the stage. 'He eats work, and he eats life,' says a friend. When he has enjoyed a meal, he may lick his plate ('He likes nursery food – cakes, sweets, jellies: he likes coming here because of the puddings,' says a BBC friend); and he devours roles, books, ideas and causes with the same appetite. He likes to be busy; he travels well, and has taken his one-man show, *Acting Shakespeare*, all over the world.

But he is not greedy for gold. He declined to make a million (pounds, not dollars) by touring the States with *Amadeus* for a year. He only replaced his moped with a Mini when he bought a house by the Thames at Limehouse, which he shares with the actor/playwright Sean Mathias.

He is unusual, even exceptional, among actors in his instinct for planning his career, deciding what he wants, and refusing what he doesn't. And he has played his chances like a game of chess. His double performance as Shakespeare's Richard II and Marlowe's Edward II for the Prospect Theatre Company made his name in 1969, but he turned down all the subsequent offers (from the National and Royal Shakespeare companies, *inter alia*) to become a founder-member of the Actors' Company, the first British theatre group successfully run as a collective. The actors took all decisions democratically; chose their plays and hired their directors; and all got the same starvation wages (as he considers them now).

It annoys him that most people in the business nevertheless perceived the company as led by Edward Petherbridge and Ian McKellen. After three years, McKellen freewheeled off again, this time to play a bunch of whopping leads in a golden period of Trevor Nunn's RSC (Romeo, Macbeth, Leontes).

There is in McKellen a duality between the star actor dedicated to perfecting his art (which means playing the best parts under the best directors in the best companies) and the good company man, the 'natural leader' (as many colleagues view him) whose energies are spread and exhilarated by communal effort. While as company man he is praised for his enthusiasm and generosity, as solo virtuoso he can be criticised for self-centredness and impatience ('mainly with himself'). And on rare occasions there is a demon in McKellen that 'can throw the whole pack of cards in the air and leave it all to chance,' says a colleague. 'Probably very exciting if you're in the audience: if you're on the stage with him, you get a terrible fright.'

There are nevertheless few actors who would not give their eyeteeth to work with him; and his devotion to his work commands affection as well as respect. 'Ian is *all actor*,' said one director. 'It's his passion – it's his life.' In his theatrical commitment – as in his oratorical aptitude – McKellen has always attracted comparisons with the great actor-managers of the past, and exerts a powerful magnetism in the mess of unemployment, competition and five-minute fame that composes the British acting profession today.

There is no doubt of the contribution he will be making to its better health from his new position at its centre (though he still hasn't got a contract or an office at the National). But he and Petherbridge will certainly be controlling a budget, choosing plays and directors, working to improve actors' conditions, and hiring new people (though as a former Equity official, he says he could never *sack* anyone). It all adds up to a measure of leadership of actors by actors rarely seen in mainstream British theatre since the days when Olivier and Richardson were running the Old Vic Company in the 1940s (until they got fired).

There is equally little doubt, however, that McKellen's contribution to his fellows can never – to him – match in importance the contribution he would always wish to make to his audiences. Central in his postcard collection is a picture of three elderly, silver-haired people sitting and smiling in an English garden: Ashcroft, Gielgud, Richardson.

'National treasures', he calls them. For this gifted, driven, indefatigable man, they embody the great goal of his career and his life: 'To end in glory, and in harness.'

BOB GELDOF

7 July 1985

For once, just once, the record industry's hyperbole is excusable. Next Saturday's Live Aid TV rock jamboree for famine relief in London and Philadelphia, with its expected global audience of a billion and its forecast revenue of £20 million, will be the biggest event in pop entertainment history.

Its progenitor Bob Geldof, a 32-year-old Irish rock star in decline, is as extravagant a figure as that bizarre half-world has thrown up: a showman of intense energy and organising ability, deeply flawed by a wild, destructive urge.

There is no doubt that his motive is genuinely humanitarian. Cheap shots accusing him of staging a cosmic publicity benefit for the once chart-topping Boomtown Rats are dismissed by people who are well aware of his exploitative skills.

Nor is there any doubt about the savage commitment with which, in the past few weeks, Geldof has bullied civil servants and corporation chiefs in a dozen countries into coughing up goods and services, from satellite time to Concorde, for the fifteen-hour electronic marathon.

Yet he is a mass of contradictions: a man without a drop of conventional show business sentimentality in his veins, an apparently well-adjusted loner in a noisily gregarious trade, an entrancingly literate conversationalist whose altruism is impossible to reconcile with his coarse cynicism, a disciplined professional whose ungovernable egotism has torpedoed his own career.

Two stories illustrate his singularity.

The day after the BBC News report last October on the Ethiopian Famine, Geldof called a friend and expounded his idea for Band Aid. 'F---ing good crack, eh, Mike?' he remarked. The friend explains: 'He wasn't thinking in terms of salvaging his rock career. By "crack," he meant working everybody up, visiting Ethiopia, meeting Mrs Thatcher and giving her the verbal, pulling a stroke on the world. It would be Billy Graham, Albert Schweitzer and Terry Waite rolled into one.' And that, of course, is what he has achieved.

The second story is about a radio programmers' national convention in San Diego in 1979. The Boomtown Rats, in America to plug an album, were topping the bill at a huge showcase gig in a sports stadium packed with the élite of US broadcasting. It was their big opportunity to break through from domestic success to the riches of the transatlantic record market.

'As soon as Bob hit the stage, he launched into a tirade against American radio,' one of Geldof's backers recollects, wincing at the memory. '"What do you

think of the people who run radio?" he shouted to the kids in the audience. "Garbage!" they yelled. "Mr Lighting Man," he called, "switch your spotlights to the balcony!"'

'Sitting in the balcony was a row of guests-of-honour, the grandees of the industry, in their crimson tuxedos. "There they all are!" Bob shouted. "Boo-oo-oo!" the kids screamed. The guests stood up *en masse* and walked out. Next day, the order went out to take the album off all radio shows. It cost Bob his success there, and the group never made it in the States.'

Geldof is exceptionally tall and thin (at six feet three inches he weighs only ten and a half stone) with long, soft features. Notwithstanding his Flemish ancestry (his grandfather was a Belgian pastrycook who migrated to Dublin), he looks more like a romantic Celt than most people of Irish descent.

This is deceptive. Despite his rebellious tone, and speech studded with juvenile obscenities, he is not someone who radiates inner tension. His outbursts, generated at moments of exaltation, are products of self-indulgence rather than compulsion. Russell Harty, who filmed with him in Ireland last spring, found him 'a comfortable man to be with'.

The son of a Dublin merchant, he spent his childhood in Dun Laoghaire, a middle-class suburb of the city. His mother died when he was seven, and he was virtually brought up by an elder sister. He was educated at Black Rock College, a notable Catholic public school. After casual jobs as a truck-driver, busker, English language teacher and factory hand, he went to Canada and worked as a pop music journalist on a Vancouver paper, the *Georgia Strait*.

He returned to Dublin in 1975 to go into the publishing business, and was negotiating a loan from the industrial development authority to launch a free sheet when he joined some friends who were forming a rock group.

It was the dawn of the punk era. Their performances were embellished by blue movies projected on to a screen behind the band and by cages of live rats fed on raw liver. At the climax of the show, these animals would be loosed on the audience 'to liven things up'. Bourgeois Ireland was gratifyingly *épaté*.

Geldof brought the six-piece group to London in March 1977. Ensign Records signed them with a £60,000 advance (it turned out to be a shrewd investment). First impressions were favourable. They had the raw New Wave sound, but the instrumentation was subtler than the crude wham-bam punk style, and the lyrics were sharp. At a time when most punk musicians communicated in grunts, the articulate Geldof was a natural for the chat-show circuit.

The early albums did well. They had two singles at No 1, *Rat Trap* and *I Don't Like Mondays*, expressing the modish self-pity of pop with more than usual eloquence. Then they began to fade. The last time they were in the top ten was early 1981.

The slide is always humiliating – and unnervingly swift. TV producers back off. Disc-jockeys become politely evasive. Columnists no longer call back. The kids stop screaming and stare. The mirror of Narcissus is shattered. For Geldof, whose impulsive candour had made him enemies in every section of the industry, it was to be gruelling.

In his *hubris*, he had publicly attacked the pop music press at concerts. (His audiences were of course, their readers.) When he had been seeking a backer, the influential disc-jockey John Peel, in whose house he was staying, generously offered to lend him £1,000. A week or two later, Peel read that Geldof had told an Irish paper that he 'didn't want to become part of Peel's perfumed paradise'.

Worst of all, he had denounced the punk movement's fuzzy pretensions to social concern. 'There's a huge dishonesty about the New Wave,' he had said to an interviewer. 'Most people get into bands for three reasons: to get laid, to get famous and to get rich.'

As Fachtna O Ceallaigh, then manager of the Rats, says: 'It was a remark that marked him down for retribution. Rock lyrics at that time were all about deprivation. Everyone was claiming they'd been on the dole. Bob exposed pop stars who had lied about the poverty of their background. He made quite a few enemies from that moment on.'

The industry has various theories about why the Rats lost touch with their audience. 'They began to see themselves as "artists",' says Peel. 'Their sound mellowed out for the American market. They were producing music for stadiums rather than pubs.'

'Bob became bored with the rock world,' says O Ceallaigh. 'Part of the Rats' success had always been his instinct for what would go. When he moved out of London, he cut himself off.' Disc-jockey Paul Gambaccini says: 'Most pop music is about unhappiness. Being settled and contented and rich is not an interesting subject.'

Phonogram, the Rats' present label, keep urging Geldof to abandon the group and go solo, as Bryan Ferry did successfully when Roxy Music went downhill, but he has refused to ditch his old friends. He once remarked bitterly that the music business was 'like playing chess against Bobby Fischer – no matter how many moves you make, you know you'll lose in the end'.

He recently told *Time Out* that he was flat broke. The last two or three albums have probably brought in little income, if any. The recent film, *Number One*, in which he played a snooker hustler, has been a commercial flop. Geldof was on a percentage.

He and his girlfriend Paula Yates, front-woman for Channel 4's *The Tube*, own a house in a fashionable street in Chelsea and Davington Priory in Kent. (They have a two-year-old daughter Fifi Trixie-Belle.) He has been dealing in upmarket antique furniture for the past three years. 'Bob can make money out of anything,' says Chris Hill. 'He's a total survivor.'

The Rats will be back among the top-liners in Saturday's concert, a forgivable piece of opportunism. But Geldof's new celebrity hasn't helped them sell records. Not long ago, he quoted de Gaulle's dictum that there is no authority without mystery, adding sadly: 'There was no mystery about us. We always seemed to be available.'

Trevor Dann of BBC2's *Whistle Test*, who admires him, says: 'In my view, this has polished Bob off as a rock star. He can't be a symbol of youthful alienation – James Dean and Mick Jagger promising a riot on stage – *and* be sending food to Africa. From now on, he's the guy who organised Live Aid.'

DAME PEGGY ASHCROFT

20 December 1987

Dame Peggy Ashcroft celebrates her eightieth birthday on Tuesday; today the leaders of her profession celebrate her. This evening at the Old Vic her oldest friends and younger colleagues will present a tribute called *Her Infinite Variety* in honour of Dame Peggy and for the benefit of her chosen charities, Help the Aged and the Save the Children Fund.

Edith Margaret Emily Ashcroft has spent six of her eight decades at the centre of the English stage. She was born in 1907, the daughter of a Croydon estate agent; her best friend at Woodford School was called Diana Wynyard. Peggy played Shylock to Diana's Portia and Cassius to her Brutus; by the age of thirteen she had decided to become an actress. In 1963 her home town offered her the compliment of a monument: she opened the Ashcroft Theatre in Croydon by reciting a poem written for the occasion by the late John Betjeman, entitled *Local Girl Makes Good*.

Anthony Quayle, a friend and colleague since the 1930s, reflects: 'Actresses before Peggy were beauties, or eccentrics, or *femmes fatales*. Peggy has always been, to some extent, the girl next door. She brings to the stage not the virtuosity of an Olivier, or the eccentricity of an Edith Evans, but one's recognisable neighbour – and that neighbour, you find, has got passions, and ecstasies, and pain. Peggy succeeds not by a display of personality, but a revelation of the workings of the heart.'

At the Central School of Dramatic Art, Peggy Ashcroft shared one of her prizes (awarded by Athene Seyler) with a fellow-student called Laurence Olivier. She was still a student when she made her first professional appearance – at Birmingham Rep in 1926, playing Margaret in Barrie's *Dear Brutus*; her stage father was Ralph Richardson. 'I was awful,' she recalled in 1977, as Richardson handed her an award for 50 years' service to the theatre. Richardson nodded. He also hailed her as 'a rare and precious gem whose beauty and brilliance has illuminated our stage for half a century'.

Peggy Ashcroft works – as she lives – with simplicity, directness, modesty and understatement. Sir John Gielgud (who has also known her for the half-century) says: 'She's terribly ordinary, in a way; but with this wonderful distinction of attack – like a little bull-calf, butting you with her head. She has a strong instinct about a part, and a clear idea of what she wants to do with it.'

Another colleague said: 'She was not a conventional beauty, which was rather lucky. It kept her on the narrow, disciplined, thorny little path towards becoming

a great actress.' Dame Peggy has recounted, with mingled distaste and pleasure, how she was once advised that she might make a film star, if she'd just get her nose straightened and her teeth fixed.

Her entrance into the British theatre was greeted with almost instant acclaim. Harold Hobson first saw her in 1929, before he became a critic. He had crossed the Pennines (from Sheffield to Manchester) to see Matheson Lang in Feuchtwanger's *Jew Süss*. In 1964, he remembered 'not Matheson . . . but the young, slim Peggy Ashcroft, alone, aloof in what I recall as a high tower, reading the Old Testament. There was a quality of tranquillity about her, an immovable sad peace . . . I felt I was in the presence of greatness.' Kenneth Tynan called Peggy Ashcroft a player 'of whom it might be said that her soul is showing'.

Such recognition – or admiration, or adoration – has never ceased; it has helped Peggy Ashcroft achieve a career in which (as a blunt colleague put it) 'she's never had to do rubbish, and she's never been bad'. She has created and recreated Shakespeare's golden girls; when she took Ibsen's *Hedda Gabler* to Norway in 1955, King Haakon gave her a medal. But she has not sought stardom; she disapproves of the abuse of the word.

As a schoolgirl she was fired by reading about Henry Irving's troupe of actors at the Lyceum; and 'as a young actress I rather dreamed of being part of a company'. Her collaboration with John Gielgud began when he directed her as Juliet for the Oxford University Dramatic Society in 1932, and she joined the companies that he formed at the New and Queen's theatres before the war. Here, and later with George Devine and Glen Byam Shaw and Michel St Denis and Anthony Quayle in Stratford and London, 'I found the life I wanted'.

She believes the best theatre is 'a matter of continuity – continuity of players, continuity of style'. The critic Michael Billington, whose study of her career will be published next year, adds: 'Her whole career is based on the quest for the kind of permanence, security and fellowship that only companies can provide'; answering in her 'the insecurity that is the mark of true talent'.

In her turn Dame Peggy bestows on a company 'a sort of glow,' says Janet Suzman. Gielgud says: 'She's a kind of fairy godmother, and a frightfully good influence. She makes everyone behave better. She's very unmalicious, not interested in the vagaries of theatrical gossip – which I rather enjoy. I've seldom seen her lose her temper; if she uses a swear word, it makes me laugh, because it's so unlike her.'

She was the first person to sign up with Peter Hall's Royal Shakespeare Company in 1960. Hall says he couldn't have done it without her; she remains an RSC director, though she has not appeared with the company since she left a golden memory in 1982, playing the Countess in Trevor Nunn's *All's Well that Ends Well*.

People speak of an element of surprise in Peggy Ashcroft. In the 1950s she showed a remarkable readiness and adaptability to move from interpreting the classics to the wave of new writers – Albee, Pinter, Duras, Beckett; in this decade she has achieved another quiet revolution by transferring her energy and talent from the stage to the screen (both small and large), and thereby achieving a popular success she had never known before.

It began when Stephen Poliakoff tempted her with *Caught on a Train* (BBC TV) in 1980 ('written with her in mind, though she didn't know it,' he admits); then came Barbie Batchelor in *The Jewel in the Crown* and Mrs Moore in David Lean's *A Passage to India*, which won the first Oscar of her career.

There is considerable courage in all this. 'If you're Peggy Ashcroft, the burden of being Peggy Ashcroft is enormous,' says Peter Hall. 'As an actor, however great, you start from nothing every time you walk on the stage. I know the agony and anguish she goes through when she does, and how she gives and gives and gives in rehearsal.'

The two are close friends. There is a fierceness in her friendship. When in 1975 she hated Hall's *Hamlet*, she said so over lunch. 'She was very upset by this and so was I.' When in 1978 he came under attack, she leapt to his defence in fury and in print.

With equal ferocity, Dame Peggy defends her own privacy: refusing interviews, questions, revelations. The most that her friends will divulge of their privileged knowledge is that she is 'very emotional'; but they insist that even they do not know if she is religious, or whether she is happy or unhappy.

All her three marriages – to the publisher Rupert Hart-Davis, the theatre producer Theodore Komisarjevsky, and Jeremy (now Lord) Hutchinson, QC – ended in divorce. She plans to move next year from the house in Hampstead that has been her home for 42 years. Her son lives in Canada, her daughter in France; there are four adored grandchildren. 'People who know the Royal Family never talk about them,' offered more than one friend in explanation.

She works both in and out of the limelight for Amnesty and against apartheid, for Russian dissidents and Chilean refugees, for the unemployed and against nuclear weapons. She is a life-long socialist. But 'it isn't a question of politics,' she has said. 'It's one of human rights.' Janet Suzman says: 'She embraces everything – movements, causes, people, children, life itself – as fiercely and wholly as she embraces the parts she plays.'

Dame Peggy Ashcroft's career is a catalogue of triumphs; for her life, 'if you made a list of the people she has known and worked with, it would cover the intellectual and artistic community of Britain for the last 70 years,' says Donald Sinden. But it looks as though we shall never know the truth of her personal experience of all these things.

'Her greatest treasure is that she remains an absolute mystery,' says Janet Suzman. Judi Dench pondered. 'It's said that you can't be more on stage than the person you are in life. If that is true – and I believe it is – then Peggy's capacity for passion, and compassion, and gentleness, and fire, are more profound than anything I can express in words.'

Anthony Quayle said: 'In 55 years she hasn't changed. She's just got into character make-up. She has the same youthful, enthusiastic attack on life. But she's the girl next door who's grown into a great woman.'

BARRY HUMPHRIES

27 December 1987

Outside the *Daily Telegraph* office in Fleet Street, Barry Humphries is waiting for a friend. As Nicholas Garland emerges (this was before he moved to the *Independent*), Humphries is having a seizure, speechless with laughter at a display of Garland's cartoons in the window, while passers-by edge nervously towards the kerb.

Garland grabs him by the arm and they walk up the street towards Simpson's Restaurant. Humphries is dressed as a Surrealist hidalgo of the 1930s in a bold-striped double-breasted suit, wide-brimmed brown fedora and spotted bow tie. To every pedestrian he passes, he says, '*Hello*, what's your name?' in the cracked, ingratiating voice of the brain-damaged.

Some smile sympathetically at Garland, assuming him to be a male nurse or caring relative. Others respond kindly to Humphries, and are suddenly entangled in mad conversation.

At Simpson's, Humphries visits the men's loo. Standing at a urinal, he muses loudly on a seldom discussed disability. 'I'm not actually *doing* a pee,' Garland hears him remark in a penetrating voice. 'I'm only *pretending* because it's sometimes very hard to pee when you're trying to. Once, when I got back to my table, the urge became so powerful that I did it right there in the restaurant . . .'

Subversion is Humphries's métier and his passion. He loves to watch the eddies of disturbance it causes. In its simplest form, it subsists in the richly elaborated scatology of his Les Patterson monologues. At a more advanced level, there are his famous sight gags, often perpetrated on planes or trains: persuading a friend to have his leg encased in plaster so that Humphries can be seen viciously kicking it, to the horror of other passengers; or surreptitiously emptying a can of Russian salad into a Qantas sick-bag, pretending to vomit violently into it, and then scooping the contents into his mouth with a spoon.

His masterpiece, of course, is his deployment of Dame Edna Everage to obliterate the boundary between fact and fantasy. It is becoming increasingly

difficult to define the plane of existence she inhabits. She began, 30 years ago, as a caricature of a Melbourne housewife, written and performed in revue by Humphries, a flesh-and-blood actor with a birth certificate, a passport and a social security number.

But she has somehow transcended her creator. Humphries often speaks of her in the third person. Much more spookily, other people find themselves involuntarily treating Humphries and Edna as independent beings. Reporters turn in extensive interviews with Edna which barely mention Humphries. 'There's no question of going up to Edna and addressing her as Barry,' says LWT's Judith Holder, who produced *The Dame Edna Experience*, 'When Barry telephones me, I find myself saying, "But Edna . . ."'

'In some odd way, Barry turns everything around,' says Garland. 'When you have a real Hollywood star like Charlton Heston coming into a TV studio to talk to someone who doesn't exist at all, and agreeing to wear a sticker saying "Chuck" to remind everyone who he is, something very remarkable has begun to happen.'

There is a fashionable theory that Humphries has become possessed by his own creation and cannot break free from Edna's terrible psychic embrace. (A perfect plot for an 1890s horror story.) 'You have to ask yourself,' says a colleague, 'whether Barry isn't very slightly loopy.' It's a bit too literary to be true. Humphries is a cerebral and deeply cultivated artist who is in complete control of his material. If the paint has slopped over the edge of the frame, it is certainly by intent.

He was born in 1934 in the well-to-do Melbourne suburb of Camberwell, where his father was a spec builder, and educated at Melbourne Grammar School, the Antipodean equivalent of a grand English public school. He won the poetry prize and a scholarship to Melbourne University.

In 1952, he helped found Melbourne Dada, whose art exhibitions and cabarets outraged Melbourne society. Humphries was expelled from the Old Boys' Association. (He has since been forgiven, and has endowed a Barry Humphries Prize 'for originality' at the school.)

His comedy began as satire on the affectations of suburbia in the vein of John Betjeman's *How to Get On in Society* and Osbert Lancaster's *Homes Sweet Homes*. It still causes unease among Australian intellectuals.

He came to Britain in 1959, and began playing character parts for Lionel Bart and Joan Littlewood – a striking presence, tall and dark, already generating the awesome energy that now enables him to hold an audience in subjection, single-handed, for over two hours.

Peter Cook, like Betjeman, admired Humphries's records on which he played Sandy Stone, a morose oaf not unlike Cook's own E. L. Wisty. Cook engaged him for a short season at the Establishment in Greek Street. Audiences were baffled by the Australian context, but Humphries attracted a coterie of aficionados which included the *Private Eye* crowd.

When Garland took the idea for the Barry McKenzie comic-strip to Cook, Cook suggested Humphries as the writer. This Aussie *Candide* ran in the *Eye* from 1964 to 1973, and spawned two movies – one of them partly financed, in a fit of absence of mind, by the Australian Government.

Humphries has brought to his ten one-man shows since 1962 the gifts of superb timing, wonderful comic invention (often ad lib) and an exacting consciousness of style derived from his own aestheticism. He is a man of profound, un-showy erudition. In the 1960s, Hilary Spurling took him on as a reviewer for the *Spectator*, where he wrote elegantly about the Gothic novels and *fin-de-siècle* culture he loves.

He has a discriminating collection of Symbolist and Expressionist art (including one room devoted to erotic art). Sir John Rothenstein, who put him up for the Athenaeum, has written an essay on Humphries's own paintings, which look like an affectionate salute to Die Brücke. He recently commissioned the French composer Jean-Michel Damase to compose a concerto for the horn-player Barry Tuckwell.

He and his wife Diane Millstead, an artist, own a large house in Belsize Village, another overlooking Sydney Harbour, and a holiday place in north Portugal. They have two small sons. (Humphries has two grown-up daughters from a previous marriage.)

He is High Church, politically Conservative, compulsively mobile and an incurable worrier. In the early 1970s, he almost destroyed himself with drink, but stopped after waking up face-down, mugged and bedraggled, on a parking lot. He sometimes addresses friends in the role of a terminally insecure neurotic. ('Would it be okay if I smiled at you so people will think we are friends?' is a favourite line.) 'It's a joke,' says one of them, 'but it communicates something about Barry himself.'

As his youth recedes, he has developed a nostalgia for the suburbia he once derided. Sandy Stone has been transformed from a butt into a sympathetic Chekhovian commentator on the passing of the old certainties. 'I suppose that strong antipathy betrays secret affinity,' explains Humphries, quoting Wilde.

Sir Les remains pure Gillray, spittle and all. Edna has long since slipped her suburban moorings and evolved into a ten-times-larger-than-life burlesque of international stardom, though retaining a tenuous gentility. (She finds Australia's Bicentenary distasteful, preferring to call it the Heterocentenary.)

Humphries is correct in denying that Edna is a drag act. The music hall tradition of travesty made its effect precisely by playing on the audience's awareness that an actor is impersonating a woman or an actress a man. Humphries, on the contrary, has submerged all male traits in his performance. This is what gives it its disconcerting charm.

Edna has become a vehicle for surreal comic imagery. Humphries's latest triumph has been to parody the narcissism of the TV chat show, which had seemed unparodyable, by inflating it *ad absurdum*. Guests enter down a vertiginous glittering staircase beneath a gigantic pair of sequinned spectacles like the eyes of Doctor Eckleburg in *The Great Gatsby*. Sometimes, they are ejected through a trapdoor *en route*. Edna's assistant is not the conventional pneumatic chorus-girl in fishnet tights but her ageing bridesmaid Madge, who seems to be petrified in a permanent existential *crise*. (On stage, at the Strand theatre, she now appears bandaged like a mummy.)

At a certain point, the show cuts loose from reality and seems to float up into a realm in which logic has melted like a Dali clock. It doesn't happen all the time. When Humphries occasionally loses concentration and goes gently aground, one feels the audience, utterly captivated, willing him to lift off again. But when it does happen, when whole sections of the auditorium are weeping with laughter, handkerchiefs wet with tears, you recognise that you are in the presence of a great artist and a generous spirit.

LENNY HENRY

26 February 1989

A rash of red noses will break out on the nation's faces next month in a bizarre and peculiarly British rite, presided over by the black comedian Lenny Henry.

Quite why we have to disguise our charity by donning clowns' noses on 10 March is too deep a question of the national psyche to answer, but Henry's place at the epicentre of it all is a wholly natural one.

One of the highlights of the Comic Relief event is a filmed report of him in Burkina Faso, the wretchedly poor West African State. Only a few years ago it would have been inconceivable for the BBC to have sent a comedian to report on such a tragedy as the Sahel drought. It's part of the changes in the attitude to Third World suffering which people like Bob Geldof and Henry have wrought – very much against the political grain – that such a potentially depressing subject will be presented at prime time to a 'fun-loving' audience of millions.

That the presenter is a huge black man – at six feet two inches Henry is actually more of a brick outhouse than his partner in a Comic Relief Romeo and Juliet sketch, Frank Bruno – would have seemed even more unthinkable. That change is solely due to the quicksilver genius and transparently soft heart of the man who is now perhaps the biggest and best-loved comic in the country.

Lenworth Henry was born 30 years ago in Dudley, in the Black Country. His natural voice is still thick with Brummie, and he has a strong sense of his West Midlands – as much as his family's West Indian – roots, something which, typically, he investigates in his humour. One of his earliest political jokes neatly skewered Enoch Powell's calls for repatriation of black immigrants: 'Powell's offering us £1,000 to go home. I'll take the money: the train fare's only ten quid from here to Dudley.' Powellite illogic was never smacked so crisply.

His mother, Winifred, has been an ever-present influence. It was she who made the move from Jamaica with some of her children – she was to have seven – back in the late 1950s, her husband, now dead, following on later. Henry now realises how hard things must have been for his mother to bring up the family with very little money. She was a cook, her husband a labourer. One of his first acts when he started to hit the big time was to buy her a new house in Dudley. A strongly religious woman, Mrs Henry is active in the Pentecostal church. Although not much of a church-goer himself, Henry shows his respect for the black Christian movement by his extremely careful treatment of it. His act may look riotously slapdash, but is in fact the product of meticulous planning, well-whittled writing and a long and sometimes painful apprenticeship.

He first realised he had a comic gift when he tried out his impressions of cartoon characters for his friends at his Dudley primary school: to this day, he does a Top Cat so life-like you can almost sniff the fish-head skeleton TC flings from his dustbin. His state schooling failed to set fire to his intelligence. He flunked the 'second part' of the eleven-plus; that he remembers which part perhaps registers the hurt. In 1984, he went some way to exorcise his wasted school days by swotting for O-levels in English language and literature (*Cry The Beloved Country*, *Henry IV Part Two*) while doing two summer shows a day at Blackpool.

He first went on stage at the Queen Mary Ballroom at Dudley Zoo, where he worked part-time as a bottle-collector. An Elvis impression, his hips snaking to 'Jailhouse Rock', was so good that his name was passed on to the *New Faces* talent-spotting programme. He won his heat, and on the strength of a few bookings packed in his job at a local engineering factory. Although Winnie disapproved at the time, within weeks she was travelling hundreds of miles on the northern club circuit to give her son moral support.

It was a bruising baptism, telling mother-in-law jokes years before he was married, working a seam of humour with deeply-ingrained prejudices about black people. At sixteen, he was too young to do anything but serve up what his audiences expected. Even so, his quality shone through his material and lucrative-seeming contract offers were made.

At a loss to know what to do, Henry went to Robert Luff, the impresario who ran the 'Black and White Minstrels', in the mid-1970s considered to be a much more innocent show than we would allow today. Luff, a moustachioed former major in the Gordon Highlanders, liked the lad so much that he became (and remains) his manager. For five years, from sixteen to 21, Henry learnt his stagecraft in ten-minute slots between the Minstrels sets. He was the real 'darkie'; everybody else had to black up. Henry now realises quite how 'weird and unsettling' it all was, but has the strength of character to acknowledge how much he learnt.

At 21, he told Luff he wanted to do something different. Henry was delighted when Luff said, 'Yes, you're right'. The relationship between the old major, now in his seventies, and the black youngster would seem highly improbable, but they have both learnt from one other. Luff cites Henry's involvement in last year's Free Mandela concert with the same pride as his own Burma campaign. (Henry's success in winning respect for black people is such that no one would dream of televising a *Black and White Minstrels Show* today.)

His great break came with *Tiswas*, an anarchic kids' television programme. For the first time in his professional life, Henry was generating his own humour, creating his own characters. The show became cult viewing, high spots being Algernon, a Rasta with a wind-sock on his head, whose calling cry 'ooo-kaaaay!' was echoed around the country's playgrounds, and a send-up of David Bellamy, popping up from his studio undergrowth, ginger-bearded and growling, 'Where wobin wedbweasts go tweet, tweet'. During the riots of 1981, it was a breath-taking punch to racist sentiment to see a black youth win hearts and minds with such gentle, happy humour every Saturday morning.

Critically and commercially, he has not taken a wrong step since. *Tiswas* was followed by an adult version, *OTT*, then *Three of a Kind* with Tracey Ullman and David Copperfield, and *The Lenny Henry Show*. Over the years, he has developed a repertoire of black comic characters, through whom he explores various aspects of the black British experience.

The sharpest observed is perhaps Delbert Wilkins, a streetwise Brixton lad who ran a pirate radio station. Junior Industry Minister Robert Atkins recently attacked the show for 'glamorising' the pirates who were really 'thieves of the radio spectrum'. He had failed to watch the end of the series, when Delbert got a job at the BBC. Atkins had to issue another statement, saying how 'delighted' he was to hear of Delbert's going straight.

Despite his working-class, 'minstrel' background, Henry shares the same values as the new wave 'alternative' comedians. Where his work differs is in the consistent quality of the writing and his accessibility: he can bring the house down at a small cabaret venue and deliver prime-time comedy to a mass television audience, without corrupting the integrity of either his characters or himself. It's a tightrope act, getting laughs without upsetting racial sensitivities: he brings it off with gutsy panache.

Henry has been condemned for 'creating black stereotypes for white people', and a few have even gone so far as to say he is racist – a view on a par with the notion that Elvis Presley is alive and well. As far as letters to the black newspapers are concerned, the scale of the protest is very slight.

His friend and fellow-comedian Ben Elton has said: 'It would be a terrible thing to exclude a group from the cultural experience by being too terrified of insulting them: that would be contra-racism'. In fact, no one judges his material more harshly for racist and sexist content than Henry himself. His next biggest critic is his wife, the comedienne Dawn French, with whom he lives happily and privately in London.

After Comic Relief, Henry will open the Lenny Henry Sickle Cell clinic at King's College Hospital. There is already a doctor whose full title is the Lenny Henry Senior Lecturer, as good a testament to his charity work as any. After that? He has conquered the world of stand-up comedy and wants to develop into films.

A whole generation of black kids now looks up to him as a role model: a great weight he bears graciously. For them, he has shown, to paraphrase Marcus Aurelius, that a man's life is dyed with the colour, not of his skin, but of his imagination.

MADONNA

1 July 1990

There is a perversity in the very name itself: almost an apotheosis of the cheapening, disrespectful age we live in. The dictionary defines 'Madonna' as 'A Lady, a Madam, a designation of the Virgin Mary'. Yet not even her most ardent supporters could claim now that any of these descriptions aptly fit the public persona of Madonna Louise Veronica Ciccone – the 31-year-old pop

megastar who will appear at three sell-out Wembley shows this month and whose already hugely profitable film *Dick Tracy* opens in London this week to the usual massive attention that now meets her name wherever she goes.

Instead, she finds herself the subject of serious analyses in classes on feminism in the United States. What does she represent? What kind of woman is she? Is she a parody of womanhood, designed to titillate men? A symbol of the new, sexually liberated woman able effortlessly to manipulate men? Or is she just a shameless fraud?

The only certainty is that she is singing and posturing her way all the way to the bank: she has made no fewer than eighteen records which have become major hits, amassing worldwide sales of $60 million. *Dick Tracy* made $23m alone in the first weekend it was released in the United States; just in Japan, she sold $14m worth of tickets on her current world tour. If she was to retire tomorrow, she would do so with perhaps $200m in the bank, properties in New York and California, a collection of serious art, three companies – and hundreds of employees on her payroll.

By any standards, therefore, she is a phenomenon – 'the most famous woman in the world', according to the American magazine *Rolling Stone*. Yet few are willing to claim she has a particularly outstanding voice, and even fewer testify to any serious acting ability; if she has one notable talent, it is for dancing. By no means everyone, either, finds her attractive either personally or professionally. In her brief marriage to the less-than-gifted actor Sean Penn, they were known together as the 'Poison Penns'.

Perhaps if she has a genius, though, it is for self-promotion. Her first album *Madonna* came out six years ago but received only a lukewarm reception; she seemed set for her Warhol-like fifteen minutes of fame and a career in the sleazier nightclubs of New York. But she slowly took off and has never looked back – repeatedly showing an ability to re-invent herself with a rapidity that manages to retain even the short attention span of a generation of adolescents who do little but endlessly watch pop videos on cable television. From blonde to brunette and back to blonde, from virgin to whore and all things in between, from pop singer to actress, from film to theatre; she has done them all with enormous, if barely explicable, success.

Her public persona, invariably, revolves around a clever, contrived portrayal of what is supposed to be her sexuality. In her latest tour programme – designed, incidentally, by her 29-year-old brother Christopher – she arises at one point from a trapdoor on stage, pouting and writhing on a red-velvet-and-gold-brocade bed, singing her first major hit 'Like a Virgin'.

Then she sings 'Like a Prayer' in a cathedral-like set, a huge cross slung down from the ceiling. Like Mae West, Marilyn Monroe, and Marlene Dietrich before her, she almost *mocks* her femininity – which perhaps helps explain why she often incurs the wrath of feminists and has a large camp following, among others, from homosexuals (though, such is her universal appeal, that has not stopped one prominent British newspaper editor from proudly displaying her photograph on his wall).

To say she is a complicated woman, therefore, is to put it mildly. Her public and private personalities often become blurred into a confused mess; she has been forced to take psychiatric treatment. Those who know her well – and there are not many – describe her as an unhappy person, confused by her success and never quite fitting convincingly into the superstar syndrome.

The clues to the Madonna phenomenon, inevitably, lie in her upbringing. She is the third child in a family of eight, brought up in a strict Italian Catholic family in the relatively isolated Mid-West. Her mother – also called Madonna – died of breast cancer when she was five, and when her father re-married three years later the young child was never able to form a fulfilling relationship with her step-mother. The young 'Nonni' went to a convent school, where she was continually told of the perils of boys and sex by the nuns. She seriously intended, in her early teenage years, to become a nun herself – and began a collection of crucifixes.

A strict father, a traumatically disciplined schooling, the lack of a firm maternal model: all clearly contributed to a person ultimately desperate to escape the repressions and parental shortcomings of home. In early adolescence she cut off her shoulder-length brown hair, pierced her ears and stopped shaving her armpits and legs; a friend from the era says she went from being the model Catholic schoolgirl to 'far out'. She now boasts that she lost her virginity at fifteen – a 'career move', she now says with characteristic attention-seeking insouciance.

The route out of her pubescent impasse, she decided, was ballet – and she took three terms at the University of Michigan studying dance there before heading for New York. The myth is that she arrived there with $35 in her pocket and told a taxi-driver: 'Take me where everything is.' He dropped her off at Times Square – and the rest, as they say, is history. She had a brief career with a dance company, followed by a flirtation with soft-porn; then, at 24, managed to start on the (New York) Soho/New Wave club circuit. *Madonna* followed a year later, and she gradually developed a cult following on radio.

But notwithstanding all this there is also a much less-publicised side of Madonna: she is a perfectionist who devotes long hours to what she does and 'works like a dog', according to one friend. She landed the part in *Desperately Seeking Susan* – her first major break in films – amid fears among the directors that she would prove the caricature of an undisciplined, cocaine-snorting rock star. Instead, when they sent a car to pick her up at six in the morning, they would discover she had already been out to exercise at her local gym at 4.30.

Privately, therefore, we have something of a neurotic introvert; publicly, the image of a sex-crazed, mixed-up woman always behaving outrageously. The publicists have been busily putting out material that her latest affair is with Warren Beatty, her co-star in *Dick Tracy* – an impression which neither has done anything to dispel. Indeed, a photographer just happened to be on hand last week to record the sight of Madonna arriving at Beatty's apartment in evening dress – and leaving in her limousine wearing nothing but a bathrobe.

So just as interest in Madonna might fade, she can be guaranteed to bounce back with a new image – always keeping just ahead of the game, always being slightly more outrageous and even blasphemous than the last time. Sado-masochism is now part of her act. And just while the rumours about Beatty are proliferating, she is hinting that she is also having a lesbian affair with a Hollywood comedienne: all part of the movie publicity circus these days.

Nonetheless, while Madonna's musical success has been phenomenal, her ventures into films have been markedly less so. She made an initially lively debut in *Desperately Seeking Susan*, but floundered desperately with Sean Penn in *Shanghai Surprise* – possibly one of the worst films ever made – and *Who's That Girl?*

But perhaps after her music, the younger generation – and here we return to the notoriously short attention-span of American youth – knows her best for her pop videos, which are often sexually explicit and calculatedly tasteless. Some depict her in sado-masochistic roles, naked and chained to beds, and so forth. In her current world-wide tour, her male singers themselves become bizarre sex objects, at one point wearing brassières to match her own. (In Toronto, the act brought in the Vice Squad, who watched glued to their binoculars.)

She shows her business acumen by combining her tour with the publicity blitz for *Dick Tracy*. Disney have spent $30m on the film, and another $10m promoting it. US critics have hedged their bets: it isn't a great movie, they say, but it is worth going to see and will make a lot of money. They seem united in one belief: it won't do Madonna's career any harm.

Yet it is hardly a healthy role model Madonna presents to all the so-called teenage-girl 'wannabees', to whom she is so vacantly nihilistic a symbol of our age. But such is Madonna's rainbow of public personas, her mania for hard work and her ruthless determination to succeed that she could end up having the last laugh on all of us. That dictionary definition, just possibly, might not end up being so inaccurate after all.